What Reviewers Are Saying About *Modern*

"If you follow this volume's clear lessons, in a year or two you will not only have the knowledge and skills needed to understand other books on ceremonial magick, you will be a practicing ceremonial mage."

—eCauldron.net

"Kraig's *Modern Magick* remains one of the most lucid and practical texts available."

—Lon Milo DuQuette, author of *Enochian Vision Magick*; *Angels, Demons & Gods of the New Millennium*; and *Tarot of Ceremonial Magick*

"Superb! Every page clearly illustrates that here is an author who not only writes about magick, but has obviously practiced it successfully. This book is a must for the beginner as well as the advanced student who wants to effect 'change' and explore the 'worlds' beyond the physical plane."

—Cris Monnastre, former student of Israel Regardie

"I am sure that there are many, like myself, who consider it [*Modern Magick*] the missing key to the Golden Dawn system."

—Roger Williamson, author of *The Sun at Night*

"This is a wonderful book!"

—David Godwin, author of *Godwin's Cabalistic Encyclopedia*

"This may well be the best book available for anyone who actually wants to begin doing magick, as opposed to merely reading about it."

—Donald Tyson, author of *The Fourth Book of Occult Philosophy* and *Enochian Magick for Beginners*

"If you are looking for an effective key to unlocking the mysteries and experience of Western magickal tradition, this is certainly an effective one."

—Kenneth Deigh, publisher and editor of *Mezlim* journal

"This is a book you will keep at the ready for research, advice, and study. It is a road map of the often confusing paths of the world of high magickal arts. Recommended!"

—Brother Shadow, *The Path*

"Gives the serious student all the tools needed to be a magician."

—Pyramid Books

"This unusual book might well have been written by Aleister Crowley himself, from whom the author draws extensively yet always responsibly... Well written, informative, and extremely practical, this is essentially a work for the doer rather than the dreamy theorist."

—William Gray, author of *Temple Magic*

"At last a book that cuts through the mysteries of one of the most mysterious subjects. Mr. Kraig breaks down many doors that have deterred so many true seekers of light by giving detailed, understandable explanations of the secrets that others have covered up."

—Brook Martin, *Sunsight News*

What Readers Are Saying About *Modern Magick*

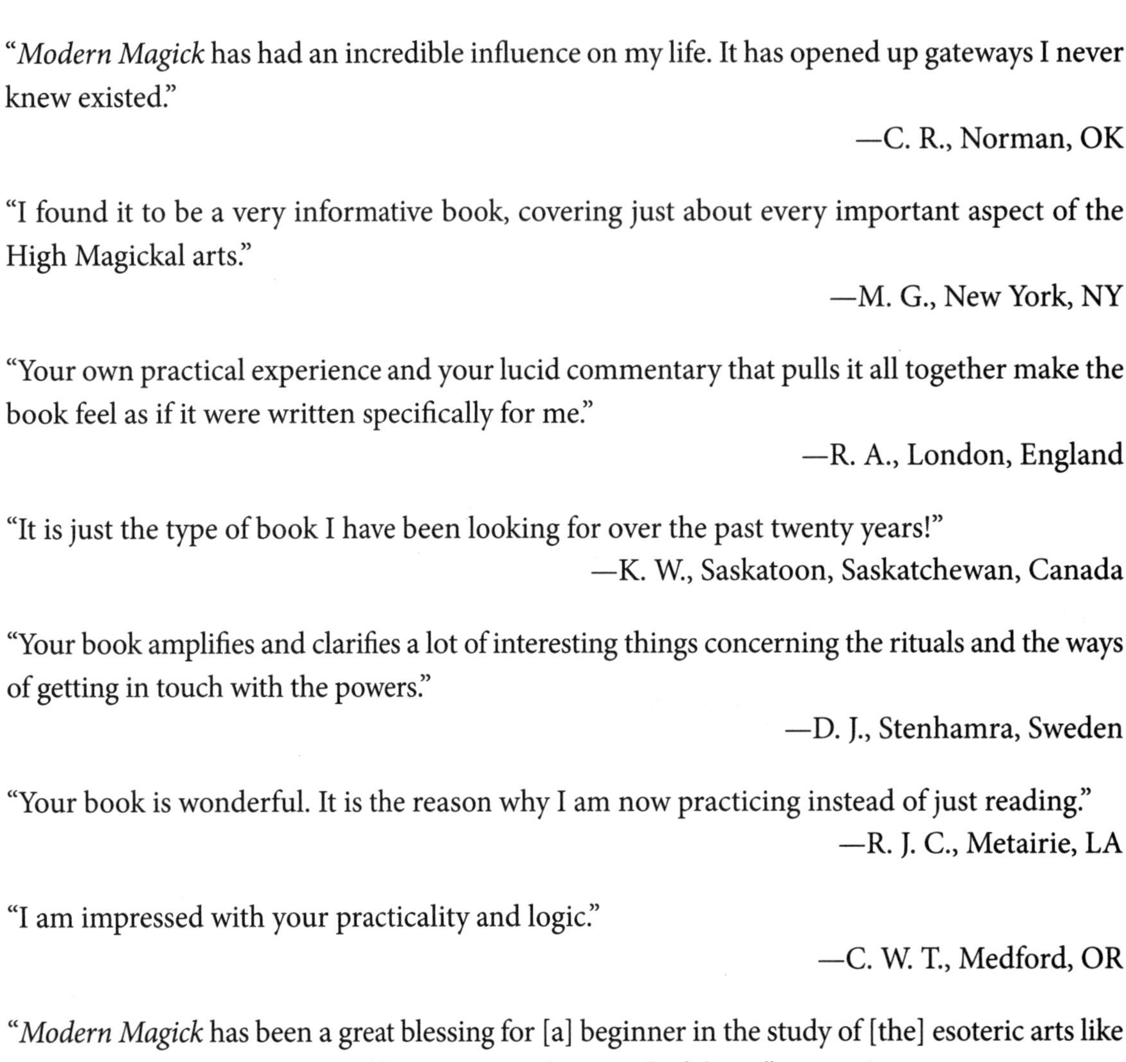

"*Modern Magick* has had an incredible influence on my life. It has opened up gateways I never knew existed."

—C. R., Norman, OK

"I found it to be a very informative book, covering just about every important aspect of the High Magickal arts."

—M. G., New York, NY

"Your own practical experience and your lucid commentary that pulls it all together make the book feel as if it were written specifically for me."

—R. A., London, England

"It is just the type of book I have been looking for over the past twenty years!"

—K. W., Saskatoon, Saskatchewan, Canada

"Your book amplifies and clarifies a lot of interesting things concerning the rituals and the ways of getting in touch with the powers."

—D. J., Stenhamra, Sweden

"Your book is wonderful. It is the reason why I am now practicing instead of just reading."

—R. J. C., Metairie, LA

"I am impressed with your practicality and logic."

—C. W. T., Medford, OR

"*Modern Magick* has been a great blessing for [a] beginner in the study of [the] esoteric arts like myself, and I deeply thank you for writing such a wonderful text."

—S. T. D., Santa Ana, CA

ARE YOU A TANTRIC?

Please answer yes or no to the following questions:

1. Do you believe there might be more than one god or goddess?
2. Do you believe that goddesses can be powerful warriors, not merely passive mothers?
3. Do you consider yourself to be Pagan or Neopagan?
4. Are you familiar with the concepts of chakras, karma, and kundalini?
5. Have you ever practiced yoga?
6. Are you looking to spiritually evolve?
7. Would you like to feel more self-empowered?
8. Do you believe each person is responsible for his of her own actions?
9. Are you seeking a Pagan tradition that has a truly ancient source?
10. Would you like to work with a symbol that has as much or more potential than the Kabalistic Tree of Life but isn't Kabalistic?
11. Do you know that Western astrology doesn't work with the planets and stars where they actually are in the sky?
12. Have you ever wondered about the ancient magick of non-Western cultures such as India?
13. Have you been fascinated by the ancient gods and goddesses of India?
14. Have you looked at Hinduism and been sort of interested, but are sure modern Hinduism isn't for you?
15. Would you be interested in discovering the sources of acupuncture, feng shui, and kung fu?
16. Have you ever studied any form of Tantra?

17. Have you ever wondered if there might be more to Tantra than just sex?
18. Have you ever wanted to travel through India?
19. Are you intrigued by the supposed power of kundalini energy?
20. Do you want to learn powerful rituals and celebrate ancient festivals?
21. Do you feel your spiritual path should be a full-time thing rather than something you occasionally do?
22. Are you ready to make positive and amazing changes in your life?

Tantra is more than what you usually hear. It is one of the oldest, continually practiced forms of Pagan spirituality. However, no spiritual system is right for everyone. Is it right for you? This test may help clarify things. Use the following key to discover whether Modern Tantra *may be your answer.*

If you answered yes to:

- 20 or more questions: You're a natural-born Tantric.
- 18 or 19 questions: You'll get a lot out of looking into Tantra as a spiritual path.
- 16 or 17 questions: Investigate Tantra. You may want to add some of its concepts to your current path.
- 14 or 15 questions: You will be intrigued by studying Tantric concepts.
- 12 or 13 questions: You may find studying Tantra intriguing.
- 11 questions or less: Although you may find Tantra interesting, it might not be your path at this time. Even so, studying Tantra will answer many of your questions—such as where certain Pagan concepts originated—and prepare you for a potential future with unlimited possibilities.

MODERN
TANTRA

About the Author

Donald Michael Kraig (1951–2014) graduated from UCLA with a degree in philosophy. He also studied public speaking and music (traditional and experimental) on the university level. After a decade of personal study and practice, he began ten years of teaching courses in the Southern California area on such topics as Kabalah, tarot, magick, Tantra, and psychic development. He was a member of many spiritual and magickal groups and was an initiated Tantric.

Foreword by Carl Llewellyn Weschcke

MODERN TANTRA

Living One of the World's Oldest, Continuously Practiced Forms of Pagan Spirituality in the New Millennium

DONALD MICHAEL KRAIG
(SHAMBHALANATH)

Llewellyn Publications
Woodbury, Minnesota

FIRST EDITION
First Printing, 2015

Book design: Bob Gaul
Cover art: iStockphoto.com/2282495/©Mr_Vector
iStockphoto.com/51523426/©AnnaPoguliaeva
Shutterstock/58287853/©Mahesh Patil
Cover design: Kevin R. Brown
Interior art: Title page and chapter Sri Yantra: iStockphoto.com/23469059/©tschitscherin
All photographs © Donald Michael Kraig's personal collection
Vitruvian Man on page 108 © Elisabeth Alba
Illustrations © Kat Lunoe on pages:
48, 50, 53–54, 56, 58–59, 61, 70, 73, 75, 76–77, 79, 81–84 *(excludes the Yantras),*
109–110 *(excludes the Macrocosmic Snowflake),*
130, 144, 153, 229, 238, 249–255, 266–267,
277, 279, 281–282, 285, 304
Illustrations © Mary Ann Zapalac on pages:
107, 208–210, 214, 221, 247–248, 276
All other illustrations © Llewellyn Art Department

Llewellyn Publications is a registered trademark of Llewellyn Worldwide Ltd.

Library of Congress Cataloging-in-Publication Data
Kraig, Donald Michael, 1951–2014
Modern tantra: living one of the world's oldest, continuously practiced forms of pagan spirituality in the new millennium/by Donald Michael Kraig.—First Edition.
1 online resource.
Includes bibliographical references and index.
Description based on print version record and CIP data provided by publisher; resource not viewed.
ISBN 978-0-7387-4016-4
1. Tantrism. I. Title.
BL1283.84
294.5'5—dc23 2015033867

Llewellyn Publications
A Division of Llewellyn Worldwide Ltd.
2143 Wooddale Drive
Woodbury, MN 55125-2989
www.llewellyn.com

Printed in the United States of America

We focus our thoughts on Ganesha, the lord with one tusk.
We meditate on Ganesha, the lord who has a curved trunk.
May the one-tusked one guide us on the path toward spiritual light.

All traditional rituals begin by calling on Ganesha (also known as Ganapati), as he is the "breaker of obstacles" who helps you achieve success in your life.

Ganesha ("Gah-nesh" or "Gah-neshuh") is usually pictured as a chubby boy with the head of an elephant. The story of Ganesha is explained in chapter 3.

DEDICATION

This book is gratefully dedicated to those who have seen Tantra for what it is, and not for that which it is not. Specifically, I would like to thank some of my most important teachers:

H. H. Sri Paramahamsa Mahendranath (Dadaji), 23rd Adiguru (chief guru) of the Adinath tradition, whose influence transcends anything he could have guessed before his great samadhi (physical death). His teachings will inspire Tantrics—especially Western Tantrics—for ages to come.

Sri Lokanath Maharaj (Michael Magee), who has been quietly sharing his knowledge and providing the true essence of Tantra while others make up fantasies or simply repeat nonsense they read elsewhere.

Dr. Jonn Mumford, a true Tantric, filled with joy, laughter, and the willingness to share his vast wisdom.

Sunyata Saraswati, an inspiring teacher of the entire mind, body, and spirit.

The initiates of AMOOKOS and its offshoots, who continue with their development and practice of the system originally presented by Dadaji and Lokanath.

Shama Helena, whose strong voice reveals the importance of energy work and Tantra.

The many fine revealers of Tantric truths over the past 150 years, from Arthur Avalon (Sir John Woodroffe) to Harish Johari.

Carl Llewellyn Weschcke, who believed that a more comprehensive approach to Tantra was long needed.

And finally, I am especially grateful to the president and members of NAMASTE, who have allowed me to present much of their Tantric system for the new millennium.

CONTENTS

ILLUSTRATIONS

CHARTS

FOREWORD

By Carl Llewellyn Weschcke

The author of this book just recently passed away at far too young an age. Two years previously, he wrote me his objectives for this book:

> The goal of this book is to present Tantra as a ***complete spiritual system***, just as my *Modern Magick* presented a complete magickal system.

I first met Don Kraig in San Diego where he shared an apartment with Scott Cunningham, author of so many of our books on magical herbs, earth magic, crystals and gems, Paganism and Wicca, and more. Scott and Don had attended college together and shared their interests in these subjects and in becoming writers and authors, which led to them both submitting their first books to Llewellyn. The rest, so to speak, is history.

From this start I knew Don Kraig for more than forty years, first as a friend, then as a contributor to *Gnostica* magazine and author of the early edition of *Modern Magick*, and on to his joining the Llewellyn staff in St. Paul as a copy writer, then as an editor of *New Times*, then as editor of *Fate* magazine, and then back to Los Angeles as an acquisitions editor, manager of the Llewellyn Encyclopedia, and copy manager for our trade catalogs.

In all these years we were good friends, sharing ideas for books we wanted to write and books we wanted to see published, and ideas and ideals about subjects of mutual interest—mainly the ***serious*** studies and practices of Magick, Tantra, Kabbalah, and the various Pagan traditions in today's *New Age*.

And we shared in the belief that the "New Age" is *REAL*, and not just a passing *phase*. For us, it is the beginning of a long-term Cosmic Cycle of challenge and response, of climate and environmental change, of the advent of amazing scientific and technological change, and a raising and *expansion* of Human consciousness—all leading towards a coming era of global civilization free of present-day religious and political conflict with individuals increasingly free of dependency on the "other."

I underlined the word "serious" in a previous paragraph for some very good reasons. *"Serious"* in the context of the *Book World* means books with *depth, breadth, validity,* and *vision*. Such a concept was always important to both of us as cultural observers, as writers, editors, and publishers. Yes, we want books that attract a substantial audience, but we write for an audience of **Doers** and **Users**, not just readers and students.

Of course I do not mean to denigrate "students" in any way—*we are all (or should be) life-long students:* individuals learning, developing, and *growing* in skills and accomplishment, thus *becoming more than we are!*—but some people are content just to know *about* a subject in an academic sense, while Don wrote for those that are Doers and User-Practitioners. Nor do I mean to denigrate more casual or curious "readers" who just want to read about subjects actively mentioned in the news or talked about among friends. Contrary to some old folklore, *curiosity* is a good thing that starts one on the path to greater knowledge and innovation.

All those students and readers are the people who can later decide to pursue these subjects in a more intensive manner, so it is important that we make our "serious" books accessible to all readers. When we say this book is a "Complete Spiritual System," we do mean exactly that, *and* ***also*** *that it is accessible and meaningful to all readers—casual, curious, student, academic, beginner, advanced, and serious practitioners.*

In other words, *you* can be confident that this book qualifies to meet your goals as a reader and then as a book that will "grow" with you as your interest may expand and deepen.

Tantra Is More Than You May Think!

Many people, perhaps most Americans and Europeans, think of Tantra only as an extended sexual performance in which men and women both learn to delay orgasm in order to experience more intense and prolonged sexual pleasure—even to the point (particularly for women) of genuine ecstasy and even altered states of consciousness leading to such extra-physical phenomenon as spontaneous ESP and Out-of-Body Experiences.

Stop for a moment and think: *Tantric Sex practices can lead to* ***spontaneous*** *psychic experiences, and altered states of consciousness.* "Spontaneous" in this context is nearly the same as saying "Accidental." Tantra, as a "Complete Spiritual System," was not given to the pioneering Tantrics as a fully developed system by angels or other "Higher Beings," *nor was any other system, evolved practice, or religion, despite the many myths to the contrary.*

Rather, as we live and "reach" for new and more complex objectives, we *grow—actually we* **evolve**—not in the Darwinian "Survival of the Fittest" sense, but in *the Human sense of "responding to the challenge" of need and desire leading to "Growth and Development through the Effort to Accomplish Specific Goals."* Humans are *Innovators, Inventors, Instigators, and Improvers:* As we seek to improve our condition or situation, making our lives richer, we are rewarded through *Inspiration* and *Intuition* to accomplish our goals and thus to develop new abilities and skills. That's how *Human* Evolution works.

Real Tantric Sex Can Lead to States of Higher Consciousness

Any activity that accidentally induces such particular psychic and spiritual experiences (as through Tantric Sex) can be turned into *serious* controlled methods of Higher Development and Attainment. **Altered States** become the means to explore *realities beyond the purely physical dimension* even as **Bodily States** provide the "leverage" to raise and focus consciousness in other dimensions that facilitate psychic empowerment and the power to "map" the non-physical universe and the "anatomy" of our own subtle bodies.

We Now Call Those Early Self-Initiates "Shamans"

Shamanism was never a so-called "primitive religion," nor was it confined to any geographic area (such as Siberia, where it was first explored by relatively modern "*Soul Academics*"), nor was or is Shamanism specific to any historic period. Shamans, men and women alike—often as couples—are the Astral Travelers who "see" where the best hunting grounds are, when and where the best fishing can be had, where the best food crops grow, and where the natural healing springs and waterfalls are. They have become energy healers, have learned the inner nature of plants and herbs, and have built a huge pharmacopeia of natural remedies and magickal herbs benefiting all of humanity.

As Shamans, and other "seekers," found ways to open hidden doors to alternative levels of consciousness and new dimensions of the non-physical universe, new systems developed and continued to evolve into those that today we know as Tantra, the Kabbalah, Taoist Cosmology and Alchemy, Magick, and Spiritism. It is from these and their related mythologies that various religions developed (and not the other way around), but those religions and later physical and psychic sciences are **not** advancements upon their roots, but are institutionalized alternatives that have largely lost their way as they became political and economic powers lacking the very spirit of those early initiates.

It is Shamanic Tantra that inspired and slowly developed into the Hindu religion that today (with over 960 million adherents) is acknowledged as the world's oldest, with a mythology still shared between Tantra, the older shamanic-based spiritual and magickal system, and the Hindu religion, the mythic-based cosmology and priest-based institution, and each together led into the development of the various Yogas and knowledge of the chakra system, the Ayurvedic system of alternative medicine, and more.

The Contrasting Role of Myth in Religion vs. Experiential Shamanism

In contrast to the developmental role of Alternative States of Consciousness leading to actual experience of the *inner realities* of the Human Person (physical and spiritual), of Nature in all its manifestations (physical and spiritual), of the universe (physical and cosmic), Myth is all together *another story!*

Mythology can best be understood as a kind of "pre-science" attempting to explain observed phenomena in familiar human terms related to the memories and culture of peoples in a relatively defined geographic area. *This is important!* The mythology of people living in a hot, dry desert is going to be different from that of people living in a pleasant coastal area. And yet there are certain similarities between those cultures (and their mythologies and shamanic experiences) that developed along major river basins like the Nile, the Tigris and Euphrates, the Indus and Ganges, the Rhine, the Mississippi, the Yellow, the Niger, and others. Such large river basins led to stable agrarian cultures, while their navigable rivers led to communication and trade with others.

The pre-history of the people living in the Indus Valley, now part of India (just as the name suggests), was that of a peaceful agrarian people experiencing Nature as bountiful and nurturing in an "Earth Mother" sense, and primarily free of contact with people of a different way of life—*until* the invasion by Aryan cattle herders with a strong military and a ruling all-male "Sky Father" priesthood. While this is a simplistic presentation, the conquering Aryans introduced a *Caste* system with male priests at the top, the male military next, then a developing trading and merchant class, and the "native" farmers at the bottom. Women lost the status they previously held to become veritable chattel of the men.

The new rulers adapted much of the previous culture's Shamanic Tantra into the new religion we know today as Hinduism—the same Gods and Goddesses, but with a switch to a mainly male god dominance over the female, and a loss of many of the personal magickal elements that conflicted with the male priesthood's political dominance over the Hindu society.

The Mythical Foundations of Various Religions Have No Historical Validity

The primary distinction between Eastern and Western culture today is the *exclusionary* monotheism of the three major religions of Middle Eastern origin (Judaism, Christianity, and Islam), with the additional element proclaiming the various mythic stories as actual history—and thus removing the *inner* spiritual dimension from the individual person to that of an external spiritual power delegated to a mythically empowered historic figure (Moses, Jesus, Mohammed) and administered by an institutional priesthood with a theology fixed to a past time.

"Religion," by its very definition of *binding together*, is the unifying of masses under institutional leadership organized around a mythical story with a dated and unchanging theology. Simply speaking, people *belonging* to the dominant religions are united by a common "belief system" of which they have little understanding, and in which they have little interest other than the emotional security of *Belonging*.

Historically, religion united people into a tribal community. The myth is the story of a religious foundation that has little to do with historical accuracy. It is, rather, a story to justify the organization of a leader and followers under a common defense shield. The group is a kind of extended family unified not by blood or genuine belief but by confidence in mutual support against any enemy—or "stranger."

The belief system was of little importance to most members of the group who would blindly follow the leader who promised protection against warring tribes. At the same time, the belief system itself became important to the leadership (1) as a means to "crowd control" and (2) as a means of self-justification for their position.

But that leadership cannot tolerate internal competition, hence personal spiritual communication and any development of psychic skills are **condemned** under the monopolistic dominance of the centralized control of Temple, Church, and Mosque. A famous example is the sad story of Joan of Arc, burned to death because she refused to recant her claim that Angels spoke directly to her in contradiction to the Church's dicta that only ordained clergy had that power.

Spirit, as an inner reality of individual experience, is forbidden other than in minor "outsider" evangelical and mystical sects.

The *Personal* Shamanic Experience at the Beginning

All religions have their foundation in personal Shamanic experience, and each has a "prehistoric" element generally called "mystical," but in actuality is also "shamanic" and "magickal." The "Mystical" is involved with the beginnings of a religion, while the pre-religious "shamanic" continues to become a "Complete Spiritual System" which necessarily is inclusive of both a Magickal and a Psychic Empowerment Program unique to its cultural origins.

The basic Mythology is a shared element to both the Religion and the originating Shamanic Beginning. But for the Religion, the mythic story is proclaimed to be **historically** real and hence is frozen in time along with its theology and eventually its rituals and dogma.

For the Shamanic Spiritual and Magickal system, the mythic elements and related correspondences, rituals, and *Vision* continue to evolve with personal experience. Nothing is "frozen," nothing is perpetuated but rather is modified as new experience deepens and broadens knowledge and practice.

Where did the original story come from? From direct and personal Shamanic experience which is tribal (geographical local) and hence its "truths" were variously unique to time and place. Hence, "my God is **not** your God," and wars often result as the interests (real estate and economics) of one group (tribe) collide with another. It is only in modern times that the belief systems of various myths have evolved into comprehensive psychological and spiritual systems independent of the organizational leadership. Thus, most Rabbis know little about the Kabbalah, most Hindu priests know nothing about Tantra, and most Christian, Islamic, and Buddhist clergy reject "unauthorized" magickal and mystical practices. While they refer to them as dangerous to the soul of the practitioner, their fear is to their own inability to "practice what they preach."

In other words, the religious clergy do not want to lose control over the individual but prefer that everyone remain among the spiritually dependent "flock."

Tantra Is Not a Religion, but a Complete Spiritual System of Personal Growth and Psychic Empowerment

As a student of Tantra and a Tantric practitioner, YOU are the empowered Priest/Priestess. You are free from external domination. You may choose to participate in a small group of like-minded individuals—a coven, a magickal order, a study group, or a group coming together for seasonal and other celebrations—but in the final analysis you are ultimately "your own guru." Your growth and advancement are experiential and not a matter of initiatory or academic degrees.

Tantra is a complete Spiritual System. More importantly, it is **not** a system derived from an older tradition, or one that is an amalgam of other traditions. Even more important, it is not one constructed for political purposes or maintained by an organizational structure.

Tantra is Shamanic and personal in origin, inspired by images and symbols experienced in altered states of consciousness. These images and symbols are those from many shamanic journeys, and each has grown in strength and meaning through repeated experiences, both of invocation and evocation. Over the centuries and millennia, experiment and direct experience have added to the complexity of the images of deities with associated signs and symbols giving each deity specific application of their energies. And those added Signs and Symbols have become "cross-indexed" as *correspondences* much in the manner of the Kabbalah. *"Here be Magick!"*

It is this that makes Tantra REAL, a technology of living that is both Spiritual and Practical, together not separate. Tantra *can* be a system of personal growth and development, *can* be a system of Magick and a method for personal

Success, *can* be a means to a deep Intimate Partnership, and *can* be a lifestyle that comprehends all that is potential to our New Age. *We are the Masters of our own Destiny!*

While *Tantra is not* a religion in the conventional Western sense, it has helped shape both Tibetan Buddhism and many branches of Hinduism. Tantric *ideas* can be found *in most of the world's mythology, in most of the world's Spiritism and Spiritual practices, in the mystical foundations of most of the world's religions—East-West, North-South. In the Far Past and Near Present.* ***We wrote our own Mysteries!***

Most "real religions" (other than those partially derived from others, such as both Christianity and Islam) were based on Shamanic experiences of live, local individuals entering into the universal Astral World. It is not the case that early Tantrics traveled the world, missionary-style, to convert the "natives," nor that all religions and all spiritual systems come from Space Travelers or Inner Plane Masters. ***We are the Source of our own Wisdom!***

Shamanism is as ancient as Humanity, and what we call Real Tantra nearly as old. Tantra survived because early people survived a very long time without interference in the Indus Valley, and when that valley was invaded by Aryan tribes bringing a different culture, the invaders integrated much of the local culture into theirs while at the same time instituting a caste system with priests and soldiers at the top and the indigenous farmers at the bottom—much in the same manner as the Catholic invaders of northern Europe and then of Central and South America integrated bits of local Pagan cultures into the Church's system of holy days and sacred places.

"*Tantra does not* have a central doctrine. The written texts are primarily practical manuals, and no one text or group of texts can be considered authoritative." This is true not only for Tantra, but for all spiritual systems and religions formed prior to the invention of writing about 4000 BCE. All modern religions are based on adaptations of various mythologies to suit the purposes of their organizers.

As a complete spiritual system, Tantra can be defined in many ways, and the author gives us this list:

> "*Tantra is* the magic of transforming your consciousness and thereby transforming your entire being. Your body is the most powerful tool for bringing about this transformation.
>
> '*Tantra is* a spiritual science. Tantric techniques have been tested and have proven effective for many centuries. If you practice diligently, you will experience results."
>
> "*Tantra is* a way of life. The Tantric approach to exploring your own consciousness is an ever-evolving process of discovery that emerges from daily practice.
>
> "*Tantra can* provide you with the means to deepen your sense of connection to self, to your partner, to all that is.
>
> "*Tantra is* a technology of mind and body that will lead you to know yourself deeply."
>
> "*Tantra is* a practical way to loosen the bonds of unconscious, habitual behavior and thereby start to live more freely and fully.
>
> "*Tantra is* the discipline of becoming yourself completely.

> "*Tantra is* pragmatic and non-moralistic. You can utilize whatever tools are at hand for the purpose of expanding consciousness."
>
> And his concluding statement:
>
> "Tantra is **the Science of Self-Exploration.**"

That's the real foundation of any Complete Spiritual System.

In the section titled "Some Tantric Goddesses of Magick," the author reveals more than what the words say. It is the Feminine that contains and provides the creative energy that is Magick, and it is by the Feminine form and her costume and ornaments that Masculine will is excited and given direction. In Anima and Animus, form is transformed, matter becomes energy, and energy under will, and Divinity manifests the World we Know.

In invoking the Goddess, and other ritual and meditative practices of identification with a particular deity, you are doing two things: (1) applying a specific deific force for a particular purpose (Magick) and (2) ultimately conditioning your lower **self** to become whole and united with your Higher **Self**.

In the mystical language of Tantra's Sri Vidya, symbols (including images of gods and goddesses and their accessories), and the Kabbalah's Tree of Life and system of correspondences, we have the underpinning of modern metaphysics, magick, psychology, divination, mysticism, and—surprise, surprise—science and mathematics! In fact, the Tree of Life acts as a structural map of the astral world, and hence a guide to inner plane understanding and action.

"One of the secrets of Tantra is that, above all, Tantra is experiential. All of the writing is meaningless unless you can incorporate the concepts into your consciousness and your actions... The ultimate guide, as with shamanic practice, is your experience, not what someone else writes or says."

The author compares the universal organizing principle of the Kabbalistic Tree of Life to the Tantric Sri Yantra. He refers to Sir John Woodroffe, the British scholar and translator, writing in the early twentieth century when India was still part of the British Empire:

> According to Woodroffe, the Sri Yantra represents both the human body and the universe. In this sense, the system of the Sri is in complete harmony with the Kabalists' Tree of Life.
>
> Because it's important to understand the concept that the Divine can be in everything, I'm repeating a basic idea here: Yantras, including the Sri Yantra, are more than the purely linear diagrams they appear to be. They actually *are* the goddess or god in two-dimensional form—they are not a symbol, an analog, a representation, or a metaphor of the Divine—they *are* the Divine. At least, this is the traditional description. I prefer to consider them a home for the Divine. They become the Goddess or God when you call the appropriate deity into the device.

Projecting the Sri Yantra onto the human body is another concept and practice comparable to a standard Kabalistic practice. It can also be seen as a technique for conscious bridging of *Inner* and *Outer*—called "individuation" in Jung's Analytical Psychology, and far more suitable for personal "Self-Transformation" or "Transformational Alchemy." Either the Kabalistic or the Tantric practice is at the base of the Complete Spiritual System of the two fundamental non-religious mystical systems.

The practice of Mantra with the Sri Yantra is another valuable meditational practice that is "core" to **REAL TANTRA**. In other words, there comes a point when *this is no longer a book about Tantra but is Tantra itself.*

"The most important 'tool' for Tantric work is the body/mind/spirit."

This is, of course, true for any "living" spiritual practice, but has been negated and forgotten in those traditions still based on religious theologies and myths frozen in time. All Magickal, Spiritual, and Divinatory "Tools" are very useful, both in symbolic form and as a means to multiplying our projection and specification of energies—but that of the trained mind is the most powerful of all. In the major religions, that mental aspect is replaced by rote gestures.

The Inner Secrets of "Esoteric Anatomy"

While knowledge of the subtle bodies and their physical and etheric connections has become relatively familiar in the West over the last two hundred years, at least to students and practitioners of various esoteric subjects, even serious students still lack a comprehensive understanding of the "Whole Picture" and are unable to fully integrate these "higher" levels into their "Conscious Awareness" for direct perception and intentional application in spiritual and magickal work.

In this book, we have a basic outline of the *esoteric anatomy* long ago experientially discovered by the earliest shamans from which pre-Hindu Tantra evolved. It doesn't really matter what the real "history" may be—whether these origins are 30 thousand years old or 30 million, whether brought to shamans in many cultures around the globe by Deific Masters or Space Aliens, or that they may be purely the result of shamanic journeys deep into inner space.

We are, unfortunately, too conditioned to look to external authority and guidance—whether to the "Distant Past" or to the "Distant Present" (anointed gurus and credentialed academics)—when the ultimate resource is personal experience. We benefit from Past explorers and teachers, but human growth and development is accomplished through personal action, not from "following the leader," no matter who or what that may be.

The More You Know, the Deeper and Higher You Can Go!

While this rule is true for any subject, the understanding of "esoteric anatomy" and subtle energy movements is a deeper matter requiring "inner work" to bring it to the same level as we have today in Western education and life style.

Just "Sex Stuff"!

The story of how Tantra was denigrated as just "sex stuff" and "black magic" is familiar in the evolution of all religions from their shamanic origins. The ordained priesthood cannot tolerate competition from the individual shamanic magician, healer, prophet, clairvoyant, etc., against the organization. Despite claims to the contrary, all religions are "anti-spiritual"—they cannot tolerate the *Inner* Spirit of the individual in place of the proclaimed *External* Deity of their Divine Myth.

In the case of Tantra, as "discovered" by the British "Victorians" in nineteenth-century Imperial India, *Sex* was just too blatant—in the newly translated literature, everywhere in *Temple* sculptures showing men and women in exotic sexual positions engaging in oral sex and even anal sex, in the art depicting busty goddesses in provocative costumes and gods responding with huge erections, and everywhere in depictions of yoni and lingam joined together.

It was all too much for British Victorians!

The author corrects the erroneous perceptions by quoting Mark Michaels and Patricia Johnson, two popular writers of what we sometimes call "Neo-Tantra," that which is primarily devoted to good and better sexuality:

> "*Tantra is* an ancient tradition that recognizes sexual energy as a source of personal and spiritual empowerment. This sets it apart from most Western traditions and helps explain why most Westerners have reduced it to its sexual elements alone."
>
> "Tantric sexuality is about raising and manipulating energy. Both of these are done with a combination of physical and mental techniques."
>
> "You can also enjoy Tantric sexuality for just the physical pleasure. But there is so much more if you involve all aspects."

Sex and Tantric Magick

When two people make love together, there is energy exchange between their chakras—with variations of the energy flow relating to their respective positions and visualizations.

The goals of Traditional Tantric sexuality, and those for practitioners of *Modern Tantra*, are parallel with the goals of Neo-Tantra, but they are not the same. All of the goals of Neo-Tantric sexual techniques are side benefits to the Tantric sexuality of *Modern Tantra*. The primary goal in traditional Tantra is to experience and realize that you and your Atman (your Higher Self) are a single unity. The key to this is to "let go" and surrender to the intensified sexual experience in the form of the Goddess.

Creation on the Spiritual Planes Results in Creation on the Physical Plane

One of the most important lessons in this book is "by understanding that everything you do has magickal results, you can literally *design your own rituals*." Even more important is that "designing your own rituals produces more powerful magick than copying someone else's *spells*." An almost universally true corollary is that "personal magick is generally more effective than group magick because of the difficulty of getting everyone to focus on one thing at the same time." This fact is rarely admitted because people try to justify leading a group, even a small one.

Worship and Invocation of the Goddesses

Another important subject is the "worship" of select Tantric Goddesses, actually an aspect of *Invocation*. Each Goddess is distinctly named, colored, adorned, costumed, postured, etc.—all of which are symbolic keys and correspondences to Her nature and the experience to have through Her. If a male "calls down" a particular Goddess to become one with his sex mate—whether through Invocation or Evocation, or some form of voluntary and temporary induced possession—she is that Goddess and is transformed by the experience, *and so is he!*

In a different perspective, the woman thus offering herself in such a ritual makes of herself a symbolic temporary "sacrifice" of her personal self to experience with her lover/priest and her circle/community the "ecstasy of the Goddess" through an extreme and extended orgasmic trance and perhaps the highest attainable union with Divinity.

The Ultimate Journey

What more can I say about this wonderful book? The *Next Step* is yours: JUST DO IT! Read, Study, Learn, Practice, Grow, and *Become More than You are, and All You can Become!*

Shortly after Don's passing, I agreed to help with some of the unfinished manuscript's few rough spots, and Don came to me in a dream—with that broad smile so characteristic of his approval and happiness—making me feel confident with my ideas. As a reader, you will find a few "unanswered questions" in the text reflecting small disagreements between us on matters of **modernization** of ancient pre-Hindu Tantra to meet the desires for **group** working of traditional couple's rituals adapted for modern Pagans.

As in all things, it is **NOT** rigid adherence to *olden ways* that we need, but *personal* realization of what works for you, your partner, and your group. Become empowered through personal experience and personal realization.

PREFACE

For over 150 years, the very mention of the word *Tantra* has conjured exotic and erotic images. The images are those of young, nubile, dark-skinned women and virile, washboard-stomached, young men participating in strange rites and sexual orgies. The images also include darkened rooms with tapestry-covered walls lit only by flickering candles; air filled with thin trails of wafting, blue-gray smoke from strange, foreign incenses; foods enhanced by pungent, exotic seasonings; and the strains of foreign music created on mysterious instruments, with exotic melodies rarely heard by Western ears.

In a way, this development in the West of imagery associating Tantra with eroticism was almost inevitable. The first widely circulated books about Tantra were published in the West only 150 years ago during the British occupation of India. In Great Britain, this was supposedly a time of horrendous sexual repression. One of the most famous stories of such public limitations was that covers were made for the legs of pianos because it was thought the curved pieces of wood used to raise the instrument above the ground looked too much like the legs of a woman.* Being human, however, the Victorians were interested in sex—*very* interested. It was okay for them to read about sexual permissiveness as long as it took place *over there*, in a foreign country populated by dark-skinned non-Christians who would do such despicable things. ("Quick, let's read some more about these horrible people!") Even though the great books on Tantra by John Woodroffe appeared in the early 1900s, at the end of the Victorian period, he still had to use the pen name "Arthur Avalon" to disguise his identity. These texts included Tantric philosophy, theology, science, astrology, palmistry, magick, government, and other topics. Most of this was ignored by those looking for titillating information about sex.

It should be remembered, however, that the Victorian age lasted nearly seventy years. It spawned four major artistic styles (Romanticism, Realism, Pre-Raphaelitism, and

* Actually, this story is a myth based on a story invented by Captain Frederick Marryat in 1839. It was a comment on *American*, not British, attitudes, but it illustrates what many believe about the British Victorians.

Impressionism). Like today in the United States, the people of Victorian England were widely split into conservative and progressive political factions. Religion consisted of the orthodox, the liberal, and (for the first time playing a major role) those who doubted religion altogether. While the notion that some Victorians (mostly the newly growing middle class) were prim, proper, and repressed certainly has some basis in reality, there was also a wild side. Many Victorians would attend salons, where they would discuss in explicit terms such things as whether women have orgasms and how best to make sure a woman or man has pleasure during sex. In the US, where many of the ideals of England were idolized, much of this period was known as the Gilded Age (circa 1866–1901). In 1848 there was what has been called the first women's rights convention in Seneca Falls, New York, where the attendees demanded such things as equal rights for women, the right for women to speak in all religious and public situations, and women's suffrage (women were not given the right to vote in the US until 1920, over seventy years later). This period was a time of change and uncertainty and not one of monolithic prudery, as is often claimed. An example revealing that sex wasn't as repressed as many think is that during this period there was a large market for pornography (mostly through private subscription).

Even so, for many Victorians, any discussion of sexuality was considered a taboo. Frequently, what interests us most are those things that are denied us, and what was denied to the Victorians was *open* expression about sexuality. To the people of the nineteenth century and even into the first half of the twentieth century, Tantra came to mean just one thing: S E X.

To those who have cursorily studied the subject (especially over the last fifty years), Tantra has come to be equated with extending the possibilities of sexuality beyond what is considered "normal" in Western society. Again, this was almost inevitable. The new popularity of sexual experimentation (the so-called sexual revolution), which began in the 1960s and '70s, had no guidance or direction. The *Kama Sutra* (a mostly worthless book of so-called instructions for sex and courting combined with a compendium of positions for intercourse often designed only for sexual athletes and having little relationship to traditional Tantra) became required reading for the younger generation, along with *Catch-22, Profiles in Courage,* and *Stranger in a Strange Land.*

The depths of scientific studies performed by the ancient Tantrics, including research in the field of sexuality, also made valued reading among active participants in the sexual revolution. The result was that people who were used to having a sex life that was limited to brief encounters in the male-dominant missionary position opened to astounding new possibilities. And so Tantra became associated almost exclusively with extended periods of ecstatic sexuality. That association presents some difficulties and the need for clarification.

The Evolution of Concepts (Neo-Tantra vs. Traditional Tantra)

Today, in the West, *any* sort of extended sexuality is called Tantra. Perhaps even stranger, the evocative mystery of the term *Tantra* has evolved into a catchword that can mean just about anything. I have seen it used to describe everything from swimming with dolphins to having sex while you roll around in mud. The word Tantra has become a code for anything even vaguely having to do with sexual practices not part of the Western traditions that evolved from the birth of "romantic love" about 800 years ago, as well as from the publicly anti-sexual morals of the Victorian age.

There has been a similar evolution of meaning with another word with which readers of the occult may be more familiar: *Wicca*. Hundreds of years ago, this was a word for a person who could bend or twist reality. With Gerald Gardner, in the 1950s and '60s, Wicca came to represent the religion and magickal practices of people trying to reconstruct ancient, pre-Christian, Celtic spiritual traditions (at the time, some thought they were identical to the Old Ways, but that is highly unlikely). When I was first brought into the Craft of Wicca, I could count the number of available Wiccan traditions on one hand. They all had similar techniques and beliefs—very similar ones. But since its modern founding, Wicca has widened its scope so much that nobody can provide a universally accepted definition of Wicca or Wiccans. *Wicca* has become a catchall term that can mean just about anything not having to do with traditional Western spirituality. For some, it has become a spiritual smorgasbord, allowing the user to pick and choose whatever is desired, resulting in such things as Christian Wiccans (also called Christopagans or Episcopagans). This is generally a euphemism for Christianity (often of the Arian Heresy variety, which denies the deity of Jesus), complete with its ideas of guilt and sin ("Self-Inflicted Nonsense") mixed with a bit of Mariolatry (where Mary becomes, and is worshiped as, a mother goddess) and sometimes combined with a smidgen of ecological awareness and activism.

There is a similar situation with the recent evolution of the meaning of the occult term *pathworking*. Originally, this word described the process and experience of projecting one's consciousness up the astral paths represented on the mystical symbol known as the Kabalistic Tree of Life. However, the meaning of the term has expanded to mean any sort of visualized journey. Now I find that I need to use the phrase *Kabalistic pathworking* when describing the original process.

Yet another example is that of the term *quantum leap*. A quantum leap in its original sense meant the *smallest* jump resulting in a significant change. This could yield surprising and unexpected results. Today, however, most people use this term to mean a giant leap forward.

These explanations of the meanings of terms as used in the past and how they have evolved away from their original meanings are not meant to be subjective condemnations. They are merely descriptions of what has occurred.

If you are not comfortable with the currently popular (albeit traditionally incorrect) definitions of these concepts, you may have problems communicating with others. Since communication is the purpose of language, using terms in ways that are traditionally correct but go against the wave of popular opinion defeats your entire purpose. I have also found that attempting to do so is as futile as trying to hold back the ocean tides with a bucket.

If we ignore the people who use the word Tantra as a catchword to mean anything they want it to mean, we are left with traditional forms of Tantra and a more popularized Tantra. Traditional Tantra (also called classical Tantra, initiatory Tantra, etc.) is far more than the study and practice of spiritualized and extended sexuality. The traditional forms of Tantra are complete systems of Pagan spirituality. As such, they include religious and magickal rites, the worship of a god and goddess in numerous forms, alchemy, natural magick, symbology, astral projection, spiritualized sexuality, ritual magick, philosophy, medicine, palmistry, astrology, divination, gem magick, martial arts, and much more.

The type of popularized Tantra that has evolved today, and which numerous people and groups are publicly teaching, is but a tiny part of traditional Tantra. Perhaps it would be more accurate to call these forms of extended, spiritualized sexuality by the term used by both the late Osho (Bhagwan Shree Rajneesh) and his contemporary, the late Georg Feuerstein: *Neo-Tantra.*

Neo-Tantra focuses almost exclusively on sexual ecstasy and pleasure; the preparation for this via such things as movement, sound, breath, and touch; and (frequently, to a greatly diminished extent) any spiritual results that may ensue from such techniques. Neo-Tantra is but one aspect of traditional Tantra. Feuerstein claimed the amount of traditional Tantric wisdom and information found in Neo-Tantra from some of these teachers (and their books) to be so small that a person initiated into a traditional Tantric system might not recognize it as Tantra at all.

Do not think, however, that I am downplaying the value and importance of Neo-Tantra. In many cases, Neo-Tantra has removed the excesses that have accrued and attached themselves to traditional Tantra as it has evolved over the centuries. This is similar to the way some who are practicing the relatively new magickal system of chaos magick have eliminated the often useless extras that have, over the centuries, adhered to ceremonial magick.

Much of what is taught by those spreading the knowledge of Neo-Tantra is part of traditional, initiatory Tantra. Some of the techniques, subjects, and methods explained by the teachers of Neo-Tantra will be covered here. However, they will be presented in the context of the full range of traditional Tantra. In this way, it is hoped you will get the best of both traditional Tantra and Neo-Tantra combined in a system usable for individuals and groups. To sum up:

Tantra, as presented in *Modern Tantra,* is an entire Pagan system originally from India. It is intended to be understood, practiced, and used by people in the West and all over the world, both today and for the rest of this new millennium.

I would urge readers to be wary of those whom I am beginning to refer to as Tantric dogmatists. Let me clearly state that there is no such thing as the original form of Tantra, true Tantra, the only form of Tantra, etc. Nobody can speak "for Tantra," and Tantra doesn't "say" anything. There are, in actuality, many different traditions or schools of Tantra. This fact, however, does not stop people from writing books, articles, and blogs claiming theirs is the only true way. This is perhaps the worst when it appears in forums on the Internet, as the more people believe that theirs is the only way, the more they tend to be bullies, at first disagreeing, then insulting, and finally comparing anyone who dares to suggest that there are alternatives to their dogmas with Hitler or the Nazis (a phenomenon known on the Internet as "Godwin's Law").

In my book *Modern Sex Magick*, I tried to present a completely Western approach to the subject without including Taoist or Tantric sexual practices. Because I have been influenced by those traditions, I'm sure some of their ideas slipped in. Similarly, although the practices and concepts presented here are traditional and derived from the practices of pre-Hindu India, at times my Western spiritual training may influence my wording or approach in the hope that it may be easier for people with a Western background to understand. While there may be similarities to some Western concepts, they are Tantric and not Western rip-offs.

What you will read here is *a* Tantric way. It is not *the* Tantric way, the *only* Tantric way, the *original* Tantric way, or the *true* Tantric way. I apologize in advance if anything in these pages gives the impression that I think or believe otherwise. I can say, however, that this system has worked for me and for many others. If you feel it calling and pulling at your soul, it may work for you, too.

Why We Don't Have a Complete Knowledge of Tantra

In the West today, we are generally not living under the sexual repression that was rampant 150 years ago (although some seem intent on reintroducing it). Therefore, you may be wondering why the many sublime aspects of traditional Tantric wisdom are absent from most Western books on Tantra. The answer may have to do with Western civilization's 2,000-year-long love-hate relationship with Christianity.

Many of the most famous Christians throughout history have told the same story: "I screwed up and was saved. You should not screw up." St. Augustine told of his wild youth in his *Confessions*, but told everyone else not to do the same. One televangelist, media mogul, politician, and billionaire has admitted that his fiancée was pregnant with his child when they got married, but tells us not to do the same. There has been an embarrassing number of sex-denied Roman Catholic priests who have been accused and convicted of sexually abusing boys, and more than one televangelist—brought down by a sex scandal—has returned to the public eye, still preaching. I find it odd that these religious leaders expect people to accept their interpretation of the religion when they did not, and often still do not, follow such rules themselves.[1] These leaders only came to accept the teachings later in life. Today, some Christians are quick to condemn homosexuals, using the excuse for their homophobia that the condemnation comes from the Bible, not from them; but they ignore the passages in the Bible about sexual impropriety, financial impropriety, and divorce. They can't accept that according to their own interpretation of their religion they are continuing to sin against their view of God's will.

And even though some Christian leaders deny it, their attitude is distinctly anti-sex. Since Christianity is the religious paradigm of the West, especially in the US, that anti-sex attitude has pervaded society. For the most part, each of us in the West—even if we were not raised or currently are not Christian—has been inculcated with anti-sex beliefs. The result has been that the scientific study of sexuality and eroticism has, for the most part, remained underfunded and hidden. And the result of not having access to scientific and erotic information about sex has resulted in a huge market for marriage manuals and books on sex as well as an enormous above-ground market for erotic photos, videos, and information (which made multimillionaires of Hugh Hefner, Bob Guccione, Larry Flynt, and a small coterie of pornographers). If so many of us in the West did not have such an anti-sex attitude, if sexual information were easily available, if erotica were included on the bestsellers lists instead of hidden under beds,

1 My surprise at the way followers continue to believe in failed leaders exists in spite of the evidence in the book *When Prophecy Fails*, by Leon Festinger, Henry Riecken, and Stanley Schachter, which shows that this attitude in followers is actually the common response to instances where a leader says something should happen and it does not occur.

there would be little need for pornography or the never-ending parade of repetitious sex manuals, as well as finger-pointing and condemnation, by self-righteous "experts."

The massive natural interest in sexuality, combined with the love-hate feelings toward what some call "Christian morality," has resulted in the current trend of equating that foreign idea, Tantra, with *anything* sexual, especially extended periods of sexual activity. Even so, aspects of the true nature of traditional Tantra, of which Tantric sexuality is but a part, have appeared in various books and magazine articles, although rarely in one place.

What *Is* Tantra?

One of the problems with understanding Tantra is that there is no universally accepted definition of the term. Perhaps by looking at several meanings of the word you will get a better idea of what Tantra really means.

One definition of Tantra is that it comes from the Sanskrit words *tanoti* ("to expand") and *trayati* ("to liberate"). According to this interpretation, Tantra is a way of expanding the consciousness in order to achieve transcendence.

Another definition is that the word Tantra comes from the Sanskrit words *tan* and *tra*, meaning "warp" and "woof," the threads that run vertically and horizontally on a weaver's loom. Thus, it is a spiritual path that is the warp and woof of all reality.

Others see the image of the warp and woof of a weaver's loom and believe it looks like the web of a spider. Therefore, Tantra is seen to mean the expanding *web* of knowledge.

Still others say that Tantra means any of the following:

Body, because unlike many spiritual traditions that ignore the physical world for some invisible spiritual universe, Tantra emphasizes our physical world and physical activities as well as the spiritual worlds.

Stretch, because the practices of Tantra, if followed, will enable you to extend or stretch your senses and abilities beyond those possessed by non-Tantrics.

Rope, because Tantra is a form of *yoga*, or "union," and this metaphoric rope ties followers of the Tantric path to the Divine as if they were knotted together with a rope.

Harp, because the magnificence and beauty of Tantric thought and practice seem like ethereal music. This music is found within the sublime wisdom that is Tantra.

Interior wisdom, because Tantra, like the earliest forms of the Kabalah, is an oral tradition. Even today, with so many books available on the subject, much of its doctrine remains hidden in the interior darkness of secrecy. Further, the practice of Tantra brings out our natural internal wisdom, a knowledge that some traditions ignore or denigrate.

With all the words written about Tantra, you would think that there is not much about it that is hidden. But the truth is that Tantra, first and foremost, is *experiential*, and books can only point out the direction; they cannot give you the experience. At best, books (including this one) are like the finger of a person pointing at the moon. You may focus on that finger, but you can never really know the moon without observing it—participating in its essence—directly. There is still much about Tantra that has never been written. It cannot be written. It can only be experienced.

The Purpose of *Modern Tantra*

I wrote this book because I want to share the nature of Tantra in its fullness. I want to give you an idea of what it would be like to live as a real Tantric every minute of every day. You see, *Modern Tantra* is not about some sexual practice or merely reading a philosophy in an ancient book. It's a way of life that can fit perfectly within a modern society while it gives you added freedom, health, and happiness. Tantrics literally wake up every morning happy to be experiencing another fantastic day. It's ancient wisdom—perhaps the oldest in the world—made practical for today. The system described in these pages is perfect for people who want to be part of a tradition that is genuinely ancient yet as modern as tomorrow, a living tradition that is available to any who find it appeals to their soul. This book will show you how to follow a Tantric path and live as a practitioner of a Tantric tradition.

I have already described how there are two major trends in Tantra, traditional and Neo-Tantric. Providing a description and some practices of both—Tantra in its fullness—is another purpose of this book.

Unfortunately, there is no way a single book could possibly contain everything about Tantra. Over the past several thousand years, so much has been written—and even more remains unwritten—that Tantric information fills thousands of books (for historical purists, this includes books directly considered Tantric and books that are precursors to what is now called Tantric). Plus, much of the information in those sources concerns ancient periods of time and has little relevance today. This means that any modern book on Tantra must actually be a *filter*, limiting what is presented to the reader. Most books on Tantra won't tell you that. I have always felt that I should be totally honest with my readers. That is why I am going to tell you what this book is *not* about.

First, this book is not about Western sex magick. Although there certainly are similarities, there are also vast differences, the most important difference being that *Western sex magick is a technology of magick, whereas Tantra is an entire Pagan system of spirituality*. For more information on Western sex magick, see my books *Modern Magick* and especially *Modern Sex Magick*.

Second, this book is not about Tibetan Tantra. There is only so much that can be covered in one book. This book will give a basic introduction to the subject and provide enough information for practice by individuals and groups. To add a study of Tibetan Tantra to this book would make a volume far too large to be clear. It would also prevent the presentation of a Tantric path as a single, practical Pagan system.

Third, unlike many books on Tantra (actually Neo-Tantra), *Modern Tantra* is not just about sex. Yes, you will find that Tantric sexuality, especially the type propounded by practitioners of Neo-Tantra, will play a role in this book, but you will also see that there is much more.

Fourth, any healing methods described or implied in this book are not meant to supersede licensed medical techniques. Rather, they should complement Western medicine. Consult with your health professional before changing your current health practices.

Fifth, and perhaps most important, *this is not the Tantra of thousands of years ago*. Tantra has evolved, improved, and changed to meet the needs of the times. *Modern Tantra* is meant to answer the needs of people for today and, I hope, for many decades to come.

What this book will attempt to show is that Tantra is to the East what Witchcraft or Wicca is to the West. Like Paganism and its relationship to Christianity, the origins of Tantra predate Hinduism[2] and have influenced virtually every aspect of Hindu culture. Still, describing Tantra as an outside spiritual system to Hinduism is not as far afield as it may sound. Thanks to the spiritual teachings of people such as Swami Vivekananda, Mahatma Gandhi, and others, there has been what is known as the "Hindu Renaissance." This form of Hinduism, especially popular among modern urban Indians, is as different from many forms of traditional Hinduism as modern Judaism is different from the practices during biblical times. Inspired by the Muslim period of Indian control and then the attitudes and spirituality of the British whose control of India followed that of Islam, much of modern Hinduism is puritanical, ascetic, and anti-aesthetic. This use of the phrase "Hindu Renaissance" comes from the writings of Agehananda Bharati. He refers to it also as a kind of "Christianized Hinduism." This is no more traditional than the Christian Wicca described earlier.

So should Westerners be interested in Tantra as a complete spiritual system? After all, many years ago, famed occultist Dion Fortune wrote that we should try to become attuned with and use the magick of the country in which we live. But with television, the Internet, telephones, radios, fax machines, and other forms of rapid communication, the entire world has become what Marshall McLuhan called a "Global Village." This is something Fortune apparently did not foresee. I believe that Tantra is now an ideal spiritual system for people in the West as well as in the East. This book, then, will introduce some of the religious, philosophical, spiritual, magickal, healing, and, yes, sexual aspects of Tantra. In *Modern Magick* and *Modern Sex Magick*, I wrote that "magick is not something you do, magick is something you are." Likewise, the more you experience Tantra, the more it will become a part of you. Tantra will become something you are. You will be a real Tantric.

One of the difficulties many people have with books on traditional Tantra is the frequent use of Sanskrit words. When I was first writing this book, I tried to avoid such words as much as possible. I discovered that working around such terms was inefficient. I realized that the colorful, euphonic, and meaning-rich Sanskrit terms would often best express my intent. I decided that they should not be eliminated. To make it easier for comprehension, Sanskrit or specialized words and terms will be immediately defined and listed in the glossary at the end of this book. Even so, when there is no need to use a Sanskrit term, I have not done so. Those of you who have already studied some Tantric books may find English words instead of Sanskrit ones. Don't get upset. Rather, please understand that this book is designed to help

2 This concept may anger some traditional Vedic-oriented Hindus who believe that all aspects of Hindu belief and tradition, including Tantra, came from the Vedas. However, the major deities found in the Vedas include Agni (god of fire), Indra (god of war, weather, and king of the gods), Varuna (god of the sky and rain), and Prajapati (Creator), deities with few temples in India dedicated to them. They are not an important daily part of modern Hinduism. On the other hand, the traditional Tantric deities, including Ganesh, Hanuman, and especially Shiva and Shakti in her forms of Durga and Kali, are some of the most important deities in Hinduism today, and India is literally filled with temples dedicated to them. I would also add the comment from his "Note to Readers" in *Essence of Tantra* by R. L. Kashyap (2007): "Tantra is often misunderstood. Inter[e]stingly enough, many religious Hindus, who often are inclined to denounce Tantra…[do] not seem to realize that many of the practices dear to their hearts like the ritual worship at home and temples, the invocation of the deity in icons, etc., are all derived and supported by Tantric Knowledge."

Westerners get past the difficulties and learn the spiritual essence and power of Tantra.

Sources

The teachings in this book come from four major sources. First and foremost, they come from ancient and evolving Tantric traditions. I do recommend books published by the Bihar School of Yoga. The second source comes from my initiatory experiences and training with organizations including AMOOKOS (Arcane Magical Order of the Knights of Shambhala) and other lesser-known groups, as well as private training and discussion with various individual Tantrics and Neo-Tantrics. The third source is my own practice and the reports and experiences of my students. And the fourth source is the modern Tantric system set forth by NAMASTE: the New Association of MAgical, Sexual, and Tantric Explorers. NAMASTE is divided into two sections: Eastern and Western. Those who follow the Western section study and practice sex magick along the lines described in *Modern Sex Magick*. Those who follow the Eastern section study and practice Tantra as a complete spiritual system analogous to what might accurately be called "Tantric Paganism."

Oy Vey! What's a Nice Jewish Boy Like You Doing in a Place Like This?

That's a darn good question. People who have read my works over the years know my spiritual interests have been oriented primarily toward Western occult traditions, not those of the East. For many years I wanted to try to keep the teachings of Western and Eastern occultism separate. Even so, because Eastern concepts have filtered into Western ideas, I included some of that information in my book *Modern Magick*. When I wrote *Modern Sex Magick*, however, to the best of my ability I eliminated any Eastern concepts, although I'm sure people will find some there. In my personal life, even though I had trained with teachers in certain aspects of Zen and Taoist practice, I wanted to keep things strictly Western. I always pointed out that the power centers used in the Kabalistic Middle Pillar ritual are similar to but *not* the same as the Eastern chakras. In my studies of the Golden Dawn system, I avoided the use of the tattvas and the tattvic tides. Those concepts—decidedly Tantric in nature—were taken from just one book, *Nature's Finer Forces* by Rama Prasad, and there was plenty to study and practice in the Golden Dawn system without them. I wanted to stay Western. *But the gods had different plans for me!*

Years ago, I ended up working briefly at a used bookstore. I purchased only one book while I worked there, a rare second edition of *Nature's Finer Forces* from 1897. Later, I met British author Gareth Knight, who gifted me with the original set of tattvic symbols that had been made and used by Israel Regardie. Eventually, while living in San Diego, California, I obtained old copies of *Sothis*, a difficult-to-obtain magazine imported from England. In one issue, there was an ad for an inexpensive version of the famous Cipher Manuscripts. These were the documents upon which the Hermetic Order of the Golden Dawn was founded. I wrote to find out if any copies were still available, as the magazine was long out of print. I received a response saying it was, and the publisher also asked if I wanted to be initiated into their Tantric order. I really wasn't all that interested—it was Eastern, not Western—but why not? Soon I found myself entrenched in a study of information and practices I had never previously seen. It was nothing like anything in the popular books on Tantra. Eventually I was granted *parampara*, the right to initiate into that order, and I wondered, *Why was this study coming so easily to me?*

I didn't know. I had resisted. I hadn't read much on these topics at all when compared to the Western occultism I had studied for so many years. This information was different... and yet it was also disquietingly familiar. I didn't understand why, but I made up my mind to find out.

I grew up Jewish (for a time, I even briefly trained to be a cantor; I led High Holy Day services for seniors and Sabbath services for kids), but the Conservative branch of Judaism in which I was raised said nothing about the Kabalah per se. Even so, as I began my in-depth studies of Kabalistic concepts, I found the material very comfortable and fairly easy to understand. I had grown up with this stuff, even though much of it had not been identified to me as being Kabalistic.

Since the Kabalah was shepherded by the Jews of ancient times, I think it's fair to ask who these people were. Most of what is "common knowledge" about the ancient Jews comes from the Bible. Are the ancient stories literally true? Unlike fundamentalist Christians, most sects of Judaism do not require the belief in the literal historicity of the Bible stories. And even if they did, the stories do not give much information about where the tribes that eventually banded together to form the Jewish religion and culture came from or, most importantly, what they believed. So who were the tribes that became the Jews?

While an in-depth study of that subject is a book in itself, I can share some of the surprising results of my research. One key source was a book titled *The Jewish Festivals* by Hayyim Schauss. The copy I have was published by the Orthodox Jewish Union of American Hebrew Congregations in the early twentieth century and was a translation of the original German. The basic thrust of the book is that the ancient Jews were a bunch of disparate tribes, each with their own holidays, deities, and spiritual practices. They eventually merged under the kings of Israel and Judea, and all of the holidays were reinterpreted according to a common mythology.

Leonora Leet reinforced this concept in *The Secret Doctrine of the Kabbalah*. The usual analysis of the key prayer of Judaism, the *Sh'ma*, is that it is a declaration of monotheistic belief:

Hear, O Israel,
the Lord our God is one God.

The original Hebrew is clear. There are three clauses to what is now called a prayer: *Sh'ma Yisroel: Tetragrammaton Elohanu, Tetragrammaton echod*. The first clause is *Sh'ma Yisroel*. *Sh'ma* means "hear" or "listen" in the form of a command, and *Yisroel*, "Israel," is the calling of everyone—all the different tribes—one people: the Jews. The second clause gives the names of two different gods. The first is the deity known as the Tetragrammaton, the name composed of the Hebrew letters yud-heh-vahv-heh (frequently called "Yaweh," although Jews do not actually say the name, replacing it with *adonai*, "my lord," or *hashem*, "the name"). This is followed by *Elohanu*. The "-nu" suffix means "our," and the deity is known as *Eloah*. Scholars refer to the followers of these two deities as the *Yawists* and the *Elohists*, respectively.

Note that this clause contains no grammatical article, no form of the word *the*. In Hebrew, the article *the* is indicated by prefixing the letter *heh* before a word. Although context can imply the verb *is* in Hebrew grammar, simply placing two names next to each other makes no such implication. That second clause simply cannot be translated as "the Lord our God" or "the Lord [is] our God," as Western ears usually hear it. It is simply two different names. The second name does have a suffix indicating possession, but it is historically treated and interpreted as a name.

In the third clause, *Tetragrammaton echod,* the word *echod* is usually translated to mean "one." However, in ancient Hebrew, there were no vowels. The same letters that form the word *echod* (aleph, chet, dalet), when pronounced *ah-chaid*—the same letters, mind you—mean "to unite." Therefore, this third clause, *Tetragrammaton echod,* clearly indicates that the two deities represented by the names Tetragrammaton and Elohanu in the second clause are now united as one deity, the Tetragrammaton. This "prayer" indicates that the people are united as one people, the Jews, with one unified culture and tradition, and that their deities are now united as one god, the Tetragrammaton.

But where did the tribes come from? Of course they came from the Middle East, but they didn't just pop out of the sands, rivers, and seas. Surprisingly, the answer first requires a trip to ... ancient India.

The Mystery of the Harappan Culture

In the book *In Search of the Cradle of Civilization* by Georg Feuerstein, Subhash Kak, and David Frawley, the authors describe the ancient Harappan culture. This culture preceded the current, well-known Hindu culture. It was based not around the Ganges River, but rather around the Saraswati. When that river dried up, the people spread out. Not too much is known about the people, because the main area where they lived is now in Kashmir, an area being fought over by at least three groups—and two of them have nuclear weapons. Archeology there can be ... uh ... *difficult.*

New archeology, however, does reveal this civilization in earnest around 6000 BCE, before Egypt or Babylon. At its height, one city of this culture, Mehrgarh (which actually arose around 7000 BCE), may have had a larger population than the combined populations of the northern and southern Egyptian kingdoms. It was a huge culture that expanded not through war, but through peaceful trade. When the Saraswati dried up, the people moved south into India and what is now Sri Lanka, northeast into Tibet and China, and west into Europe.[3] Some authors (see, for example *Ann Moura's New History of Witchcraft* and *Origins of Modern Witchcraft*, both by Ann Moura, *The Celtic Druids* by Godfrey Higgins, and the works of John Aubrey and William Stukeley) believe that the travelers from India became the Druids. The word *Druid* may be based on two Sanskrit terms meaning "tree" (*dru*) and "wisdom or knowledge" (*vid*), an apt description of the Druids who did have the wisdom of the trees.

The pre-Hindu spiritual system of ancient Harappa was not goddess-based, although it did have goddesses. The primary deity was Shiva (or a proto-Shiva), hence the spiritual system is considered *Shaiva* or *Shaivite*, although he did have a goddess/consort. The spiritual system has similarities to Hinduism but appears to be much closer to traditional Tantra.

The term *Tantra* actually comes from a series of books collectively known as the Tantras, published between about 500 and 1800 CE. Westerners gave the name *Tantric* to people who followed concepts from those books. Of course, those ancient people didn't call themselves Tantrics any

3 According to the Aryan invasion theory, light-skinned invaders from the north (so-called experts have given over twenty starting locations for this mythical group) drove dark-skinned Dravidians out of the Indus Valley. However, there is no archeological evidence to support this, and modern genetic research completely refutes it.

more than ancient Celtic Pagans called themselves Wiccans or Pagans.

There are two basic beliefs as to the origin of Tantric traditions. One held by some scholars is that, like Buddhism, Tantra was a response to the repressive Brahmanism of India. Further, since the first Tantric books didn't come about until hundreds of years into the modern era, Tantra was seen as a later addition to world spirituality.

But Tantrics themselves have always maintained that Tantra was an oral tradition. *Of course* there wouldn't be any books, as people spread their ideas through word of mouth, not through writing! In fact, concepts of Tantra appear in all of the sacred books of India, including the oldest, the Rig Veda, which at a minimum dates to about 1200 BCE. Some scholars point to that book's description of astronomical events that occurred much earlier, dating the book (or its sources) back as far as about 8000 BCE. Some claim it is even older. This means that the earliest forms of Tantra—what I call "proto-Tantra"—may be 10,000 or more years old. This makes Tantra one of the world's oldest Pagan spiritual traditions that has been continuously practiced by a large culture.

One of the best-known historians of the ancient Jews was Flavius Josephus. He was Jewish and survived the destruction of Jerusalem in 70 CE. He became a Roman citizen, an action that gave him the freedom to become a historian of Judaism as well as an apologist for the actions of his original people, the Jews. Toward the end of the first century, he wrote a book called *The Antiquities of the Jews*, giving their supposed history from Adam and Eve and generally following the Bible. In it he quotes Aristotle (384–322 BCE) as saying that Jews are derived from the Indian philosophers and are known as the *Calani*. Clearchus of Soli was a student in Aristotle's school. In his book *De Somno*, he elaborates on the story of how Aristotle discovered this information, but the basic concept remained the same.

Megasthenes was a traveler who became an ambassador for Seleucus I of Syria to the court of Chandragupta Maurya, the first unifier of India, before that ruler's death in 288 BCE. According to Godfrey Higgins, in the first volume of his massive *Anacalypsis*, Megasthenes wrote that the Jews were an Indian tribe or sect called *Kalani*, basically agreeing with Aristotle and Clearchus.

Higgins also claims that Ur of the Chaldees, the home of Abraham mentioned in the Bible, was actually Ur of the *Chaldeans*. "Chaldean," he continues, is actually "Kaul-Deva," or the Holy Kauls, a Brahmanical caste of India. The Kauls (or Kaulas) today practice what is considered to be a Tantric tradition.

Higgins writes that the tribe of the Brahmin Abraham was expelled from or left India and settled in Goshen in Egypt. Finally, he states, "The Arabian historians contend that Brahma and Abraham, their ancestor, are *the same person* [emphasis added]."

Is this possible? There are surprising similarities between Brahma and Abraham:

- Brahma is often pronounced "Bram." In the Bible, Abraham is initially named Abram.
- *Ab-bram* means "Father of Bram."
- Abraham's wife is Sarah. Brahma's consort is Sarah-swati.
- Saraswati is Brahma's sister. In the Bible, Abraham introduces Sarah to Pharaoh as his sister.[4]

4 When a Jewish boy reaches thirteen years and goes through the rite of Bar Mitzvah, he reads a section of the Bible. The section I read is called *Ley-ech L'cha*. In it, Abraham identifies his wife as his sister, as mentioned here.

- A tributary of the Saraswati River is the Ghaggar. Sarah's servant is named Hagar.
- Ishmael, the son of Hagar, is said to live in "Havilah." Although the exact location of this area is debated, some claim it is in India.

Why Did Abraham Leave Ur?

Higgins wrote that Abraham was either expelled from or left India. Let's assume this is accurate. The question is, why? A clue might be found in the biblical book of Joshua where God says that Abraham was on the "other side of the flood" and God then led him to Canaan. The phrase "other side of the flood" might mean "after the flood of Noah," but it might also mean the opposite of the nature of a flood. Could this mean a drought? Did a drought force Abraham to leave Ur?

In the article "Indic Ideas in the Graeco-Roman World," Subhash Kak dates the drying up of the Saraswati that I just briefly described as "around 1900 BCE," and says that this "led to a major relocation of the population." He also points out, "It is soon after this time that the Indic element begins to appear all over West Asia, Egypt, and Greece." Abraham (assuming there was an actual person of that name who did some or all of the things described in the Bible) was born as late as 1955 BCE or as early as about 2170 BCE. This matches the time frame of the Harappan relocation due to the drying up of the Saraswati.

As his death approaches, Abraham asks the "children of Heth," the Hittites who rule Jerusalem, to sell him a burial plot. Their response is interesting: "Thou art a prince among us." The Hittite language is not Arabic, it is Indo-European. It has been speculated that their home was in India. Is it possible, then, that Abraham was actually an Indian priest bringing his faith to the Middle East?

The Proto-Tantric Link to the Kabalah

Many people reading this will be familiar with ethnographer, anthropologist, and author Raphael Patai. His book *The Hebrew Goddess*, very popular among Western Pagans, provides evidence that the Jews worshiped a goddess until the destruction of the second temple in 70 CE. That title is just one of the dozens of books Patai wrote that were published between 1947 and posthumously in 1998.

In his book *The Jewish Mind*, Patai indicates a direct connection between Tantra and the Kabalah. He writes that the Kabalah resembles "certain Hindu schools" [the early Shaiva, or what I have called proto-Tantric] more than any other religion. He describes how author Gershom Scholem described the teachings of eleventh-century Kabalist Abraham Abulafia as a Judaized version of Indian yoga, equating Abulafia's rules for postures, sounding combinations of consonants and vowels, and certain methods of reciting them with various yogic techniques. "The similarity [to yoga] even extends to some aspects of the doctrine of ecstatic vision, as preceded and brought about by these practices."

Other parallels Patai points out include the idea of a non-manifest deity who eventually manifests, and the idea of emanation (in the Kabalah through the sefirot of the Tree of Life, and in Tantra through the tattvas). Most spiritual traditions see the male as outgoing and energetic, while the female is passive and receptive. Curiously, both Tantra and the Kabalah reverse this. The well-known Pillar of Severity on the Tree of Life is considered feminine, while the Pillar of Mercy is masculine. Shiva is considered a physical form, while Shakti, his consort, is the animating energy.

Patai also says that Kabalists were supposed to be aware of the sacred aspect of having sexual relations. It is incredibly similar to Tantric concepts of sexuality. And finally, both the Kabalah and Tantra have theories of reincarnation that are similar.

Tantra—or rather, proto-Tantra—clearly came before the Kabalah, but Patai refuses to acknowledge a direct link. He will only go so far as to say that Kabalists in thirteenth-century Spain knew of Hindu concepts and yoga. While that's certainly true, I don't think it represents the complete truth of the relationship. In *Between Jerusalem and Benares*, Frances Schmidt writes, "For the Jews of the Hellenistic and Roman period [circa 330 BCE–70 CE], India did not remain the farthest corner of the world . . . Jews and Indians could have come into direct contact through commercial and diplomatic overland and maritime intercourse."

Going back even further, Professor Hermann Oldenberg, in *Ancient India: Its Language and Religions*, wrote, "In the Vedic ages [long before the books called the Vedas were actually written] writing was not known...the Indians probably learned to write from Semites." Personally, I think this may have been a belief based on Western elitism and racism. As far as I can tell, it was probably either the other way around (from India to the Middle East) or there was a mutual sharing.

So why does a study of Tantra come so easily to a Jewish kid like me? As a result of the evidence described here, I am forced to make the conclusion that the tribes that would unite as Jews, or at least one of them, came from ancient India into the Middle East some 4,000 years ago as a result of drought and the drying up of the Saraswati River. Perhaps their journey was a model for the biblical story of the Exodus. Further, the philosophy, techniques, and beliefs of pre-Hindu India, in my opinion, clearly influenced the ancient Jews and especially Jewish mysticism as eventually manifested in the Kabalah. One author, Sid Jefferies, even shows how the earliest forms of the Hebrew alphabet seem to be derived from the Harappan alphabet. I will clearly state my belief that the ancient Pagan system of traditional Tantra is one of the sources of both Judaism and the Kabalah. Its study by Kabalists and Pagans may come easily to students of those systems. When I stopped fighting it, studying and practicing that system came easily to me.

Is This Just Some Form of Bowdlerized Hinduism?

As I have stated, Tantra comes from pre-Hindu sources. Many things in Hinduism were derived from Tantric practices and beliefs. Eventually, forms of Hinduism became far more important to the masses. This is similar to the way that Christianity eventually became more important than the Pagan systems in Europe.

But Tantra as presented here is *not* Hinduism. Although Hinduism is actually a wide collection of traditions and beliefs, often with varying beliefs and practices, there are three things that give a general definition of Hinduism:

1. Hindus accept and revere the books known as the Vedas. Tantrics honor the Vedas, but they are not the source of Tantric belief.
2. Hindus believe that the means or ways to salvation are diverse. Tantra is not about salvation, as there is nothing to be saved from.
3. The number of deities to be worshiped is large. There are some Tantrics who agree with this. However, the system of Tantra as presented here follows the ancient tradition that there is one deity

> who manifests in a multitude of forms. Worshiping or honoring one of those manifestations is the same as worshiping the ultimate deity.

Tantra is about liberation of mind, body, and spirit. Sexuality is just one part of this liberation. For some, this journey on the path of liberation is short. For others, it is longer. The speed doesn't matter—all those who wish to follow this path will eventually get there. If you are ready to join me and the tens of thousands of other Tantrics around the world, I welcome you to the journey with the word that has been used for thousands of years: *Namaste!* ("That which is of the gods in me recognizes and acknowledges that which is of the gods in you.")

....

Note: Some of the concepts presented in this preface originally appeared in an article I wrote for *Hermetic Virtues*, an online journal.

ONE

Myth and Mythos

Put some people together and you have nothing more than a group of people. What can bond them into something more than a collection of individuals is not, as some people believe, due to a bloodline. Rather, people bond as a result of a common set of experiences and beliefs. These experiences can be contemporary or they may be modern versions of stories (often highly altered) about events that were said to have occurred in the past, sometimes eons ago. The bonds created by the common experiences of platoon members during war are often stronger than the ties of brothers and sisters. The life-threatening nature of war experiences can make those bonds even tighter.

When spiritual groups first start out, they frequently have such bonding based on common experience. In recent times, the story of the birth of the Church of Jesus Christ of Latter Day Saints (commonly known as the Mormons) was just such a bonding experience. It begins with a far-sighted leader who supposedly has a revelation from God. He is killed and his people, fleeing religious persecution, face incredible difficulties as they travel across a vast land. When they finally find a place to stay, a natural disaster seems like it will wipe them out. But they are saved by a miracle. By joining that church, you become part of the continuation of those experiences and the resulting beliefs, attitudes, and values.

I am not going to debate whether those events happened as described. What has happened is that members of that religion believe the story. Usually such stories become exaggerated over time. The historical becomes the mythic. The mythic becomes the *mythos.*

What is a mythos? It is an interrelated set of myths and beliefs that manifest in the group's values and attitudes. Let me explain further. Virtually every culture or group has a mythos. Often, the attitudes and values of the mythos are reflected in a people's arts—painting, theater, sculpture, music, etc. *Myths* are not merely stories; they have impactful meanings to the people who believe them or simply know them. They, too, exemplify the temperament, beliefs, and principles of that people. The myths/art and the associated attitudes/values combine to make the mythos of a people.

Jews, Christians, Buddhists, and Muslims all have their myths and mythos structures. Mystical groups, from Rosicrucians to Golden Dawners, from Thelemites to the numerous sects of Witchcraft, from Freemasons to, well, you name it, each have their myths and mythos. You might take some time to consider this: What myths do you follow? What mythos do you accept?

Hinduism is replete with myths and stories about gods and goddesses and their interaction with humans. Some, such as in the epic *Mahabharata* (of which the famous *Bhagavad Gita* is but a tiny part), are extensive. Others are short stories that illuminate a single facet of life. Generally speaking, all are considered acceptable to Hindus, even when the myth is not part of the religious or spiritual tradition followed by a particular person.

In the West, our myths have been far more straightforward. They do not deal with hundreds of deities, or at least not with so many deities simultaneously. The great myths of Homer, the Jewish Bible, and the Christian Bible are each linear and tell a more or less complete story.

One of the intentions of this book is to explore the nature of traditional Tantra as a complete Pagan system that can be followed, in whole or in part, by Westerners today. Therefore, it, too, must present a linear myth and mythos. Such a myth does exist. It is a glue that holds together several Tantric groups. It is the mythos that, in various forms, presents the paradigm that allows initiates to say, "This is Tantric; that is not."

Unlike most other spiritual groups, the Tantrics of NAMASTE acknowledge that the myth I am about to share is just that: a myth. Other groups, such as AMOOKOS, have described a similar story, but limit it to a paragraph or two. The myth that follows, admittedly and unashamedly, is an expansion and amplification of the shorter stories.

Even so, there may be valid historical aspects to this myth. For example, documents from AMOOKOS reveal that satellite photos indicate an ancient civilization existed in the area now called the Gobi Desert, the supposed location of the valley of Ananda-La. But it would be too expensive to have an archeological dig in the middle of that desert, so it has never been excavated.

Whether or not a civilization like that of Ananda-La ever existed on what is now the Gobi Desert is irrelevant. What is important is that this story—this myth—explains why Tantrics are the way they are and why non-Tantrics are the way they are. It is the living mythos of *Modern Tantra*.

Just as the Kabalah, being kept by the Jews for thousands of years, has Jewish aspects to it, so, too, does Tantra, as presented here, have many Hindu aspects to it. Some readers may be surprised that the numerous gods and goddesses of Hinduism play little part in the following myth. There is a good reason for this.

Hinduism has been called a monotheistic religion with thousands of deities. The ultimate deity is *Brahman*, "all that ever was and all that will ever be." (*Brahman* was originally pronounced "Brach-mahn," with the "ch" being a guttural like the German in the word *ach*. It is now generally pronounced "Brahm-ahn" and shouldn't be confused with *Brahma*, the Hindu creator deity.) The correct pronoun when speaking of Brahman is "it," because by calling it "him" or "her," we are giving Brahman qualities that are limiting. Brahman manifests in numerous forms, including the male triad (Brahma, Vishnu, and Shiva) and their many female counterparts, including the Mahavidyas; forms of Shiva and Shakti (including Kali, Durga, Lakshmi, and Parvati); and other deities such as Ganesha. Each deity has his or her own meaning and purpose. Thousands of books have been written about them. Chapter 4 explores and explains in greater detail deities linked to traditional Tantra.

But the present book is not primarily about the play of the gods and goddesses, although some aspects will be covered later. Rather, it is about how you, the reader, can become a Tantric, part of the growing family of contemporary yet traditional Tantrics around the world. Thus, the myth that follows is about people and *their* interplay, not about gods, goddesses, and their relationships with humans.

Yes, the story that follows is a myth. Its value is that it identifies the mythos, the pattern of basic values and attitudes of many Tantrics, including those who follow the living system that is *Modern Tantra*.

Preface: Creation

In the beginning, there was naught. There was no time. There was no space. There was no lack of time. There was no unspace. There was no order. There was no chaos. There was no wet. There was no dry. There was no hot. There was no cold. There was no above. There was no below. There was no in. There was no out. There was no left. There was no right. There was no war. There was no peace. There was no hate. There was no love. There was nothing: no thing.

And unbidden, from within the nothing, came a stir, a throb, a vibrant pulsation. And thus it was that love was born. But it was not the love that people have for another person or thing. Nor was it the "love for all" that so many today claim to profess. For this love was an energy, pure beyond belief, pure beyond understanding, pure beyond comprehension. It was from no one and it was directed to no one nor to any thing. Yet it was, and is, the source and foundation of all love in the physical and non-physical universe.

And it came to pass that within the nothing the pulsation of love experienced a reflection of itself. The physical universe functions with opposites, and this reflection was the polar opposite of the pulsation of love. And the opposite of love is not hate, but an absence of that love energy. And so it was that the pulsation of love came to consist of a flowing, an outpouring, a smooth transition from love to not love and back to love again. And lo! So was born *anandalahari* ("ah-nahn-dah-lah-hah-ree"), the "wave of bliss" (see illustration).

And so it was that the anandalahari started everywhere and nowhere and went to the ends of the universe. But there was no way to express the energy of love nor to receive the energy of love. So the energy of the wave began to rest at the points where it would change direction, forming the *samatribhujananda* ("sahm-ah-tree-boo-juh-nahn-da"), the "triangle of bliss" (see illustration).

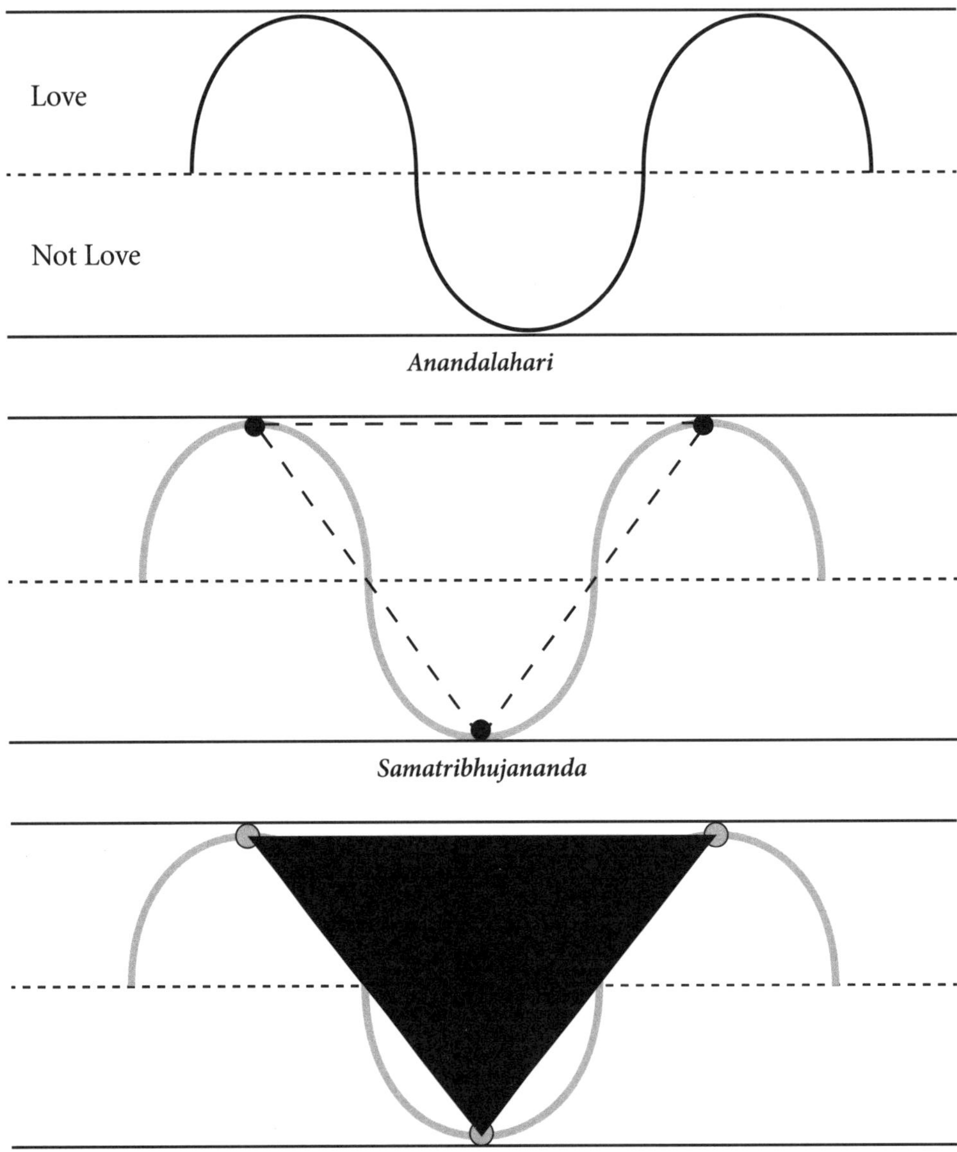

Anandalahari

Samatribhujananda

The Cosmic Yoni

And it came to pass that rather than smoothly flowing in waves, the energy of love began to move directly from point-of-power to point-of-power to point-of-power, following and forming the path of least resistance. And thus there came to be formed the cosmic yoni, perfect in its perfection, without flaw or blemish (see illustration). And the cosmic yoni, formed as it is of perfect love-beyond-love, was a pathway from the infinite *not* to the infinite *is*. And so it was that from the nothing came love and from love came the Divine, ready to manifest.

The Divine wanted—*needed!*—to share its source, its love. But there was nothing to share with. So the Divine manifested Brahma, the creator. And Brahma was bursting to tell of his love, but there was no air for the vibration to sound. So Brahma was content to make a soundless sound, the source of all sound, *nada brahma*. And from this was born his consort, Saraswati. But she longed to hear Brahma's love for her, so through her yoni she gave birth to air.

Together they lived in a beautiful world. Brahma rode on a magical white swan (*hamsa*) that could derive spiritual beauty from the world around it. Saraswati, goddess of learning and knowledge, she who created the letters of the alphabet, loved to hear Brahma recite his love for her. Thus was born *mantra*. And the mantra must be repeated over and over, for it would only last for the time it took to be sounded. Thus was born *japa*, the repetition of mantra. But it was not only mantra that would not last. Indeed, nothing would last.

And the Divine was sad that nothing would last, and so, through the energy created by the union of Brahma and Saraswati, and by way of the cosmic yoni, there was created Vishnu, the preserver. Vishnu lies on an ocean of milk, and his dreams keep in manifestation that which Brahma created. To keep Vishnu alert came Lakshmi, his consort, who massages Vishnu's legs. Vishnu preserves, but without Lakshmi he can do nothing. She brings good fortune.

The sound of Brahma is fleeting, so the vibrations of the sounds created physical signs, *yantras*. And lo! The mantras are deity in the form of sound. And lo! Yantras are deity in physical, two-dimensional form. Be not confused by those who say they are but symbols or mere representations, for the *true* mantra and the *true* yantra are as much of the Divine—more!—than are any of the other images of the gods.

And from the joyful couplings of Brahma and Saraswati and of Vishnu and Lakshmi have all the people, places, and things of all the sheaths of the universe been formed. But it came to pass that there was too much.

And so, as a product of the couplings of the divine couples, the cosmic yoni brought forth and into being Shiva, the transformer, and Shakti, the energy that empowers Shiva. And with them came time. And with time came the passing of physical life. The three deities (*Trimurti*, pronounced "try-mur-tee") and their consorts created all life from the non-physical, maintained it, and transformed it back into the non-physical. All are vital for a healthy universe. To deny one is to deny all. To honor one is to honor all. Shiva is Brahma is Lakshmi is Saraswati is Shakti is Vishnu. And all are Brahman.

With time came multiple forms. Shakti was also seen as Kali, she who brings death, and Kali Ma, the mother of us all. Vishnu was also seen as dark-skinned Krishna, player of the flute and lover of the many milkmaids; lo, he is honored for his virility.

Thus was the coming of the gods, time, space, air, water, earth, the plants, and the animals. Thus was the coming of men and women.

Part I: Ananda-La—the Source of Wisdom

It was a time before time, when the rivers were cool and the water sweet, the air smelled of fragrant flowers and herbs unknown today, and the tiger and crane, lion and wolf, were yet young. And it came to pass that one species of animal, the humans, began to become self-aware. They learned that they were not the same as other animals or even other humans. They joined with others of their kind for protection and for procreation, forming clans. Sometimes they had a hard life. Sometimes things went more easily.

Most of the clans were nomadic. They would go where the weather was gentle and the fruitfulness of the land was great. One such clan, the Laced Triangles clan, seeking escape from a particularly harsh and snowy winter, pushed north through a narrow mountain pass. There they found an enormous mountain-encircled valley, a valley so big it contained its own hills and valleys.

And the weather in the valley, protected by the giant mountains, was mild and the trees were bent over with delicious fruit. The clan head, Anandanath ("Uh-nahn-dah-naht"), and his wife and clan co-head, Parvatikalidevi ("Pahr-vaht-ee-kahl-ee-dehv-ee"), decided that it was time for a change. "From this day forth, this is our land," Anandanath said. "From this day forth, we are no longer clan heads, we are the king and queen of this land. And it shall be known as the land of Ananda-La ["Uh-nahn-dah Lah"]."

And so it was that the Laced Triangles clan settled into the enormous valley of Ananda-La. The mountains that surrounded the valley not only brought it a temperate climate but also helped protect it from enemies. Ananda-La was so big that it was blessed with smaller but highly fertile valleys, fish-filled rivers, and a wide variety of natural vegetation. Crops grew easily, and the flocks of sheep and goats, cattle and camel, were as numerous as the stars of the clear night skies. The once-nomadic clan grew into a large civilization, developing writing, art, theater, music, architecture, education, philosophy, ethics, agriculture, healing techniques, astronomy, mathematics, and many more aspects of an advanced society.

The people of that time were over seven feet tall and their natural lifespan was many hundreds of years. It was not uncommon for men and women to have the pleasure of playing with their great-great-great-grandchildren. Their houses were simple, as the weather was mild, the most deluxe being large, surprisingly elegant yurts. The graciousness of Brahman allowed the people of Ananda-La plenty of time for pleasure, and often they would dance around the bonfires and make love late into the night.

The government of Ananda-La was simple. First came the rulers, a king and queen who made the laws, and their advisors. Next came the judges who enforced the laws. Finally, there were the appellates, who made sure the judges acted fairly and there was not even the slightest sign of corruption. To be a judge or an appellate was a great honor, and each adult citizen of Ananda-La was expected to serve as one or the other for a period of five years.

The appellates never had to look at the actions of the rulers, for as long as people could remember, their leaders had been wise, kind, just, fair, artistic, and clever. In honor of the founders and first rulers of Ananda-La, each king took the name Anandanath and each queen took the name Parvatikalidevi. As part of their tradition, they kept large numbers of soldiers in the major passes that led into Ananda-La. This show of force prevented any invasion. As a result, Ananda-La had been at peace with its neighbors for as long as anyone could remember, and that, dear reader, was a very, very long time.

The population of Ananda-La grew, and with the gifts of education and physical health, the civilization prospered. Different people thought of different ways to improve life in Ananda-La, sometimes getting into strong disagreements over how the country should evolve. In every generation it was the duty of the wise King Anandanath (who could not rule without the agreement and consent of his consort, Queen Parvatikalidevi) to always seek a balanced middle path. When people simply could not find a way to agree, the king and queen would grant one of the opponents a new area to live. The valley was so large that even after many centuries of peace and growth there was more than enough room for all. Since the people had no spiritual, emotional, or physical ties to any particular area of land (other than Ananda-La in general), the policy of granting a distant property to prevent disagreement was an accepted practice. The result was that the people of Ananda-La had a great deal of diversity of thought. The schools were filled with people of all ages. This diversity, tempered by the wisdom of the rulers, helped to make Ananda-La vibrant and strong.

In the time just before the *Great Change*, the royal couple had a son and a daughter. The first was born in what today would be called early April. She was a wild child, always experimenting with boundaries and wanting to know how things worked. Her favorite questions were "Why?" and "How?" Both Anandanath and Parvatikalidevi, as well as the daughter's teachers, would patiently answer her questions. And she was named Schambhaladevi ("Sham-ball-uh-dehv-ee").

The next year, during the time that would today be called early May, their son was born. He was the opposite of Schambhaladevi. He was not interested in the whys and hows, he just wanted to know what to do. Where Schambhaladevi would toss her toys around, he would line them up and see if he could move them while keeping them in order. And he was given the name Agarthinath ("Uh-gar-tee-naht").

Like the other children of Ananda-La, Schambhaladevi and Agarthinath grew up strong and educated. Schambhaladevi often spoke with the scholars. They would bob their heads over her uncannily intuitive understanding of everything from physics to philosophy. Agarthinath was more at home with the workers, and frequently designed devices that could make their labors easier and safer. Both were beloved of the people.

Part II: The Coming of "That One"

When a country is as happy and prosperous as Ananda-La, it is inevitable that it will become the target of those who are envious, hateful, and less prosperous. To prevent an invasion and destruction of the country, some scientists and wizards created a weapon that would destroy everything from where it was placed to beyond the end of sight. They believed it would make even thinking about attacking Ananda-La out of the question. It was this weapon, known as Shivanayanajala ("Shee-vuh-nai-ya-nah-jal-ah"), that resulted in the *Great Change*.

Wars, up to this time, had been based on the idea of small or large numbers of soldiers fighting other small or large groups of soldiers. But what do you do about one angry person? To this day it is forbidden to speak his name, and those who speak of him refer to him only as "That One."

And it came to pass that a single man with a donkey came to do business in the largest marketplace of Ananda-La. "Fine grain!" he shouted, as he moved toward the market. Finally, he found someone to buy all of his bags of grain. "You have made a good deal," That One told the buyer.

As That One hurriedly left the market with his money, the purchaser looked in the bags of grain. In the bag he had inspected there was, indeed, fine grain. But the others merely had grain at the top of the bag. As he dug through he found that beneath the grain was straw and dirt. "I have been cheated!" he shouted. Citizens, proud of their country and their laws, came out of their homes and businesses. They quickly captured That One, and he was brought before the judges.

And it came to pass that the judges convicted That One of trying to cheat at commerce. His sentence: a year in prison. "I am innocent," he said. "I did not do this." As a result of his protestations of innocence, his case was given to the appellates. They, too, found him guilty. For his false protestations he was sentenced to an additional year in prison.

"I am innocent," he said again. "I did not do this." His claim led to a judicial hearing before the king and queen. After hearing and seeing the evidence, the queen reminded the king of a minor law. The king nodded and said there was one thing that neither the judges nor the appellates had considered: That One was not a citizen of Ananda-La. The king and queen conferred again, then the king, making a just ruling for the victim, and to protect the people of Ananda-La, said, "Here is our judgment. You shall repay the man whom you tried to cheat. In payment for the time and effort of the judges and appellates, you shall forfeit the good bag of grain and your donkey. And you are exiled from Ananda-La for life."

And it came to pass that four judges took That One to the border. Along the way they did wrongly smite That One with their hands and staves. And when they neared the pass in the mountain rim of Ananda-La, they stripped him naked and drove him past the soldiers guarding the border by throwing rocks at him. The soldiers laughed at That One in his torment. "I shall have my revenge!" shouted That One.

And in the generations to come, the teachers would explain that sometimes, when a person does wrong, rather than feel ashamed and contrite, he or she becomes filled with anger and rage toward those who discovered the wrong. Filled with such emotions and enraged by his wrongful suffering and humiliation in front of the soldiers, That One spent years seeking a means to achieve his revenge. It was not until he was old and gray that he learned of the Shivanayanajala device. "My revenge is at hand!" he cried.

And it came to pass that That One returned through a pass in the mountains surrounding Ananda-La that was so small, so rock-filled, and so narrow that it was left unprotected. Because he was old and gray, nobody recognized him and he was able to slip into crowds and talk with people at the fairs and markets. Although the people who had created the Shivanayanajala device tried to keep its location secret, a secret shared never remains a secret. So it came to pass that That One discovered its hiding place. His rage, building for decades, emboldened and sent the strength of youth through his aged body. He slew two unsuspecting guards. "Finally, vengeance is mine!" he cried, as he moved toward the giant device. Suddenly, pain filled his chest. That One looked down and saw the head of a spear bursting from between his ribs. He had not known of a third guard. The third guard had come up behind That One and thrust so hard with a spear that it went through That One's back and came out the front.

And so it was that That One died. But neither pain nor imminent death would stop his enormous rage, and with his last breath did he stumble forward and trigger the Shivanayanajala device by using the techniques he had bribed others to teach him. His hatred and desire for revenge so consumed him that even in death he was willing to destroy so much and so many.

And the Shivanayanajala device was incredibly powerful. But it was not like the destructive devices of today. It required over twenty-one weeks to actually build up to a destructive peak. A device that, once triggered, takes weeks before it explodes may seem odd to the people of today. But to the people of Ananda-La, who lived hundreds of years, a few weeks pass as do a few minutes today.

The Shivanayanajala device was very large and could only be moved with great effort.

However, once it was triggered it automatically sealed and could not be disarmed. It drove large, spiraling poles deep into the ground, taking movement of the device that was formerly difficult into the realm of impossibility. When what That One had done was discovered, and it was realized that there was no way to reverse the build-up of the device, the queen sent word to all parts of the land: for the people, culture, and tradition of Ananda-La to survive, it was time to leave their homes.

And lo, there was much wailing and crying. Even though they felt no allegiance to any particular location in Ananda-La, they loved the beauty and majesty of their land. They had also traded their fine goods with many other peoples and learned from them of the harshness outside their valley. Now, gone would be their homes. Gone would be their possessions. Gone would be the clever items that made their lives easier than those in the areas outside of Ananda-La. Everything would be gone.

But the people of Ananda-La were pragmatic. For their culture to survive, they must escape the sure death and destruction of the Shivanayanajala device. The king and queen called their children for a conference. "Princess Schambhaladevi and Prince Agarthinath, long have you been the voice of youth in Ananda-La. You are honored, loved, and respected by the people," said the king.

The queen continued, "For our people to survive, they need the fire of youth and energy."

The king took her hand. "Your mother and I are over 250 years old," he said. "We no longer have that energy. We are the past. Besides, we love this land. We *are* Ananda-La."

The queen looked at her children with a loving smile. "We will not leave." The prince and princess protested, but the queen held up her hand to silence them. "Our decision is final. Now *you* must lead the people of Ananda-La to safety."

And many tears were shed, but eventually all came to see the wisdom of the king and queen.

And it came to pass that most of the people prepared to leave, led by Princess Schambhaladevi and Prince Agarthinath. Most of the people over 200 years of age decided to stay in Ananda-La, as did some of the younger people who could not bear to leave their beautiful land.

But before the people left, there was time for one last thing, a final ritual. As per tradition, Schambhaladevi was given the name Parvatikalidevi and Agarthinath was given the name Anandanath. Thus, they became the new rulers of the people of Ananda-La.

And lo, there was much talking among the people. For previous to this time, only a husband and wife took the names of the rulers. The new King Anandanath put his arm around the new Queen Parvatikalidevi and told his people that new times would require new traditions. However, there was no further time to talk of this, he said, for the exodus must begin as soon as possible.

The people of Ananda-La had been great investigators of the physical world. One of the things they had discovered was that there was a vast system of caves under the mountains, today called the Himalayas, which formed part of the rim of their valley. It took 146 days for all the people to reach the safety of the caves. And it was not too soon. Less than a day later, the device went off. For fourteen days, the night was turned to day. A great foehn swept across the land and onto the mountains, resulting in countless snow slides. And then, for an additional fortnight, the temperature outside the caves seemed to be that of the sun. In spite of the heat, the days became as black as night; darker, as neither the sun nor moon nor stars could be seen through the ash and dust that filled the sky.

Part III: Under the Himalayas

And it came to pass that the darkness did last for six years. And after the constant external darkness ceased, the heat did last for yet another seven years. And lo, it was yet twenty more years ere the temperature returned to normal. And it took three more years before anything would grow under the sun.

It is said that the secrets of how to make the Shivanayanajala device are still known by some Tantric adepts in a secret order, but they have vowed to give their lives before making one or telling how one could be made to someone who was not part of their order.

Within the caves under the Himalayas the temperature stayed constant and comfortable for the survivors of the Shivanayanajala device. Safe from the heat and the unstable conditions outside the caves, they were able to use torches to provide light enough for their meager crops and small herds. There was not a great deal for everyone, but with sharing, trust, and work, all could survive. Within a few years they were even starting to improve on their personal comforts. But as life beneath the Himalayas improved, a new problem arose.

For a large, thriving society with lots of room, such as that of Ananda-La, diversity of thought and deed makes for a culture that is strong and vibrant. But if you take those strong, independent people and put them in a small, walled-in situation, such as was the case under the Himalayas, such diversity leads to divisiveness. At first, everyone worked together to make sure all could survive and to rebuild their society. But once a level of stability had been established, the disagreements of the people came to the fore. How were the survivors of Ananda-La to think, act, believe? When large fights began to break out, the queen and king knew they must act for the survival of their people.

The previous several years had been most difficult for King Anandanath. Although he loved his sister, he did not love her as a wife. As beautiful as she was, he found the notion of sex with his sister to be improper and distasteful. She, on the other hand, saw their importance as symbols for their people. She loved her handsome brother, and for years was distressed that he would not make them king and queen in actuality—producing princes and princesses—as well as in name. Now, the violence among their people presented a new responsibility and tasks that they knew they had to accept and resolve.

And it came to pass that the brother and sister rulers called a mass meeting of all the people. They met in the enormous common hall, the largest cavern under the mountains. It was big enough to hold most of the surviving population of Ananda-La. There, Anandanath and Parvatikalidevi each stood up and shared what they believed. They were kin. They would always be united. But they were also individuals with different ways of thinking and acting, which mirrored the thoughts and beliefs of the people. Rather than being one united group, they would divide into two. The people should decide which side they would follow.

And it came to pass that by the time the day was over, the people had chosen sides. They had divided the caverns into two sections, with the large cavern they were in, now called Anandavishnu-La ("Uh-nahn-duh-veesh-new-lah"), being the one place of meeting shared between the two sides. The separate sections, in honor of the names of their king and queen when they were prince and princess, were called Schambhala-La and Agarthi-La. The entire complex was named Sangara-La ("Song-gahr-uh-lah").

Parvatikalidevi and Anandanath, like many of the rest of the people in the caves, hugged and kissed and cried. Then they led the divided people into the two separate sections of the caves. For many, the destruction of Ananda-La was called the *Great Change*. But the truth was that it was this moment that marked the real Great Change. For in truth, a country is more than land. It is actually the sum total of its people. And as of this moment, the people were divided. The spirit of Ananda-La had survived the effects of the Shivanayanajala device, but it could not survive the basic nature of the people. Ananda-La was no more.

Part IV: The Departure from Sangara-La

And it came to pass that the people of Sangara-La not only survived, but thrived under controlled conditions. Joy was expressed over new births and sorrow was expressed over the passing of loved ones. The new children grew up to be shorter in stature and lived shorter lives.

And the sadness was great between Anandanath and Parvatikalidevi. For although they loved each other in different ways, they still loved one another. Now they barely saw each other. They grew old separately. Although each had lovers and consorts, neither married. Neither had children. But they made sure that their people were safe and healthy.

And sixteen more years came and went. The citizens of both Schambhala-La and Agarthi-La had made forays outside the caves and longed, once again, for the sun on their faces and the sweet smell of fresh air. But the king and queen resisted this. They knew that when they left the caves, they would have to lead their peoples in different directions. They knew they would never see each other again. This they did not want.

And it came to pass in the fifty-sixth year of their lives under the Himalayas that the crops did not grow. And lo, there was much sorrow. For fifty-six years, there was safety and limited comfort. But the king and queen realized that there was now no choice. The people had to leave their isolation and protection.

But the brother and sister could not bear to leave each other. And so it was determined that they would stay and the people of Sangara-La would leave under the guidance of their judges, who henceforth would be known as "chieftains."

And there was great rejoicing and great sorrow. But within a week, only Anandanath and Parvatikalidevi, as well as their retinues, were left in the caves. For decades, people would come seeking the mystics of the mountains for their wisdom. That wisdom became legendary. It was said that they lived to be 324 years old, but their bodies were never found. People still seek them and their wisdom today, journeying to the Himalaya Mountains. With their passing, Sangara-La, as Ananda-La before it, became only a memory and the stuff of which legends are made.

The chieftains initially led their tribes back to the location of their ancestral home, what had been the valley of Ananda-La. But the Shivanayanajala device had worked all too well. The land that had been so beautiful and fertile was now nothing but sand. The rivers that had once flowed through the land and been filled with fish were gone. The mountains that had surrounded and protected the valley were now nothing more than wind-swept dunes. For a month they encamped in what was now a bleak desert. And the people wept, for even those who did not remember the beauty of Ananda-La had heard stories of its magnificence.

And during the month the chieftains met in a central encampment. The chieftains represented all of the various beliefs of the people. Knowing they could not survive as a large group in this desert, they made a momentous decision.

And it came to pass that the chieftains each led their tribe in a different direction. They went to lands now known as India and China, Japan and Tibet, Europe and Africa, as well as the Middle East and places in between and beyond. Everywhere they went, they left their language, their sciences, their arts and philosophies, their spirituality and their hopes, their desires and their dreams.

Schambhala-La and Agarthi-La are no more. Ananda-La and Sangara-La are no more. But the beliefs and traditions of those people became the source of Hinduism and Buddhism and their Tantric variations, and they influenced the sciences, arts, philosophy, and spirituality of people all over the world. They live on even today.

The Mythos

It is important to understand that the myth of Ananda-La does *not* take sides, nor does it imply that the philosophy of Schambhala-La is better or worse than that which was practiced in Agarthi-La. Different people need different things at different times in their lives. Not to have the appropriate philosophy and teachings available would hurt a person who needs them. It's good that both are available.

Be that as it may, it is the philosophy and beliefs of the people of Schambhala-La that are of most interest to us here. They are, mythically, the precursors of Tantra. To understand those beliefs, it may be easiest to compare and contrast the beliefs of Schambhala-La and Agarthi-La. Again, however, I want to emphasize that neither is a *better* set of beliefs. They are merely different, and each is appropriate for the person who needs it.

Scientific Method vs. Superstition

"Don't walk under a ladder. It's bad luck." We've all heard that numerous times. When we were children, we may have asked that most important of questions: "Why?" The answer probably fell into one of two major categories, the pseudo-scientific (somebody on the ladder might spill something on you or you might bump the ladder and knock somebody off) or the traditional (it's been passed down for generations as being bad luck).

Perhaps, like me, you found those answers unsatisfying. Is it okay to walk under a ladder if you can see that nobody is on it? Why has this belief been passed down for generations? Perhaps, like me, you were a natural-born Tantric. When I was young, I tested the theory by setting up a ladder and walking under it. I was nervous the first few times I went through it, but I discovered that no bad luck was associated with my transgressive act.

This is the basis of the scientific method. You start with a theory (walking under a ladder gives bad luck). Then you test it (walk under a ladder). You look at the results to see if they either support or disprove the theory.

The scientific method is also the system of Schambhala-La, the system of Tantra. Tantric rituals, in a very real sense, are scientific experiments. If they work, continue to use them. If they don't work, either change them so they will work or simply don't use them.

There is a story about a man who noticed that his wife cut off both ends of a roast before she cooked it. He asked her why. "That's the way it's done, isn't it?" she asked. He responded that he had never seen such a thing before. "Well, that's the way my mother did it, and she taught me to cook. I'll see what she has to say."

The next day the woman asked her mother about it. The mother replied, "Well, that's the way it's done, isn't it?" The woman told her mother that her husband didn't understand this and wanted to know where she learned it. Her mother said, "Well, that's the way my mother, your grandmother, did it, and she taught me to cook. Go see what she has to say."

The following day the woman asked her grandmother about this. The grandmother, laughing, explained, "There's no need to cut off the ends. When your grandfather and I were young and poor and had a small child, we had only one very small pan. It was all we could afford. The only way I could get a roast to fit in it was to cut off the ends. Your mother must have seen me do this when she was a little girl, assumed that a roast must be cooked that way, and taught it to you."

The cooking technique of the granddaughter, indeed, is a form of non-Tantric thought, a method followed by the people of Agarthi-La. Somebody did something out of necessity for her personal situation and others copied it without asking why. Over years and decades, the original reason was lost and people simply followed the superstition.

Religion vs. Spirituality

Today, in the West, most people equate religion with spirituality:

Are you spiritual?

You bet! I go to church every Sunday morning.

But spirituality is *not* religion. Spirituality concerns your personal relationship with the Divine, the God and Goddess, the Source of All. Religion in the West tends to consist of sets of formalized beliefs marked by structured patterns that, for many, have lost any sort of spirituality. Just as elementary schools should be places where children learn, so too should synagogues, churches, mosques, and cathedrals be places where people go to commune with the Divine. Unfortunately, it is often true that children don't learn at school, and people are indoctrinated with fear rather than receiving spiritual succor from religious groups.

With Tantra, mythically derived from the system of the people of Schambhala-La, there is most definitely a religion, complete with deities and beliefs. However, the nature and methods of the religion involve meditation (communication with the Divine), personal responsibility, spiritual development, and self-empowerment. The religious leaders are teachers from whom followers can learn. Further, since each Tantric is expected to link with the Divine by way of any of many techniques, the experience can yield new information. That means Tantra is evolving. Among Tantrics there is the recognition that stagnation is the breeding ground of decay and death.

The people who came from Agarthi-La, people who are not Tantric, fall into organized religious structures. Rather than having teachers and scientists as their leaders, they have priests who tell them when and how to worship as well as how to think and act. The question "Why?" is either forbidden or responded to with comments that are illogical, superstitious, or a poor attempt at justification. For example, rather than meditate, they pray (one-way supposed communication with the Divine, frequently asking for something they don't really feel they deserve).

As with all groups, there are hierarchies in both Tantric and non-Tantric groups. However, in a Tantric group people are free to move up or down the "open hierarchy" at any time. In non-Tantric groups, there is a definite pecking order, and it is quite difficult to move out of one's caste and up through the hierarchy.

I doubt if there is any pure Tantric religious group without instances of a more fixed hierarchy. However, they tend to be far more open than non-Tantric ones. Thus, the techniques and methods of all religious groups tend to blend both Tantric and non-Tantric methods. This is good, because different people need different things. If a person needed a tight structure where he would be told how to think, act, and believe, it would be wrong to force him into a group that did not have such a non-Tantric structure. He would be lost, unhappy, and certainly no closer to having a personal relationship with the Divine.

Alternatively, a person who needs the freedom and personal responsibility inherent in Tantric religion would be lost, unhappy, and no closer to having a personal relationship with the Divine if thrust into a highly structured, non-Tantric religious group.

Both types of religious structures are needed.

Magicians vs. Priests

In the religious history associated with the time of Jesus, another figure stands large: Simon Magus. Indeed, some scholars believe that Simon Magus was so respected that some of the acts attributed to his magicks evolved into the biblical tales of miracles performed by Jesus.

Whether or not Simon Magus actually existed is not important for this discussion. What is important is to look at what happened. Specifically, any magician, as typified by Simon Magus, is a threat to power structures, including those (perhaps *especially* those) of controlling (non-Tantric) religious organizations.

Magicians have the ability to alter or change reality. As such, they realize that anything they do may have unforeseen side effects. They also acknowledge that they are responsible for their actions and all of the results of those actions. As soon as you realize you are free to do anything (although you must also face the consequences of your actions), you are a danger to authorities. You don't have to obey them. You may be punished for your action, but you are still free to do it. No wonder religions that are dominated by central authorities fear magicians! If one person doesn't have to do what the authorities say, why should anyone do what they say?

And Tantrics are magicians. A magician changes reality by using little-known techniques to alter his or her mental, physical, emotional, and spiritual environment. Tantra is not just about sex. There are also techniques of magick, some of which will be revealed later in this book.

The magickal abilities, called *siddhis*, result from the practices and techniques taught within Tantric schools. Throughout history, as a result of their original, freethinking ways, Tantrics have been seen as leaders. Meanwhile, the non-Tantrics have traditionally flocked to those who tell them how to act and think. This is all good, as societies need followers and leaders.

The manifestation of this dichotomy in the West is similar. Priests and ministers *tell you what to think and how to act*. Magicians *ask you to think and to act*. Which type of person is your leader? Which type of person are you? Perhaps you already are a Tantric and just didn't know it!

Appealing vs. Intriguing

All people need things to believe in. The more closely these things represent reality, the more mentally healthy a person is said to be. Non-Tantrics look for appealing, easy answers. Acupuncture triggers endorphins that get rid of pain. That's simple, but it is certainly far from complete. Acupuncture can also be used to cure many diseases and ailments and help maintain health. To understand it requires a knowledge of energy paths and how to find and stimulate appropriate points along those paths. The first description is appealing because it is simple to understand. The latter is intriguing because it implies an entire energy structure within the body that few people in the West understand. Chinese acupuncture is derived from the Tantric healing system and physiological studies combined in what is called *Ayurveda* ("Ay-yur-veh-duh").

Yoga? That's a way to stretch the body. But a Tantric realizes that what most Westerners call "yoga" is actually just one form of yoga, *hatha* (correctly pronounced "haw-tuh") *yoga*. There are actually several types of yoga. Further, yoga not only stretches the body, it stretches the mind. It can help a person awaken power centers and energy paths within the body. Again, the first description is appealing because it is quick and easy. The latter is intriguing because it describes a complex system of energy paths and power centers.

Non-Tantrics love the appealing, easy answer. In the West, their philosophies can be fully explained on bumper stickers. Tantrics understand that the universe is not that simple. They are willing to explore more complex concepts that lead to a deeper understanding of reality.

Conclusion

One of the purposes of this chapter has been to give you an idea of what differentiates a Tantric from a non-Tantric. Tantra is not just about sex. It is about freedom, responsibility for one's actions, and magick. It is about rejecting ideas that are no longer valid. It is about discovering if there is any value to perpetuating a superstitious belief. It is about healing and divination. It is about spiritual science. And within those topics has been the study of sexuality, including how the pleasure of sex can be enhanced and how sexual practices can lead to spiritual enlightenment. Tantrics have been studying sexuality for thousands of years. In the West, scientists have been actively studying sexuality for less than 150 years.

According to one famous text, the *Mahanirvana Tantra*, we live in a dark age for which the books known as the *Tantras* provide the best source for spiritual development. In India, time is not seen as linear, with a starting and an ending, but rather as circular, with an enormous, repeating cycle. According to another text, the *Bhagavata Purana*, an avatar (incarnation) of Vishnu—his last avatar—will be born in Schambhala-La (Shambhala). The birth of this avatar will mark the end of this dark age and the beginning of a golden age of enlightenment.

Of course, as I hope I've made very clear, the myth of Schambhala-La is just a myth. So too are the gods and goddesses (although I believe the energies they represent and their manifestations of divinity are real). How, then, can an avatar be born in Schambhala-La and mark the beginning of a new age?

Taking this story literally—being a fundamentalist—is appealing, but yields impossible questions. Where can we find this city? What will the avatar look like? What signs will indicate that the avatar has arrived?

A Tantric will look at the exact same story and come to a far more complex, a far more intriguing, conclusion. Schambhala-La doesn't exist as a physical city. For a Tantric, the city of the myth is but a symbol of a spiritual place. It exists in the heart. It lives in the soul. It infuses those of us called to visit Schambhala-La with the potential for freedom and bliss. No matter where we are, we can make our world a dark, horrible place or we can make it light and spiritual and full of joy. The choice is ours.

....

If you would like to find joy in life rather than seeing only darkness, you can find many ways to do so. *Modern Tantra* can lead you on that path.

TWO

Tantric Philosophy

As stated previously, I cringe when I hear expressions such as "Tantra says . . . ," "According to Tantra . . . ," and others of the like. Tantric philosophy and ideas have evolved for thousands of years. No single individual, group, workshop, or book speaks for all of Tantra.

One of the major ways to look at Tantra is in two divisions: the *Vama Marg* (reversed or left-hand path) and *Dakshina Marg* (right-hand path). In the West, the right-hand path of occultism is often seen as representing a magickal path of good and moving toward the Divine. The left-hand path is seen as evil. This may be due to the Latin origin of the word for left, *sinister*, which means both "left" and "unlucky." The word *sinister*, in modern English, has come (by way of Old French and Middle English) to mean "to hint at or portend evil."

In Tantric traditions, however, the definitions of the terms are much different. One description of Tantra is that it leads to the Divine by the same means that lead others to spiritual evil. Thus, Tantra has been called the "path of the fall." What takes others *from* the spiritual path leads the Tantric *to* the godhead. In order to do this, some Tantrics will spiritualize taboo acts and then practice them, freeing the practitioner from preconceived notions or limiting beliefs and showing that anything can be made spiritual. This breaking of taboos is practiced symbolically by some Tantrics who follow the Dakshina Marg (right-hand path) and literally by those who follow the Vama Marg (left-hand path).

As explained in the previous chapter, neither Vama Marg (the system mythically traced to Schambhala-La) nor Dakshina Marg (the system mythically traced to Agarthi-La) should be viewed as superior to the other. Indeed, some traditional books point to the notion that the practice of Dakshina Marg Tantra is necessary before a practitioner can move on to the practices of the Vama Marg, while others claim that the opposite is true.

Even so, there are still many differences between the practitioners of these two divisions of Tantra. Nobody can speak for both or describe them in the same breath.

Here is another example of divisions of traditional Tantra. I had the honor of being initiated into (and later receiving the right to initiate into) a tradition of Tantra known as the *Adinath* tradition. This tradition is one of nine traditions that are part of what is known as the *Navanath* lineage. Even so, there are vast differences between the nine divisions. The Adinaths, for example, seem to follow and represent what is commonly thought of as Vama Marg. The *Pagal Naths*, or "crazy lords," another subsect of the Navanath tradition, are known for doing odd behaviors in public as an attempt to awaken people from their everyday consciousness. In this they are more focused on methods similar to some of those taught by the Armenian-Greek mystic and spiritual teacher George Ivanovich Gurdjieff {c. 1866–1949) than on what we commonly think of as Vama Marg Tantra.

Here we have two sects that come from the same lineage, but that are so different that nobody can describe all of their beliefs as a single system. What I am describing in *Modern Tantra* is one particular system. It will agree with the beliefs of many Vama Marg Tantrics, but not all of them. Similarly, many Neo-Tantrics will agree with some of what is presented here, but perhaps not all of it. As you become more involved with any particular Tantric path, you may find some differences and some similarities. Therefore, please do not take what I am presenting here as laws written in stone. Rather, they are based on my initiations, my personal study, my personal work, my work with various groups, and comments from students. As they write on the Internet, "YMMV" (Your Mileage May Vary).

The Wheel of Time

Most mystical traditions believe in reincarnation. This is found in Hinduism, Buddhism, Shintoism, mystical Judaism (the Kabalah), Spiritualism, Shamanism, Theosophy, Wicca, and even some early sects of Christianity. Part of this results from just looking at the universe. Seeds turn into plants. The plants bloom, go to seed, and die. Much later, the seeds from the plants come back to life. Both wild and domesticated animals are born, mature, and die, only to have females give (re)birth to new life. There is a universal pattern of birth, life, death, a pause, and seeming rebirth. If this happens for plants and beasts, why not humans, too?

If we reincarnate, perhaps endlessly, we must be struck by a series of questions. How long has the universe existed? What is the mechanism for reincarnation? Why do we even incarnate?

The Yugas

The Tantric view of time is that the universe is constantly going through cycles. These form a mammoth *kalpa*, or Day of Brahma, that takes 4,320,000,000 years before repeating. Each kalpa is subdivided into fourteen *manvantaras* (age of

Manu[5]). Each one of these is divided into seventy-one *mahayugas* (great age). A mahayuga lasts about 4,320,000 years. A mahayuga is divided into four *yugas*.

The first part of each mahayuga is known as *Satya Yuga*. This is seen as a golden age of righteousness that lasted 1,728,000 years. During this period, people were free of evil and hate. They had very long lives of up to 100,000 years and were physically beautiful, incredibly strong, and so tall (about 30–38 feet) that they were called giants.

The second yuga, beginning at the end of the first, was the silver age called the *Treta Yuga*. Righteousness decreased among the people by one-fourth, so it is also known as the ¾ Yuga. Strength, beauty, and longevity also decreased. Now the average lifespan of a human was "only" 10,000 years. This period lasted for 1,296,000 years. The Treta Yuga marked the introduction of religious rites and ceremonies, replacing individual spirituality.

The third yuga is called *Dvapara*. Righteousness was decreased by half from the Satya Yuga. Evil and good were now about equal. Beauty, strength, and longevity decreased. People only lived to be about 1,000 years old. This period lasted for about 864,000 years.

The fourth yuga is that of *Kali*, darkness. It is said to have begun at midnight between the 17th and 18th of February 3120 BCE, and it will last for 432,000 years. This age is characterized by viciousness, weakness, and disease. Human life will only last 100–120 years. People will only be 5'–6'3" tall.

5 Manu is an archetypal figure similar in mythic function to the Jewish Adam. He is the forefather of all humanity and in some traditions is seen as the person who instituted religious practices. Like Noah, he was saved from a great flood. The deity who saved him was Vishnu or Brahma.

Today, in the Kali Yuga, we have the most unrighteous of times. According to the *Mahanirvana Tantra*, written hundreds of years ago, in this age people will earn respect simply by owning things and will tell lie after lie to become successful. Sex will be the only way people will be able to enjoy life, and people will confuse the outer trappings of religion with true spirituality. That description of our age, made hundreds of years ago, sounds accurate to me.

The ideal spiritual texts for the first yuga are the Vedas. These are the famed books of sacred Hindu knowledge. There are three primary ones, the *Rig Veda*, the *Yajurveda*, and the *Samaveda*. Although the Vedas are also appropriate for spiritual guidance during the second yuga, it is believed to be more difficult to practice the techniques described therein. The spiritual texts for the third yuga are the *Puranas*, a group of post-Vedas spiritual books, and during this period the Vedas are no longer good for accomplishing spiritual goals. Finally, the ideal spiritual texts for the current age, the Kali Yuga, are the Tantras.

Tantrics see this world as being wonderful. If this is the least righteous of all the ages, how can this be?

Life *Is* Wonderful

In many spiritual and religious traditions, life on Earth is seen as horrible and vile. The goal is to learn to ignore the physical world as much as possible. In some Christianity traditions, believers are told to be *in* this world but not *of* this world, and even that Satan is the god of this world. In many sects of Buddhism and Hinduism, life is seen as a way to experience pain and suffering repeatedly through multiple lifetimes until we can get off the wheel of rebirth and no longer incarnate. Indeed, those who no longer need to incarnate on our horrible planet but do so in order to help others are known as *Bodhisattvas* and are due great honors.

And who can disagree with such an attitude? Children all over the world suffer with horrendous diseases. They labor long hours for pennies a day. Wars and "disputes" kill tens of thousands of people during "good" years. People are locked for years in prisons for minor crimes, while those who destroy the lives of tens of thousands of people are rewarded or see no punishment at all. We pay taxes to corrupt politicians. We buy insurance, betting against our own health and safety. As our bodies age, they become infirm and we lose not only the appearance of youth but also the abilities of youth. And then we may suffer the indignities of long, lingering pains leading to death—if criminals do not kill us first. If we are lucky enough to have a long and relatively healthy life, we will certainly lose friends and loved ones to illness, accident, and time. We are fated to be alone, scorned by youth and perhaps hidden in a "home" until we die. Living in this world can perhaps be summed up best by the bumper sticker "Life sucks and then you die." Death is called a "release" from the sorrow and woe of living.

How could anyone disagree? Life is harsh and painful. Let me share a bit of my life. I watched my father die when I was six. My mother immediately had a nervous breakdown. My grandparents died from slow, lingering, painful diseases. My brother was a victim of serious diseases and had to experience several major surgeries and amputations before suffering a painful death. Another close relative, a former competitor in cross-country running, developed a disease that put him on crutches or in a wheelchair. My good friend Scott Cunningham died of a frightening and lingering disease on the day my parents sold the home in which I grew up. These two events occurred on my birthday in 1993. A few years ago, my mother had a sudden brain hemorrhage and died without my having a chance to say, "I love you. Goodbye." My brother-in-law died of a lingering disease. On January 17, 2000, I came down with Bell's palsy, a disease that temporarily paralyzed the left half of my face. Two weeks later, on Super Bowl Sunday, I died and was brought back to life by some excellent doctors and paramedics. Even so, I now have a chronic disease that may eventually cripple me, blind me, or result in the amputation of my legs. One might ask, "Don, why don't you just give up? The pain and suffering in this life is just too great. All is but sorrow and woe."[6]

But to many Tantrics, including myself, all of life is beautiful. Our universe is wonderful, exhilarating, the ideal place to live, love, learn, and spiritually evolve.

So are Tantrics blind to the reality around us? How can Tantrics love this world when there is so much pain and suffering?

Tantrics are *not* blind. In fact, we are just the opposite. Instead of seeing the world as random happenings pushing us back and forth and over which we have no control, Tantrics see an underlying reality of beauty, peace, love, and enlightenment. The question we must ask, then, is why doesn't everyone see this inner reality?

6 I have *not* given up. All the symptoms of Bell's palsy ended, and I have no sign of the disease. When I left the hospital after dying, I was injecting large amounts of two different types of insulin daily under the skin of my legs or stomach. Due to ritual work, visualization, nutritional patterns, exercise, and the good wishes and energy of friends and loved ones, that was quickly brought down to only thirty units of one type of insulin. For years now, I have no longer needed to inject insulin. Instead, I take a tiny pill once a day. I anticipate a time when I will need no drugs for my diabetes and look forward to an eventual cure or total remission.

Maya, Kleshas, and Vidya

The answer is that we are blessed and cursed by the goddess Maya. Behind what we call reality—the physical world—is the true reality: the spiritual world of pure energy in motion (vibration). But the goddess Maya dances and plays with the energies and finer matter of the inner reality, creating what forms our common, physical, consensus reality. One of the differences between Tantrics and non-Tantrics is that Tantrics see through the *maya*, the illusion, while non-Tantrics are caught up in the intoxicating beauty of her dance.

The reason most people see the world as terrible and filled with pain is because the dance of Maya disguises our ability to see the beauty of the real, spiritual world. Maya manifests in our lives in the form of five types of "pains" (*kleshas*), or blockages, that prevent us from seeing how wonderful life is and keep us from evolving spiritually.

I contend that the basis of all the kleshas, what prevents us from seeing through the maya, is *avidya*, ignorance, or the lack of knowledge (*vidya*). Vidya also means such things as, science, philosophy, logic, and metaphysics. Some say it includes the knowledge of soul or of spiritual truth. One legend even describes a pill called *vidya*. This pill, when swallowed, allows you to ascend to heaven. Metaphorically, taking the pill vidya (gaining knowledge) will let you see that heaven truly is here on Earth. Suffering with a lack of knowledge, avidya, keeps us blinded by maya and seeing the world as a terrible place. By overcoming the klesha of avidya, we can discover the real beauty of the universe. More on this as we examine all five kleshas.

The Five Kleshas

False Ego (Asmita)

The first klesha to look at is the false ego, *asmita* ("ah-smee-tuh"). Today, virtually all psychological literature makes it clear that having a strong ego is important to maturation and individuality. The *false* ego, however, is a misinterpretation of who we are, a misinterpretation we accept as fact. It is composed of false beliefs about ourselves and our relationship with the universe.

This false ego entices us to see "reality" as the link between ourselves and the world of maya. It allows us to see our higher self as being nothing more than our lower self. It allows us to believe, as the bumper sticker says, that "whoever dies with the most toys wins." In fact, maya is an illusion. Although our higher self and our lower self are parts of a unitary being, they are not the same. Due to reincarnation, the number of toys we have is irrelevant and does not matter. What matters is how we evolve spiritually.

One of the major beliefs of the false ego is the notion that we all have free will. Actually, we each only have the *potential* for free will. We are constantly battered by unconscious whims and desires that influence and control us. Psychotherapists around the world are kept busy by people attempting to discover the nature and source of the unconscious motivations that limit and control them. Not only do these unconscious motivations control us mentally, they also often control us physically. Many ailments that prevent us from performing various actions are rooted in our unconscious minds. In some cases, such as with agoraphobia (a fear of public or open places that can become so severe that panic attacks result, preventing a person from leaving home), the control of the unconscious over our actions is clear. How can we have free will if our unconscious does not let us go out the door?

In my case, the effects of my subconscious on my body were a bit more subtle. When I was young, I developed severe allergies to pollens, along with what is called "athletic asthma."

This stopped me from enjoying what I used to do daily—run and play in the overgrown fields and hills near my home. Sometimes I would do so anyway (the natural Tantric within me), and more than once I had to be rushed to the hospital to receive a shot of adrenaline so I could breathe instead of struggle for breath through fluid-filled wheezes.

As is the case with many youthful asthma and allergy patients, I eventually outgrew it. But as it ended, my mind/body played another trick on me. The skin on the fingers of my right hand started to dry, scale, and flake off. Sometimes the scaling was so deep that I would bleed. It was very painful. It was as if my body was trying to stop me from doing the things I enjoyed—playing music and writing. Sometimes when I would play keyboards in a band at a club, I would get so involved in the playing that I would totally ignore the pain (again, a very Tantric thing to do). At the end of the set, I would look down in the club's dim light and see that the white keys were streaked in black—they were covered with my blood!

My mother took me to an expensive dermatologist. He took skin scrapings. I was diagnosed as suffering from eczema or contact dermatitis; he didn't know which. I was treated with creams, ointments, drugs, and ultraviolet light. At night I had to put the ointments on my hand, cover it with a cotton glove, and cover the mess with a plastic bag. The skin problem would go in cycles of getting better and worse, but it didn't go away.

Then I turned to one of my skills—speaking—to make a living. My hand started to heal, but I developed a small, nagging cough, making regular speaking difficult.

Until I was about thirty-five, my body was fighting me. How could I have free will when something was causing all of these problems? Treating the individual problem was simply not working. I had to find the cause and treat it.

My mother, as a result of a casual conversation, revealed what I now believe was the real cause of these issues. I had misremembered my own history. I had thought that my asthma and allergies developed about a year after my father's death. To my surprise, my mother informed me that this was incorrect. In fact, my first allergy attack occurred *one week after the death of my father*. In a flash of insight, I realized that for three decades my childhood feelings of sorrow, abandonment, loss, lack of understanding, etc., had controlled me. It was not until I understood what had happened that I stopped having outbreaks of coughing or eczema.

By discovering what was controlling me, but finding out what was part of my deepest self, I moved one step closer to true free will. Part of the process of Tantric work is discovering those parts of our unconscious that control us and then discharging (through understanding and physical, mental, and spiritual work) the power they have over us. Thinking we are in control when we are not is part of our false ego and is based on a lack of information about the reality of who we are.

Perhaps the easiest way to understand this klesha, the false ego, is to compare what we think of ourselves with what our friends and loved ones think of us. On a scale of 1–10, are we friendly, loving, caring, generous, silly, ill-tempered, dogmatic, wise, clever, etc.? Where your answers about yourself do not match those of people who know you well is where your false ego is ruling and possibly misleading you. The wider the disparity (you rate yourself a 10, while people who know you rate you a 1), the more your false ego is in control.

Ignorance (Avidya)

The second klesha to examine is ignorance, *avidya* ("ah-vihd-yuh"). Ignorance is different from stupidity. A simplistic description is that an ignorant person doesn't know that one plus one equals two, while a stupid person may know that one plus one equals two but doesn't know that one penny plus one penny equals two cents.

Ignorance itself isn't bad. We can study, learn, and work to overcome ignorance. It is our self-centered refusal to recognize our ignorance that prevents us from understanding the universe and our place in it. This prevents us from understanding the energetic nature of the universe and how it is hidden from us by maya. Ignorance lets us think love and possession are the same thing. It equates religion with spirituality. It prevents us from becoming enlightened.

For thousands of years, people in India have studied the nature of the body. One of the things they have discovered is that there are various energies that pervade the body, follow paths within the body, and pool to form vortices of power. As long as we are ignorant of these, we cannot help ourselves heal, energize, and become enlightened.

If you do not know that you need medical care, how will you get that care? You won't request it. If offered, you won't take it. Refusal to end ignorance is stupidity, and such stupidity can cost you your life. Ignorance, however, can lead to knowledge when you realize that in some area you are ignorant. If you want a job in computers and are ignorant of how they work, you know you must get an education in the field. One of the things I like to tell students is:

The realization of ignorance is the beginning of wisdom.

People who know they are ignorant can do something about it. People who are ignorant can change. Change is much more difficult for people who are stupid and do not accept the reality of their ignorance. Such people are unlikely to change. A five-year-old who is ignorant of how to read, but wants to learn, is wonderful to work with. A twenty-year-old who is ignorant of how to read, and refuses to take the time to learn (due to egotism, not caring, etc.), is justly called stupid. I love working with ignorant people. I do not like being with stupid ones. I suppose that is a personal klesha (repulsion) I need to work on.

In *Modern Tantra* there are five traditional types of ignorance:

1. Ignorance of the value of your time and the refusal to take advantage of opportunities offered you.
2. Ignorance of your true inner self and the refusal to do the work necessary to discover your inner nature.
3. Ignorance of believing you are only a physical body and nothing more.
4. Ignorance of living in a state of anger for short or long periods, as anger only harms you (mentally, physically, emotionally, and spiritually) and takes you away from a spiritual path.
5. Ignorance of assuming that life ends at physical death and that the essence of who and what you are does not continue.

As I wrote, I believe that ignorance is the source of all the kleshas, the key to the blockages that keep you from succeeding in any aspect of your life. It allows you to become distracted from your path by everything from politics to TV, from the pursuit of worldly wealth to an unrealistic assessment of what is, and is not, important.

Repulsion (Dvesha)

The next klesha we will look at is repulsion, *dvesha*. To explain the idea of repulsion, let's examine scents. For a second, think of the most repulsive scent possible. What happens to you when you smell it? Does it make you gag? Does it make you want to run away? Do you actually move away from a repulsive scent?

I find the smell of vomit repulsive. Just a whiff and I start to gag and feel a desire to vomit myself. And frankly, I hate the feeling of having to vomit. I hate actually vomiting even more. (I would add that in India, regurgitation for the purpose of purification is not an uncommon practice. I have a long way to go before I master that technique!)

But if we look at this a bit deeper, we will discover something quite interesting. There is absolutely nothing wrong or awful about the scent of vomit. Rather, something in my past allows it to trigger something physiological in me. There is nothing wrong with the smell; it's just a smell. But for some reason I have made it a horrible experience.

To generalize this, we could use this expression:

Nothing is horrible in itself
save that we make it so.

This, of course, is a version of a speech in Hamlet where he says, "For there is nothing either good or bad, but thinking makes it so: to me it is a prison." Indeed, our taking of something that is neither good nor bad and making it so horrible that it physically bothers us can be like a prison keeping us from freedom and happiness.

Many people find snakes or bugs repulsive. There is no reason to do so. Most snakes and bugs are benign to humans; in fact, they are helpful to the ecology. They are not horrible. They are neither good nor bad. They simply are. We put qualities on them that we consider horrible and repulsive. Some sects of traditional Tantrics in India have members who live among the rotting corpses, bones, and ashes of cremation grounds in order to prove that nothing is horrible in itself. Some go so far as to have sex with the corpses.

I do not advise anyone to attempt this because of sanitary issues and because here in the US (and probably in most countries) it is against the law. But the idea remains the same: if you are repulsed by anything, find out the reason why and overcome it. This may not be easy. Examining one's motivations is not often direct or simple. Sometimes it is emotionally painful. However, perhaps the easiest way to deal with repulsion is to concentrate on that which repulses you and see what emotions it brings up. Free-associate based on those emotions. Allow your mind to move from association to association, even if they do not seem related to the original item. You may be surprised to discover the real source of the repulsion. Hypnotherapy and neuro-linguistic programming can also help you break the links between neutral stimuli and unwanted responses to those stimuli.

I'm not suggesting you should actually do something that repulses you. You do not have to practice something or try it even once in order to overcome a repulsion to it. All you have to do is mentally think about it, see what is the nature of the repulsion you have toward it, and work with that cause until the repulsion to that smell, idea, practice, etc., is gone.

Years ago, I experimented with this concept while I was studying music at the University of California, San Diego. There is a musical interval known as a *tritone* (an augmented fourth)[7]. This was considered so discordant that in

7 The sound of the augmented fourth is heard in the first two notes of the song "Maria" from the musical *West Side Story*. The third note resolves the tritone to a more sonorous pitch.

Western music, until the end of the Renaissance, it was nicknamed *diabolus in musica*, the "devil in music." For a class, I wrote a piece of music I named "Tritonus." It consisted of harmonies and melodic lines based around the tritone interval. After several minutes, you became used to the sound, and to the listeners' ears it was no longer discordant. As a musical joke, the end of the piece resolved into a common, very harmonious major chord. But because the piece focused so strongly on the tritone interval, the listeners' ears became used to its disharmony, and that normally sonorous final chord sounded discordant and out of place. I succeeded, through repetition, in making something that normally sounded bad sound good, and something we so often consider musically good to sound bad. I had ended one repulsion and started another. Nothing is horrible in itself save that we make it so.

There are other cases where practice can help us overcome repulsions. Here is an example that is sometimes used by comedians. A man and woman have a long session of passionate sexual activity. During their lovemaking they lick and kiss virtually every part of each other. Before they go to sleep, he says, "Honey, can I use your toothbrush?"

"Eww," she responds. "That's disgusting."

They have just kissed and licked each other's most intimate parts. They have kissed deeply, what is popularly called "sharing spit." But she finds the thought of them sharing a toothbrush repulsive. It seems odd, yet many people feel this way. Perhaps you've experienced this.

Passionate, open-mouthed kissing, the "sharing spit" just described, is popular among many people. But the notion of sharing the saliva of another person in a different context is often considered repulsive. This repulsion can be overcome by consciously sharing saliva with a partner by passing it back and forth while kissing.

Another fluid some are repulsed by is sperm. People can begin to overcome this repulsion by smearing the sperm on their bodies (see my *Modern Sex Magick* or *Modern Magick* for ways of doing this to create magickal talismans). Because oral sex is now common (remember, it was a taboo for many people barely sixty years ago, and many people still do not practice this form of sexuality), many women are familiar with the taste and texture of sperm. Many, if not most, heterosexual men, however, find the thought of having sperm in their mouths repulsive. This can be overcome by a woman kissing a man after she has given him oral sex where he has ejaculated into her mouth and she either swallows or spits out the ejaculate. At first, he will only get some of the flavor of his sperm. Later, she can keep some of it in her mouth and pass it to him during the kiss (a popular current urban slang term for this practice is *snowballing*).

Similar practices can be done with women's lubricative and ejaculatory fluids and, yes, even menstrual blood. In the West, those who practice the consumption of bodily fluids for spiritual purposes usually transform these substances through the use of heat, primarily by cooking. However, it is usually safe for a person to drink his or her own urine (urine is sterile). There is a long tradition of this in India, practiced by no less than Mahatma Gandhi and his followers at his *ashrams* (religious communities). He was known to greet people in the morning, saying, "How is your urine today?" I have a booklet on this technique that refers to consumption of one's urine as *Rasa Tantra*.

Does that practice sound horrible? Remember that nothing is horrible in itself save that we make it so.

Retention (Raga)

The next klesha we will look at is retention, *raga* ("rah-guh"). This is the experience of being attached to any physical thing. What happens is this: You experience something and it sets up a response in you. That response may be that you like the way something looks, smells, sounds, feels, tastes, etc. As a result of this positive response, you try to repeat the experience. It is this desire to repeat the experience that is attachment, or retention. We may try to buy, own, or possess this object of desire. This object may be a car, a book, a painting, a person, or any other thing.

This attachment to something or many things bogs us down, controls us, and prevents us from being free. Here, once again, is an example from my life.

Years ago, before the change from vinyl records to compact discs, I had a huge collection of large 33⅓ rpm albums and 45 rpm singles. Some were rare "picture discs" (they had images or photos embedded into the vinyl). Others were made on softer vinyl that improved the sound quality by holding more sound information, but they would wear out more quickly than other records. Still others were rare albums imported from England or Japan. Some items in my collection were quite unusual. For example, I had a copy of the original 45 rpm single of the Rolling Stones performing a song that had been written by the Beatles' Lennon and McCartney, "I Wanna Be Your Man."

Because my records were valuable, I took excellent care of them. I purchased special protective inserts that I put the albums in before returning them to their cardboard sleeves. I also kept the original paper inserts because having them increased the value of the albums. Then, to protect the outer sleeves of the albums, I bought special plastic holders for them. I made sure that I always kept the albums vertical because laying them flat was supposed to damage them. I would rarely play the albums made of softer vinyl so they wouldn't wear out.

And then I lost my job. Suddenly I needed some extra money. The only things I had of value at that time and that I could quickly and easily sell were the albums. Oh, how it hurt to have to pick out the ones I could bear to sell! Eventually I had no choice. I had to sell almost all of them.

As I sold them, something unexpected happened. A weight was lifted off my shoulders. I came to the conclusion that *I did not own the records, they owned me!* I treated them in special ways. I cared for them as if they were children. I was a slave to what I saw as their needs.

As I sold each album, I felt lighter, freer. They no longer possessed me. I was becoming free. No longer was I attached to them. I still have a lot of CDs, but I never had the attachment to them that I had with the records.

In India, there is a tradition among the orthodox Hindus of getting rid of attachments by becoming a renunciant. A monk practicing renunciation is entitled to only a bowl for begging, a change of clothes, and the right to sit under the shade of a tree. By having nothing, the renunciant is supposed to get rid of attachment to the world. He is supposed to become free and spiritual.

Unfortunately, it doesn't always work that way. In fact, I hazard to guess that it doesn't work that way for most renunciants. Giving up tangible things is only the physical trapping of renunciation. Just because you don't own something doesn't mean it won't possess you. Have you ever *really* wanted something you didn't already have? A particular car? Tickets to a concert? A certain lifestyle? Then you have attachments to it even though you do not have it. And because of *avidya*, ignorance, you may be attached to something even though you are not consciously aware of the attachment.

You do not have to get rid of your possessions, as I did with my record collection, to free yourself from attachment. All you need to do is develop the *attitude* of non-attachment. This will bring you freedom of thought, word, and deed. You can raise a family and own a home, car, and TV and still be the master of yourself and the things you own. Keep them? Lose them? It doesn't matter because you are detached and free.

As a result of non-attachment, you become unaffected in the face of the trials and tribulations of life. After all, what are these difficulties save the play of maya in your life? When you get caught up in daily difficulties (maya), you cannot see the greater reality. The more you are attached to this world, the less you can see into the greater, real world. Get rid of your mental attachments to your few physical things and become open to the greater universe, with its many billions of things.

This brings us to a Tantric view of love and romance. As mentioned in the previous chapter, love is an energy. It pervades the universe. You can tap into it and dwell in it. You can share it with others. True love multiplies; it never subtracts. The more you experience it, the more there is.

If you are like most people, either you loved or, if she is still alive, you love your mother. Because you love her, you want her to be happy and healthy and have interesting experiences. The same is probably true of the way you feel about your father, your friends, brothers and sisters, and other relatives.

But when it comes to boyfriends and girlfriends, wives and husbands, the situation changes. "You are mine," says the so-called romantic. Is this really good? Is this not treating the person you most passionately love as if he or she were a tube of toothpaste, a set of tires, or a record album? Is it really love or merely a desire to possess?

"I saw you flirting at that party," says the angry lover. But why is he upset? The flirting made her happy. She didn't leave and go home with the person she was flirting with. Why does the lover feel angry? The answer is that he is afraid someone might take away his "possession."

And that is true. She might leave him. But she might leave him whether she flirts or not. His attachment to her is like that of a person who owns an automobile. You have to protect it because somebody might steal it. Or they might just scratch it.

But a lover or spouse is not a car. The other person chooses to be with you or not be with you. Trying to control a person and limit his or her freedom seems to be just the opposite of what you would do if you really loved that person.

Let's take it one step further. If you want your lover to be happy and have wonderful experiences, why limit him or her from having sex with another person? Are you afraid that your lover will find somebody who is better sexually than you are? That can happen whether you allow it or not. In most cases, people come together for more than sex. They find some sort of fulfillment with that person of which sex is only a part. Would your car drive off with another person because that person is a better driver? If your lover leaves you for a better lover, then there was actually very little keeping you together anyway. And perhaps it would help you to see your ignorance about sex and allow you to start learning to be a better lover!

What I am presenting here is the notion of love and non-attachment. You can have both. Then, when you find a real love, you will come together out of true love, not out of a desire to possess that which cannot be possessed. You both will choose to be together rather than demand obedience and attachment. You both will be free to grow and your love will only enhance that, growing as you grow. You can consciously *choose* to have one partner rather than being terrified that you *must* only have one partner out of fear of losing that partner. Love does not require jealousy or fear.

Clinging to Life (Jivitvasajya)

The last klesha we will examine is clinging to life, *jivitvasajya* ("jih-veet-vuh-sahj-yuh"). I think it is fair to say that most people want a long, quality-filled life. But there is one thing that is undeniable. Our physical bodies, due either to accident, age, or illness, will eventually cease to function. This is yet another thing that unites all humans: sooner or later, our bodies will die.

There is nothing wrong with wanting to live a long life. For example, getting exercise on a daily basis and having good nutrition will help us live longer, healthier lives. Having regular sex and moving the energy within us helps to keep us young, healthy, and energetically vibrant. All of these things are good.

But there are people who think that doing all or some of these things will help them live *much* longer lives. Some people will exercise for hours every day. They may get up early, go to a gym and exercise, go to work, jog at lunch, exercise at the gym after work, and then go to sleep. Why? To live a longer and healthier life. Unfortunately, with all that exercising they may have *no time to actually live that life!* They are so busy trying to avoid death and illness that they are kept from the world (like an ill person) and have no life (like a dead person).

I am not saying that such people should stop exercising. But it is important to realize that no matter how much you exercise, no matter your nutrition choices, one day your body will die. That means every hour you exercise is time spent away from your family, time spent away from your friends, time spent away from appreciating nature and music and art, time spent away from following a spiritual path. If given the choice of going to a museum with someone you love or spending a couple of hours at the gym in the hope of extending your life a few moments, which would you choose? I know the decision I would make.

Let's look at another situation. A person lives in a city and is afraid to come out of his house because ten years ago, during a nearby robbery, a person was killed. By staying inside, this person believes he is avoiding the possibility of being killed in a robbery. This person also avoids the possibility that a car will jump the curb and smash into him, killing him. But for all practical purposes, by hiding in his house to cling to life, by not experiencing the world, he may as well be dead. This clinging to life prevents him from living.

Now, I am *not* implying that people should take stupid chances! Walking on the edge of the roof of a fifteen-story building with no safety equipment is stupid. Driving while impaired by lack of sleep, alcohol, drugs, or focusing on texting is dumb. Always making poor food choices and not taking care of your health is not wise. We should protect ourselves by wearing safety equipment, avoid things that impair our judgment while driving, and do things for our health. But fearing death so much that we won't go out of our door because of something that happened ten years ago or because a car might leap the curb is foolish. Could something bad happen? Yes. But when the chances of it happening are so slim, there is no reason to let our *unreasonable* beliefs and fears control us.

Frankly, something like that could have happened to me. I still remember the first day I passed the test and received my driver's license. That evening I begged my parents to let me borrow the family car and, for the very first time, go out driving on my own. It was pouring rain in a rare Southern California thunderstorm. I was so excited that I talked them into it with wonderful teenage logic: "I have to learn to drive under these conditions sometime. Why not now?"

So there I was, driving slowly in the heavy rain. At times it was coming down so hard I could not see more than a foot or two beyond my front bumper. My lights reflected back off a curtain of falling water.

Most teenagers see themselves as immortal. They do not conceive of their own death. I was one of them. But the amount of rain was much more than I was used to. I started driving slowly back home.

I got to the top of the Charnock Avenue hill near my home when it happened. The entire car flashed with a bluish-white light and the engine stopped. Aliens? I don't think so. I believe I was hit by lightning. I was saved because an automobile is an ideal safety structure from exterior electricity.

Rather than this making me terrified of driving in storms, it made me feel more secure. Your chance of being hit by lightning, depending upon the source you read, is about 3,000,000 to 1. By being hit by lightning, I had just improved my odds incredibly against ever getting hit by lightning again. (The annual number of people in the US who get hit by lightning, depending upon the source, is listed as ranging between 41 and 300.)

If it is your desire to follow a Tantric way of life, I urge you to self-analyze and determine if some of your actions are based on clinging to life to such an extent that your beliefs and actions are no longer reasonable. If so, you might want to consider ways to overcome this klesha. Remember, all of our bodies will die. It makes sense to take care of ourselves so we can live long, healthy lives. But clinging to life so strongly that we end up avoiding experiencing life is not wise at all.

Karma

While the Tantric attitude that this is a wonderful world and a wonderful life may now be a bit more understandable, it's still important to accept the fact that we have experiences we describe as pain and suffering. There are wars with massive death and destruction. Innocent children suffer from terrible diseases and abuse from those who should show them love. Even if we can accept that these things happen in our world, at one time or another we have to ask ourselves a simple question: *Why?*

> *Why* does the person who cheats
> in business go unpunished?
>
> *Why* are non-combatants
> killed and maimed in wars?
>
> *Why* do infants suffer
> from horrible diseases?

The answer to such questions in most Western traditions is most frequently a non-answer: "We don't know." "It just happens." "It's God's will." "That's the way the world works." "They'll be rewarded/punished in heaven/hell for what has happened to them and for what they've done here on Earth." The last type of response does imply there will be some cosmic retribution or reward, but as to causes for these things... well, it's just chance, coincidence, or bad luck. And that's not an answer at all.

In the past few years, there has been an upturn in awareness of what has been called "wealth consciousness," or the "law of attraction." Simply put, this law states that what you think about and act upon you draw to yourself. If you focus on poverty, you draw poverty to you. If you focus on wealth, you draw wealth. The truth, however, is that if you're poor, then sitting in a corner and thinking about wealth isn't going to help pay your rent. *You have to do something!* But what? Obviously, what you have been doing isn't working. What lessons are there in the poverty you're suffering? Once you learn what's wrong, you can discover how to move toward wealth. In other words, instead of viewing your poverty as a curse or punishment, you can see it as something educational. You don't like it; therefore, instead of dwelling on it, you need to figure how best to end it. If you learn the lessons of poverty, you can move toward wealth. And that type of learning is the basic idea of *karma*.

(The following information is based on an article I wrote for the Llewellyn Encyclopedia, www.llewellynencyclopedia.com, and is used by permission.)

Many people use the term *karma* without truly understanding what it means. "It's my karma to be poor," they say. Or instead of "poor," they say "ill" or "lonely." In doing this, they make karma appear to be the same as what is usually called "fate." It is not. In fact, the original notion of karma is quite the opposite of fate.

The term *karma* simply means "action." There is nothing in the definition that indicates fate. In a spiritual context, it means that everything you do will cause a reaction. If you do something good, you will receive something good. If you do something bad, something bad will happen to you.

There are two important aspects of this definition. First, it means there are no "lords of karma" watching over the process. There is no one to judge you. Further, it means that your intent plays no part in the working of karma. Whether you planned to harm someone or it was an accident, if you harm someone there will be a karmic result. Yes, even if it was an unintended action, you are still responsible for it. This is similar to the concept that if you drop a pebble in a quiet body of water, waves will appear from where you dropped the rock. It does not matter whether you intended to drop it or why you dropped it.

Second, with karma, the reaction to your action need not be instantaneous. I'm sure you have seen someone who has acted poorly and seemed to profit from those actions. The response to an action may take weeks, months, years, or even several lifetimes.

Types of Karma

1. Sanchita
2. Parabdha
3. Agami
4. Kriyamana

Traditionally, there are three types of karma. First, there is *sanchita karma*. This is the collected karma from all of your past lifetimes. Some people consider *parabdha karma*—that portion of sanchita karma you are working on in this lifetime—to be a fourth type of karma, but I consider it an aspect of sanchita karma.

The second type is called *agami karma*. This is the karma you have created in your current life. It differs from parabdha karma in that you are not working on it (that is, trying to work it off), you are just acquiring it. The third type is called *kriyamana karma*. It is the karma you create and work off immediately, popularly known as "instant karma." For example, park your car illegally and you get a ticket.

Working Off Karma

The key to understanding karma is the concept of "working it off." Through self-study, introspection, and other means such as divination and hypnotic past-life regression, we can discover the actions that caused our karma and how to overcome it and never face it again. Karma, then, can be seen as *the great teacher*. When you face something negative caused by karma, the goal is not to make you suffer; it is not to punish you. Rather, it is to awaken you and tell you that for your own sake you need to change. Indeed, the goal of karma is to make us better, more caring, more loving, more spiritual people.

Once you discover the cause of your karma, the means of working it off can become quite self-evident. Are you poor? What can you learn and put into practice from your poverty? Are you in ill health? What can you learn about life as a result of the illness, and how can you share this information with others?

There are other means of working off karma, including charity, performing rituals, and even reciting certain magickal words hundreds of thousands of times. Some of these will be covered later. However, the most common way to deal with unwanted effects of karma is to *learn the lesson that karma wants you to have and act on that information*, often doing the opposite of what initially caused the karma. There is no good or bad karma, there is just karma. How we interpret it makes it seem good or bad. What we do about it makes it important.

The Gunas

As mentioned previously, it is believed by some authorities that the Druids, or their progenitors, came to Europe from India. Certainly the Druids did more than simply lead spiritual rites and guide the people. They had beliefs they introduced that had not been seen in Europe previously. They didn't just amplify, they brought in new things.

One of these things they brought was a focus on concepts associated with the number three. Indeed, many of the teachings of Druidism came in the form of the famous Druid Triads. Where did these come from? Is it possible the threefold focus came from India? I don't know, nor do I claim it as a fact. But the triadic format that is found in many systems—the Tao yin-yang of China, the pillars of the Kabalistic Tree of Life, and even the part of the philosophy of Georg Wilhelm Friedrich Hegel (1770–1831) known as dialecticism (also called the Hegelian dialectic or the thesis-antithesis-synthesis theory)—may have its roots in ancient Tantric concepts, including that of the three *gunas* (see illustration).

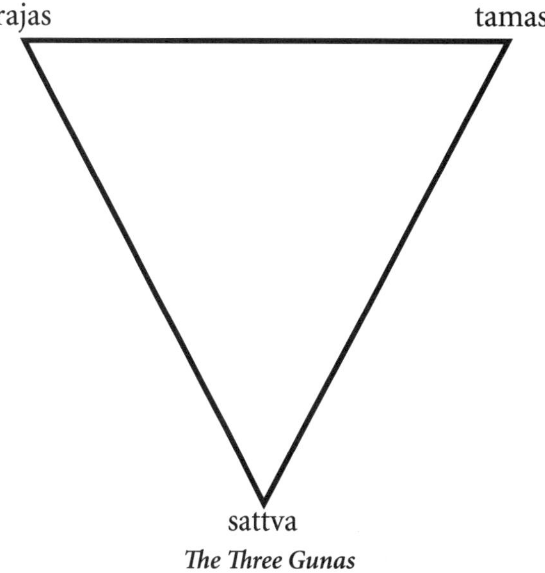

The Three Gunas

It is true that we hear a lot of the word *Trinity* in Christianity. However, it was unknown to the original Christians of the last part of the first century. The word *Trinity* was coined by Tertullian (c. 155–c. 220 CE), but not exactly in the same way as is accepted today. The current idea of the Trinity in Christianity was fought over until the Council of Nicea in 325 CE, and it took longer than that to filter down to the churches and believers. According to the *New Catholic Encyclopedia* (volume IV, p. 295), "[O]ne should not speak about Trinitarianism in the New Testament without serious qualification." The volume further states that the orthodox version of the Trinity was "the product of 3 centuries of doctrinal development," and only became part Christianity "in the last quadrant of the 4th century."

Here in the West, which is so heavily influenced by Christianity, we are far more likely to speak in terms of dualities: good and evil, up and down, left and right, happy and sad, and so on. This is more along the lines of Aristotle (384–322 BCE), who heavily influenced Christianity and saw the universe in opposites, such as the physical world (which he described in his work *Physics)* and the non-physical world (which he described in *Metaphysics*).

The frequent use of triadic concepts certainly may have originated with the ancient Tantrics. The archetype of this is found in the three *gunas*, or tendencies, which are energies that drive things in nature: *rajas, tamas,* and *sattva.*

Rajas is the guna of action and dynamism. The more of this tendency you possess, the more you are driven to act on things. It gives you the desire to acquire new things and the fear of losing that which you have. The combination of desire and fear leads you to act. Rajas deals with moving energy, including light. It is the nature of change.

Tamas is the guna of inertia, inaction, and dullness. Dullness can relate to concepts of darkness and ignorance. There is nothing wrong with rest, but a person (or animal or thing) who has a great deal of tamas is too inactive, heavy, and unmoving. Tamas resists change.

Sattva is the guna of balance and order. A person with this tendency is calm but alert. Thus, sattva is a balancing of the tendencies of rajas and tamas. It is the tendency toward harmony.

The concept of the three gunas is used in understanding yourself and your actions. It can be used in the preparation of food and in the layout of your home. It can help you understand your physiology and help determine the best healing methods for individuals, etc.

A person who has an athletic build and is energetic, who perhaps plays a lot of sports, is rajavic. Such a person is an adrenaline junkie and may enjoy excitement and risky behavior. A tamasic person is slow, heavy, and thoughtful—or lazy. Think in terms of a river: a narrow one is rajavic and moves quickly and is easily turned. A large one is tamasic and moves slowly but is difficult to turn.

Being rajavic or tamasic is neither good nor bad; it simply is. If you are starting a business, you might look for people who are rajavic in nature to get it moving quickly. They would also be able to change direction quickly in order to confront and overcome new challenges. But once it's going and your business is beginning to become successful, you might look to hire tamasic people, who, once started, are difficult to stop or change.

In chemistry, there is a concept known as "dynamic equilibrium." This is an ever-changing balance. This, perhaps, is a good description of a person who is sattvic. Such a person can easily exhibit more or fewer of the qualities of rajas or tamas. A person who is sattvic tends to be thinner and, perhaps, "airy." The archetype of the hatha yoga practitioner, especially to Westerners, is someone like this. How else can you get into those pretzel-like positions? In reality, however, it is health and flexibility that allow ease in achieving hatha yoga *asanas* (positions). A slender, inflexible person has difficulty achieving asanas, too.

Need more energy or want your passions excited? Eat foods that are rajavic. These are foods that are sour, dry, hot, bitter, or salty. Eating fast is also rajavic. Have too much energy? Eat foods that are tamasic, such as onions, meat, overripe foods, or garlic. Drinking alcoholic beverages and smoking tobacco are also tamasic, as is overeating and heavy foods such as potatoes and starches, things that might slow you down. Sattvic foods calm and purify the mind, balancing the rajavic and tamasic energies within you, and they help create an even flow of energy. Such foods generally have a sweet taste and include dairy products, honey, whole grain cereals and breads, fresh vegetables, fruits, nuts, and legumes.

It might seem that sticking to sattvic foods is ideal. Indeed, a sattvic diet is often recommended for practitioners of hatha yoga, which is so familiar to Westerners. But if you're filled with the energy of the rajas guna, it might be better to counterbalance with a tamasic diet before switching to sattvic foods. Likewise, if you're very tamasic, a rajavic diet might be better before switching to sattvic foods.

Of course, nobody is purely based in one guna, so understanding the gunas as they go through you, combined with knowing the gunic nature of any particular food, is more valuable. Similarly, no food is purely of any one guna. For example, a ripe orange will have some areas that have tiny amounts of rot, even if your eyes can't see it. Thus, although a ripe orange is basically sattvic, it also has some elements of tamasic energy. Be sure to do more research on foods and their energies and consult with a medical doctor or licensed dietician before changing your diet.

In a person, the effect of the three gunas constantly evolves. If you look at the triangular diagram of the gunas shown in this book, you can see their relationship. Rajas and tamas, when joined, becomes sattva. Sattva and rajas result in tamas. Sattva and tamas result in rajas.

The Five Elements (Tattvas)

The gunas are tendencies or qualities that are found in nature. However, everything in the universe also has certain physical qualities. From the divine universal energy, or *prana,* evolved the five elements, or *tattvas*, which, in combination, form everything in the universe and through which the gunas function (see illustration). These five "elements" are not the same as the elements found on the periodic table of elements, as shown on the chart that hangs in high school science classes. Rather, they are the coalescence of five forces found in the physical world. In our modern world, it might be more accurate to call them elementary forces, but I'll call them elements to follow tradition.

Akasha

Akasha is the Sanskrit term for spirit, ether, (sometimes spelled *aether*), or space. It could be called the "source element," as all of the other elements come out of the energy of akasha. Visually, this tattva is represented by an egg shape, sometimes described as an oval, that is colored indigo (in the color spectrum, indigo is between blue and violet). Traditionally, akasha is associated with sound and the sense of hearing. If you look at chapter 1, you'll see that this makes perfect sense, as according to the creation myth, it was vibration or sound that was the source of everything. A tool used to represent akasha is the bell, which is frequently used in Tantric rituals. Alternatively, a trumpet or horn made from a large conch shell is used. These items, as well as those listed for the other elements, are described in more detail in chapter 7. Some people have related akasha to cosmic radiation. It has the quality of space, into which all things manifest.

Meditation on the tattva symbol of akasha is very easy. Make a copy of the tattva (see the illustration for an example), and after preparing yourself with banishing and purifications (either those of your choice or ones described later in this book), simply stare at the image. Allow yourself to mentally "fall into" the indigo egg, or perhaps imagine yourself walking through it as if it were a doorway, and simply allow it to take you where it will. Meditation on the akasha tattva is wonderful for strengthening your link to the Divine. Including it as a focus for magickal rituals is good for bringing things together, including people, plans, and prospects for the future.

Vayu

Vayu, the tattva of air or wind, is said to evolve out of akasha. Visually, it is represented by a blue circle. If akasha is the unlimited space of the universe, then vayu fills that space with its powerful energy. It is associated with the sense of touch. Its tool is the dagger, which cuts through the air and also cuts through the kleshas that block us from achieving all our goals, including those that are oriented toward moving ahead on the physical plane and those oriented toward advancing spiritually. It introduces the quality of movement or locomotion into the space of akasha.

Meditation on the vayu tattva symbol, using the technique just described for akasha, can help you obtain clarity of mind and purpose. It can help you attain inspiration and is great for overcoming mental blocks and the inability to find a way out of current situations. It's also great for triggering new beginnings.

Tejas

Tejas, the tattva of fire (or, on a more cosmic level, solar energy), comes next. Visually, it is represented by a red triangle with a single point down. It is related to light and color as well as the sense of sight. Tejas introduces the quality of expansion to the universe. Fire applied to anything causes it to expand. A tool used to represent tejas is a lamp. Traditionally, this is a lamp filled with purified butter known as *ghee.* Instructions for making ghee are in chapter 7.

Another form of lamp uses small chunks of pure camphor burning in small wells or indentations. Of course, you could also use a candle or any other type of lamp.

Meditating on this symbol (as described for akasha) is great for helping you develop passion for something, as well as anything to do with passion, including sexuality. It's also good for increasing energy and for personal transformation. If you feel like you're lacking courage, meditate on this symbol.

Apas

Apas is the tattva of water. Just as water is the natural opposite of fire, apas is the opposite energy of tejas. Therefore, it is the energy of contraction or gravitation. In contrast to the sharp points of the fire tattva, the tattvic symbol for apas is a lunar silver crescent, appearing like a bowl. Its representative tool is a container of water. It can be a bowl or chalice. Traditionally, the special vase used for this is a *lota* bowl. *Ganga jal,* the water traditionally used in the lota, is taken from the Ganges River.

Meditating on the apas tattva symbol is an ideal way to obtain answers for all questions of the emotions, romance, and the heart. It can help give you insights into what is going on in your unconscious mind and help you clarify issues dealing with the unconscious. It can help you learn to live with change and help with emotions such as love, caring, and compassion. It can give you hope and help you overcome fear. It may also help you have more vivid dreams, as well as remember your dreams better and interpret their meaning with greater clarity.

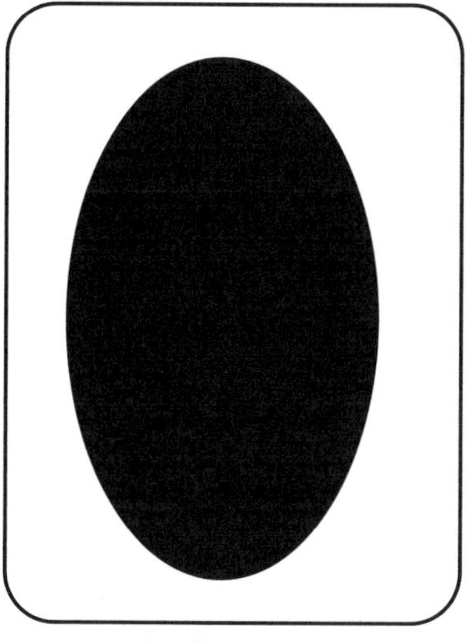
Akasha–Spirit

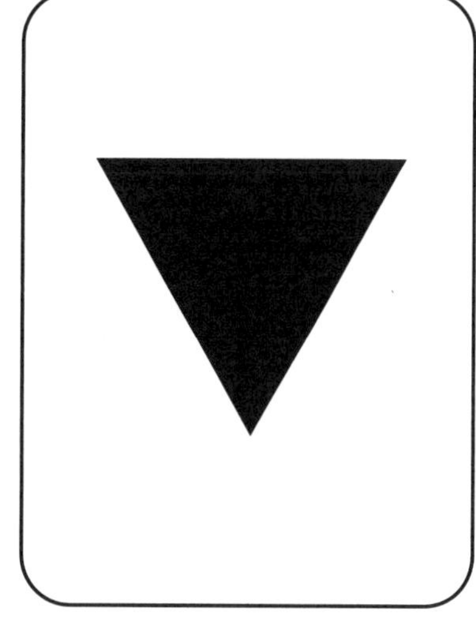
Tejas–Fire

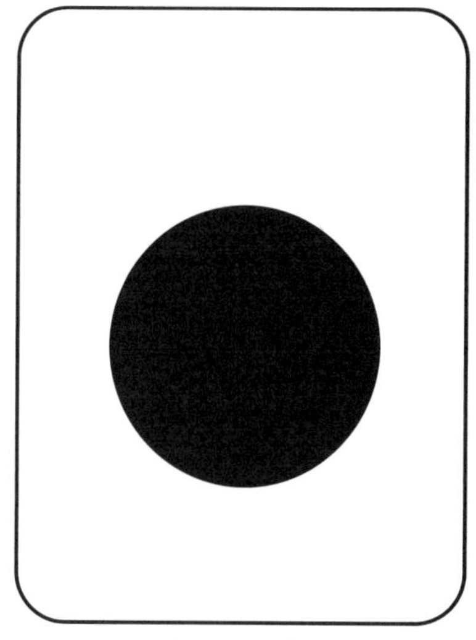
Vayu–Air

Prithivi–Earth

The Tantric Elements

Akasha .... Indigo (Oval)
Apas .... Silver (Moon)
Prithivi .... Yellow (Square)
Vayu .... Blue (Circle)
Tejas .... Red (Triangle)

The Tattva symbols shown on this page are based on scans of the Tattva symbol cards handmade by the late Israel Regardie. He gave them to famed occultist and author Gareth Knight in the late 1960s or early 1970s, and Mr. Knight generously gave them to this author in 1991. They are based on teachings from the book *Nature's Finer Forces* by Rama Prasad.

Apas–Water

The Tantric Elements (Tattvas)

Prithivi

Prithivi is the tattva of the element of earth and represents both magnetic and geomagnetic energy. It is symbolized by a simple yellow square. It is described as being the opposite of akasha. Akasha gives room for locomotion, while prithivi resists it. It is the solidity and weightiness that we conceive of when we think of a mountain or giant rock. It is associated with smell, and its tool is incense. Frequently, a small handful of incense sticks will be used during rituals, filling the air with earthy scents.

The mystical diagrams known as *yantras* frequently have an outer square, showing how the energies of the image are kept within it. This square should remind you of prithivi.

Meditating on the yellow square symbolic of prithivi will help you with all things on our earthly, physical plane. It's good for money and finances, home and security, and giving a concrete reality to anything you are working to achieve.

There is far more to the tattvas than can be described here. There are also some alternative tattvic systems. An advancement on the use of the symbols is to superimpose one over the other. Thus you can have apas of prithivi, or water of earth, and tejas of akasha, or fire of spirit. Reversing which symbol is superimposed on the other—prithivi of apas, or earth of water, for example—will give a different effect and different results when used in meditation or magick.

The concept of the tattvas and the tattvic tides, described in the next section, is little known and little used in the West. It was introduced to Western occultists primarily in the book *Nature's Finer Forces* by Rama Prasad, originally published in 1894. The leaders of the Hermetic Order of the Golden Dawn considered the concepts so valuable that in the same year they introduced a brief version of the information from Prasad's book as part of their teachings.

However, one of the things I would like to stress again is that Tantra is not just about theory, philosophy, and spiritual concepts. While you can certainly learn a lot about Tantra from books, the true essence of Tantra is experiential. Don't just think about it. Try out the suggested meditations. Try working with the tattvas. If you are currently involved in Western forms of magick, try incorporating the tattvic tides into your regular work.

One of the things I like to say when I give workshops is that you shouldn't just take my word for anything. Instead, I encourage you to try it out. Work with it. See how using something I'm sharing changes your life for the better. Experiment. Play. Have fun. Do. The original concepts of Tantra didn't come from a book. They were the results of fearless experimenters traversing the unknown. Luckily, today there are people who have done the work and already tried these things out. The trailblazers have already made a path for you. But thinking about the path won't get you to the end. Only taking a chance and walking down that path will get you to your goals.

Tattvic Tides

Using the tattvas in magick can be very powerful. It can help enhance any ritual you do. But the tattvas are not simply external things or a set of symbols. They are composed of very real energies. Each of us has a set of energetic cycles that we go through. The most famous of these are the cycles known as circadian rhythms that we go through daily. They affect us mentally, emotionally, spiritually, biologically, hormonally, physiologically, and more. There are also cycles that last much longer, such as women's menstrual cycles. The studies of these cycles are known as chronobiology.

The energies of the tattvas, similar to the energies in a human, go through fairly rapid cycles. These cycles are known as the *tattvic tides*.

The cycle of these tides begins at dawn every day. First, the energy of akasha (spirit) fills the universe. Doing magick for anything associated with spirit for the first twenty-four minutes following dawn, while that tattvic tide of akasha is "in course," will enhance the magick. This is also a perfect time to do any sort of devotional practice to the gods.

After the first twenty-four minutes, the tides change and the power of vayu (air) is in course and becomes the strongest. This is the time to do magick associated with this element. Following vayu comes tejas (fire), apas (water), and prithivi (earth). Each of the tides lasts twenty-four minutes, so one entire cycle lasts for two hours. This is repeated twelve times during the day. The chart shown here gives you an example of how this works for the first half of a day when dawn occurs at 5:00 AM.

Naturally, the times and tides of this chart would continue for another six cycles until the following morning. This chart would need to be adjusted according to the time of sunrise locally for you. Readers familiar with the *planetary hours*, such as described in *Modern Magick*, will note that since the tattvic tides are based only on dawn and the five elements (and not on sunrise, sunset, and the planets), the computations are much easier.

Time	Tattva	Time	Tattva	Time	Tattva
5:00–5:24	Akasha	9:00–9:24	Akasha	1:00–1:24	Akasha
5:24–5:48	Vayu	9:24–9:48	Vayu	1:24–1:48	Vayu
5:48–6:12	Tejas	9:48–10:12	Tejas	1:48–2:12	Tejas
6:12–6:36	Apas	10:12–10:36	Apas	2:12–2:36	Apas
6:36–7:00	Prithivi	10:36–11:00	Prithivi	2:36–3:00	Prithivi
7:00–7:24	Akasha	11:00–11:24	Akasha	3:00–3:23	Akasha
7:24–7:48	Vayu	11:24–11:48	Vayu	3:24–3:48	Vayu
7:48–8:12	Tejas	11:48–12:12	Tejas	3:48–4:12	Tejas
8:12–8:36	Apas	12:12–12:36	Apas	4:12–4:36	Apas
8:36–9:00	Prithivi	12:36–1:00	Prithivi	4:36–5:00	Prithivi

The Tattvic Tides (Akasha = Spirit, Vayu = Air, Tejas = Fire, Apas = Water, Prithivi = Earth)

The Path of the Fall

One of what might be the most amazing and totally original aspects of Tantric philosophy is the way you find a path to the Divine. In most spiritual traditions, you are expected to become more and more godlike. If your religion says, "Do not eat a certain food," you don't eat that food. If your faith tells you, "Do not listen to non-religious music or dance," you are considered more spiritual if you don't listen to non-religious music and don't dance.

With Tantra, it is understood that everything in the universe is a manifestation of the Divine. Therefore, everything is sacred.

But we each have our own taboos. Tantra is not the primary spiritual practice for most people, and therefore there is a process of *unlearning* beliefs you currently possess. In some spiritual systems, drinking alcohol is forbidden. To many practitioners of that tradition, drinking becomes a personal taboo. Such taboos, however, actually have the effect of keeping you away from finding the sacred in the activity of drinking. Therefore, breaking taboos is a powerful way to find the spiritual in everything and free yourself from past limiting beliefs. In those traditions that allow the use of alcohol, drinking to excess is usually forbidden. Breaking this taboo—getting drunk as part of spirituality—is a part of some Tantrics' spiritual practice. But as you may imagine, simply breaking taboos doesn't help you find or travel a highway to the Source.

The goal is to see the Divine in what is forbidden. Therefore, by experiencing what is forbidden, you are experiencing the Divine. It's not simply drinking the forbidden wine that makes a difference. It's not getting drunk that makes a difference. Rather, it's making that wine sacred through various rituals and then partaking of the sacrament. Similarly, simply having sex with someone who is not your spouse doesn't make you a Tantric. Tantra is not about cheating on a partner. Before participating in a Tantric ritual that might involve sex with someone who is not your regular partner—what is normally considered a banned behavior—you and your spouse (or regular partner) should be open about what you are doing. Make sure both of you are okay with this. Then the new partner is made sacred; s/he is honored as a manifestation of the God/dess and is even worshiped as such. Your sex with this person becomes sacred, open, and honest rather than something sordid and merely cheating. As you can imagine, some Tantrics do not have regular partners in order to avoid potential difficulties, while others limit their work, by choice, to their current partner.

As mentioned earlier, because of this breaking of taboos, Tantra has been called the "path of the fall." By that, it is meant that if, through ritual, you make sacred those beliefs and behaviors that most people think would take you away from what is spiritual, those beliefs become holy and those acts become spiritual and sacred.

Other than finding the spiritual in all things, there is another, very practical use of breaking taboos—one that could literally save your life. Let's imagine a person who has a behavior that threatens his or her existence, perhaps alcoholism or excessive gambling. Nobody simply does these things. Rather, there is some unconscious reason or reasons that drive the person. Often it is because the individual is unhappy and looking for something. And sometimes this emptiness leads to such behaviors because the person is seeking the transcendent—underlying all of our wants and needs is often a desire to find the Divine.

So what a Tantric who has an unwanted behavior might do is seek to find the Divine within the unwanted behavior. With every drink, you are drinking the Goddess. With every roll of the dice, you are touching the God. Surprisingly, after a relatively short time, the mind begins to realize that what you've been searching for isn't the drink or the dice, but the Divine that is in them. Attachment to the behaviors fades while devotion to the Divine takes over.

Another way of describing this process is by calling Tantra the "path of reversal." The profane is reversed and becomes the spiritual. In Tantric sexuality, there is a secondary meaning to this concept of reversal.

In most non-Tantric sexual activity, the men usually have a single, explosive, genitally focused, combined orgasm and ejaculation. Women may have a single orgasm or multiple ones that are also explosive and genitally focused. For both, the result is generally nothing more than a quick release of tension and the very brief experience of pleasure.

With Tantric techniques (some of which will be described later), instead of an *explosive* orgasm/ejaculation, the man can experience just the reverse: an *implosive*, full-body, singular orgasm or multiple orgasms. He may or may not ejaculate, and rather than be limited to a few minutes of frantic friction, there are extended periods of sexual activity and pleasurable sensations that lead to transcending ordinary experience. The woman Tantric can also experience such orgasms with similar results, as well as have copious ejaculations that have a sweetness indicating the production of the mysterious spiritual substance known to Neo-Tantrics as *amrita*.

However, the real purpose of Tantric sexual practices is not merely to enhance pleasure or simply to produce amrita. Rather, it is to change the focus from the physical to the spiritual. It is to find the Divine in your partner, yourself, and the sexual activity. The increased and extended pleasure is just a wonderful collateral benefit.

If mere sexual activity or rituals that include sexual activity made us spiritual, most adults would be enlightened. Of course, the evidence of our experience shows that this is certainly not true. So what exactly is it that changes sexual activity into something spiritual? What is it that can turn drinking or gambling into a realization of the Divine? The answer is found in becoming aware of (or manifesting), increasing, and directing the universal spiritual life force that flows through the universe and through each of us. Learning how to do this is an important practical aspect of Tantric sexuality. Yes, it can be done through visualization and breathwork, but that can take many months or years of practice. Tantric sexual practices can help you achieve this much more quickly. This will be discussed later.

Return to the Natural

So why go through all of these meditations and practices? It is because of karma, the kleshas, and our conditioning that we are no longer able to see the true beauty of the world. The philosophy behind the techniques described so far has the ultimate goal of returning you to where you should have been all along. *We should be able to find joy in life naturally.* We should be able to be naturally spontaneous in our devotions, our practices, and our lives. But most of us are far removed from the natural way our bodies and minds are meant to be. Most of us aren't Tantrics because we have lost the natural way.

In Sanskrit, the word *sahaja* ("sah-hah-dja") means "spontaneity" or "being natural." It's a state of being joyful in life, part of which includes seeing all things as being divine.

Are you joyful in life? *Joyful* is not the same as *happy*. Joyfulness is an approach to life that sees the beauty and the Divine everywhere and in everything. The sahaja experience can be overwhelming and enlightening. It is part of traditional Tantra and a state of complete freedom and peace.

One of my teachers, Dadaji, compared the concept of sahaja to that of the naturalness of a tree. Trees don't need to be told how to grow. They don't need rules to learn to spread out their roots and branch out with thousands of leaves. But we have forgotten our "primordial perfection." The meditations, exercises, and practices described in this book can help lead us back to this state of naturalness where meditations, exercises, and practices are no longer needed but are performed when desired.

Traditional Tantra is a path of naturalness, a path that can help bring out the true you, a path of sahaja.

What Will You Get from This Book?

The traditional Tantra described here is not merely a varied set of practices. It is not intended that you should pick and choose which techniques to follow (although if that is what you want to do, go ahead).

The idea is that if you practice the techniques, meditations, rituals, etc., described here, you will eventually reach a state of sahaja. If you hadn't already guessed, there is more to traditional Tantra than just naturalness.

When you achieve sahaja and have knowledge of magick, when you see the Divine in everything—including yourself—and can change what you don't like to meet your desires and wishes, then you are truly a traditional Tantric. You have a connection to the Divine, you know who you really are, and you have the power to make changes in your life. Does this sound like anything you may have heard of before?

If you follow or are familiar with Thelema, the system of the followers of Aleister Crowley, you will see similarities to the concept of the Knowledge and Conversation of the Holy Guardian Angel leading to the basic rule of Thelema: "Do what thou wilt shall be the whole of the Law." Discover who you really are and do whatever you need to do in order to manifest it. "Do that, and no other shall say nay."

The ancient Sanskrit term that corresponds to this is *Svecchachara* ("S'vek-cha-kar-uh"), which means "the path of doing one's own will." With the techniques, meditations, and rituals of traditional Tantra, you can follow this path, a path of perfect freedom, joy, naturalness, spontaneity, and personal responsibility.

Traditional Tantra is not directly related to Thelema, and certainly precedes it. However, it is in harmony with many Thelemic concepts, and there are traditional Tantrics who are also Thelemites. Perhaps it would be appropriate to say that traditional Tantra includes precepts that are pre-Crowleyan Thelema.

Some of you reading this may recognize a similarity to the Wiccan Rede:

Eight words the Wiccan Rede fulfill,
An it harm none, do what ye will.

This is the original version of the Rede from 1964, written by Doreen Valiente (and probably taken from Aleister Crowley either directly or by way of Gerald Gardner). There is at least a fifty-year tradition that stresses the "harm none" aspect of the Rede. But that is not the way of Tantra.

An example of the difficulty of harming none is given in the very non-Wiccan book *Illusions: The Adventures of a Reluctant Messiah* by Richard Bach. In it, the teacher/messiah, Donald Shimoda, tells the student, Richard, that he is free to do whatever he wants. Richard replies by saying that's true as long as you don't hurt anyone else. Later, from the bushes, a very dramatic vampire, complete with cape and Lugosi-esque accent, begs Richard to let him bite him and get some blood. Richard refuses, even though the vampire tells him of the great pain he'll experience without blood. Shimoda points out that Richard has done harm to the vampire in order to protect himself. Carrying this out, he tells Richard that he is free to do whatever he wants.

Silver RavenWolf, in her book *Solitary Witch*, deals with this problem by saying that you have to balance things for the greater good. So it would be okay to do harm if by not doing it you would allow greater harm. This redefines the concept of "harm none" and is acceptable by her many fans. I would point out that this is somewhat similar to the Jewish idea that you are supposed to follow the 613 commandments given in the Jewish Bible, but you are also commanded to break any of them if it will save a life or improve health.

This concept of breaking rules and doing something deemed bad or transgressive in order to achieve a greater good is not the way of Tantra, either.

The Tantric concept of Svecchachara indicates that you are free to do whatever you want. There's no need for equivocation, "weasel words," redefinition, or explanation. There's no need for any guesswork (what, for instance, is the "greater good"?). However, Svecchachara makes very clear that *you are responsible for whatever you do.* First you have to learn what you really want to do by eliminating the kleshas in your life and the maya they create. Then do what you want. That's unlimited freedom. But you are completely responsible for what you do. Freedom and responsibility are a basis for the philosophy of traditional Tantra.

THREE

Gods and Goddesses

In the preface to this book I asked, "What's a nice Jewish boy like you doing in a place like this?" I explained that not only are there similarities between Tantra and the Kabalah, but that it's quite possible that Tantra influenced both Judaism and Kabalah. Sure, that's heretical to many, but being a heretic is quite common to both Kabalists and Tantrics.

However, there's another point that I have to bring up in relation to the deities of Tantra. In the West, we basically have two types of deities in the major religions: ones that have no physical appearance, as in Judaism, and those that appear as humans, as in Christianity.

Even the Pagan deities of the West look like humans, although they may, at times, appear as animals. A few, like Medusa, are malformed, but this is the exception and those that either are human or were human in appearance are the norm.

Going back further to the Egyptian pantheon, we see deities who are part-human and part-animal, but their images are almost always two-dimensional and very stylized. We can live with that. The ancient deities of India, however, are a different story.

How can a silly monkey be a powerful warrior? How can a fat boy with the head of an elephant be an important god? And why do they have three eyes and all of those arms? What are those weird things they're holding? And if you want to get grim, what about Kali, with the dripping blood, necklace of heads, and belt of human arms? That's just gross. For many Westerners, the deities of ancient India are just too weird.

As described earlier, there is one deity with numerous forms. The physical appearance of each form directly represents the energies it manifests. So don't be shocked by unusual characteristics. As you'll see, everything is symbolic of certain energies. Use the images as a key to unlocking manifestations of divine energy. Do that and these ancient deities can quickly become new friends.

Tantra is a complete spiritual system. As such, it has its own set of deities. There are many, many deities in the Tantric pantheon, and in this chapter you will meet a few of the more important ones.

But before sharing that, I feel it is important to look at the very nature of the Divine. After all, how can we talk about the gods without agreeing on what the gods are? In lectures, I have described some of the Tantric gods and goddesses, but have found that simply explaining them has been unsatisfying to my audience. I finally discovered why this is: the very notion of the Divine is different between Tantrics and most Westerners.

So before describing some of the gods and goddesses, I'm going to make a comparison between the Tantric notion of the Divine and the Western notion of the Divine.

The paradigm of the Western notion of the Divine is found in the form of Christianity. Some people would ask, "Why not Judeo-Christianity?" The answer is that there is no such thing. It is an invention trying to make Christianity appear to have Judaism as its source and thus turn Christianity into an older tradition than it actually is. Let's look at some of the basic vital and intrinsic differences between Judaism and Christianity:

Judaism	Christianity
1. One deity.	1. Three deities mysteriously called one.
2. Personal responsibility.	2. Jesus takes responsibility for your actions.
3. All can achieve heavenly reward.	3. Only Christians achieve heaven.
4. No place of eternal punishment.	4. Hell.
5. Messiah is an era (Messianic) or a worldly leader (not a god). Will bring world peace and is yet to come.	5. Messiah (God in human flesh) already came and will come again.
6. Many books considered sacred, even new ones.	6. Only Bible is sacred.
7. No images or icons allowed.	7. Some sects have images, icons, relics, etc.
8. A religion and a culture. You can be an atheist, without religion, and still be involved in Jewish culture.	8. A religion only. A person cannot be an atheist or a Pagan and also be a Christian.
9. Reincarnation part of Jewish mystical belief.	9. One life and then "sleep" until the Resurrection.

Differences between Judaism and Christianity

Of course, because there are numerous sects of Christianity and several Jewish traditions, these differences do not always hold true. But enough of them hold true to show that Christianity, although its leaders claim otherwise, is not an evolution of Judaism. True, early Christians were Jewish, and Christianity does use some of the Jewish holy writings. But if that were the only thing necessary to have a "Judeo-Christian tradition," then it would be appropriate to say that there is also a "Judeo-Christo-Islamic-Satanic tradition," and I doubt if most people, let alone most Christians, would accept that belief.

Whether you are Christian, Jewish, Muslim, Pagan, atheist, or of some other faith, if you grew up in the West, and especially in the US, you have lived in a society that is a de facto Christian society. Sunday is the day of rest, not Saturday (as in Judaism) or Friday (as in Islam). There are Easter and Christmas holidays that everyone in school receives (even though these holidays have been given new, non-sectarian names). Sorry, no time off from work or school for everyone on Samhain, Rosh Hashanah, Beltane, or Ramadan. So if you will accept this basic notion that this is a de facto Christian society, we can compare the Tantric notion of the Divine with that of mainstream Christianity. In this way, you will learn some of the basic ideas and will be able to compare them with your own thoughts.

Christianity	Tantra
1. God exists in heaven or is "eternal," meaning he is outside our universe.	1. The ultimate divinity (Brahman) is an infinite spirit who is the universe.
2. God is properly addressed as "he."	2. Brahman is beyond limitations and can be described as "it." Brahman is God, Goddess, gods, and goddesses.
3. Humans are victims of original sin, and only through Jesus Christ can they be saved.	3. We are all manifestations of the Divine. There is no "original sin" and no need to be "saved."
4. To believe in God, you must accept the words of prophets and Jesus that are in a book, the Christian Bible.	4. God is experienced personally, right now, in the moment. Other people's words and books can only give ways for us to have this experience.
5. Only those who believe in Jesus go to heaven to be with God.	5. The unity of the higher self (Atman) with the ultimate divinity (Brahman) can be experienced now.
6. God will not tolerate the worship of other gods or beings.	6. All of the deities, all of the gods and goddesses, are Brahman. Worship any or all of them.

Differences between Christianity and Tantra

Christianity (cont.)	Tantra (cont.)
7. God takes his created universe very seriously.	7. Brahman considers the universe a wonderful place to play (Lila). It hides inside each of us and encourages us to seek the Divine.
8. God enforces his commandments through force, intimidation, and fear.	8. Divinity loves us all and encourages, never punishes. However, we are all subject to education via karma.
9. God is formless, and all images and icons should be destroyed (although many sects have them).	9. Divinity, like water, can fill any container. Therefore, worship it within icons and images, for it is there, too.
10. God's laws are arbitrary and are interpreted by his representatives on Earth, yet are considered eternal.	10. Laws change as needed by individuals at the time. Spiritual laws transcend scriptures, books, and codes.
11. Because we are a creation of God, we must follow his commands.	11. Because we are united with God, we should search for meaning, substance, and spirituality in our lives.
12. Extreme regimentation. Follow the rules of the sect.	12. Extreme individuality. Truth comes from within.
13. Beliefs must be spread. Other beliefs must be destroyed.	13. Seek truth in your own way. Destroy nothing. It might help another. There are many paths to the Divine.
14. Since we are mere matter and devoid of divinity (or only have a "spark" of the Divine within us), so too are all other things in the universe.	14. Since God is infinite, it is in everything. It is in us and in all things in the universe.
15. God is stern and grim. All holidays that have not been secularized (such as Christmas) are dry and severe.	15. Manifestations of the Divine can be lovable and joyful. The Holi festival (where people spray each other with colored water or powder) is an example of that joy.
16. Religion is an exterior practice that helps lead people to God.	16. The Divine is already within us. Spiritual traditions such as Tantra teach how to bring what is inside (but hidden) out.
17. God reveals himself only to certain people.	17. Through various spiritual techniques, we can all discover the reality of the Divine.

Differences between Christianity and Tantra (continued)

As you can see, the very nature of what is considered to be "God" in Tantra is quite foreign to the mainstream of Western theology. However, more and more people are discovering that the traditional theology of Western society no longer answers their questions, no longer fulfills their needs, no longer satisfies their souls. It is my hope that for them, this book will bring an alternative that strikes like a lightning bolt and makes the body quiver with an intuitive understanding that spiritual truth can be found within and does not require any prophet beyond what is in the heart.

One final note: Tantra evolved over eons and over vast distances at a time when travel and communications were difficult. As a result, there are many descriptions and stories about the deities. What follows is meant to give you a basis for Tantric practice and, hopefully, will spark your interest in doing further research. Don't be surprised if you find slightly different, wildly different, or even contradictory stories, descriptions, and methods of worship for the deities. Those differences indicate what the people of that area at that time needed to learn. Seek out the deities yourself and see what they tell you.

Brahman

There is a famous question, often asked by children, that is naive and obvious yet wise: "If God created everything, who created God?" In many spiritual traditions, this is incredibly difficult to answer, and some of the proposed solutions are convoluted at best, as well as confusing and not very satisfying.

The Tantric answer is simple: Brahman. Brahman ("Brah-mahn") has no form and no qualities such as gender, appearance, or size. Brahman is the source of time, space, matter, energy, and life. Brahman is unchanging, although everything that comes from Brahman may change. Brahman is absolute reality.

According to one of the oldest of the Hindu sacred books, the *Mundaka Upanishad* (part of the better known *Atharva Veda)*, Brahman is infinite and everything that is finite comes from the infinite. To those familiar with Kabalistic concepts, Brahman is analogous to the *Ain Sof.* The Ain Sof, the source from which all things—as represented by the Tree of Life—manifest, is generally not described save to mention that the very name means "without limit" or infinite. Brahman is also described as the "godhead."

Because Brahman is infinite, perhaps the ultimate form of worship of Brahman is simply contemplation on the nature of infinity and a limitless being, the source of everything. Brahman's mantra, which can be repeated to help in this contemplation of the godhead, is "Aum."

Ganesha (Ganapati)

Ganesha ("Gah-nesh" or "Gah-nesh-uh," with the accent on the second syllable) is one of the most popular deities. He is the god of success and often identified as the breaker of obstacles. If things are not going your way, try chanting his mantra, *Aum Gam Ganapataye Namaha*, the traditional 108 times, or a multiple of that number. You might also use just his bija mantra, *Gung* or *Gam*. Alternatively, chant either mantra whenever you think of it. Ganesha won't necessarily get rid of the obstacles to your success, but he will help you get around them, perhaps by showing you alternatives you didn't know were available.

I really like this story of the birth of Ganesha. After a night of passion, the god Shiva went off to war (some say hunting), and his wife, Parvati, gave birth to Ganesha (some say he was born an adult, but he is often shown as a child). Ganesha quickly became a strong warrior and the guardian of his mother's private chambers.

Well, Shiva eventually returned and wanted to see his wife. At the door was Ganesha, guarding the way. Ganesha didn't know Shiva, and wouldn't let him in. Shiva didn't know this was his son, and was ticked off that this unknown fighter wouldn't let him see his wife. The result was inevitable, and the fight between them was brief. It ended when Shiva won by chopping off Ganesha's head.

So Shiva went in to see his wife, who proudly asked him what he thought of his wonderful son who was guarding the door.

Oops!

Well, now it was Parvati's turn to be ticked off. As part of her anger, she refused to have sex with Shiva until he brought his son back to life. Shiva vowed to do so by using the head of the first living being he saw. Now, I'm sure he was thinking he'd see some nice, nondescript person, but instead he saw an elephant. So he cut off the elephant's head, put it on Ganesha's shoulders, and brought him back to elephant-headed life.

Ganesha is seen as a breaker of obstacles, as the obstacle to his returning to life (and the obstacle to Shiva having sex with Parvati!) was overcome not in the obvious way, but in a way that was unexpected and unique.

But there is more to Ganesha than that. Shiva is the highest guru (*adi-guru*), or teacher, of Tantra. He wouldn't share the secrets of Tantra with anyone, even Parvati, his spouse. However, she knew his weakness: he liked sex. So while they were having sex, she would ask him for some of his secrets. He would say that he could not refuse her and would reveal to her the secrets of Tantra. Meanwhile, Ganesha would be hidden in the room and would write everything down.

So although Shiva is the god of Tantra, Ganesha is the sharer or teacher of Tantra. He is credited, therefore, as being a god of teachers, wisdom, learning, and writing. He is also known as the Lord of Beginnings, and many rituals—even if dedicated to other deities—will begin by honoring him.

Ganesha Deity

Ganesha Yantra

Ganesha is also the destroyer of vanity and selfishness. Even though he must have a massive appetite to feed his big belly, the "vehicle" that carries him around is a small mouse. You can see the mouse in many images of Ganesha. The mouse is eating, even though the mighty Ganesha could easily crush him and take his food. But Ganesha realizes the value of everything, including a little mouse, and works with him rather than fight him. We, too, should care for the weak, meek, and needy. We can respect the smallest among us, even if we disagree.

Ganesha is usually pictured with one of his tusks broken off. He did this himself so he could act as scribe to the seer Vyasa and use it to write the *Mahabharata*. It also represents the concept of keeping what's good and getting rid of the unnecessary. This concept is also represented on the Hanged Man card of the tarot.

Ganesha's big head represents the idea that you should "think big," while his big ears and small mouth indicate that you should listen more and talk less. His large potbelly symbolically means that you should peacefully think about (digest) everything that comes your way, whether it is good, bad, or indifferent. In one hand he holds an ax to cut off the bonds and attachments that keep you from your spiritual path. In another hand he holds a rope to pull you closer to the godhead or a goad to drive you toward the Divine. As an offering, Ganesha loves red flowers. His simplest mantra is *gam* ("gahm"), and chanting it can help you eliminate obstacles in the areas of health and financial affairs such as jobs and businesses, as well as obtain wisdom.

Shiva and Shakti

The primary deities of Tantra are Shiva and Shakti. Some Tantrics, the *Shavites*, focus on Shiva as the ultimate form of God. Others, the *Shaktas*, focus on Shakti, the female aspect. They have different practices and beliefs, but have one thing in common: they are all Tantrics.

Shiva

Shiva is the ultimate male deity of Tantra and the ultimate teacher of Tantra. In the *Mahabharata*, he has 108 titles or "names." In the *Shiva Purana*, it is revealed that he has 1,000 names. Usually these names (as with many names of the Tantric deities) are descriptions of Shiva or of his skills and abilities. Curiously, if you look closely, you'll find that the numerous names contradict each other at times, implying that Shiva has powers and abilities that are contrary to his very nature. But there is a reason for this. As you contemplate the different titles and conflicting qualities, you come to realize that Shiva has any quality or energy you might need.

Shiva is frequently called the God of Destruction; however, it would be far more accurate to call him the God of Transformation. Everything evolves. Everything changes. Shiva is the god of that change. He is death only in the sense of a caterpillar dying so that a butterfly can live. This is similar in concept to the meaning of the Death card of the tarot. He is the first teacher of Tantra and hatha yoga.

Perhaps the best way to understand this god is to look at a typical image of Shiva and the symbolism associated with him.

Shiva is naked, perhaps covered by an animal skin. His own skin is grayish blue. The color of his skin is that of the ashes of cremations. This shows that although Shiva is the source of everything in the world, everything eventually dies (and is reborn) and cremated or turns to dust/ashes. But he is not the ash—he transcends the physical world.

Shiva's hair is matted. The result of the matting is that the hairs, instead of being separated, are joined together in bunches. This represents the union of mind, body, and spirit, the goal of yoga. Shiva is the god of yoga.

Water shoots out from the top of Shiva's head. This represents the source of the Ganges River. It is believed that bathing in the Ganges can remove karma. Thus, Shiva is also the master of karma and is capable of removing it from those who are dedicated to him.

Shiva is shown with three eyes. In fact, one of Shiva's names is *Tryambaka Deva*, or "Lord with Three Eyes." The two normal eyes represent the ability to see the physical world. The third eye, often shown turned ninety degrees between his other eyes, indicates knowledge of the spiritual world and the power that comes from that knowledge. This third eye is said to destroy all "evil." Here, evil means working against what is spiritual. For example, evil can be seen as trying to live forever rather than recognizing that all things in the world live and die; they transform, just as Shiva is the god of transformation.

Shiva's eyes are half-closed. It is believed that when Shiva opens his eyes, a new cycle of life begins; when he closes his eyes, it indicates the end of a cycle. Thus, with half-closed eyes, Shiva is shown in mid-transformation. And since we constantly open and close our eyes, it implies that these cycles continue forever. The partially closed eyes also present the image of the meditative pose of a hatha yoga practitioner, and Shiva is the Master of Yoga.

Shiva Deity

Shiva Yantra

Shiva wears two large earrings. These rings are frequently worn by Tantrics of the Nath tradition. Typically, women wear the ring in the left ear, while men wear one in the right ear. This indicates that Shiva the Transformer is not just male or female, but has the powers of both. Both are required for creation.

There is a snake around Shiva's neck. The snake is a symbol of Shiva. It represents the idea that Shiva is the master of yoga and Kundalini energy, which is often described as a serpent.

Shiva has necklaces made of rudraksha seeds. These seeds are believed to have many spiritual and healing powers. Different seeds have different numbers of sections or faces. Some seeds are so rare and are considered so powerful that they can individually sell for many hundreds or even thousands of dollars. Here, they show how Shiva can use various spiritual laws just as rudraksha beads have various numbers of faces. In fact, one of Shiva's names is *Rudra*, "he who is uncompromising." The necklace has 108 beads. You'll discover the meaning of this number in chapter 7, "Tools of Tantra."

Shiva's right-hand mudra. Shiva's right hand is shown in the position of granting favors and grace. He also destroys ignorance and helps wisdom become awakened in his followers.

One of Shiva's symbols is the trident. In Sanskrit, it is known as a *trishul*. The three tines represent knowledge, action, and will, the keys to creation. The sharp points also indicate Shiva's ability to destroy ignorance.

Shiva's drum. Shiva is often shown with a drum that looks something like an hourglass. The drum, known as a *damaru* ("dah-mah-roo"), has two conical sides that meet at a single point. It represents conscious and unconscious minds, manifest and unmanifest existence. Although the two sides of the damaru have different sounds, because of the design they blend together in one sound. This union of opposites is a key to spirituality and magick.

Near where Shiva sits or stands is a water pot. The pot is made from a gourd. To transform a gourd into a water pot, you must carefully remove all of the inner fruit and clean the outer skin. Similarly, we need to eliminate the attachments we have to the phenomenal world by cleaning our inner selves of ego, desire, fears, etc.

Nandi the bull. In many images of Shiva, you will see a bull named Nandi. He represents ignorance and power, indicating that Shiva removes ignorance and gives power to his followers.

Shiva sits on (or may wear) the skin of a tiger. This shows that Shiva is the source of potential energy. Shiva's partner, Shakti, *is* the energy, but the *source* of the energy is Shiva. It is only together that they can create. It is traditional for Tantrics to meditate and work certain types of magick while sitting on a tiger skin. Today, it is illegal to export tiger skins from Asia, as tigers are an endangered species. Modern Tantric practitioners will often use artificial tiger skins or rugs designed to look like the skin of a tiger.

The Shiva Lingam. Symbolic of Shiva is the Shiva lingam. This is a long oval of smooth stone, traditionally taken from a particular location in the Narada River after the running water has polished it smooth. The lingam is obviously a phallic symbol, representing the creative power of Shiva. Although often available by itself, it is traditionally partially inserted into a yoni stone. The yoni stone looks like an elongated slot that has been opened to form a circular depression, mirroring the appearance of female genitalia. With the lingam inserted into the yoni, this is clearly an image of sexual intercourse between the God and Goddess, indicating a method of high spirituality and the importance of Tantric sexuality.[8] Lingams have been found in the ruins of the Harappan culture. Shiva is not always associated with a yantra, although you can use the one illustrated here. You can also meditate and contemplate either his image or the image of a lingam.

One of the most famous mantras for Shiva is *Om Namah Shivaya* ("Ohm Nah-mah Shi-vai-yah"). In fact, it is so famous that it has a title, *Panchakshara* ("Pahn-chak-sha-ruh"), which means "having five syllables." This may seem odd since it clearly has six syllables. However, the last syllable, as Westerners would pronounce it, is said almost silently, like a quiet "uh" that is almost swallowed. Some people transliterate the mantra as "om namah shivay." It doesn't have a direct translation, but it loosely means "I honor Shiva." In this instance, "Shiva" refers to your higher self, so it is bringing your attention to the idea that you are more than your everyday consciousness. You are special. This mantra can be used for purification.

Shakti (Durga, Parvati, Kali)

While the Western tradition has the male as active and the female as passive, the Tantric tradition is just the reverse: the male energy is that of form, while the female energy is that of action. Shiva is form, Shakti is energy—pure energy. Shiva can be described and given an appearance, but how can you show an image of pure energy? It can't be done.

And yet, to the ancient Tantrics, that pure energy could manifest in different ways. Thus, the energy was given different forms that represent different aspects of that pure energy. They are considered consorts of Shiva. They are wildly different, but they are all the same. They are manifestations of the great goddess, pure Shakti energy. They can loosely—*very loosely*—relate to the maiden-mother-crone aspect of the Goddess found in many Western Pagan traditions.

Durga is a warrior goddess. She was born when the world was under attack by the greatest of evil demons. Fearing they might lose the battle, the male gods created Durga, giving her all their powers. To win the battle, Durga created Kali from her forehead. It was she who was able to slay the demon and save the world.

---

8 Several years ago, I celebrated a holiday dedicated to Shiva at a yoga center. There was an enormous Shiva lingam there, gloriously embedded in a yoni stone. I think that most of the people at the celebration had no knowledge of working with such an image or its meaning. They were only familiar with the practice of hatha yoga. The festival featured the chanting of mantras dedicated to Shiva and honoring him with gifts by putting them on the lingam. These "gifts" consisted of such things as water, flower petals, and yogurt.

As soon as the yogurt was applied to the top of the lingam, the celebrants began whispering. The symbolism of thick white goo dripping down a hard, upright, slender oblong rock was quite obvious! The head yogi of the center realized what people were thinking and quickly tried to explain away the obvious symbolism by talking about the purity of the color white, etc. I don't think many people were fooled.

Part of the festival was chanting joyous Shiva mantras all night long. However, we had to stop around 2:00 AM, when the police came in and broke up the celebration. We were making too much noise! Within a year, the yoga center moved to a less suburban location.

Durga Deity

Durga Yantra

Durga is incredibly beautiful and powerful and is usually shown riding on a tiger (linking her with Shiva). Her weapons include Shiva's trident, a scimitar, a bow, a conch shell, and the circular weapon known as a *chakram*.[9] Durga's name actually means "invincible," and she can be prayed to for assistance in destroying your personal demons, specifically poverty, suffering, hunger, bad habits, disease, injustice, cruelty, laziness, and separation from the Divine. Her bija mantra is *dum* ("doom"), and working with it can bring you energy (i.e., Shakti), power, protection, health, victory, and wisdom.

I loosely associate Durga with the maiden form of the great Goddess. I associate *Parvati* with the mother aspect of the Goddess. Parvati is gentler and less wild than Durga and corresponds to the ideas of fertility, marriage, devotion to one's partner, and, of course, power (Shakti). Parvati is the Tantric goddess of love.

Parvati Deity

9 Yes, *Xena: Warrior Princess* fans. There really is an ancient weapon of that name and appearance.

If not baring her breasts (a sign of divinity), Parvati is often shown wearing white, indicating that she is pure. If her vehicle is shown, it is a lion. (Since she was originally a goddess of the Himalayas, it was probably a mountain lion at first, but now she is usually shown on a typical lion of the plains, or a tiger.) Her weapons are the same as those of Durga, except she has a crossbow or sword instead of a long bow. Her bija mantra is *hrim* ("hreem"). She has no commonly accepted yantra.

Finally, in the crone aspect, is *Kali*, the darker (and therefore "later") and transformative form of the Shakti energy. Kali is described more thoroughly in the section about her within the discussion of the *Mahavidyas* in chapter 4.

Ardhanarishvara Deity

Ardhanarishvara

While it's impossible to adequately describe the pure energy, Shakti, in the form of a goddess, there is a slightly similar situation in modern Western Neopaganism. While most Neopagan traditions focus on a Goddess and a God (perhaps as the head of a pantheon of deities), some believe that beyond these two there is an ultimate, unknowable, single divinity that is neither male nor female. Those Neopagan paths that follow this belief have a system that is known as *panentheism*, the concept that the supreme deity is transcendent (the unknowable deity beyond the God and Goddess) and immanent (the God and Goddess), whom we can personally know.

This concept of panentheism is not entirely foreign to the better-known Western religions. For example, in Judaism there is a transcendent deity who sometimes becomes manifest and communicates directly with individuals or indirectly through the agency of the angels.[10] However, the transcendent deity is never pictured. That is why Judaism is known as *aniconic*—it doesn't have a physical representation of the transcendent deity and even forbids such an image.

One of the deities of ancient India was a combined form of Shiva and Shakti, male and female, form and energy. This deity is known as *Ardhanarishvara* ("Awrd-hahn-awr-reesh-vawr-uh"). Its image is that of a person divided vertically, with one half being male and the other half female. It clearly shows that although it is possible to speak of Shiva and Shakti as separate beings, they are, in actuality, linked and inseparable. Where there is one, there is always the other.

10 *Angel* is from the Greek word *angelos*, which means "messenger."

The name *Ardhanarishvara* is actually composed of three words: *ardha*, which means "half," *nari*, which means "woman," and *ishvara*, which means "god" or "lord." Therefore, the name is literally "the deity who is half goddess and half god." As with many of the ancient Indian deities, Ardhanarishvara is often shown with more than two arms to indicate the deity's powers. Usually, these are presented in pairs. Curiously, Ardhanarishvara is sometimes pictured with three arms, one on the female side and two on the male side. One of the male hands is in the mudra that dispels fear, while the other holds the trishul, Shiva's trident. The hand on the female-Shakti side holds a mirror or small pot. Alternatively, she may carry a sunflower or noose. Other images have different numbers of arms.

The importance of Ardhanarishvara is that it shows we can—indeed, we must!—discover the opposite side of ourselves and unite with it. This linking of our self and our shadow is what the psychologist Carl Jung called the process of *individuation*, a necessity for becoming a healthy and balanced adult. It is this linking of opposites within us that is also a key to magick and to Tantric sexual practices.

Similarly, many of the practices of hatha yoga have a goal of uniting the physical body with the Shakti energy. Thus, Ardhanarishvara is representative of the inner practices of this form of yoga. The androgynous nature of Ardhanarishvara from thousands of years ago also implies what biologists have only recently learned and psychologist Sigmund Freud revealed: during gestation we are both male and female, and it is natural to have androgynous aspects, no matter our gender. It therefore shows understanding and respect for people who are androgynous, bisexual, transgendered, etc. The Tantric tradition honors and respects the sexuality of all people, as long as it does not involve the mental, physical, or spiritual abuse of others. Ardhanarishvara is one of the oldest and most common forms of deity found in Indian art, and is the presiding deity of the third-eye chakra.

The union of Shiva and Shakti in Ardhanarishvara is considered (according to the text titled *Kularnava Tantra*) to be the highest form of Shiva. It is also the union of the incoming and outgoing breaths. The sounds that are automatically made by the breath are "ha" and "sa." Therefore, the mantra for Ardhanarishvara is the famous *Sri Paraprasada* ("Shri Pahr-uh-prah-sahd") mantra: *hamsa*. This mantra is unique in that it is not actually spoken. Rather, it is simply heard in the incoming and outgoing of the breath. Focus on the breath and hear it as it comes in: *ha*. Listen to the breath as it goes out: *sa*. Focus on both and your breath automatically chants the mantra *hamsa*. This can bring unity and peace to your life. It can lead you to deep meditative states and even various magickal powers. Ardhanarishvara does not have an accepted yantra, although some use the Sri Yantra.

Other Tantric Deities

Hinduism, a development of Tantra, has been described as "a monotheistic religion with thousands of gods and goddesses." In Tantra, although there is the understanding that there is only one ultimate deity, it is also recognized that the godhead manifests in thousands of ways. Each is called a god or goddess. Even the letters of *Devanagari*, the alphabet of the Sanskrit language, are referred to as *matrikas*, or "little goddesses." There are fifty letters in this alphabet, a number matching the lotus flower petals in the metaphoric lotuses that make up the six chakras of the body (below the crown chakra). Each of the matrikas has powers. In symbolic drawings of the chakras—showing the chakras as lotus flowers with different numbers of petals—each petal has a Sanskrit letter on it, a little goddess, each representing one of the powers of that chakra.

Unfortunately, the discussion of the matrikas is for another time and place. Here, however, are just some of the deities that are worked with by many Tantrics.

Hanuman

In mythic and spiritual literature, there is a tradition that warrior gods and heroes always have a flaw, sometimes leading to a great action. Samson's passion for Delilah resulted in his downfall, but he was able to destroy his enemy's rulers as he died. Hercules, while driven temporarily mad (thanks for nothing, Hera!), killed his wife and children and had to spend a dozen years performing incredible labors in penance.

Hanuman ("Hahn-you-mahn" or "Hahn-oo-mahn") is mentioned here, as he is perhaps the greatest mythic warrior in Indian tradition. As a child, he was wild and received an odd curse: even though he was a great warrior of incredible strength and invulnerability, he was fated to forget his powers and abilities unless someone reminded him that he had them.

In the famous story the *Ramayana*, Hanuman joins with the god Rama as the latter searches for his wife, who has been abducted by a demon. As part of the story, Hanuman is sent to a mountain in the Himalayas to get an herb that will restore life to the brother of Rama. Unable to easily find it, he *lifts the entire mountain* and brings it to Rama so that the brother's life can be restored.

Besides being incredibly strong and invulnerable (when he remembers it), Hanuman is also known for his deep devotion and love of the Divine in the form of Rama and his wife, Sita. Oh, and one other thing: this great and invincible warrior looks like a monkey. Hanuman is frequently referred to as a monkey god. Sometimes he is imaged as a strong young man with the face of a monkey.

Hanuman Deity

This sounds odd, especially to most Westerners. After all, aren't monkeys silly, fun-loving animals like we've seen in all the movies? That's exactly the point. Our minds are constantly running, metaphorically jumping between limbs of a tree, from one thing to another. The only time we can turn off the superficial, ego-oriented aspects of our minds is when we are reminded that we have higher abilities and powers, and part of achieving those abilities and powers requires the quieting of the mind, or the bypassing of our normal, daily consciousness.

Hanuman represents pure devotion and surrender to the Divine. If Hanuman, as a monkey, seems to represent an animal that acts foolishly, it is because he represents the Divine Fool as shown on the tarot card the Fool, who is abandoning common "wisdom" and beginning a journey to find what is spiritual.

Hanuman also represents the higher aspect of the universal spiritual energy known as *prana* ("prawn-yah"). Prana is sometimes falsely equated with the breath or air because the energy can be controlled and manipulated through the control of breath. Indeed, Hanuman is known as the Son of the Wind. Developing the strength of Hanuman—having strong pranic energy—will allow you to overcome all of your obstacles and enemies (inner and outer) in order to achieve your goals. It is said that Hanuman could become as large or as small as desired in order to achieve his goals. Honoring a statue (*murthi*) of Hanuman (he really likes offerings of sweets and fruits, especially bananas, of course, as well as wearing the color red) can help you gain energy, curiosity, and enthusiasm, as well as overcome obstacles and achieve goals. Warriors will especially honor and appreciate the favors of Hanuman, both actual soldiers and people who replace warfare with competition, such as boxers, wrestlers, ball players, etc.

Ganesh helps you overcome obstacles by finding alternatives. Hanuman helps you struggle through opposition. It is wise to call on the god you need at the appropriate time. Hanuman's bija mantra is *praum* ("prah-oom").

Dhanwantari

We live in an age where we are farther than ever from the sources of natural foods and more deeply embedded in increasingly toxic environments. Compound that with sedentary lifestyles isolated from the rhythms of nature and an aging population and the result is a vast increase in ill health. Surprisingly, one of the key contributors to ill health is the result of modern miracles found in Western medicine. How has Western allopathic medicine increased ill health? Many of the people who would have died in their youth or later in life from diseases and medical problems that ravaged the world (and in some places still do) not only remain alive but achieve old age. Along with increased longevity, however, has come an increase in both chronic and acute medical ailments.

I am not suggesting that we should let people die as some form of bizarre eugenics experiment that will improve society's overall health. Nor am I suggesting that people who reach eighty, ninety, or one hundred years of age or more should just suffer with ill health and live with pain and anguish (while enhancing the retirement plans of executives of multinational pharmaceutical corporations and for-profit hospitals and medical insurance companies). Instead, I am urging just the opposite.

One of the traditional purposes of Tantra has been the extension of life, a long life that is filled with vitality and health. Tantra is filled with methods to heal ailments and keep people healthy, from hatha yoga and breathing practices to medical techniques (Ayurveda) and alchemy. It is only natural, then, that there should be a deity associated with health and healing. That god is known as *Dhanwantari*, and he is needed now more than ever to help those who are ill.

Dhanwantari Deity

Dhanwantari ("Dahn-wahn-tah-ree") is considered one of the first healers of ancient India, and the source of traditional Indian medicine. He is credited with the discovery of such things as antiseptics and plastic surgery. You can seek his blessings for continued good health or for healing. Prayers can be made to him for yourself or for others.

Dhanwantari is imaged as having four arms. In one hand he holds a mortar and pestle, a primary tool for doctors and alchemists to mix herbs and potions. In another hand he holds a scroll that contains the secrets of Ayurveda. If you are devoted to Dhanwantari, he will share these secrets with you. In his third hand he holds a vase (*kalasha*, pronounced "kah-lash" or "kah-lash-uh") that is said to hold *amrita* ("ahm-ree-tah"), the elixir of health and immortality. His fourth hand is shown in the mudra that grants blessings—in this case, the blessings of health and well-being.

Around his neck is a long necklace made of herbs that are used in healing, maintaining health, and extending life. In paintings he is often shown coming out of an ocean. This ocean, symbolically, is the source of life, knowledge, enlightenment, and the elixir of life itself. It is our blood.

The mantra for Dhanwantari is rather long. However, here is a loose translation of the mantra that you can memorize or read for health, healing, and longevity:

Om
I pray to the great god Dhanwantari,
who holds the kalasha that is filled
with the amrita of immortality!
Dhanwantari, you can
remove all diseases.
Dhanwantari, you can
remove all fears.
You are the preserver of the three
worlds—body, mind, and spirit.
It is you who desires
us to remain well.
You are even empowered
to heal my true soul.
Honored, honored, honored are you.
Hail to the lord of Ayurveda!

Lakshmi

Lakshmi, also spelled Laxmi ("Lock-shmee"), is the beautiful goddess of prosperity and wealth. As such, she is frequently shown with a pile of golden coins in front of her. She has a golden complexion. Sometimes she holds a pot from which pours coins into the pile of wealth at her feet. She is dressed in beautiful clothes, and her hands show the mudras of giving blessings and eliminating fears.

Lakshmi will give wealth of any kind to those who seek it. This is not limited to wealth in terms of money. It can also relate to property, wisdom, health, etc. However, Lakshmi is primarily known for being the goddess of financial wealth and for helping people when they need money.

Even though different artists and different traditions will show Lakshmi with different associations, the one that is always shown is the lotus. This can range from her simply holding a lotus to her sitting upon an enormous one. This is a key to understanding Lakshmi... and a key to understanding why you're unhappy.

According to several Tantric traditions (and this has been carried into both Hinduism and Buddhism), the reason you are unhappy is that you are attached to things and beliefs. When these do not meet your expectations, you become frustrated and unhappy. You believe you should be treated fairly at work or school, but it doesn't work out that way so you become unhappy. You believe that if you work hard, you should get a raise, but it doesn't work out that way so you become unhappy. You expect someone to do their assigned work, but they don't and you become unhappy. You expect that because you love someone, that person will love you forever, and when that doesn't work out you become unhappy.

It would seem, then, that the cause of unhappiness is our unwillingness to accept as fact a simple expression: *What is, is.* That doesn't mean you can't work and strive to change things and make them more to your liking; it simply means that if you live without attachments and expectations, you will have massive amounts of happiness. Does that mean you cannot have something you want? Does that mean you should forget loving someone and having him or her return your love forever? Absolutely not. Rather, it means that yesterday is only a memory and tomorrow is only a dream. The only thing we can be sure of is what's going on right now. We can love with all our heart *right now.* We can strive to achieve a goal *right now.* Aleister Crowley described this as living without the "lust of result." Live in the now and create a better tomorrow. If the tomorrow you want happens, fantastic! If it doesn't happen, that's simply what is, and what is, is. If it's not what you want, work to change it... or work to change yourself.

Lakshmi Deity

Lakshmi Yantra

The lotus, which rises from the mud into the clean air as something beautiful, shows that we can be spiritual in a material world. We can be spiritual everywhere. We do not have to be brought down by the cares and problems of everyday life. We can be above them. We live in the world, we revel in the world, we find beauty and spirituality in the world. This is one of the essential lessons found in many strains of traditional Tantra.

So honor, be devoted to, and worship Lakshmi to acquire and maintain wealth. However, Lakshmi gives only a hand, not a handout. To obtain Lakshmi's assistance, you must indicate that you want her help by doing something besides begging. She gives her help to those who work to get ahead. It is also said that she only helps those who keep their houses clean. That means you should make sure your home is not dirty or overly messy. After all, if you won't even take care of your home, no matter how modest it is, how will you take care of the gifts of Lakshmi? A dirty home is a sign of laziness and indicates that you really don't want to get ahead. If you need to find a note or message, you will have difficulty doing so if your office space is a mess.

Keeping your house clean also means keeping your heart and spirit clean. This certainly means being focused on your goal and accomplishing it by helping others, not by taking advantage of those who may be easy to deceive.

Lakshmi is also worshiped to bring peace of mind. Although wealth and inner peace do not necessarily go hand in hand, for many—especially Westerners—it is difficult to be spiritual when you're worried about where you will get your next meal. Her bija mantra is *srim* ("shreem").

Saraswati

Saraswati ("Sahr-uh-swah-tee") is one of my favorite goddesses. She is usually shown playing a musical instrument known as a *veena* (pronounced "vee-nuh"), a long instrument that appears similar to the better-known (in the West) sitar. It represents her mastery over arts and sciences, especially music.

So why do I like her? I started learning the piano before I began school. Over the years I have publicly performed on instruments including piano, accordion, string bass, organ (from the Hammond B3 to massive church pipe organs), synthesizers, and theremin. I have performed classical music, including singing in choirs and madrigal groups, and with rock bands, including opening for acts ranging from Great White to Elton John. Music has been a very important part of my life, so I'm quite drawn to Saraswati.

Saraswati, however, is the goddess of far more than music. She represents the ability to express yourself in speech, music, or writing. She is usually pictured with swans, and they are considered her vehicle. A myth states that if you offer a swan a mix of water and milk, it will drink only the milk. This means that Saraswati is capable of distinguishing between good things and bad things that are offered, and will choose only the good.

Of course, the swan is white, as are Saraswati's clothes, indicating her purity.

It is her purity that gives her beauty, so she is viewed as being beautiful. She doesn't have as many gems and decorations as some other goddesses because she values wisdom over attachment to physical things. She has four arms, representing the intellect, the ego, the mind, and alertness. Her mala necklace is made of crystal, representing what she values: spirituality.

Saraswati is often shown with one or more peacocks. Symbolically, the peacock is seen as having even greater pride and arrogance than is justified by the magnificent display of its colorful tail feathers. Since she controls the peacock, the message is that we should not be overly proud of any physical beauty we may possess—real beauty comes from within and is understood with the heart, not merely seen with the eyes.

Saraswati Deity

Saraswati Yantra

Saraswati's bija mantra is *Aim*, and is said to bring knowledge, creativity, and mastery of communication skills, including writing prose and poetry, music, public speaking, etc. The key to the type of knowledge and wisdom she offers can be found in her very name. It is based on two Sanskrit words: *sara*, which means "essence," and *swa*, which means "self." She is especially honored by teachers and students, scientists and scholars, as well as poets, writers, speakers, and musicians.

There is another special aspect to Saraswati that ties up this section on Tantric deities. It is also believed that she is one of the oldest goddesses in the world, the goddess of a river. Rivers, of course, often bring prosperity and fertility. It was only later that she was associated with the creative sciences and arts.

And the river she is associated with, of course, is the Saraswati, the river that was the source of greatness and power for the Harappan culture described earlier in this book. As that culture is the source of Tantra, Saraswati is very definitely a Tantric goddess, and creativity, fertility, artistic skill, musical ability, and prosperity are definitely a part of Tantra.

Other Deity Concepts

Ishta Devata

One of the challenges of Tantra as a Pagan tradition is not that there is a dearth of deities, but rather that there is a feast of gods and goddesses. Some Western Pagans select one or two deities to work with consistently, while others flutter from one deity to another, often moving from one pantheon to another. For some, the latter pattern can prevent spiritual development. By constantly looking through numerous pantheons and deities, they never find a single deity or even a set of deities to link with. They never feel the blessings of working consistently with a specific set of gods and goddesses. Even so, not selecting one deity or a group of them to work with certainly satisfies some people, but it leaves others seeking more.

Although some Tantrics work primarily with Shiva and some work primarily with one of the basic forms of Shakti, there are no rules concerning this. Still, it is suggested that if you want to follow Tantric tradition, you select one deity to work with on a regular basis. This doesn't mean that you should not or cannot work with others—indeed, that is encouraged. It also doesn't mean that if you decide to work, say, primarily with Durga that you cannot call upon Saraswati when you need her or Dhanwantari when you need him. Again, you are encouraged to do so.

This chapter is only a most basic introduction to the deities of the Tantrics. There are many more. And as briefly mentioned earlier, deities are often described with different characteristics/powers, some of which are even contradictory. That's all okay. Remember, Tantra evolved over many centuries and the traditions evolved to meet the needs of practitioners.

Still, it is suggested that you select one deity as your primary focus. In Sanskrit, the word *ishta* ("ish-tuh") means something that is cherished. *Devata* ("deh-vuh-tuh") means a deity. Therefore, your *Ishta Devata* is the deity you cherish the most. It is your favorite deity, the one you choose to work with.

Remember, it can be any deity. You can choose one from the descriptions given here, or you can study other books and find a different one. And yes, although the ones described here are traditional Tantric deities, there's no reason that you cannot use one from another pantheon—Egyptian, Greco-Roman, Islamic, Jewish, Christian, Celtic, Norse, or any other. In fact, you can actually *invent* a deity. After all, the deities are only manifestations of Brahman, and if the power of Brahman can be brought into a statue or picture or even a linear design, why not make up your own Ishta Devata?

To work with the Ishta Devata, begin by doing research. Then make an altar to your chosen deity. What should be on this altar? Again, there are no rules. If the deity is well known, you might want to at least have a picture or statue of that deity. Sound is an important part of Tantra, so you might also include a bell, cymbals, or a gong. If you decide to buy a gong, be aware that there are differences between Indian-made gongs and Tibetan ones. Indian ones sound rich and sonorous, to bring the deities to you. Tibetan ones sound harsh and clangorous, as their sound is designed to frighten away demons.

You might also want to have such things as a cup or pot for water, some lamps such as oil lamps or candles, an incense burner, a conch shell (to represent the goddess), or a larger conch trumpet (you may want to learn how to play it) to help banish your area and call the deities. Traditionally, you could have a plate to hold offerings to the deity, such as fruit, rice, yogurt, or flowers. You might also want to include your deity's yantra. Traditionally, there are actually some strict rules concerning the creation of a yantra, including the material of which it is made and whether you begin your drawing from the inside going out or from the outside going in. However, you can certainly use just a paper one—you can draw it yourself. Think of the deity as you make it. Traditionally, paper yantras do not maintain their power for long, so after you use it, burn it and create another one for your next session. I'll share more about altars later.

You might also like to have some type of chalice to hold wine that you can drink and use to honor your deity with a libation. I use a *kapala* ("kah-puh-luh") that is described in greater detail in chapter 7.

Your altar can be as simple or as complex as you like. It can be small or large. Do you have too many items to place easily on your altar? No problem! Just make a small stand or little table so your altar has more than one level. Do what is in your heart for your Ishta Devata. Have fun as you design your altar. Do the best job you can. Don't compare it to the altar of anyone else. Well, actually, you *should* look at other altars for ideas about what you could add or what you don't know. Just don't rank yours as better or worse than any other altar you see. Do the best you can. Suggestions for how to work with some of the items on your altar were given earlier in this chapter.

And have fun. That doesn't mean you should act stupidly or without reverence. It means you should enjoy what you are doing. Seeing your altar should make you smile. Cleaning your altar might cause you to break into a spontaneous song. That would make Saraswati very happy.

Atman

One of the basic concepts of traditional Tantra is that your true self, who you really are—your "soul," if you will—is usually hidden by a variety of things. It is covered up by your false notions of who you are (the Tantric concept of the false ego) that are not in harmony with your spiritual essence. It is hidden by karma that prevents you from seeing your higher reality. It is lost because of your attachments to false beliefs and physical things. One of the goals of traditional Tantra is to break through all of those things that are keeping you from discovering who you really are. Many of the techniques of Tantra have this as a specific goal.

There is a name for this higher self, the ultimate and real you. It is *Atman* ("Aht-mahn"). The word itself is related to the concept of breath, so breathing techniques are often involved in helping you discover your own true self, your soul, your Atman. This book will share some of those techniques in later chapters.

But there is a powerful secret concerning Atman. You are unique and an individual. Everyone else is different from you. Your Atman is not their Atman. (All living things have their own Atman.) But what does this have to do with Tantric deities? Simple. Your Atman and Brahman are one and the same! Your individual soul is identical to Brahman.

So why aren't you eternal like Brahman? Why can't you create whatever you want like Brahman? Why can't you do whatever you want like Brahman?

You should know the answer by now. Things like the (false) ego, attachments, false beliefs, karma, the kleshas, maya, conditioning etc., keep you from realizing who you are. They keep you from achieving all that you want to achieve and doing whatever you want to do. They keep you from reality.

The techniques of Tantra include ways for you to have an extended and healthy life (alchemy), create whatever you want (magick), and do whatever you want to do (following the path of doing your will: Svecchachara). Tantra is a spiritual path with practical results that can improve your life in this world and, as a result, improve the world.

Some Tantric Goddesses of Magick

In India, magick is a practice particularly associated with Tantra. Although all of the following goddesses are aspects of the Goddess, by attuning yourself to the qualities, power, and energies (shakti) of these Goddess aspects, you can gain the power and energy of that goddess and use it for magick. To work with this list, visualize the following goddesses as described. They are each sitting upon Shiva, who is prone, white, naked, and smeared with ashes. Make the visualization as clear and complete as possible. In your visualization, make each goddess beautiful according to your concept of beauty.

When the image is as clear as possible, involve yourself in the visualization. See the goddess blessing you and bestowing her energy and gifts upon you. Use all of your senses: What does it feel like? What does it smell like? What else do you see? What do you hear? What do you taste?

Kriya Shakti

Pronunciation: "Kree-ya Shahk-tee"

Appearance: Kriya Shakti's skin is black like rich, fertile earth. She is *digambara*, "clothed in space" (naked). Enlightened, she has three eyes and two hands. Around her neck is a garland made of sapphires, and she is smeared with purple unguent. She is smiling, and her smile lights up her face and dark eyes.

Purpose: For physical, spiritual, emotional, mental, and magickal energy.

Energy: Akasha, the fifth element, also known as spirit.

Jñaña Shakti

Pronunciation: "Nya-nya Shak-tee"

Appearance: Jñaña Shakti's skin is pure white, like freshly fallen snow. Her face gives a feeling of pleasure when you look at it. She has three eyes. One hand is slightly open, giving favors or boons, while the other is raised with the palm forward to dispel fear. She is decorated with ornaments in her hair, on her arms, around her waist, about her ankles, and with a necklace, all featuring perfect white pearls.

Purpose: For knowledge, especially as a reflection of inner wisdom.

Energy: Lunar influences.

Iccha Shakti

Pronunciation: "Eek-cha Shak-tee"

Appearance: Iccha Shakti's skin is as red as the fire from a million suns. Her ornaments are rubies and also rudraksha berries, but she also has bracelets and anklets made of gold. She has three eyes and two hands. She is young and filled with energy. This is seen by the way she holds her body. She is smeared with red powder.

Purpose: For working with your will.

Energy: Solar influences

Pita Devi

Pronunciation: "Pee-tah Deh-vee"

Appearance: Pita Devi is very slender and has a nervous energy, indicated by her restless eyes. She is digambara (naked), revealing yellowish skin smeared with yellow powder, which is why she is sometimes known as the Yellow Goddess. Around her neck is a quartz necklace. She holds a book in her right hand and a mirror in her left. Pita Devi rules ambiguity, herbs, cleverness, language, alliances, speed, and duality. Her secret name is "Look forward, not back." Serving her are eight *yoginis* (subgoddesses) with names that mean Skill, Acuteness, Duplicity, Leopardess, Authoress, Craftswoman, Brightness, and Impulse.

Purpose: For improved thinking and knowledge.

Energy: The influences of the planet Mercury.

Nila Shakti

Pronunciation: "Nee-la Shak-tee"

Appearance: She, too, is digambara, and you can see her violet skin, but just barely. It matches the darkness around her, making her almost invisible. Nila Shakti is known as the Sapphire Shakti. She wears gems of polished jet and holds a bowl of shattered glass in her right hand and a mask in her left. Masks, shock, detachment, isolation, hermits, and anchorites are ruled by her. Her secret name is "I do not exist." Her yoginis are named Isolation, Hermit, Detachment, Darkness, Mask, Vampire, Death, and Split.

Purpose: For detachment. This gives the ability to deal with the ups and downs of life without suffering the pains non-Tantrics associate with living in the world.

Energy: The influences of the dwarf planet Pluto.

Rakta Devi

Pronunciation: "Rahk-tah Deh-vee"

Appearance: Rakta Devi is red and slender, with a boyish and strong figure, like an Amazon. She is naked and has three eyes. Unlike some of the other Tantric goddesses, she appears angry. In her right hand she holds a sharp knife, and in her left a *buckler*, a small shield. She is justifiably known as the Goddess of the Color of Blood. She rules those things signified by the names of her attendants: Anger, Stamina, Blood, Knife, Castrator (yikes!), Murderer, Conqueror, and Vigorous.

Purpose: For vigor. Also for magick of destruction. This does not necessarily imply only negative things, such as fighting and war. Digestion in the stomach and the natural decay of leaves and dead plants on a forest floor are also forms of destruction.

Energy: The influences of the planet Mars.

Aruña Shakti

Pronunciation: "Ah-roon-yah Shahk-tee"

Appearance: Aruña Shakti is naked and has three graceful, gazelle-like eyes. She has exceedingly long and elegant dark hair. She wears opal. In her right hand is a bowl from which smoke emerges, and in her left hand is a crystal intended for skrying. She is known as the Magenta Shakti. Her attendants' names signify the powers (shaktis) of the goddess: Romantic One, Dreamer, Passive One, Confused One, Undecided, Misty, Serpent Girl, and Roe-Deer.

Purpose: Work with Aruña Shakti when doing dream work, dream interpretation, and trance work. Also good for sammohan (hypnosis) and for inspiring the imagination.

Some work with her for help in deluding others . . . or themselves.

Energy: The influences of the planet Neptune.

Harina Devi

Pronunciation: "Hahr-ee-nah Deh-vee"

Appearance: Harina Devi is a wonderfully beautiful goddess with three eyes and two hands, fair hair above a sweetly smiling face, and an alluring, curvaceous figure. In her right hand is a flower, and her left hand is lowered and extended, the sign of giving. She is sometimes known as the Green Goddess and is considered a goddess of love and affection. Her yoginis are Synthesis, Harmony, Placidity, Joyfulness, Love's Ointment, Adorned with Peacock Feathers, Sexual Priestess, and Child-Artist.

Purpose: Work with Harina Devi for magickal goals involving love, sensuality, and sex.

Energy: The influences of the planet Venus.

Karbura Devi

Pronunciation: "Kahr-boo-rah Deh-vee"

Appearance: Karbura Devi is a large, fleshy woman who is surprisingly angular. She has three eyes, wears a necklace of crystal, and has an air of haughtiness about her. She is smeared with a dry, blue powder. She threatens with a stick in her right hand, and with her left hand she holds a child to one of her breasts. She is known as the Grey Goddess. Her yoginis are Analysis, Control, Love's Screw, Dominatrix, Count, Hierarchy, Compulsive One, and Robot.

Purpose: Karbura Devi is a goddess of control. Working with her will give you the ability to control all things, including yourself.

Energy: The influences of the planet Uranus.

Malini Devi

Pronunciation: "Mah-lee-nee Deh-vee"

Appearance: Malini Devi is a sweet lady who is naked and natural, smiling broadly. She wears only high-quality gold and jewels. When she is not smiling, her tongue is out and touches her lower lip. She has three eyes. When you visualize her, see her using her right hand to shower you with gold. In her left hand is a bowl full of choice food. She extends this in offering to you. Malini Devi is also known as the Flower Goddess. Her yoginis are Tongue, Assimilator, Expansion, Optimistic One, Vain, Fortune, Largess, and Generosity.

Purpose: She is the great giver of wealth on every level—financial, spiritual, erotic, wisdom, etc.

Energy: The influences of the planet Jupiter.

Asita Shakti

Pronunciation: "Ah-see-tah Shahk-tee"

Appearance: Asita Shakti is an old lady, resentful of the youth and potential of others. She has a dark and melancholy appearance, with disheveled hair showing a lack of personal attention. She has three eyes and two hands and is digambara. Her body is dry and rough; her breasts are pendulous. She is smeared with black powder. In her right hand is a cord. She uses this to restrain people and bring them back to a spiritual path. In her left hand is a skull, the container of the brain and a reminder that egotism is a waste of time. She is called the Black Goddess; however, she is also known as the Great Limiter. Thus her yoginis are forms that can limit us: Rejection, Limitation, Caution,

Responsibility, Melancholy, Servitude, Sorrow, Darkness, and the Dusky One.

Purpose: Work with Asita Shakti for all rites that restrict or terminate.

Energy: The influences of the planet Saturn.

FOUR

The Mahavidyas

While Durga is the strong form of the goddess consort to Shiva (Kali is even more powerful), the sweet version of his mate is Parvati.[11] Parvati is a goddess of the harvest and a protector of women. Always depicted as beautiful, she is also a goddess of love and lust. In fact, her matings with Shiva at times become so wild and intense that the entire universe shakes, frightening even the rest of the gods and goddesses. Although not a warrior, Parvati is no meek and mild little lady. She can appear calm and discreet, but behind closed doors with Shiva, she is a wild woman who revels in her power and sexuality.

As with all the symbolism of these deities, even their wild couplings have meaning. This indicates that, like humans, Parvati and Shiva could become overpowered by their emotions and feelings. There is a Bengali account of Parvati calling Shiva an irresponsible dope smoker who is incapable of looking after himself! After one fight, Shiva threatened to leave. So Parvati made ten different forms of herself to guard each of the directions: the four cardinal points, the four cross-quarters, plus above and below. As a result, no matter which direction he turned, there was a form of Parvati. Each of the ten would block his way by revealing important spiritual truths (which is why they are called "wisdom goddesses"). He was so entranced by their wisdom and his resulting spiritual enlightenment that he stayed. The *Dasa* (ten) *Mahavidyas* are ten fundamental aspects of the ultimate cosmic mother goddess.

Another way of looking at the Dasa Mahavidyas is that they are a way in which the pure energy of creation, the Shakti energy, manifests itself in seven developmental stages

11 Note: The first part of this chapter was derived, in part, from an article I wrote entitled "Dasa Mahavidyas and the Tree of Life" for the online journal *Hermetic Virtues*.

that correspond with the chakras. The final three aspects represent the way Parvati withdraws creation back into herself.

Kali: She Who Is the Eternal Night

The first Mahavidya created is Kali. Each of the ten has a two-dimensional image known as a *yantra*. In the West, we are likely to think of a yantra as a symbol representing the goddess. The word *yantra* is actually Sanskrit for "machine" or "device." The Tantric interpretation, however, is that this is not a symbol at all. A yantra *is* the goddess in a two-dimensional linear form. As such, it is worthy not just of great honor, but of actual worship. Some may think that worshiping geometric images is a silly, archaic concept. But since deity is everywhere, why not see it in a linear diagram?

How should we worship Kali and the other Mahavidyas? If you have ever seen a real Hindu or Tantric ritual (*puja*), you may have seen such things as giving flowers, milk, or clothes or waving a flame in front of an image of the goddess or god. These techniques are a good way to start. But the ultimate form of worship is not to do something with, for, or to the deity, but to understand that you and the deity are not separate, are not two different things. Such a form of devotion can be experienced and performed anytime and anywhere.

But why do this? Very simply, worship of this sort leads to knowledge of the deity. By better understanding a deity, we better understand ourselves and our place in the universe. Perhaps no form of wisdom can be a higher form of worship. This gives new meaning to the words over the ancient temples: "Know Thyself."

Kali Deity

Kali Yantra

The name *Kali* is derived from the word *kala*, which means "time" and "blackness." Kali is frequently shown as having dark blue or black skin.

The color white reflects all wavelengths of light, while black absorbs them all. Thus, it could be said that Kali has absorbed within her the potential of everything, including everything unknown, everything known, and everything that can be known.

Since we humans are not eternal (*eternal* originally did not mean "lives forever," it meant "is outside of time"), we experience everything through time. To do that, we must have life and the energy that allows life to continue. Thus, as "time," Kali is also the life force energy.

All things that live have certain qualities. Specifically, they are born, they mature, and they die. Kali has been called the Goddess of Yogic Transformation. But the transformations in life, alchemic in their nature, include such concepts as putrefaction and destruction/change. Such things can be terrifying to us, so the image of Kali is that of a terrifying woman. Perhaps she is terrifying to men because she is totally in her power.

When we see things as being terrifying, we generally think of them as being evil. But Kali is above and beyond all concepts of good and evil, positive and negative. She is pure ecstasy that provides perfect satisfaction.

To mentally focus or meditate on Kali, visualize her image. Kali is usually pictured as being black or blue in color. Around her neck is a *mala*, a set of 108 prayer beads. Kali's mala is made of human skulls rather than beads, however, indicating all of the problems she has slain. Her skirt is made of human arms, and her earrings are corpses. Her own arms show her carrying things such as Shiva's trident, a flaming bowl, a curved sword, and a head that she has just removed with the sword—transformation, indeed! Some versions show her making gestures (*mudras*) that indicate her giving favors and dispelling fear.

When working with her yantra, you may follow this format. Start by drawing your yantra (from the center triangle out) or obtain a copy of any size, and put it in a frame of some sort so that it can have water sprinkled on it. Place it on an altar or on the cleaned floor so when you look at it you will be facing east. Cover it with a cloth, or turn it upside down. Also for the altar you will need a candle or oil lamp, some incense and an incense holder, a small pot or bowl to hold water, a leaf from any living plant to sprinkle the water, a flower, and a piece of fresh fruit. You may add anything else you want to the altar. There are no dogmatic rules.

1. Prepare yourself by taking a bath or shower and putting on clean clothes. Some may prefer to remain *digambara* (clothed with the directions of space), or naked. As you do this, listen to pleasant music that will help you adopt a positive state of mind.
2. Go to your altar and sit down, facing the east.
3. Light the candle or oil lamp (you may have several if you wish) and the incense. Reveal the yantra by uncovering it or turning it over so you can see it.
4. Focus on the yantra as you do the following:
    a. Dip the leaf in the water in the bowl or pot and sprinkle yourself with it to purify yourself. Sprinkle the yantra to purify it, too, with the element of water.

b. Wave the incense in front of the yantra as an offering of scent and the element of air.

c. Do the same with the candle or lamp as an offering of light and the element of fire.

d. Hold up the fruit as an offering of the element of earth.

e. Hold up the flower as an offering of the element of *akasha* ("ah-kash" or "ah-kash-uh"), or spirit.

5. Allow yourself to surrender completely to the will of the deity. Chant or simply repeat the deity's mantra 108 times. You can do this very quickly.

6. Close your eyes (if they're not already closed) and ask that the deity bless you. Ask for any desires you wish to be granted. Be specific and make sure that the deity can work with your wishes.

7. When you are ready, thank the deity in your own words, bid the deity goodbye, then cover the yantra again or turn it over.

   According to tradition, Shiva told Parvati that working with yantras is very powerful and is as essential to the gods as oil is to oil lamps.

....

Kali's simplest mantra, or bija mantra, is *krim* (sounds like "cream"). Repeating it helps you uncover the essence of Kali. It is also said to help you attain physical strength and health, remove black magick, and find success as well as the solution to difficult problems. Saturday is Kali's special day.

Tara: She Who Is the Starry Goddess of Compassion

The second Mahavidya, Tara (Sanskrit for "Star"), is also important as the Buddhist goddess of compassion. Her name means "deliverer" or "savior." She is not a redeemer or savior in the way Christians think of Jesus. Rather, she delivers and saves knowledge and wisdom. She willingly provides the wisdom that allows us to save ourselves. Another of her titles, appropriately, is "The Saving Word."

That Tara and Kali are close is indicated by their appearances. Both are naked or wear a limited amount of clothing. Both have necklaces of heads that have been freshly cut, representing the destruction of the false ego. Both have tongues sticking out. They both dance on a body. But while Kali is pure, undifferentiated energy (which can sometimes be experienced as chaotic), Tara brings some order and the first concept of positivity to that undifferentiated energy, for Tara is the power of the incoming and outgoing breath, the power that allows us to control universal life energy, or *prana* ("prawn-yah"). The first sound we make, the sound of the breath, is also sacred. As described earlier, it automatically forms "ham" on the inhalation and "sah" on the exhalation. This forms the sacred mantra of *hamsa*, the Divine Swan, or the equally famous Tibetan version, *so-hum*.

Thus, it is from Tara that comes sound—and with sound come words, with words comes communication, with communication comes knowledge, with knowledge comes wisdom, and with wisdom comes enlightenment.

Tara Deity

Tara Yantra

In Tibetan Buddhism, Tara is worshiped as the manifestation of compassion.

To meditate on Tara, you can focus on her yantra or on her image. Tara, as an evolution of Kali, is deep blue in color, albeit not as dark as Kali. Also like Kali, Tara has matted hair, indicating that she has used energy in the passion of love. Around her neck she has a garland of human heads, indicating the wisdom she will offer, and she has several serpents for ornaments, indicating that her consort is Shiva. Again like Kali, Tara is often depicted dancing on a corpse, indicating her focus on the spiritual rather than the physical, and that she destroys all that is negative. Sometimes she stands within a burning funeral pyre, again indicating that she can help you destroy all negativity and everything that is negative. She has four arms and carries a sword or head chopper and a scissors, as well as a severed head. These indicate that she can help you remove your false ego, which prevents you from accepting the wisdom she offers. The scissors, specifically, indicate that she cuts away the attachments that keep you from finding happiness. She also holds a lotus. The lotus grows up from the muck at the bottom of a lake to produce a magnificent flower. It represents the potential of the soul.

Tara's bija mantra is *trim* (sounds like "treem"). Repeating it helps you uncover the essence of Tara. Tara is known as the Goddess of Tempestuous Seas, and since seas, or water, metaphorically relate to life, it is Tara who helps us over rough seas and through life's difficulties. Her bija mantra is also said to help you attain wealth and fame, happiness and success.

A longer mantra is *om hreem streem hum phat. Hreem* is a sound of purification and transformation. *Streem* is a sound of the archetypal feminine and is used to develop strength for new births and sustaining those new creations. *Hum* is for protection and knowledge and gives spiritual perception. *Phat* (pronounced like "top hat" with the leading "to-" removed) protects and removes obstacles, and is also known as the thunderbolt mantra. Thursday is Tara's special day.

Tripura Sundari: She Who Is Sixteen Years Old

Tripura Sundari ("Try-poor-uh Soon-dah-ree") is also known as *Lalita* ("Lah-lee-tuh"), "she who plays." Her yantra is the famous Sri Yantra, described in more detail in the next chapter. She is known as the Beauty of the Three Worlds (mental, physical, spiritual). The beauty results from the light of the vibratory energy that comes through her, and through all things. By understanding the source of her beauty, we are better able to understand and find the beauty that exists in all things.

There is a story that Shiva made fun of Kali's dark skin, so she ran off to meditate until her skin lightened. A wise man found her and told her that Shiva was going to marry another goddess. Not knowing she had achieved her goal, she ran home and saw a reflection of herself, now with light skin, in Shiva's heart. Thinking it was another goddess, she flew into an angry rage.

Shiva told her to look again. What she saw was a reflection of herself. Her light skin (representing spirituality) was always there, just beneath the dark (representing physicality). He said that she was beautiful in the three worlds, so she was *Tripura Sundari*. But he would also call her *Sodashi* because she was like a sixteen-year-old woman. This represents the culmination of a period of growth.

Unfortunately, many people are too caught up in just one of the worlds—the physical—to understand where beauty really comes from and that the very concept of beauty is dependent solely on our personal perceptions. We can truly appreciate and understand the beauty in other people and things only when we appreciate and understand the beauty within ourselves. It comes from our own inner light that is charged by universal energy from Tara. When we see beauty, we are seeing a reflection of ourselves. If we see ugliness in things or people, it is also a reflection or our perception of our own ugliness. As above, so below. As within, so without.

"She who plays" is a mother goddess. She invites our playing and love, but we often fail to understand and get caught up in the physical world, attached to people and things, resulting in our being locked in suffering and sorrow. From her, though, we learn that such things are misunderstandings of reality and, at most, only temporary. She awakens the joy in our lives and awakens us to the bliss that is really the basis of all things.

There is an entire mode of working with the Sri Yantra that is discussed in chapter 6. For now, for the purpose of focus and meditation, you can use that yantra or Tripura Sundari's image, which is that of a young girl of sixteen. She is also known simply as "sixteen" (*Sodashi*) or as "The Young Girl" (*Bala*). Tripura Sundari combines the power of Kali with the knowledge of Tara and her own blissful self from her spiritual understandings. She takes the Shakti energy and moves it from merely existing in our physical world and allows it to move through our five senses. Visually, she is a young girl sitting on a lotus, which itself is on the body of Shiva. Shiva is lying on a wide throne. Sometimes the throne is shown as being made of five gods (Brahma, Vishnu, Rudra, Indra, Sadashiva) representing the five senses. She holds a bow made of sugarcane. Its arrows are the personification of sweetness. She is gorgeous and beautiful. It is she who gives shape to our desires. Desires descend through our five senses of perception: sound, touch, vision, smell, and taste.

Tripura Sundari Deity

Tripura Sundari Yantra (Sri Yantra)

As the first part of her name, Tripura, implies, she takes on three forms: physical, subtle, and transcendent. Therefore, Tripura Sundari's bija mantra is threefold: *aim klim sauah* (sounds like "aim kleem sau-uhm," where the "sau" sounds like the "sou" in *sour*). Aim is for the power of wisdom, klim is for beauty and delight, and sauah is for spiritual transformation and transcendence. Repeating this mantra helps you achieve deep levels of spirituality and victory over personal demons. Tripura Sundari is popularly worshiped by women seeking to marry.

Bhuvaneshvari: She Who Is the Creatrix of the World

Bhuvaneshvari ("Bhoo-vah-nesh-vah-ri") is the "Queen of the Universe," the true mother of all worlds, the cosmic womb. Kali is time, and Bhuvaneshvari is space, into which all things manifest. Before her, there was energy. Now, matter and physicality finally emerge.

Worshiping this Divine Mother promotes a broader vision of the universe. She helps us transcend concepts of nationality, race, gender, religion, class, and so on. In short, she allows us to manifest the understanding of Tripura Sundari, allowing us to have perfect mercy for all.

Another name for Bhuvaneshvari is *Maya*, the goddess of illusion. Her dance makes those who have not achieved understanding become locked in meaningless prejudices. But with understanding we see her for what she is, just doing her part in the larger dance of reality. Thus, we find her divine love, which gives everything and everyone the space to be just what they are.

Bhuvaneshvari represents the Shakti energy that moves out to take on names and forms, the forces and powers that manifest as our physical world. As such, she is also the goddess of physical phenomena.

Bhuvaneshvari Deity

Bhuvaneshvari Yantra

As with the other Mahavidyas, you can meditate on Bhuvaneshvari's yantra or her image. The image of Bhuvaneshvari is as beautiful as that of Sundari, but her skin is the color of the rising sun, filled with reds, oranges, and yellows merged in power. She has flowing black hair, and her lips are red and full. The crescent moon crowns her head, and she possesses three eyes. As usual, the central eye relates to the third eye, which opens as your understanding of the universe opens. Two of Bhuvaneshvari's four hands traditionally hold a noose, to trap illusions and carry them away from you. One may also hold a goad, to drive you on your spiritual path. Her other hands form mudras indicating the granting of favors (fingertips down, showing the palm) and the dispelling of fears (fingertips up, again showing the palm).

Bhuvaneshvari is said to have a slim waist and thighs below beautiful, firm breasts smeared with the scents of sandalwood and saffron. Her arms are made for embracing. Yes, this description is overtly sexual. That is only natural, as Bhuvaneshvari is the Queen of the Physical Universe and the created world. This also should remind you of the Tantric concept that the physical world is not something terrible, a place to escape from or a "veil of woe." Rather, it is a wonderful place of joy and bliss. With the gift of seeing through the maya, Bhuvaneshvari lets us completely appreciate the world she has created, including all of its beauty.

Bhuvaneshvari's bija mantra is *hrim* (sounds like "hreem"). Repeating it helps you uncover her very essence. This mantra, related to the heart, is also said to help you prepare for all spiritual practices and increase kundalini energy. Friday is Bhuvaneshvari's special day.

Chhinnamasta: She Who Cuts Off Her Own Head

If you thought the image of Kali was frightening, you haven't met Chhinnamasta! The name, pronounced "Ch'heen-uh-mast-uh," means "a severed head," and her image is that of a naked woman who has cut off her own head. But wait, it gets even more weird!

Chhinnamasta holds her own severed head in one of her hands. From her neck are spurting streams of blood. Out of the mouth of the severed head is stretched a long tongue. The head seems to be ecstatically drinking one of the streams of her own blood.

There is something very strange about this image (well, besides the obvious). The appearance on the face of Chhinnamasta is not one of horror, terror, or pain. Instead, she appears to be happy or even in a state of bliss. This reminds me very strongly of the image of the Hanged Man in the tarot.

The Hanged Man is shown hanging by his ankle, not his throat. He is blissful, even though items are falling, or have fallen, from his pockets. He is a *willing* sacrifice, giving up something in order to be open to something even better. It's the letting go of the old to make way for the new.

Similarly, Chhinnamasta is seen as the power of sacrifice and courage. Being a willing sacrifice, even when you know that you will get something better, requires a great deal of courage, and Chhinnamasta has it.

Another story as to Chhinnamasta's creation is that the gentler form of Kali, Parvati, heard her two attendants asking for food because they were starving. Always willing to share, Parvati cut off her head and let them drink from the streams of blood, so some images show two others drinking with her.

Chhinnamasta Deity

Chhinnamasta Yantra

If we do not give things up when it is time, nature decrees that we will suffer. Many animals sacrifice their winter coats for lighter summer coats. It's the giving up of one thing for another. If you don't sacrifice what you need to give up, if you don't let go of your baggage, you will suffer. That's simply the way it is, even though it may seem like a severe punishment.

Use either Chhinnamasta's yantra or her image for meditation or focus. As with the previous forms of the Mahavidyas, Chhinnamasta's body is that of a sixteen-year-old adorned with a garland of severed heads. The age, of course, is symbolic and is not meant to represent a pedophile's obsession—assuming pedophiles are also into headless, auto-cannibalistic victims. Chhinnamasta's age is a code. It is related to the cycles of the moon and menstrual cycles—specifically, a period of sixteen days from the beginning of the new moon cycle.

Chhinnamasta's large, firm breasts are covered with lotus petals, and her hair is matted and spread out to look like bolts of lightning. At her feet are the bodies of *Kamadeva* ("Kah-mah Dey-vah"), the god of love, and *Rati* ("Rah-tee"), his consort and the goddess of love, entwined in intercourse. This symbolizes the sexual and kundalini energy that Chhinnamasta embodies.

It is also the first time in this pattern that we see a form of the goddess standing on two people rather than one. They are making love, showing that Chhinnamasta is bringing the kundalini energy into the physical universe. Also, because the goddess of love, Rati, is above the god of love, it indicates that she is in control. This shows that although Tantric adepts are encouraged to enjoy the bliss of sex, they should be in control of their urges rather than letting those urges control them.

Chhinnamasta's bija mantra is *hum*. Repeating it helps you uncover her essence. It is also believed that it will help you overcome sorrow and disappointment, as well as demolish the false ego (a main cause of suffering). It can help you master your senses. Saturday is Chhinnamasta's special day.

Bhairavi: She Who Is the Goddess of Decay

Bhairavi ("Bye-rah-vee") is known as the Warrior Goddess.[12] The divine wrath and anger she represents is specifically focused against impurities that are within us. Inwardly she helps us destroy problems that keep us from spiritual evolution. Externally she gives us the strength and insight to defeat anything ranging from bad vibes to people who work against our spiritual well-being while we traverse our individual paths to enlightenment. So in a very real sense, Bhairavi helps give us rebirth and resurrection as we quit the dark and seek the day.

According to one source, Bhairavi's name is a composite of three Sanskrit words: *bharana* (to create), *ramana* (to protect), and *yamana* (to disgorge). Thus, she is more than a goddess of destruction; she also is a goddess of creation and maintenance.

The Christian Bible uses the concept of the Word to represent Christ, the resurrection deity. In John 1:1, it says, "In the beginning was the word, and the Word was with God, and the Word was God." If, however, we look at this strictly from the wording (no pun intended), it is clear that the concept of words and speech are important to the notion of creation. This is reflected in Genesis 1:3

---

12 Note: Some writers switch the order of Chhinnamasta and Bhairavi in the evolution of the Dasa Mahavidyas. The order presented here is the one given in the classic text known as the *Todala Tantra*.

where it says, "And God said, 'Let there be light.' And there was light." In the practice of magick—as in the working of a "spell"—this is also true.

Unfortunately, this has resulted in horrible misconceptions of magick. In so many novels, films, TV shows, and comic books, there is the image of a power-hungry dabbler mumbling and poorly pronouncing a few special words, resulting in demons jumping out of the ground or popping out of the air to do this person's bidding. If this were true, every book on magick in the US would be banned under the Patriot Act! Obviously, there is far more to magick than just speaking the words. They must be backed with some sort of power or energy.

Bhairavi Yantra

Bhairavi Deity

Bhairavi not only is a warrior goddess, but is also the goddess of the power of speech when it is filled with raw potential energy (i.e., possesses the element of fire). It is said that she can use her empowered words to eliminate all opposition (to spiritual evolution). Her image often shows her enraged, riding a donkey, and her mouth filled with the blood of demons. She holds a sword in one hand while giving blessings and removing fears with two others. Her fourth hand holds weapons such as a thunderbolt or trident.

One of the best-known forms of Bhairavi as a warrior is that of Durga, described earlier. Durga is shown riding a lion, a symbol of the fire element. Astride the lion she carries and uses her weapons to save us from all difficulties and blockages to our personal spiritual growth. These blockages can be our own internal demons, but they can also include external forces such as disease and death. She may not be able to eliminate those outer forces, but she can help change our understanding of them so we learn from them rather than merely suffer from them. Bhairavi is also seen as the ultimate warrior goddess, *Chandi* ("Chahn-dee"), the destroyer of opposition. Chandi would assist Kali in the destruction of demons.

Bhairavi is a goddess who helps bring change. Perhaps the ultimate form of this change is when the pure Shakti energy evolves into energy that can change us physically, emotionally, and spiritually. The old and unneeded decays to leave room for a new creation. This energy that has the potential to change us is known as *kundalini.*

If you don't use Bhairavi's yantra for meditation/concentration, focus on her image. As usual, she is very beautiful. Her head has a garland of flowers, and she is smeared with red paste, although her skin already is said to look like the red rays of a thousand suns. She has three eyes and a beautiful face, with the type of smile that is said to slowly appear. She wears white gems, and sometimes her hands are shown holding milk, which nurtures our bodies, and a book, which nurtures our minds.

Like Tripura Sundari, Bhairavi is said to rule over three worlds. Therefore, her bija mantra is threefold: *hsraim hskrim hsrsauh* (sounds like "sraym" with a leading breath, "skreem" with a leading breath, and "srr-sau-uh" with a leading breath). Repeating this helps you uncover the essence of Bhairavi. It is also said to help you attain excellence in speech, as well as dynamism and drive to accomplish goals. It will allow you to discover your true goals and move toward them without being interrupted by attachments to minor things. It helps you discover hidden inner negative energy, discharge it, and release your spiritual fire. Bhairavi's special day is Wednesday.

Dhumavati: She Who Is the Goddess Who Widows Herself

The seventh Mahavidya is Dhumavati ("Doo-mah-vah-tee"). Dhumavati is the oldest of the Mahavidyas. She is a grandmother goddess, giving honor and respect to the wisdom that comes with age. To have lived this long, she has overcome all of her failures and realized that each failure had within it one or more things to learn. Combined, these learnings have given her knowledge and wisdom she can share so we can become victors in life.

The word *dhuma* means "smoke," and Dhumavati's name means that she is composed of smoke. So her nature is to obscure things. How, then, can she share her long lifetime of earned wisdom? The answer is that in order to obscure one thing, you must reveal another. When you obscure superficial desires, you reveal inner needs and can develop spiritual goals. Those superficial desires can take your focus away from your true spiritual goals. Dhumavati's obscuration actually helps you to focus and achieve your goals. She is worshiped by those who think of themselves as helpless, afflicted with hunger, and suffering the terrible pangs that accompany birth... and death.

The other nine Mahavidyas have consorts. Dhumavati, however, is the Widow Goddess. This means she is pure, feminine energy, with no aspect of the masculine. Nothing in our physical world is purely male or female, positive or negative, electric or magnetic, yang or yin, etc. Everything is blended. As part of this metaphor, in most Western teachings, the masculine/positive/electric concept represents pure energy, while the feminine/negative/magnetic concept represents pure form. As I've already pointed out, in Tantric traditions the opposite is true. The female is considered pure energy and the male is considered pure form. There is a saying that exemplifies this concept: "Shiva is a corpse without Shakti."

While for some people, not having a partner indicates freedom and independence, it can also have the opposite effect. Some people need a partner. Dhumavati can be generalized into the sensation of wanting what one doesn't have, being a beggar eternally and desiring physical things.

Use Dhumavati's yantra or her image for concentration and/or meditation. She is usually shown as an old woman, tall and very thin, the color of smoke. She is wrinkled and unattractive, with long, uneven teeth, several of which are missing. Her hair is a matted mess. Picture Kali as an old, weakened woman. She wears old, dirty clothes (taken from a corpse in a cremation ground) that don't hide her sagging breasts. In one hand she holds a winnowing basket that is used to separate usable grain from the grain's husks or chaff by tossing the harvest in the air. It represents the ability to separate what is bad and unusable from what is good and practical. Dhumavati rides in a type of chariot or cart that has a crow, a symbol of death, on it. She is seen to be sad, quarrelsome, and angry and is associated with ignorance. Can you get past those blockages, often in the form of physical things, to find your spiritual way?

Dhumavati's bija mantra is *dhum* (sounds like "doom"). Repeating it helps you to uncover her essence. It is also said to help you eliminate anything blocking your spiritual path, your adversaries, and to attain health, wealth, strength, and good fortune. Using this mantra creates a sort of protective spiritual smoke that hides you from any type of negativity, even hiding you from death. Dhumavati's special day is Saturday.

Dhumavati Deity

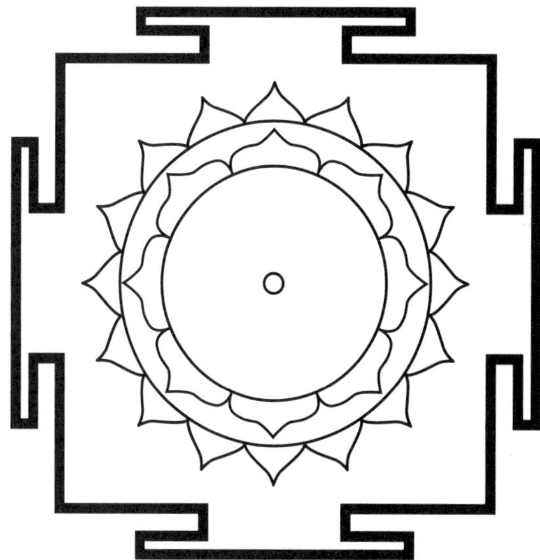

Dhumavati Yantra

Bagalamukhi: She Who Grasps the Tongue

When pure, undifferentiated sound (represented by Tara) manifests as light, Tara becomes Bagalamukhi ("Bah-gah-lah-moo-kee"). This light is stunning, effulgent, ultimately powerful and glorious, making Bagalamukhi a wonderful and powerful goddess. To look at the evolution of the Mahavidyas, consider the concept of sound (Tara) made manifest as speech (Bhairavi) that becomes so stunningly powerful (as Bagalamukhi) that it silences all others. Bagalamukhi represents the hypnotic powers of the Goddess that instantaneously stop others in their tracks. Symbolically she helps you quiet the voice that constantly goes on in your head and allows the inner voice from your higher self to come through. It is here that the Shakti energy has turned inward. It changes individuals who have lived in ignorance and misery by allowing them to achieve a state of bliss. With Dhumavati, people yearn for relief from the pains of life. With Bagalamukhi, people rediscover that they are divine and are encouraged to seek spirituality.

Whenever you have to debate others or simply present your position to others, Bagalamukhi is the goddess to call on for support. Sometimes that "other" person is an aspect of yourself that keeps you from your spiritual path.

Because of this stunning, hypnotic power, Bagalamukhi can be considered an "inverter." If people would speak against you, she inverts their speech into silence. She reveals their "knowledge" for the ignorance it truly is. She makes the powerful powerless and turns your defeats into victories and your opponent's victories into defeats.

Dhumavati represents a focus on physical things. Bagalamukhi shows the power of the non-physical, helping you to refocus on the spiritual and the understanding that there is a part of you that is divine.

Meditate or focus your devotion on Bagalamukhi's yantra or her image to gain her graces. Many images show her skin as yellow, and her clothing may be depicted in a similar color. She sometimes wears trinkets that are yellow and has yellow flowers in her hair. She may sit on a throne made of the yellow metal gold. Around her throne are red lotuses. With one hand she is reaching out to grab the tongue of her demonic foe. With her other hand she holds a mace so after she has him by the tongue, she can smack him on the head.

Bagalamukhi's bija mantra is *hlim* (sounds like "leem" with a leading breath). Repeating it helps you to uncover her essence. It is also said to protect you from enemies, especially fierce ones. Therefore, it will help you achieve victory, fame, and success. Some people pronounce it "hrim." Bagalamukhi's special day is Tuesday.

Bagalamukhi Deity

Bagalamukhi Yantra

Matangi: She Who Loves Pollution

Matangi ("Mah-tahn-gee," with the "g" as in "goose") is the goddess of articulating or communicating inner knowledge and is therefore the goddess of art, music, and dance, a Tantric goddess similar to Brahma's consort, Saraswati. Both play a *veena* ("vee-nuh"), a stringed musical instrument about four feet long. Both are symbolized by rain clouds, thunder, and rivers. However, Matangi is focused on inner knowledge and bestows talent and expertise, whereas Saraswati offers more common learnings. Saraswati rules the ordinary, while Matangi rules the extraordinary. Matangi shares in the transformative power of Kali and Shiva. She is also the goddess of teaching and counseling.

Matangi is the color of dark green emeralds, like the color of the deep sea. She has three eyes and is said to be radiant, like the moon. However, when she walks, her steps are said to be like those of an infuriated elephant. Her eyes are shown as rolling under the influence of alcohol. She carries weapons that are used to fascinate and subdue her enemies. She may hold in her hand a parrot, representing speech and the fact that humans are unique because of our broad and innate natural ability to speak. She is sometimes called the *Mantrashakti,* the goddess of words. Her throne is covered or perhaps is made of gems with the symbolism of a lion. You can use this image or Matangi's yantra for focus and/or meditation. Matangi is "the giver of results."

Matangi Deity

Matangi Yantra

In a story about Parvati, the goddess assumes the form of a human in the lowest class of people, those who are associated with death, impurity, and pollution. In this form she is known as *Matangi*, a symbol of how intention can make anything sacred.

Matangi's bija mantra is *aim*, a mantra also sacred to Saraswati. Repeating it helps you uncover the essence of Matangi. It is claimed that it will help you gain wisdom and lead to perfection. It may also lead to marriage and a happy married life. Matangi's special day is Sunday.

Kamala Deity

Kamala: She Who Is the Last But Not the Least

The tenth of the Dasa Mahavidyas is *Kamala* ("Kah-mah-lah") or *Kamalatmika* ("Kah-mah-laht-mee-kah"), the Lotus Goddess of Delight and the power of perfect happiness. Delight and happiness, especially in our physical world, may seem out of place or at least not very attainable. However, as I pointed out earlier, the Tantric concept does not view the physical world as something terrible, a place to leave, or a "veil of woe." Rather, it is a wonderful place of joy and bliss. Kamala represents true self-awareness.

Kamala is a Sanskrit word for lotus. In this, she is like the goddess of the lotus, *Lakshmi* ("Lahk-shmee"), the consort of Vishnu the preserver deity. Lakshmi is also the goddess of wealth, beauty, and love. Some say Kamala *is* Lakshmi, but she is never shown with Vishnu, so there are differences. For example, Kamala is not dominated by Vishnu, as is Lakshmi. Kamala is independent and liberated.

Kamala, as ruler of love, beauty, and bliss, is also similar to Tripura Sundari, but Sundari deals with a more subtle form of love, beauty, and bliss, based on a positive self-image. Kamala deals with the outer form of beauty as a manifestation of the inner. It's a subtle difference, but it is there. Because of the focus on the outer, Kamala is directly related to the earth, as the earth contains the full physical manifestation of the Divine.

Kamala Yantra

Kamala will aid you in whatever you wish to do and help you achieve your goals. This is not for spiritual goals, but for worldly ones: financial success and security, family and loved ones, etc. However, these goals should be outward manifestations of your spiritual life and not merely temporary desires based on supposed needs or wants caused by attachments, egotistical wishes, or even what could be considered fetishes or neurotic desires.

As with the other Mahavidyas, you can meditate on Kamala's yantra or on her image. Kamala is beautiful, and her skin tone is the yellow of Bagalamukhi combined with the browns of the earth, yielding a golden tone. Kamala is shown wearing beautiful silks and has a crown of gems. Two of her hands form the mudras of granting favors and eliminating fears. Four pure white elephants—the largest animals on land—bathe her by pouring jars of water or the earth's nectars over her. The nectars represent unity with the Divine (yoga), virtue, wealth, and knowledge—a union of the mental, emotional, spiritual, and physical worlds. In her other hands Kamala holds lotus flowers, representative of life and fertility on the physical plane. She stands on a lotus herself. You can meditate/focus on this image or on Kamala's yantra to seek her wisdom and favors.

Kamala's bija mantra is *shrim* (sounds like "shreem"), the same as that of Lakshmi. Repeating it helps you to uncover the essence of Kamala. It is also said to enhance creativity and help you become more aware of physical beauty as a manifestation of the Divine. It can help you achieve gracefulness and fertility in thought and deed. It is said to grant all of life's highest goals. Monday is Kamala's special day.

In the images of the Mahavidyas, you may have noticed that they don't completely match the descriptions. Such images are almost always incomplete. Artists will focus more on one aspect than another, stressing that aspect of the particular goddess. If you were drawing images of the goddesses, which aspects would you emphasize? Also, artists may come from traditions that use different descriptions of the goddesses than those given here. They're not wrong, they're just different.

....

Because the Dasa Mahavidyas are guardians of the ten directions of space, some Tantrics use them for banishings. Here is one I created a few years ago and have used successfully many times:

Banishing by the Mahavidyas

1. Begin by chanting **Om** until you feel centered and calm.
2. Walk or turn to the east. Offer incense, a flame waved in this direction, the thunderbolt mantra, and/or something similar. Say: **Chhinnamasta, goddess of divine satisfaction, watch over the eastern gate of this chakra of bliss.**
3. Walk or turn to the south. Offer incense, a flame waved in this direction, the thunderbolt mantra, and/or something similar. Say: **Kali, goddess of spiritual transformation, watch over the southern gate of this chakra of bliss.**
4. Walk or turn to the west. Offer incense, a flame waved in this direction, the thunderbolt mantra, and/or something similar. Say: **Bhuvaneshvari, goddess who rules the universe, watch over the western gate of this chakra of bliss.**
5. Walk or turn to the north. Offer incense, a flame waved in this direction, the thunderbolt mantra, and/or something similar. Say: **Bagalamukhi, goddess of**

communication, watch over the northern gate of this chakra of bliss.

6. Walk or turn past the east, completing your first circumambulation. Continue on to the southeast. Offer incense, a flame waved in this direction, the thunderbolt mantra, and/or something similar. Say: **Dhumavati, great grandmother, watch over the southeastern gate of this chakra of bliss.**
7. Walk or turn to the southwest. Offer incense, a flame waved in this direction, the thunderbolt mantra, and/or something similar. Say: **Tripura Sundari, threefold goddess of beauty and bliss, watch over the southwestern gate of this chakra of bliss.**
8. Walk or turn to the northwest. Offer incense, a flame waved in this direction, the thunderbolt mantra, and/or something similar. Say: **Matangi [shout her name], goddess of sound and energy, watch over the northwestern gate of this chakra of bliss.**
9. Walk or turn to the northeast. Offer incense, a flame waved in this direction, the thunderbolt mantra, and/or something similar. Say: **Kamala, great goddess of unfoldment, watch over the northeastern gate of this chakra of bliss.**
10. Walk or turn to the southeast to complete the circle. Then walk or turn to the west of your area and face east. If you are moving as opposed to just turning, walk to the center of your area. Look up. Offer incense, a flame waved in this direction, the thunderbolt mantra, and/or something similar. Say: **Tara, great goddess who brings hope and help when all seems lost, watch over the gate above this chakra of bliss.**
11. Look down while still in the center of your area. Offer incense, a flame waved in this direction, the thunderbolt mantra, and/or something similar. Say: **Bhairavi, great warrior goddess, watch over the gate below this chakra of bliss.**
12. Again, chant **Om**. Inhale deeply and sound this mantra using your full and slow exhalation. Allow your senses to reach out and make sure that your area is banished. Repeat the chant until you feel balanced.

In closing this section, I think it is interesting to look at the message that underlies the ten great powers: They are all dangerous women. They do not stand on convention. They're associated with death and transformation. None of them are subservient to males.

To quote historian and Harvard professor Laurel Thatcher Ulrich, "Well-behaved women seldom make history." The Mahavidyas are the driving force behind *lots* of history.

These women, these goddesses, are subversive. They share the Tantric concept that living according to social norms forced upon you by society, friends, custom, religions, etc., does not lead to liberation and spiritual freedom. Tantrics often appear to be the same as those who have been marginalized by society: the misfits, the improper, the outsiders, the unique. It is by cutting through the boundaries of what is allowed or accepted, by doing what is unexpected or frowned upon, that the Tantric discovers new approaches to the world and to spiritual development.

One learns techniques so that, when mastered, they can be abandoned. This is what leads to true freedom.

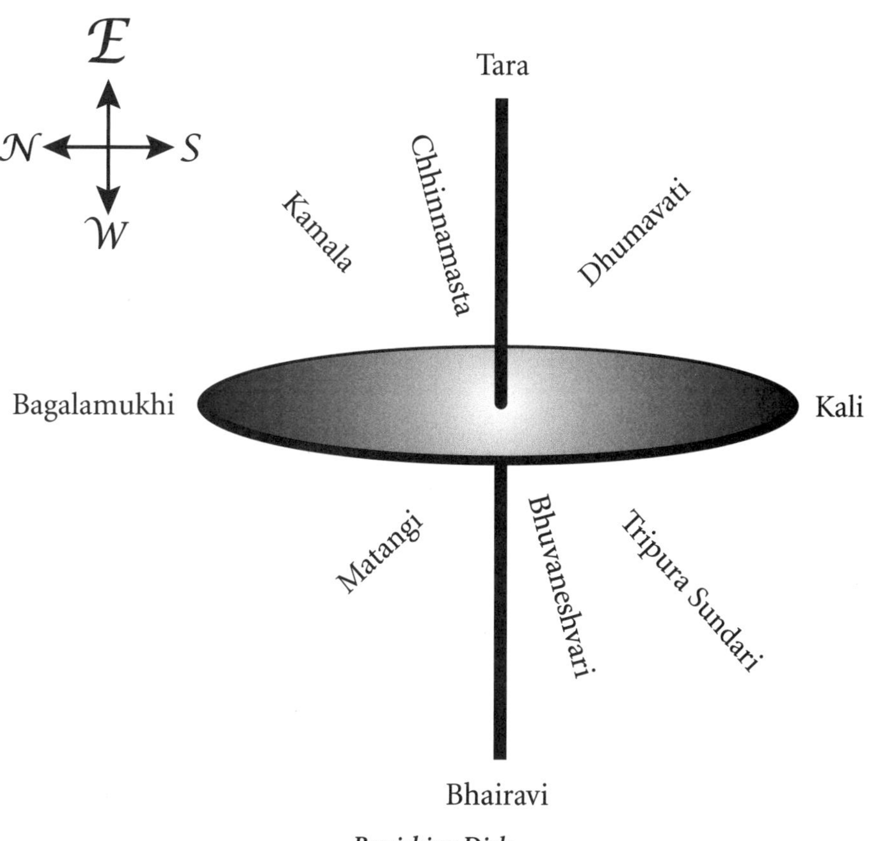

Banishing Disk

FIVE

The Mystical Key, Part I: Sri Vidya

I have seen estimates that up to 85 or 90 percent of all sensory data comes through our eyes. As a result of this physiological phenomenon, it was inevitable that the mind would primarily think in images or symbols rather than words (or perhaps because we think in images, we focus on visual sensory input). When you say or think of the term *tree*, for example, your mind has within it an image (or many visual images) of a tree or trees. You know what is meant by the word *tree* because you have this knowledge. If you never had an image of a tree, then you would not understand the word until either you observed a tree or perhaps somebody explained what a tree was and you could create an image of a tree within your mind.

This is one reason why nonvisual *concepts*, such as honesty, love, reliability, patriotism, democracy, etc., are more difficult to understand and describe than are *things*, such as a tree, a doll, or a ball. There is no image that can fully explain what those concepts mean. Instead, your mind usually has to collect a series of images to do this. An understanding of such concepts only comes through learning and experience.

Unfortunately for communication, people may have different sets of images to define the same terms. Thus, even if you use one term—a popular current term, for example, is *family values*—it may have different meanings to different people. In neuro-linguistic programming, this concept is exemplified by the phrase "the map is not the territory." Politicians take advantage of this by using emotion-laden phrases without defining them. A politician can say, "I'm for a stronger educational system!" which may make you want to vote for him even though what he means by this is to "turn the schools over to private businesses" while you think he means to "give greater public funding to schools," or vice versa. That is why it is important to completely explain symbolic concepts.

Wiccans often use the pentagram as a symbol for their beliefs. Some Christians use a cross or crucifix in the same way. Today, Jews use the *Mogen David* ("King David's Star"), a six-pointed star composed of two interlocking triangles, as a representative symbol. Earlier in Judaism, a candlestick with seven branches represented the faith.[13]

Unlike Judaism and Christianity, Tantra (which is far older than either of those religions) has no single, primary text. *But it does have a symbol.*

As a comparison that may be familiar to many readers, the Kabalah (the mystical underpinnings of Judaism and much of Western—even Pagan—magick) has a traditional symbol that has played an important part in the practices and philosophies of mystics and magicians for two thousand years or more: the Tree of Life. The most popular contemporary version of this diagram shows ten circles connected by twenty-two pathways (see illustration).

The Tree of Life can be seen as a key to the universe. It is in complete harmony with everything from Newtonian physics and quantum mechanics to astrology and tarot cards. To a person who understands the image, it contains symbolism explaining many spiritual belief systems, including those of Judaism, Christianity, Hinduism, Buddhism, and Taoism. It explains everything from the nature of psychology and why we forget most aspects of our past lives to business plans and guides for romantic relationships. It can be used as a map to the astral worlds. It can reveal the meaning of complex concepts such as Einstein's general theory of relativity and the Hegelian Dialectic. The Tree of Life corresponds to the physical body and can be used for everything from strengthening the aura to spiritual healing.

To say this simple symbol is a handy tool revealing complex concepts to those who understand it is an understatement. One famous occultist referred to it merely as a sort of giant filing cabinet for storing related aspects of mystical information. But as you can see from just this brief mention, the Tree of Life is far more than just some sort of astral database! (For more information on the Tree of Life and its uses, see my *Modern Magick*.)

Virtually all spiritual systems have some sort of symbol. Countries have symbols—the flag of the country—too. Such flags are often revered much as the cross is by many Christians and the Torah is by many Jews. In fact, in the Pledge of Allegiance, citizens of the US first pledge their allegiance "to the flag of the United States of America" before pledging allegiance to the country. Now, obviously that refers to the concepts represented by the flag, for who wants to vow allegiance to some pieces of cloth that have been sewn together?

With all of the images of deities in India and hundreds of two-dimensional symbols (yantras), there is one particular symbol, more than any other, that represents and embodies the ideas of Tantra. With this symbol as a guide, you can do everything that you can with the Tree of Life, and, as I think you will see, even more—much more.

13 This lamp is called a *menorah*. Many people think a menorah is the special candelabrum used during the festival of Hanukkah. In actuality, that multi-branched candle holder is called a *Hanukiah*.

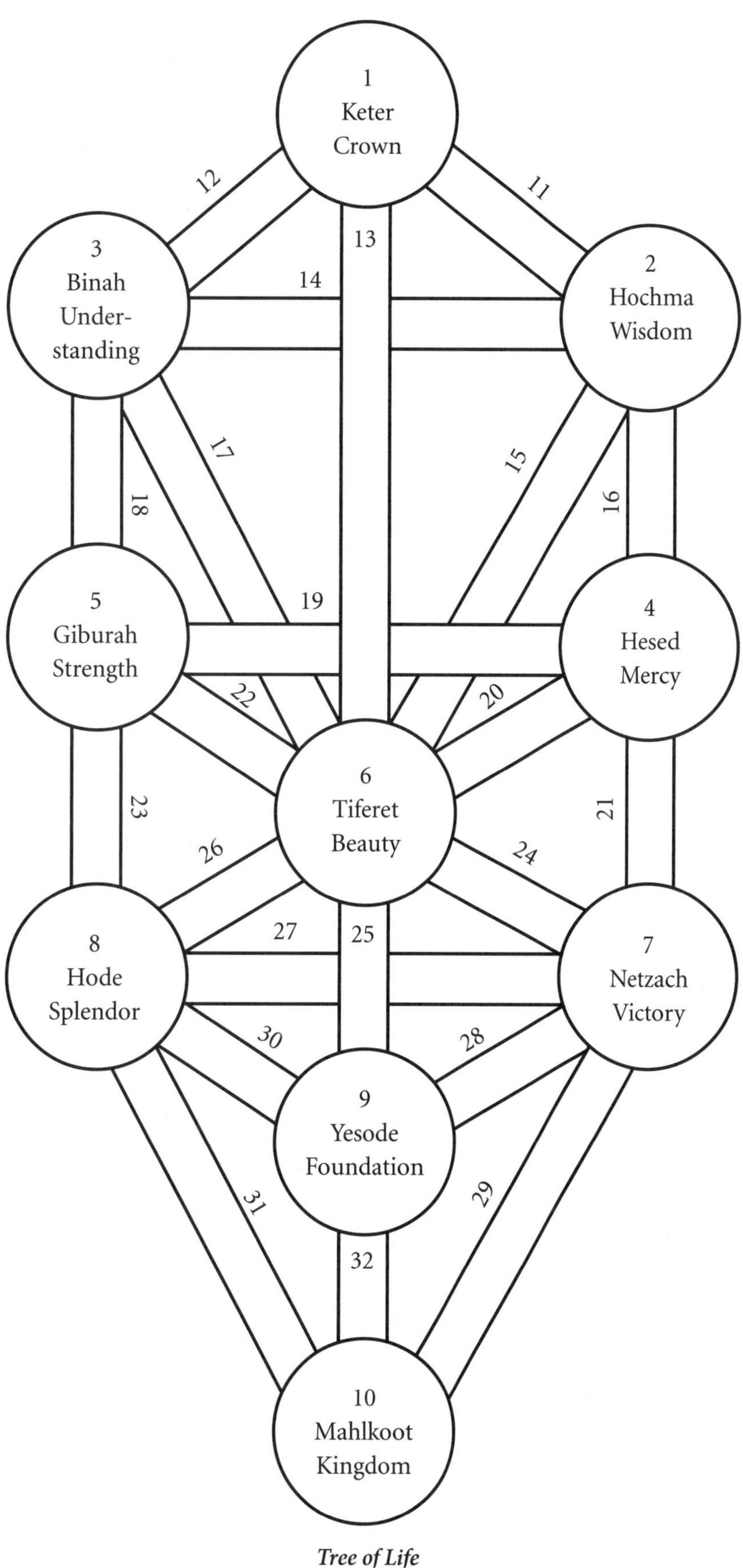
1
Keter
Crown
2
Hochma
Wisdom
3
Binah
Under-
standing
4
Hesed
Mercy
5
Giburah
Strength
6
Tiferet
Beauty
7
Netzach
Victory
8
Hode
Splendor
9
Yesode
Foundation
10
Mahlkoot
Kingdom
11
12
13
14
15
16
17
18
19
20
21
22
23
24
25
26
27
28
29
30
31
32

Tree of Life

This symbol is the *Sri Yantra* ("Shree Yahntrah"), and the study of the wisdom hidden in the symbol is known as *Sri Vidya* ("Shree Vihdyuh"). The Sri Yantra is arguably the most meaningful symbol in Tantra and is sometimes called the "king of all yantras." It is certainly one of the most popular symbols in all of India. There are actually some Tantric sects where practitioners worship it. I'll describe why, and give an inkling as to how, later.

The Sri Yantra

The Sri Yantra

The Sri Yantra is an interlocking set of triangles surrounded by symbolic lotus petals, circles, and, finally, an outer "square" with invisible doors that serve as entryways to the symbol's many secrets. I would contend that as powerful and useful as the Kabalistic Tree of Life can be, the Sri Yantra is like the Tree of Life on mega-steroids. This may upset some of my Kabbalist friends, but I hope what you read here will convey the Sri Yantra's value and power.

This chapter has been the most difficult of anything I've ever tried to write. When I first started, I wanted to share *everything* I knew about the Sri Yantra. Right now, on my desk, I have about a dozen books exclusively about this image. In my library I have many more books that include short passages or long chapters on the subject. I also have numerous papers and documents about the possibilities and potentials of working with this figure. I give an introductory workshop on this symbol that takes two days for me to present.

Slowly, and regrettably, I came to realize that just as there are many individual books that deal only with the Kabalistic Tree of Life, an in-depth discussion of the Sri Yantra for Westerners would take at least a full book. That's far more than I can effectively include here.

Please do not think I am hiding anything. The goal of this book is to present Tantra as a complete spiritual system. Just as my *Modern Magick* presented a complete magickal system and didn't spend half the book on the Tree of Life, neither shall this book use hundreds of pages examining the Sri Yantra. The subject is so voluminous that a full explanation of it, one that will explain far more of its intricacies, warrants one or more books of its own.

I hope that your reading of *Modern Tantra* will lead you to books by other authors. In the future, I intend to write at least one book that goes far more deeply into Sri Vidya. Until then, please refer to the more in-depth books named in the bibliography.

I have to add, though, that studying Sri Vidya—while stimulating, intriguing, and enlightening—will never reveal the real secrets of the Sri Yantra, most of which have never been published in any language. As an analogy, while there have been many thousands of books written on Tantra, one of the secrets of Tantra is that, above all, Tantra is *experiential.* All of the writing is meaningless unless you can incorporate the concepts into your consciousness and your actions. And if what you learn from your practices contradicts what some writer, including me, scribbled on paper, then you are right and all the writers are wrong. Of course, you may only be right for your own life, but that's part of the path of Tantra. The ultimate guide, as with shamanic practice, is your experience, not what someone else writes or says.

So why was this chapter so difficult for me to write? As any author can tell you, including more is easy. The hard part is determining what you are going to *exclude.* I have rewritten this chapter several times so that it will begin to give you insight into the symbol without being so overwhelming (what is currently referred to as a "data dump") that your eyes will glaze over. I've regrettably had to exclude some things that, at the time I wrote them, I felt were vitally important. Upon rereading the chapter, however, I saw that they only got in the way of making *Modern Tantra* accessible to as many people as possible. I now believe, after so much time spent with this chapter, that it is complete enough and provides practical techniques for working with the Sri Yantra. As of this writing, it certainly contains far more than you will find in any other popular book available in the West.

The following pages provide a basic introduction to the symbolism of the figure and a few methods of working with it. This way, you will be able to experiment with it and perhaps become as amazed at its potential and practicality as I am. With this information, if you wish, you can incorporate its wisdom and applications into your spiritual practices no matter what path you follow. And if you choose to follow a more Tantric spiritual path, it can become a guiding light on your personal spiritual journey, just as the Tree of Life guides so many Kabalists.

There is one more thing to add before moving on to the next section of this chapter. Previously I mentioned what I call the "proto-Tantrics." These people lived in the northeast part of India. Their society existed as long ago as 10,000 years or maybe even longer, with established cities at least 8,000 years old. They worked with the Sri Yantra (or its predecessors) for at least 5,000 years. Tantra has evolved over the centuries, and it was inevitable that different "schools" or traditions with different interpretations of the Sri Yantra would develop. If, in your studies, you come across something that is different from the information presented here, please do not think that either one is incorrect; they are simply different interpretations of the same thing made by people trying to understand the figure's depth, beauty, and intricacies. I suggest meditation on, study of, and practice with the image to find out what is right for you. That is far more important than adhering to what I (or any other author) present for you to read, study, and consider.

An Overview of the Design of the Sri Yantra

The Sri Yantra (also called the *Sri Chakra* or just the *Sri*) is composed of an outer "square," technically called the *bhupura* ("boo-poo-rah"), with "gates" in the center of each side. Within the square are three concentric circles, two circles of symbolic lotus petals, and nine intersecting *trikonas* (triangles). The four triangles that point upward represent Shiva, the male aspect of the Divine, and the five pointing downward represent Shakti, Shiva's female counterpart.

At the center is a point commonly known as the *Bindu.* It is the union of Shiva and Shakti, and is actually composed of three aspects (and thus is sometimes more accurately called the *Tribindu*). This point, then, is technically composed of a blur of three colors: red (representing Shakti), white (representing Shiva), and pink (representing their union). However, in most cases it is shown as a single black, or sometimes red, point.

As you will learn in this chapter, the intersections of the nine trikonas form forty-three triangles. The eight-petaled lotus represents the "lotus of creation." The sixteen-petaled lotus represents the sixteen "days," "fingers," or *kalas* of the moon. I'll share more on this in a moment.

The Sri Yantra can be approached in one of two ways: from the Bindu in the center to a gate on the outer square (an outward expansion called *projection*) or from a gate toward the Bindu (inward involution called *absorption*). The importance of these concepts will also be explained later.

Interpretations of the Sri Yantra

While commenting upon the symbol, Sir John Woodroffe (under the name "Arthur Avalon," author of numerous books on Tantra from the late Victorian era) claimed that by working regularly with the Sri Yantra, the lines of the figure that are initially interpreted as being external to the practitioner become *internalized* as a pure mental state. It literally transforms the mind, and the practitioner comes to see everything as divine. Eventually, the practitioner comes to realize that he or she is the Sri Yantra. The body's nine apertures (two eyes, two nostrils, two ears, the mouth, the anus, and the urethra or urethra/vulva) correspond to the nine chakras, or "circles," of the Sri Yantra. This is why the human body can be considered an "island of nine gems," a metaphor for this nine-chakra system. How the two extra chakras relate to the human body will also be discussed.

To Kabalists, the Tree of Life represents both the universe, called the macrocosm, and the individual, called the microcosm. Kabalists also follow the famous concept based on the Tablet of Hermes: "That which is above is as that which is below, and that which is below is as that which is above, only after a different manner."

According to Woodroffe, the Sri Yantra represents both the human body and the universe. In this sense, the system of the Sri is in complete harmony with the Kabalists' Tree of Life.

Because it's important to understand the concept that the Divine can be in everything, I'm repeating a basic idea here: Yantras, including the Sri Yantra, are more than the purely linear diagrams they appear to be. They actually *are* the Goddess or the God in two-dimensional form—they are not a symbol or representation of the Divine—they *are* the Divine. At least this is the traditional description. I prefer to consider them a home for the Divine. They become the Goddess or God when you call the appropriate deity into the device. If you desire to have the deity in the yantra for a long time, it can be carved into stone or etched into copper, bronze, silver, or gold. For more temporary use (and often for magickal purposes), it can be drawn on a large leaf or paper or even scratched into the soil. Woodroffe believes that the Sri Yantra should be in every home, as it will bring happiness, prosperity, and health. In India it is highly popular and seen everywhere. As a popular explanation for it being ubiquitous, it is often simply called a good luck symbol.

The contemporary author S. K. Ramachandra Rao has published several books on the Sri Yantra. Here are some of the ideas he presents about the sigil:

1. The Sri can be used both to activate and to direct energies within and outside of the practitioner. Although Ramachandra Rao doesn't use the terminology, this is a basic concept of magick.
2. The Sri is a "psychocosmogram." The universe is symbolized by the figure, and by working with it, you can make changes in the universe. Again, this is a description of magick.
3. The Sri can function as a model of transformation. This can occur from the inside out (projection) or from the outside in. (Note: In *Modern Tantra* this is called "absorption." Ramachandra Rao calls it "concentration.") Perhaps most importantly, this transformation leads to integration of the spiritual and the physical, human and Divine.

According to one brief text, *Quintessence of Sri Vidya* by T. V. Kapali Sastry, the goal of physical and mental practices using the Sri Yantra is "self-realization." The author writes that this means realizing that you are the Goddess herself. Meditation on the Sri Yantra, as described later in this chapter, can help you achieve this realization.

There are many goddesses in multiple forms who are linked to the Sri Yantra. However, according to *Quintessence*, the ultimate deity adored through working with the Sri Yantra is the Divine Mother herself. This ultimate mother is the progenitor of all beings in all universes, including all gods and goddesses. She has a thousand names, but is also beyond names.

The author also describes how the Sri Yantra can be viewed as the source of manifestation. The book describes the process of manifestation with the Sri: first there is a desire, from the desire comes a throb, and from this vibration comes a point, the Bindu. The Bindu becomes threefold and forms a triangle, the innermost triangle of the Sri Yantra that is, in fact, a cosmic *yoni* (female genitals) and the source of all manifestation. This brief description is similar to the myth described earlier in the book you are reading.

Quintessence adds that the "light of lights" (a rather Kabalistic-sounding expression) that comes through the cosmic yoni, for the purposes of manifestation, ends up in a threefold classification known as moon, sun, and fire. This sounds like some mystically wonderful but ultimately meaningless philosophical babble, but actually it is very exact. According to a tradition into which I was initiated, people working with the chakra system initially used only three chakras, and they were associated with the sun, the moon, and fire. Therefore, in metaphoric language, the author has described the birth of an individual's energetic system via the Sri Yantra.

Finally, *Quintessence* points out that the Sri Yantra, and therefore Tantra, is a very practical system, advising you to remember the world while you strive for the Divine. It adds that your practices are incomplete unless you can link your growing spirituality with the physical world and your life. As I wrote in *Modern Magick*, "Magick isn't something you do, magick is something you are." Likewise, although you may choose to do things that are Tantric in nature, the goal of studying and practicing Tantra is to *become* a Tantric in your approach to life. Tantra, too, isn't just something you do, it is something you are. To truly be Tantric, the philosophies and practices of Tantra should pervade every aspect of your life. They can improve all aspects of your life.

According to the book *Vamakesvarimatam*, as translated by Sri Lokanath Maharaj (Michael

Magee), the overall goddess of the Sri Yantra, called *Tripura* (or, more completely, *Tripura Sundari*), is the "ultimate primordial Shakti." Shakti is the Tantric concept of the Goddess, and Tripura is the ultimate form of Shakti. (Note that various Tantric texts are often filled with hyperbole of this kind. Therefore, it's not surprising to read in a book about the Sri Yantra that the goddess who is the Sri Yantra is also the ultimate form of Shakti.) Tripura is said to be the source of the "three worlds" (body, mind, spiritual energy).

This book continues to make clear that the Sri Yantra is focused on the goddess. Without the Shakti energy of the goddess, Shiva cannot act. When united with Shakti, Shiva becomes imbued with power. This is followed by a curious statement: "Only by union with Shakti is subtle Shiva known ... and neither karmas nor pleasure are known (without her)."

I find this absolutely astounding, and it requires a bit of explanation. There is a concept known as *Sandhya Bhasha* ("sahnd-yah bahsha"), an expression that literally means "twilight language." A similar English concept would be "to hide in plain sight." Specifically, it refers to the idea that a seemingly obvious statement contains a code for something deeper. If you don't understand the code, you won't understand the mystical meaning. It was quite common for early Tantric works to be written in this style, leading to misinterpretation.

In this case, the words sound like a discussion of qualities of a distant god and goddess, something you might find in any book or writing on Pagan spirituality. But the code takes us deeper.

The prerequisite for understanding that passage is the knowledge of two simple concepts: *Each of us can become aware that we are Shiva. Each of us can become aware that we are Shakti.* The statement, then, clearly means that by uniting with our counterpart, we become imbued with power, we can clear out unwanted karma (through obtaining knowledge), and we experience pleasure. In Western terms, this is a clear expression of sex magick.

I would point out that this seems like it is only talking about a heterosexual pairing, but as I stated, each of us can manifest as Shiva or Shakti. It's the Shiva/Shakti *energy*, not the physical gender, that matters.

Does this interpretation seem like I'm exaggerating? There's more. *Vamakesvarimatam* continues:

Shiva's sun mandala,
(the masculine aspect of the
second, or sexual, chakra)

having opened,
(sends out masculine/
electric/outgoing energy)

melts the moon mandala,
(opening the female aspect
of the second chakra)

causing a flow of birth-nectar-liquor,
(resulting in enlightenment
and the flow of a spiritual-
magickal fluid called amrita)

with its blissful and gladdening ...
(This fluid has spiritual and
magickal powers.)

She becomes Shiva, with no
qualities, no characteristics,
devoid of the form of Time.
(Together, the partners become as
one, and experience enlightenment.)

Although this can be interpreted as a powerful form of sex magick, it does not necessitate physical sexual contact. The key is that we are dealing with spiritual energy, not physicality. Certainly physical relations can be used for this, but mere sexual expression, without knowledge and intention, does not lead to enlightenment. If it did, all people who have sex would be enlightened sex magicians, and the condition of the world indicates that isn't the case.

More Details on the Design of the Sri Yantra

All true yantras, not just the Sri Yantra, are the deity in two-dimensional, linear form. As a form of the God or Goddess, they reveal concepts of infinity, time, space, and polarity. They also represent a mathematical version of ritual practices. In some systems of traditional Tantra, yantras form the core of those practices and are integral to worship and magickal practice. In those and other Tantric traditions, the Sri Yantra is considered the king of all yantras. Magickally, it is considered the most potent spiritual means of accomplishing all that is desired.

Another name for the Sri Yantra is the *Navayoni Chakra* ("Nah-vah-yoh-nee Chah-krah"). *Nava* is Sanskrit for "nine" (the figure is composed of nine central interlocking triangles) and *yoni* means vulva (symbolized by the triangle). The *Bindu* dot in the center is seen as the nucleus of the combined Shiva (static) and Shakti (dynamic) energies condensed into an infinitely powerful point. This Bindu expands and creates. The static and dynamic energies separate, forming two additional points, which, by joining the first one, create a triangle. The multiplication of this triangle forms the Sri Yantra. Thus, this yantra literally defines the creation process. You might want to spend some time meditating on the Sri Yantra with this in mind.

When looking at different versions of the Sri Yantra, you will note everything from slight to dramatic differences in coloring. Some experts will tell you that the colors don't matter, so please don't adopt what I am about to share as some sort of dogmatic truth. It is simply the system with which I am most familiar. Try it! If it works for you, fantastic. If it doesn't work for you, experiment until you find something that does. Then share the results of your experiments with all.

Please look at the full-color version of the Sri Yantra on the cover of this book. The outer "square" is composed of three lines colored white, red and yellow. Inside of this is a yellow space known as a "ground." Together, this threefold system (you will see the concept of threes repeated many times in this image) is said to be symbolic of the entire cosmos that is threefold in nature: physical, mental, and spiritual. There are goddesses associated with points on each of the three lines of the outer square. These lines are sometimes described as the three cities of Tantra. Here is the square and the ground:

Yellow Periphery of the Sri Yantra

Concentric Circles of the Sri Yantra

Within the "ground" are three concentric circles called the *mekhalas* ("meh-kah-lahs"), or girdles. In this version they are yellow, green, and red. Again, the triad represents the three worlds or cities, but the yellow ground between the square and the girdles makes a big difference. That large yellow ground is the dwelling place of Maya, the goddess of illusion who enchants the three worlds. Again, each of the circles has goddesses associated with them. They are collectively known as the first chakra of the Sri Yantra. Some people consider the mekhalas, ground, and outer square to be the first chakra.

Inside these circles are two more concentric rings. The outer ring is the second chakra and has sixteen symbolic lotus petals colored blue. The inner ring is the third chakra with but eight red petals:

Blue Sixteen-Petal Lotus of the Sri Yantra

Red Eight-Petal Lotus of the Sri Yantra

Ten Red Triangles of the Sri Yantra

Fourteen Blue Triangles of the Sri Yantra

Ten Blue Triangles of the Sri Yantra

Inside this red ring are nine interlaced triangles that form forty-three triangles as a result of their interaction. On the outside, colored blue, are fourteen triangles forming the fourth chakra of the Sri Yantra. It is said to be the chakra that bestows all auspiciousness. When you wish to work on practical methods of spiritual evolution (or think about theories concerning it), you work with this chakra.

Next come two rings of ten triangles each, the outer red one and the inner blue one. Together they are where your inner realizations will begin to unfold for you. Working with the outer fifth chakra will help you accomplish every purpose in life. Working with the inner sixth chakra, sometimes called "the great protector," can help protect you from many difficulties.

Eight Red Triangles of the Sri Yantra

White Yoni Triangle of the Sri Yantra

Even deeper is a chakra composed of only eight red triangles. This seventh chakra is said to be helpful in removing physical and mental problems, and can help you rid yourself of unwanted and unneeded desires and infatuations:

When you can work your way through this area of the Sri Yantra, it is believed that you are free of all earthly bonds and stand on the threshold of ultimate realization. In this there is a similarity with the Kabalistic concept of "crossing the abyss."

The eighth chakra is said to give all accomplishments. When you have worked your way to this level of the Sri Yantra, you are on the verge of complete spiritual realization:

The ninth and final chakra or power zone of the Sri Yantra is the Bindu, the virtual Holy of Holies, the sanctum sanctorum. Here is found divine union within total bliss. Here you merge with the universe and become one with the cosmos. Enlightenment? Nirvana? Samadhi? Names become irrelevant as you become pure joy:

Sri Bindu of the Sri Yantra

In some versions of the Sri Yantra, all of the triangles are drawn in red, representing the color of radiant energy as well as the dynamic and fiery elements of cosmos. In those versions the Bindu has no color, representing the finest, most ethereal form of spiritual light. Some versions of the Sri Yantra have different colors based on the artist's imagination, the material on which he or she paints, or simply the colors that the artist has available.

Approaching the Sri Yantra

For a moment, let's go back to T. V. Kapali Sastry's *Quintessence of Sri Vidya*. In it, the author gives some basic requirements for successfully working with the image. Here are my interpretations of his requirements from a more openly Tantric point of view:

1. *To work with the Sri Yantra, you should be a "worshiper of beauty and grace."* This means more than simply seeking out beauty. It means the development of the ability to see beauty in everything, even things that others might not consider beautiful.
2. *To work with the Sri Yantra, you should "reject ugliness in all its forms."* This means more than some sort of external ugliness (ugliness of appearance or action), but goes into rejecting ugliness in thought, word, and deed.

   This combination of seeing beauty in everything and denying that ugliness exists returns us to the concepts of the kleshas described earlier in this book. If you don't understand the concepts, I suggest that you go back and reread chapter 2.
3. *To work with the Sri Yantra, you should not "court squalor and poverty."* Many spiritual systems imply that wealth or even having nice things is an impediment to spiritual disciplines. A typical example of this is the quote from the Bible that says, "Money is the root of all evil." However, the Bible doesn't really say that. Rather, it says, "The love of money is the root of all evil." It is not money or things that take you away from the spiritual, but rather, it is the *desire* for these things. This is identical to the meaning of the klesha of attachment. Even if you don't have certain physical things, you might still want them. That longing for "stuff" can take you away from a spiritual path. It doesn't matter whether you have things or not, it is whether you desire them. I previously described this in the discussion of the kleshas.

   Although some Tantric traditions support giving up all possessions, other traditional Tantric paths recognize the difference between a practitioner owning things and the things owning the practitioner. If your goal in life is the acquisition of things, then yes, they can and probably will keep you from a spiritual path. However, as I have written elsewhere, it's hard to be spiritual when you're not sure where your next meal will come from! *Suffering does not result in spirituality; it just results in suffering.* Extended fasts and even self-mortification are not a part of working with the Sri Yantra or Tantra.
4. *To work with the Sri Yantra, you should be optimistic about life and cheerful.* So many people are quite content to be negative and seem to love sharing their negativity with others, bringing down everyone's mood and energy. This is not the path of a person working with the Sri Yantra or of Tantra. Rather, you should have ultimate faith in the belief that the Goddess will help you move things and events in your favor or help you turn around unwanted things and events and improve them.
5. *To work with the Sri Yantra, you should be clean in body, mind, and spirit.* Bathe before doing work with the Sri Yantra. Wear beautiful clothes and, if you wish, adorn your body. Eat delicious foods.

Tantra is a path of the experience of true enjoyment in life, and this should be shown in everything you do, everything you eat, everything you wear, everything you are. This is about experience, not gluttony.

6. *To work with the Sri Yantra, you should respect the Goddess in all her forms.* In many cultures, women are treated poorly, ranging from receiving lower pay and fewer job opportunities to the cultural acceptance of body mutilation and rape. In some countries, women are actually punished for being raped, while the rapist is let free. In certain cultures, women are punished for the crimes of others in their family through being gang-raped. These horrible actions are unacceptable and must be strongly resisted and denounced by any true Tantric, for all women are manifestations of the Goddess. The Goddess flees from any location where women are mentally, physically, emotionally, or spiritually abused.

   Although this has obvious meaning, there is a deeper meaning, too. The Goddess—or the goddess *energy*—exists in us all. Anything you do to help that energy form of the Goddess manifest is a way of honoring her. Anything you do to prevent her manifestation is a way of showing disrespect.

7. *To work with the Sri Yantra, you should "live a life of absolute sincerity."* This refers to the concept of having personal integrity. It means you should not be deceitful, you should not lie, you should not be a hypocrite. This sounds like something that is easy, but I assure you it is not. Being what the author calls "absolutely sincere" means practicing what has come to be called "radical honesty." This concept is simply that honesty is always the best policy.

   Unfortunately, some people treat honesty as a metaphorical stick with which to brutally attack others rather than a way to share truth. For example, telling someone who is dying (yet is terrified of death), "Yeah, you're dying," is truthful, but is also a horrible and vicious approach. Sharing with the person (if you believe it) that every living thing eventually dies and death is just a stage of existence we all must go through, one that will lead to rebirth without pain or suffering and a life filled with energy and potential joy, is a way to begin honestly answering by sharing truth without being cruel.

8. *To work with the Sri Yantra, you should understand the dance of Maya.* Maya is a goddess of such breathtaking beauty that her "dance" takes us away from seeing reality. The "dance of the senses" may prevent us from seeing the spiritual world that is all around. As Tantrics, we can fully enjoy the world via our senses and also understand that there is far more to life in the invisible spiritual worlds.

9. *To work with the Sri Yantra, the mind should be quiet.* This has two meanings. First, we all have opinions, prejudices, preconceived beliefs, and so on. It is valuable to recognize and understand them because they actually limit us. They form a tight little box that surrounds us and prevents us from experiencing more—physically, emotionally, and spiritually. If

we think, "What I believe is the way things are and everyone must understand this," we should immediately ask ourselves, "Why?" It may be that what we believe is based on logic and reason. But it is also possible that our ideas are based on false beliefs that prevent us from experiencing life and freedom to the fullest. We should eliminate, one by one, each of our limiting beliefs, and we should do this as soon as we become aware of them. This can be done when we become aware of them during meditation and realize they are beliefs, not reality. We can choose to discard whatever is not helpful.

Second, each of us has an inner voice that is constantly talking, talking, talking to us. Even when we're quiet, it talks to us. One person told me that she refers to that voice as "the babbler." When we still that voice, we open our ears—and our hearts, minds, spirits, and souls—to a greater voice. This is a basic concept of true meditation. When you do this, the goddess of the Sri Yantra will take you as her own. One day you may discover that you have been on a potent spiritual path without even realizing it. It will be the path she has for you, and she will guard you, care for you, and love you as you walk the path.

One of the most common methods of meditation is the use of a mantra. So for the next part of this chapter, let's examine one such technique.

A Mantra for the Sri Yantra: *Om Hrim Strim Hum Phat*

There are many mantras associated with the Sri Yantra. Others are dedicated to the goddess (Tripura Sundari) associated with the yantra, the many subgoddesses (devis), or just the powers of the yantra. This mantra is a simple, general-purpose, positive mantra for the Sri Yantra that can be performed while gazing at the image.

Traditionally, it should be repeated 108 times. This is facilitated with a *mala*, a string of 108 beads plus one extra large bead, the meru bead. While looking at the yantra, hold the beads across your left hand, palm up. Start at the meru bead and move one bead with your fingers for each single repetition of the mantra. When you come to the meru bead again, you have completed one "round."

As you repeat the mantra, you'll find that you start speeding up. This is natural and appropriate. As you speed up, get quieter. Often, the repetition of mantras by Tantrics is described as "mumbling." Eventually you may end up repeating the mantra silently. I'll provide more information on malas and their use in chapter 7.

The purpose of this particular mantra is to bring balance, purification, wisdom, clarity, sustenance, and more. Here are some brief specifics for each word of the mantra:

Om—This word is so important that it has its own symbol, the *omkara,* included with the Sanskrit alphabet. It is said to be the initial source of all sound and of the divine power of vibration. To remind us of its importance as the basis for all vibration, it is said at the beginning of numerous mantras.

The Omkara

Hrim—This is the vibration of purification and transformation. It is the mantra of Parvati and Kali, consorts of Shiva. It is also the mantra of Sundari, the beautiful one. Tripura Sundari, the thrice-beautiful one, is the goddess of the Sri.

Strim—This is the sound of pure shakti energy. It is action and movement that pushes you toward achieving your desired goals. It can be harnessed for new beginnings and new births as well as for sustenance.

Hum—This sound is used for divine protection, knowledge, and clarity. Where Strim can power you in any desired direction, the energy from this sound can help you cut through the illusions caused by maya that prevent you from seeing reality. Thus, it can help cut through confusion and a lack of direction.

Phat—This is the thunderbolt mantra! This powerful mantra provides protection and destroys obstacles. It can be used by itself for banishings in the ten directions. It occurs at the end of some mantras, as it has the power to concentrate the force of the other parts of the mantra.

Pronunciation

Om begins at the back of the throat and ends with the closing of the lips. In this way it covers all sounds capable of being made by the human voice. Focus on the initial vowel sound to project its energy to others. Stress the final "m" to absorb its energy within you. This is especially good for healing work. To reveal the pronunciation of Om, it is often spelled Aum.

Some people pronounce it "ah-oom," while in other places it may be pronounced "um," "ung," "ahng," or something else. This has to do with the various dialects found throughout the Indian subcontinent and into Tibet. As with all mantras, experiment with vibration, then let your heart and spirit reveal what is the correct pronunciation for you.

Hrim sounds like something between "rim," as in the description of the top edge of a drinking glass, and "ream," as in five hundred sheets of paper. However, it begins with the "h," an empty, aspirated, breathy sound.

Strim sounds like "stream" and rhyming with "trim."

Hum sounds as it is spelled, or as the joke goes, "What you do when you don't know the words."

The thunderbolt mantra, *phat*, is a bit more difficult to describe. Think of quickly saying the words "top hat." Then remove the initial "to-" in "top." Thus, you get "pat" but with the empty, aspirated "h" sound (like you get when the "h" starts a word, such as "hello") inserted between the "p" and the "a." Phat is *not* pronounced "fat."

Deeper Still

Tripura, the triple goddess, rules the outer square of the Sri Yantra. In one tradition, the three rings represent the three Divine Mothers sometimes seen in statues intended for worship—the *Shakti Trimurti*—consisting of Saraswati, Lakshmi, and Parvati. It also reminds me of the three "mother letters" found in the Kabalah and the three forms of the Goddess: maiden, mother, and crone.

As I wrote earlier, the Sri Yantra is considered by many to be the king of the yantras, although considering all of the goddesses associated with it, calling it the queen of the yantras might be more accurate! The Sri Yantra is the supreme yantra. All other traditional yantras are believed to be derived from it. Therefore, it could be said to both include and transcend all other yantras. That means the benefits of all other yantras, individually and collectively, are manifested with the Sri Yantra. It is claimed by some that the Sri Yantra was divinely revealed. While that's a beautiful metaphor, I must dispute that based on history. Earlier versions of yantras that may have developed into the Sri Yantra have been discovered. Still, when you think about the amazing and magnificent complexity of the Sri Yantra (I've barely scratched the surface), the way the yantra evolved into its present form is a great and joyous mystery.

As a side note, you've probably heard of *mandalas*. These are beautiful and symmetrical drawings. Although yantras are also symmetrical and, therefore, are mandalas, not all mandalas are yantras. Mandalas are beautiful drawings. They are not a deity in two-dimensional form unless they are also specific yantras. The Sri Yantra is the body of the Great Mother Goddess and should be treated as such.

This concept of the Sri Yantra being the Goddess gets tricky. The Goddess is the Sri Yantra, but if you need a point to say where the Goddess's energy resides, it is in the Bindu at the center. She is the center and is the entire image.

Similarly, she permeates the entire universe. This Great Goddess acts in five ways, all of which emanate from the Bindu of the Sri Yantra. They are:

1. The emanation of the universe from the uncreated, primal source.
2. The projection of creative energy into the universe from that source.
3. The emanation of the energy that preserves the created universe.
4. The withdrawal of those energies to allow dissolutions and endings.
5. The holding of the withdrawn energy awaiting its use in the next cycle.

Note how this corresponds with the development and return of the energy as described by the action of the Dasa Mahavidyas, the ten wisdom goddesses described in chapter 4. I would also point out that this ancient Pagan tradition showing the Goddess having the threefold function of life—creation, maintenance, dissolution—has been subsumed into the functions of the Brahma-Vishnu-Shiva triumvirate of male deities found in modern Vedic Hinduism. This is similar to the way that aspects of Pagan goddesses have been absorbed into the functions of a male deity in modern Western monotheistic religions. Like other forms of Paganism, working with the Sri Yantra within traditional Tantra truly honors the Goddess and also acknowledges the God.

Acting as a Tantric Student of Sri Vidya

There is a word that means a great deal to me: *praxis*. It means "putting theory into action."

As you learn the philosophy, wisdom, and techniques of Tantra and Sri Vidya, there are certain concepts I believe you should put into practice:

- **Every day you should show respect for the world.** Do something that helps you, others, and the environment.
- **Love and respect your life and the lives of every creature.**
- **See the manifestation of the Divine in everything.**
- **Trust yourself and cultivate faith in yourself.** Know that nothing is impossible because you are supported by the Divine.
- **Keep yourself and your surroundings beautiful.** Make the area where you meditate especially beautiful.
- **Do what you must do.** This goes beyond Crowley's famous axiom "Do what thou wilt shall be the whole of the Law." It means you are free to do *whatever* you want to do. However, you are also responsible for whatever you choose to do.
- **Never feel guilt for your actions.** Guilt is often caused by the feeling that you have committed a sin, but sin is just an acronym for "Self-Inflicted Nonsense." If you do something that bothers you, understand that what happened, happened. You cannot change that. You can make amends, if appropriate, for things you realize you should not have done. You can resolve not to repeat things you now believe you should not have done. But there is no reason for or value in feelings of guilt.
- **Don't be hard on yourself for your rate of spiritual advancement.** Don't focus on thoughts such as *I should be doing more* or *I should be advancing more quickly.* Spiritual development is not a steady line on a chart. It occurs when it does. Be grateful for each advancement, but don't punish yourself with feelings that such advancement doesn't happen fast enough. It will happen when it happens.
- **You have an amazing and limitless capacity for advancement. Don't undermine it.** For example, don't accept spiritual intimidation from others. You are just as good as anyone else. Fire or dismiss teachers who tell you that you are weak or slow and they will "fix" you. You are not a broken machine. A person who tells you things like that is primarily a businessman, not a teacher.

  False teachers like that will use many tricks to deceive you. One of the primary tricks is their ability to push one of two major "buttons" in a person: fear and guilt. They trigger such responses in followers to take advantage of them. Don't let any person—and especially don't let any so-called teacher—instill fear or guilt in you. Fire them! Let them go! If they know more than you and have more spiritual skills, it only indicates that you lack information and practice. It does *not* mean you are inferior.
- **Finally, remember that your spiritual practices should not be a hardship.** They should bring you joy and bliss. Don't let any form of self-discipline in your spiritual (or mental or physical) practices become torture. Or as I like to say, "If it ain't fun, why bother?"

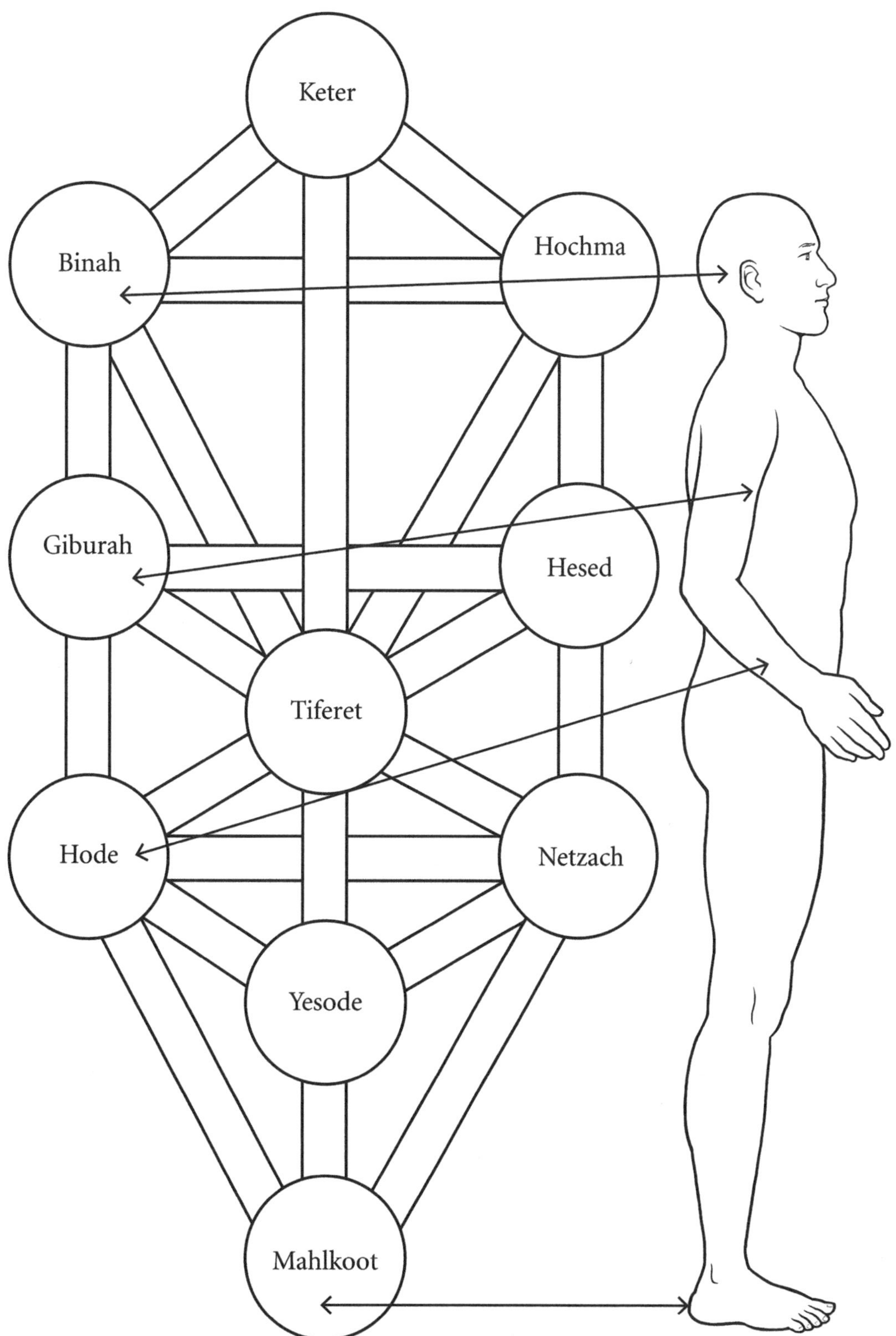

The Kabalistic Tree of Life Projected on the Body

The Sri Yantra and the Human Body—2D

On the Kabalistic Tree of Life, various areas of sephiroth on the Tree represent etheric power centers on the body. Looking at the Tree, it is as if a person backed into it, absorbing its beauty and wisdom (see illustration).

Similarly, the Sri Yantra can be projected onto the body (see illustration). Where two lines cross in the triangles, it is called a *sandhi* ("sahn-dee") point. More important are the locations where three lines intersect. These are called *marmas* and are considered to be where life energy accumulates and resides.

It is said among martial artists that the points on the body that, when struck, can harm or kill are the same points that can heal. Indeed, the marmas and other points are used in powerful healing techniques, including the use of vacuum (cupping), pressure (acupressure), needle insertion (acupuncture), and even phlebotomy or bloodletting for healing (wet cupping). These techniques are still practiced in India and became the basis for similar techniques in China.

It is believed that all of the important points of the human body are also found in the Sri Yantra. Therefore, by meditating on the Sri Yantra, a martial artist or healer can access the location of every vital spot in the human body.

For those who are interested in some of the "magickal edges" of occultism, author Kenneth Grant has gone into greater detail as to how the marmas can be used in sex magick. Basically, by stimulating the marmas on a woman, her body is triggered to produce powerful magickal fluids that can be used with great magickal efficacy. The key to the marmas is the Sri Yantra. I'll be describing more of the uses of marmas, especially for healing, later.

Symbolic Representation of the Sri Yantra Projected on the Human Body Using the Vitruvian Man

The Sri Yantra and the Human Body—3-D

There is a wonderful, small book that really helps open minds about the nature of the universe and reality entitled *Flatland.* It was written in 1884 by a British mathematician, theologian, and schoolmaster with the repetitive name Edwin Abbott Abbott (1836–1926) using the pen name "A Square." In it, the main character is a square in a two-dimensional universe, having length and width but no thickness. He ends up visiting our three-dimensional world, and when he returns home and describes the properties of the three-dimensional world, his fellow two-dimensional denizens think he's insane.

Originally written as a satire about the strict hierarchy of classes in Victorian England (personally, I prefer Oscar Wilde's hilarious play *The Importance of Being Earnest* for this purpose), it is better known for trying to explain the concept of understanding different dimensions. Reading this book for this purpose can be quite mind-expanding.

And that leads to the question "Is it possible to extend two-dimensional images into the third dimension?" Charles Stansfeld Jones (1886–1950), using the pen name Frater Achad, did this for the Tree of Life in his amazing book *The Anatomy of the Body of God*, where he projects the Tree in multiple directions, creating an amazing appearance of a multidimensional "macrosmic snowflake" crystal (see illustration):

The body can be divided into two main parts: the head and trunk, and the legs. The spinal cord, which supports the trunk and goes into the head, is the "axis" of the body. In Tantra, the mystical *Mount Meru* is called "the axis of the earth." The spine is called the *Meru Danda*, "the axis staff."

The Sri Yantra, in three dimensions, is considered to be a form of Mount Meru and is sometimes called the Sri Meru. (Mount Meru, or *Sumeru*, is a metaphorical home of the gods, like Mount Olympus. It is also symbolic of Shiva's spine and energy pathway, and your own spine.) Therefore, in the tradition of "as above, so below," the Sri represents the body. Or more accurately, the human body encases a spark of the Divine as its living soul, and as the Sri Yantra is the Divine, it means they are literally one and the same. So if we meditate on any of the aspects of the Sri Yantra, we are manifesting those qualities within ourselves. Here is a sample of how to begin to use the Sri Yantra (see final illustration).

The Macrocosmic Snowflake

A 3-D Sri Yantra

Sri Yantra in 3-D Projected on the Body

SIX

The Mystical Key, Part II: Sri Magick

Beginning Magickal Work with the Sri Yantra

In the Sri Yantra tradition, every part of the Goddess's body is sacred. By looking at and meditating upon a part of her body, represented by a *devi*, or minor goddess, you can create change. In this beginning system, that is exactly what you will do.

Step One: Banish your area. You may use the Mahavidya banishing described in chapter 4 or any other banishing. Sit in a comfortable position, facing east. Your Sri Yantra should be in front of you.

Step Two: Focus on the issue you wish to deal with. In the outer lotus, starting at the bottom and moving counterclockwise, the petals represent the following:

- The five elements: earth, water, fire, air, ether
- The five senses: hearing, touch, seeing, taste, smelling
- The parts capable of grasping: the mouth, the feet, the hands
- Three more associations: the anus, the genitals, and changing of the mind

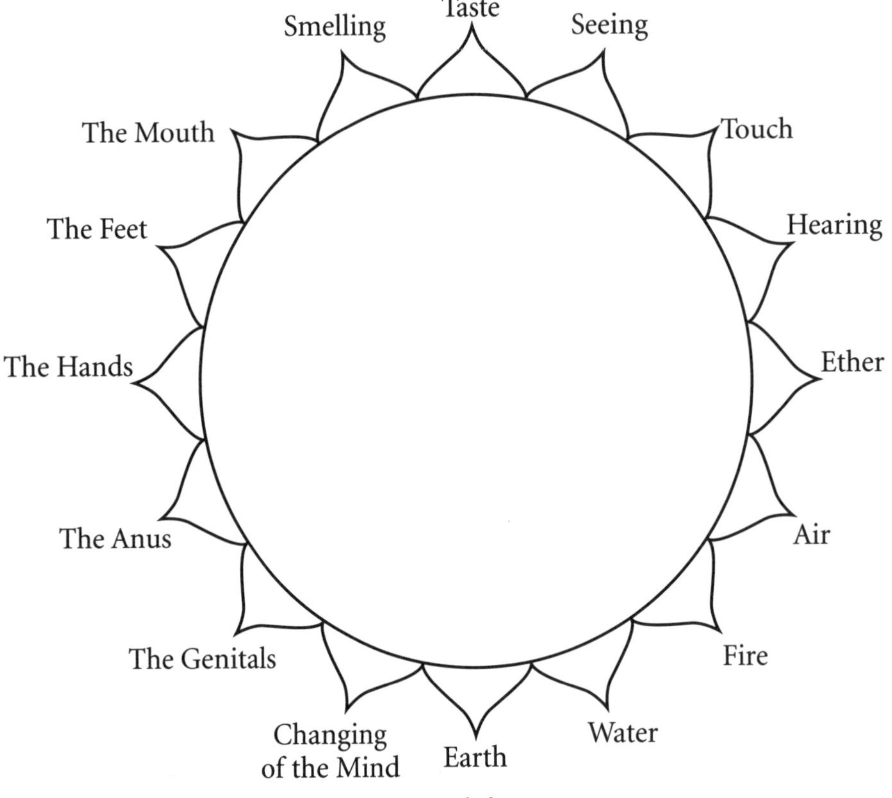

Sixteen-Petaled Lotus

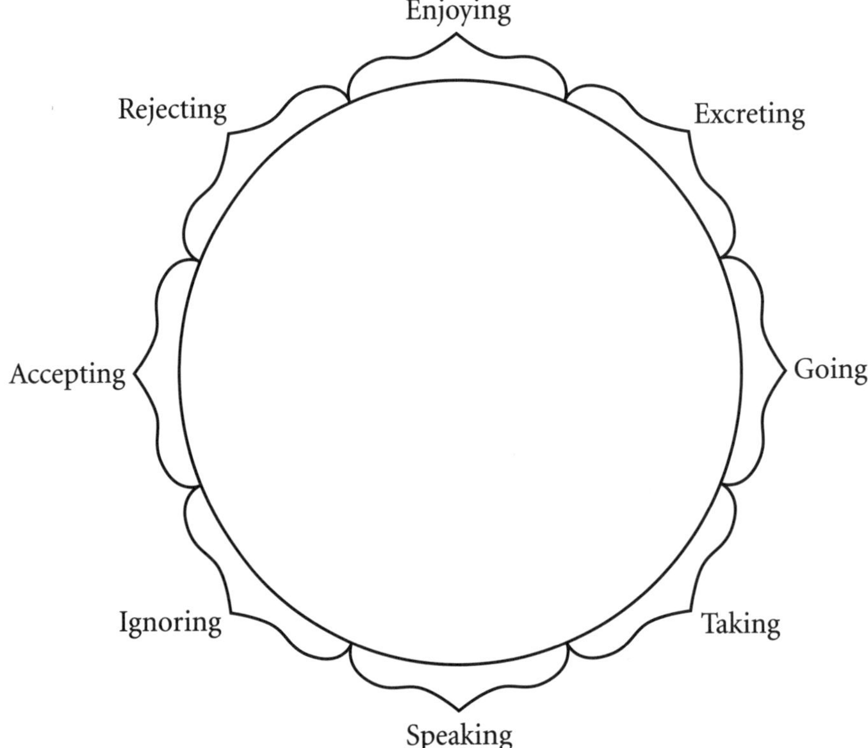

Eight-Petaled Lotus

Associations for the eight-petaled inner lotus also begin at the bottom and go counterclockwise. They are speaking, taking, going, excreting, enjoying, rejecting, accepting, and ignoring.

The use of elemental magick can be very powerful. Here are some associations taken from my *Modern Magick* that will give you information on which element is good for various purposes:

Air: Schooling, memory, intellectualism, teaching, tests, divination, communications, travel, writing, organizing and organizations, groups of all kinds, theorizing, drug addiction.

Earth: Money, jobs, promotions, business, investments, material objects, fertility, agriculture, health foods, ecology, conservation, stock market, antiques, old age, museums, buildings, construction, progress, the home, the physical world, daily necessities such as food and clothing.

Fire: Success, sex, passion, banishing some illnesses, military, conflicts, protection, courts, law, police and sheriff's agencies, contests, competitions, private detectives, dowsing, treasure hunting, gambling, athletics, strength, good health, war, terrorism. On a more personal level, anything related to the Freudian "id," including the lower emotions of absurd desire and lust (i.e., too much desire or lust), anger, and violent emotions. Also things having speed.

Water: Higher forms of love and the deeper emotions such as compassion, faith, loyalty, and devotion. Also friendship, partnerships, unions of any kind, affection, contract negotiation, beauty, rest, recuperation, meditation, spirituality, healing wounds, restoring growth, childbirth and children, the home, receptivity, family, swimming, diving, fishing, ancestors, medicine, hospitals, doctors and nurses, clairvoyance.

Ether (also known as *akasha* or spirit): Spirituality, the Divine, magick, change, transformation, alchemy, unification, balance, the soul.

Notice that a few of these listings seem duplicated, appearing in more than one of the elemental categories. As an example, the home is listed under earth and water. This is not an error. Rather, it allows you to more closely define the terms. Under the element of earth, the home refers to a structure, the building in which you live. Under the element of water, the home refers to the qualities of home life: love, stability, support, etc.

As you may have guessed, the associations for each lotus petal may be taken either literally or symbolically. For example, excreting can deal with removal of body wastes or eliminating anything that is no longer needed in your life.

Step Three: Once you have established your focus on the appropriate petal for the issue at hand, respectfully ask the devi (goddess) of the petal for help in dealing with the appropriate issue. When you have finished asking, stop. Be quiet. Listen. The response may come immediately, in a dream, or over time. Be open and ready to accept what you learn.

Step Four: If you do not have any sticks of incense burning, light one. Take the stick of incense and wave it in a clockwise circle three times in front of the image.

Step Five: Banish the area again.

That's it. This meditation is pretty straightforward and doesn't require a lot of extra work. The most challenging part of the magick is to determine which petal should have your focus.

Worship of the Goddess of the Sri Yantra

Traditionally, there are four ways to worship the goddess who is the Sri Yantra. I think there should also be a combination of the four, but I'll leave that for you to work out.

The first three, even if done mentally, are considered *projective*, or external, methods. They are focused on the nurturing, protective, and healing aspects of the goddesses of the Sri. Note, however, that the Sri is considered to be external to the practitioner.

The Fiery Path of the Mind

One of the basic rituals of Tantra is one that is found in almost all ancient practices: the fire ritual. One such ritual is described later in this book. It consists primarily of building a fire and "giving" to it symbolic items. This practice is found in varying forms among ancient Pagans around the world and is practiced by modern Pagans. Ancient Jews also practiced it in the Temple in Jerusalem, and the practice of lighting ritual candles by Jews and Catholics may be a remnant of the practice.

The ancient Tantric fire ritual follows this pattern. Perhaps the most unique feature of the Tantric system is the special container for the fire—or the care taken in building an area for the fire—that is used in the ritual. You can use a havan kund copper fire pit as described in the next chapter or just a square fire pit, simply dug in the ground or made of bricks. If made of bricks, it can be made above ground or laid into the ground.

This form of worship is a variation of the magickal ritual just described. Have the Sri in the east and the fire pit between you and the image. By focusing on a part of the Sri Yantra, with an understanding of the goddess there, you are linking to the goddess of that part of the Sri as you present gifts to the fire. You can use the beginning concepts described in the previous section or the alternate and more exacting goddesses described later in this chapter. You can also offer any type of gift you like. For some practitioners, it is incense. For others, it is performing a task in honor of the goddess. This task can be an active act or set of acts (such as working at a charity) or a sacrificial act wherein you do not do something (such as not eating your favorite food for a period of time).

You do not need to have an actual fire to follow this path of worship with the Sri (technically, this mental technique is known as *Samayachara*, "Sah-mai-yah-char-uh"). You can do the entire ritual in your mind—an astral version of this technique, if you will.

Some modern Vedic Hindus believe that this is "their" system and you must be initiated into their tradition in order to use it. Tantrics laugh at such posturing among those trying to control others. From a Tantric point of view, spiritual leaders should lead and help others on their personal paths toward enlightenment, not control them.

The Worship of Three Forms of the Sri

When you understand even some of the concepts of the Sri Yantra and that it *is* the Goddess, it follows that you can simply worship her. This second way to worship the Goddess is through the recitation of mantras in her honor. It can also be done through the use of incense, a special lamp (*diya*) bringing light, and the sounding of a bell (*ghanta*).

These tools and their use are described in the next chapter.

There are generally three forms of the Sri Yantra that can be used for this purpose. The first is the colorful two-dimensional image just described. The second is with the use of a three-dimensional version of the Sri. Alternatively, an image of the Goddess herself, a *murthi*, in the form of a statue or drawing, can be used.

The third form, however, is different. Remember that we are supposed to honor all women as manifestations of the Goddess. In this mode (technically called *Dakshinachara*, "Dahk-sheen-uh-char-uh") of working with the Sri, a real woman is used as the Goddess Sri. The woman is usually seated on some sort of raised platform, and the Goddess is invoked into her. Because she is so sacred, it is only her feet that are honored. They may be washed, blessed, kissed, censed, etc. In more secretive Tantric traditions, however, the honoring of a woman as the Goddess is more focused toward the second chakra. See the material on the yoni tantra in the last chapter of this book for details.

The Sacred Path of Tantric Union

This third way of worshiping the Goddess (technically known as *Kaulachara*, "Kah-ool-uh-char-uh") seems to be the obvious next step. Since the Goddess is in each of us, the Sri Yantra in any geometric form is replaced by a man, a woman, or a couple. There are no limitations in the way the Goddess is honored, from bathing her to giving blessings, censing, kissing, or more, as long as it is in honor of the Goddess.

Absorption into Sri

For most people, even among Tantrics, the Kaulachara method of working with the Sri is as far as they will go. There is a fourth way of worship, (technically called *Vamachara*, "Vah-muh-char-uh") which to me seems the inevitable, transcendent result of continuing with the third path.

The Goddess has many faces. Perhaps most often we see her as a loving, kind, and healing goddess. But she also has a face of dissolution and destruction, a necessary part of existence on the physical plane.

In this mode of worship, we allow ourselves to become absorbed into the Goddess. Her destructive face removes our false egos and the illusions of *maya*. With these blockages removed, the kundalini energy can rise freely to the crown chakra, opening the way to enlightenment as we literally become one with the Goddess.

Many people consider this path to be dangerous. No wonder! Most people cling tenaciously to their false egos and their concepts of reality that are heavily influenced by maya. To strip these aspects of consciousness from a person who is not prepared for it is like shoving a person out on a circus high wire without a net. It can be terrifying to the unprepared.

Most commentators make clear that none of these four methods of worshiping the Sri Yantra is superior to the others. They are all available so that a person can choose which method he or she needs at any particular time. However, it seems to me that there is a natural evolution from one method to another. I suggest beginning with the first and moving on only when you are ready, and only if you wish to do so.

An Alternate Rite

This version is particularly suited to asking the Goddess for help with emotional issues.

Step One: Bathe, then clean and banish your area. Place the Sri Yantra in the east, covered with a cloth of any color.

Step Two: Light some incense and candles or small lamps (*diyas*: see chapter 7). Use as much incense and as many lamps as you like.

Step Three: Offer a fresh flower and a piece of fresh fruit to the Sri.

Step Four: Take the covering off of the Sri. If you have an image of a particular deity you also want to include (such as your Ishta Devata, as described in chapter 3), you should do so.

Step Five: Take a container of water (such as a kailash) and a leaf from any tree. Use the leaf to sprinkle yourself with the purifying water. Then sprinkle the Sri Yantra and deity image.

Step Six: Close your eyes. Ask the Goddess and your deity to bless you and grant your wishes. Then ask for the specific thing(s) you want help to achieve or change.

Step Seven: Thank the Goddess and your deity for their help. Put away the image of your deity and cover the Sri. Eat the fruit and put the flower in a vase on your personal altar. Banish the area to close the rite.

Advanced Magick with the Sri Yantra

Working with the Devis (Goddesses)

As I wrote earlier, this material on the Sri Yantra has been the most difficult of any I've ever written. How much should I include before my readers' eyes start to glaze over because I've given too much information? In the past I've often said that I'd rather leave people saying I gave too much information than too little, but there comes a point where too much is daunting and will put people off. Today I no longer want to share too much information and I certainly don't want to provide too little. I want to share the right amount of information and I want to share it in a way you can use. With what I've shared so far on the Sri Yantra, you have a large amount of potential work you can do.

Another way of working with the energies of the petals of the lotuses is by identifying with the specific goddess who is located at or *seated* in each petal. Because this version comes from a different tradition, you'll notice that in some instances the powers of the goddesses of each petal are different from the ones listed in this chapter. One system does not invalidate the other; they simply are different.

However, it can be confusing to share multiple systems. I like to say that the system I've shared so far is easier but more exoteric. It's not as precise as the following system, but it's a good place to learn the concepts and begin working with the power of the Sri.

If you are feeling challenged by the concepts and possibilities of the Sri Yantra I've presented so far, you can pass over this section and not attempt to work with it—for now. Instead, move on to the following section. Or better yet, return to the beginning of this book and study it some more. By the time you get back here, you may be ready for it.

If, however, what you have read makes sense to you and you have successfully worked with some of the practices described, you will find this alternative and more advanced look at Sri Yantra work compelling. It covers how to access the goddesses of the outer lotus ring and the goddesses of the outer ring of triangles. My hope is that it will whet your appetite for more information on the Sri Yantra.

The Sri Yantra

Although images of the Sri Yantra usually show the outer square as completed or sealed, the initiated version, which I have used in this book, shows it open in four directions. In order to get into the Sri Yantra, rather than simply looking at the appropriate section, you travel through one of these four gates. If you visualize this image in three dimensions, you can say that these are the gates of the cardinal directions—east, west, north, and south. (Note: In the 3-D version, there are actually six gates, with an additional one above and below the figure; but for our purposes we just work with four visible gates.)

Guarding the northern gateway at the top of the image is Shiva. You enter through this gate when you are looking to obtain *wisdom* directly from the devas. Guarding the eastern gate at the right is the ancient sky god Indra. Visualize Indra as a man with four arms, carrying a thunderbolt and riding a white elephant. Indra is known to slash open the clouds with his thunderbolts in order to release the rain. The key here is the concept of the sound of the thunder. So you enter this gate if you wish to learn more about *mantras* directly from the goddesses themselves. The mantras they provide can help you find solutions in the areas they control.

At the bottom, southern gate is Vishnu, the preserver. The deities are preserved by our dedication to them, so enter through this gate if you wish to devote yourself to a goddess and learn directly from her what you need to do to honor her. This path of devotion is known as *bhakti yoga*.

Finally, at the western gate to the left, is Brahma. You enter through this gate when you want to discover *rites and rituals* for working with a goddess.

Note: The gates we aren't dealing with are the path of words (below) and the path of liberation (above).

In this system, we approach the Sri Yantra from the outside and move inward. It is believed by some that this will invariably awaken the kundalini. You can also worship by allowing the Sri Yantra to radiate its energy outward to create prosperity and harmony in your life. One way to do this is with the repetition of the mantra given earlier as you use the mala to count your repetitions and use the Sri Yantra as a focal point for your visual attention.

The number of potential correspondences between the deities and the Sri Yantra dwarfs the few that are used with the Kabalistic Tree of Life. Since this chapter is intended to introduce you to the Sri Yantra and not overwhelm you, I'm not going to include all of those correspondences and Tantric goddesses here. Instead, my goal is to give you both the flavor of working this way with the Sri Yantra as well as practical uses for this type of practice.

In a moment I'll give you an example of a technique you can use. First, however, I need to share a bit more theory.

Although the Sri Yantra looks like it is only a symmetrical geometrical image, virtually every part of the figure is representative of something else. The outer square represents the enclosing walls or fence of the Tantric practitioner. The three lines—white, red, and yellow—each have a set of *devis*, or subdeities, that are nothing less than aspects of the Goddess.

When dealing with deities who are not part of the familiar Western pantheons, I have always considered that a key to understanding them is to try to get into the minds of the people who named the goddesses. A goddess with a name that in English is *Agitate*, for example, means to stir things up and get them going. *Melt* means to break things down so they'll merge and come together. *Madden* means to create an unstoppable desire to do or achieve something. I'll be giving more specific examples later.

When looking at all the goddess associations on the Sri Yantra, you will see that some of the names are repeated on various levels, or chakras (in this case, meaning "circles" or "rings," but also associated with the famous set of major chakras described more fully later), of the image. Sometimes the names are modified. This is because the powers of each aspect of the goddess, as represented by the name, indicate the power of the goddess modified by the chakra. This is similar to the way in astrology that a planet's meaning is modified by the house it's in or the way the meaning of a tarot card is modified by its position in a spread. Here, for example, a goddess dealing with growth in the first chakra (dealing with survival issues) will have different powers than the goddess of a same or similar name in the fourth chakra, associated with love. The gate you choose to enter—to learn mantras rather than rituals, for example—also modifies both the individual meaning of the goddess and the meaning of the chakra.

Although there are several goddesses of the gated square, I'm not going to explain them here for two reasons. First, their locations in the outer square are irregular and challenging to place and remember. Second, they deal with things in the external, physical world and are not relevant to this specific magickal work. The important thing to consider about the square, because it deals with the outer world, is that we can misinterpret things due to maya.

The "girdle" of three circles relates to the first chakra. It has to do with survival, grounding, stability, fears, self-preservation, etc. The circles also relate to other triads, such as body-mind-spirit and the three major deities and their consorts.

Next comes the second chakra, a wheel of sixteen symbolic lotus petals. There is a goddess who oversees this entire wheel. She is the red-skinned goddess who is named Tripureshi. You can obtain all of the effects of the influences of this chakra of the Sri Yantra by visualizing Tripureshi in the center of the lotus petals. She is draped in fabulous gems and carries a mala (symbolic of spirituality) and a book (symbolic of wisdom). You can meditate on her by using her mantra: *Aim Klim Sauh.*

But if you want to be more precise, you can work with one aspect of the Goddess at a time. These devis or shaktis are known as the *nityakalas* ("nit-yuh-call-uhs"). Visualize each as having four arms. In three of their hands they hold a noose (to destroy the false ego), an elephant goad (to drive you forward on your spiritual path), or a pot full of nectar (to feed wisdom to your soul). With the fourth hand they each make the sign of giving (fingers together and pointing up, with the palm out). Like Tripureshi, they are very red.

Each devi or yogini is in one petal. To use the following list of names, start at the bottom of the wheel and move counterclockwise, seating one devi in each petal. Their names represent powers or qualities you can cultivate and strengthen, or regulate and control. These powers are modified by being associated with the second chakra, which has to do with the emotions, desire, fluidity, mental and physical flexibility, and healthy sexuality. The goddesses are as follows:

1. *Kamakarshini*
   ("Kah-mah-car-shee-nee"),
   procreation, attraction, lust
2. *Buddhyakarshini*
   ("Bood-yah-car shee-nee"),
   mind, decision making, discrimination
3. *Ahamkarakarshini*
   ("Ah-hahm-car-uh-car-shee-nee"), ego
4. *Shabdakarshini*
   ("Shab-dah-car-shee-nee"), sound
5. *Sparsakarshini*
   ("Spar-sah-car-shee-nee"), touch
6. *Rupakarshini*
   ("Roo-pah-car-shee-nee"), vision
7. *Rasakarshini*
   ("Rah-sah-car-shee-nee"), taste
8. *Gandhakarshini*
   ("Gahnd-hah-car-shee-nee"), smell
9. *Chittakarshini*
   ("Cheet-tah-car-shee-nee"),
   mind, intellect
10. *Dhairakarshini*
    ("Dai-rah-car-shee-nee"),
    courage, steadiness, valor
11. *Smrityakarshini*
    ("Smreet-yah-car-shee-nee"), memory
12. *Namakarshini*
    ("Nah-mah-car-shee-nee"), name
13. *Bijakarshini*
    ("Bee-jah-car-shee-nee"),
    seed, growth, semen
14. *Atmakarshini*
    ("Aht-mah-car-shee-nee"),
    self, etheric body
15. *Amritakarshini*
    ("Ahm-ree-tah-car-shee-nee"),
    immortality, revivification
16. *Sarirakarshini*
    ("Sah-ree-rah-car-shee-nee"),
    mortality, the physical body

Consider the names (or, more accurately, the meaning of the names just given) in relation to the second chakra. *Ahamkarakashini* is about the ego modified by one aspect of the chakra, its focus on mental flexibility. Is your ego dogmatic and closed or open and fluid? *Smrityakarshini* allows you to look at how you have used your emotions and other second-chakra associations in the past and consider how to use them in the future. I'll let you contemplate and consider the others.

The next ring of eight lotus petals also has goddesses associated with each petal, and their association with the third chakra modifies them.

Next comes the first ring of the forty-three triangles of the Sri Yantra. The presiding devi is the bright red and very beautiful *Tripura Vasini*. She radiates light and energy as bright as a thousand suns, has large breasts that rise with her breath, and holds a book and a mala.

The fourteen shaktis of these blue triangles are known as the *arkashanis*, or "attractors," and are associated with the chief *nadis*, or energy paths, of the body, of which the Ida, Pingala, and Sushumna are the most famous. They are proud, wanton, young, red, and decorated with gems. They hold in their hands the typical devices, including a noose, an elephant goad, a mirror (to reflect the true self), and a wine cup full of nectar.

These goddesses, again starting at the bottom of the ring and moving counterclockwise, are as follows:

1. *Sarvasanksobhini*
   ("Sahr-vah-sank-so-bee-nee"),
   the force that stirs or agitates.
2. *Sarvavidravini*
   ("Sahr-vah-vihd-rah-vee-nee"),
   the force that makes things melt or flood.
3. *Sarvakarshini*
   ("Sahr-vah-car-shee-nee"),
   the force that attracts.
4. *Sarvahladini*
   ("Sahr-vah-lah-dee-nee"),
   that which is pleasing and makes people joyful and brings delight.
5. *Sarvasammohini*
   ("Sahr-vah-sahm-moh-hee-nee"),
   the force that deludes.
6. *Sarvastambhini*
   ("Sahr-vah-stam-bee-nee"),
   that which obstructs or immobilizes and keeps things in place.
7. *Sarvajhrumbhini* ("Sahr-vahj-room-bee-nee"), that which gives you needed rest to unload what is not needed, such as toxins, almost exploding them away.
8. *Sarvavasankari*
   ("Sahr-vah-vah-sahn-care-ee"),
   that which brings things under control.
9. *Sarvaranjini*
   ("Sahr-vah-rahn-jee-nee"),
   the force that lets you see things as you will, resulting in ecstasy.
10. *Sarvamadini*
    ("Sahr-vah-mah-dee-nee"),
    that which maddens, puts you out of control, or intoxicates.
11. *Sarvathasadhini*
    ("Sahr-vah-tah-sah-dee-nee"),
    that which helps you accomplish all things that need to be done and fulfill desires. That which makes one prosperous.
12. *Sarvasampattipurini*
    ("Sahr-vah-sahm-paht-tee-pooh-ree-nee"),
    brings all forms of prosperity.
13. *Sarvamantramayi*
    ("Sahr-vah-mahn-trah-mah-yee"),
    embodiment of all mantras.
14. *Sarvadvandvachayankari*
    ("Sahr-vahd-vahnd-vah-chai-yahn-car-ee"), destroyer of all forms and types of false duality.

This ring of triangles and goddesses is associated with the body's fourth chakra, *Anahata*, the heart chakra. It deals with love, relationships, self-acceptance, balance, and compassion. So *Sarvasammohini* will give us information or ritual or wisdom about false relationships where we think we are in love but are deluded. *Sarvasampattipurini* helps our relationships and love prosper and grow.

Set up your ritual area as in the previous ritual. This time, however, visualize or imagine yourself traveling into the Sri Yantra through the gate for the appropriate purpose of the ritual. You may wish to greet and thank the god who is guarding the gate. Then imagine or visualize yourself moving to and literally sitting in the petal or triangle that matches the purpose of the magick. Traditionally you will follow a counterclockwise direction, spiraling in, rather than going directly to the petal or triangle where your goal is located. Talk to the goddess there. Thank her for her wisdom. Repeat her name 108 times or in multiples of 108 (use your mala to assist in the counting) as if it were a mantra. Give her an active (what you will do) or sacrificial (what you will cease doing) gift in exchange for her favors. Leave the way you came. Circle the Sri Yantra with incense as in step 4 of the previous ritual, and conclude with a final banishing.

The Nine-Chakra System

If you follow these concepts to their conclusion, you will discover that the Sri Yantra deals with nine chakras and not the usual seven. I'll go into more depth on the chakras later in this book, but I'd like to describe the eighth and ninth chakras here, since they involve the Sri Yantra.

The pathways of the body's energy are called *nadis*. The most famous one of these is the *Sushumna* nadi. This goes straight up the spine and is linked to the seven major chakras. The other two famous nadis, the *Ida* and the *Pingala*, flow with their solar and lunar energies around the Sushumna.

Free flow of spiritual wisdom from the godhead goes through the Brahma nadi that is *inside* the Sushumna nadi. That the Brahma nadi is inside the Sushumna shows how fine and ethereal it is. Because it is so fine, it can easily become blocked, and in most non-Tantrics, this is usually the situation.

The *vhirkuti* ("veer-koo-tee") and *trikuti* ("try-koo-tee") chakras are even subtler than the famous seven chakras, and are attached to the Brahma nadi. The Brahma nadi can be opened in a variety of ways, including the use of mantra, yantra, pranayama, Tantric sexual practices, gift of the Goddess, etc. Together, these two chakras are beginning and advanced aspects of the *kailasa* chakra, or guru chakra (*gu* = darkness, *ru* = remover). In other words, these two separate chakras are actually part of, or aspects of, an encompassing chakra.

If you stand up straight and draw a horizontal line back from the third-eye chakra between the eyebrows and vertical line down from the crown chakra at the top of the head, you'll discover that they meet on the Sushumna nadi in the center of the head. This is the location of the combined eighth and ninth chakras. Their importance will be covered later in this book.

A Brief Aside Concerning Gurus

A common Tantric saying is "There is no Tantra without mantra." The knowledge and use of mantras is very important in Tantra.

There are different types of mantras, ranging from those that are well known and public to those that are specifically designed for an individual's use. Some have said that practicing an individual or secret mantra that has been obtained "illegitimately" (from a book, by overhearing it, by being told it by someone who is not a guru, etc.) is worse than futile—it is the equivalent of Brahmanicide (killing a priest).

Frankly, I think this concept may have been invented by a self-styled guru who made a living... I mean, who shared spiritual wisdom by selling... I mean, by giving out mantras. Traditionally, a specialized mantra is supposed to be obtained directly from and only from your guru. But if you don't have a guru, how do you get your mantra(s)?

The answer is that a human guru is only supposed to be used until your *guru chakra*—your direct connection to wisdom from the Divine—is aroused and enlivened. Then you can get your own accurate wisdom, including valid personal mantras, directly from the source.

I pay homage to the Sri Yantra.
I pay homage to all who
teach Sri Vidya.
I pay homage to all who
teach wisdom.

Another Way to Work with the Goddesses of the Sri Yantra: The Puja

The word *puja* is a Sanskrit term that translates as "reverence," "adoration," or "honor." Also spelled *pooja*, it is used to indicate a ritual or rite. In regard to the Sri Yantra, there are two main types of pujas: the creation method and the dissolution method. In the dissolution method, each devi is worshiped and then visualized as being absorbed into the next devi. This is continued until all the devis of the Sri have been honored and absorbed into Lalita (another name for Tripura Sundari), the presiding devi. In the creation method, you begin by worshiping Lalita. From her, the next devi is extracted and worshiped. From this devi, the next is extracted and worshiped. This is continued until all of the devis are seated in their appropriate places on the Sri Yantra.

If you think about it, either of the puja forms could literally take hours. However, you don't have to do that here. Simply start with the last devi of a chakra, honor her in your own way, and visualize her being absorbed into the next devi. Repeat for the entire chakra and conclude with Lalita. Alternatively, reverse the process.

Meditation on Yourself as a Form of the Sri Yantra

Traditional Tantra as presented here is not meant to be considered as just another philosophy or theology. It is alive and living within each practitioner. The same is true of the Sri Yantra. I've hinted at how it relates to the body. Some practitioners hold that the highest form of working with the Sri Yantra is to bring it within you. At the end of chapter 5, I showed images of the Sri Yantra in both 2-D and 3-D versions projected against the human body. The purpose of the next ritual is to move that from being a concept to becoming a part of you.

Part One: The Three Awarenesses

Awareness One: Until you have practiced this several times, my experience indicates this is best done lying down, with your arms straight out to the side so that your body forms a cross. Visualize the outer square of the Sri Yantra on yourself with its south door at your knees. In this meditation, the south door is the door of *dharma*, the discipline of following your spiritual path. The east door of the Sri should be visualized as being just beyond the tips of the fingers of your left hand. This is the door of *kama*, or desire and lust for all aspects of life and personal growth. The west door is *artha*, or understanding. It is just beyond the tips of your right hand's fingers. Finally, the north door is *moksha*, or liberation from the illusions of maya. It is located far enough above your head to form a square with the other doors.

Awareness Two: Next come the three rings that form the girdle of the Sri Yantra. These rings should just graze the top of your head (the location of the crown chakra (*Sahasrara*), the finger tips of both hands, and just below the groin where the root chakra (*Muladhara*) is shown as it projects forward from the lower tip of the spine.

The Lotus Visualization

Awareness Three: Now, visualize a circle from your *Ajña* chakra (third-eye or brow chakra) to *Svadisthana* (genital chakra). This circle passes through the right and left wrists. Take a moment and allow the circle to evolve into sixteen blue lotus petals. Allow adjacent pairs of petals to merge, and let the color shift through purple to red, ending with eight red lotus petals.

A. Focus on the petal at your left wrist. This is the link between you and the goddess who gives you the sense of smell. Say: **I bless the goddess for her gift of smell so that I might inhale the fragrant sweetness of the three worlds.**

B. Move your attention clockwise to the petal between your left wrist and your groin. This is the link between you and the goddess who gives you the sense of taste. Say: **I bless the goddess for her gift of taste so that I might savor the delicious flavors of the three worlds.**

C. Move your attention to the third petal over the groin. This is the link between you and the goddess who gives you the sense of vision. Say: **I bless the goddess for her gift of sight so that I might see the visual beauty of the three worlds.**

D. Now move your attention to the fourth petal between your groin and your right wrist. This is the link between you and the goddess who gives you the sense of touch. Say: **I bless the goddess for her gift of touch so that I might experience the physical presence and reality of the three worlds.**

E. Now move your attention to the fifth petal over your right wrist. This is the link between you and the goddess who gives you the sense of hearing. Say: **I bless the goddess for her gift of sound so that I might hear the ineffable music of the spheres, the vibration that causes the manifestation of the three worlds.**

F. Now move your attention to the sixth petal at the right of your head. This is the link between you and the goddess who gives you your mind. Say: **I bless the goddess for her gift of my mind so that I might use every aspect of myself to experience the majesty of the three worlds.**

G. Now move your attention to the seventh petal between your eyebrows. This is the link between you and the goddess who gives you your intellect. Say: **I bless the goddess for her gift of intellect so that I might use my mind to help myself, my community, and the environment of the three worlds.**

H. Finally, move your attention to the eighth petal by the left side of your head. This is the link between you and the goddess who gives you your identity. Say: **I bless the goddess for her gift of my identity so that I might see how I am both separate and united with the three worlds.**

Part Two: The Visualization of the Five Triangles

Step One: Visualize from your third eye to your navel five concentric equilateral triangles. Each should have one point down, toward your feet. They indicate the power of Shakti, the power of the Goddess.

A. Meditate on the first and outermost triangle. The point at the navel represents willpower. The point at the right shoulder represents wisdom. The point at the left shoulder represents action. Concentrate on them being unified and merging with your *physical* body. What does each concept mean to you?

B. Visualize a second triangle, within and about the width of your three central fingers smaller than the previous triangle. Again, the point at the bottom represents willpower, at the right armpit is wisdom, and at the left armpit is action. Concentrate on them being unified and merging with your *vital* body, that part of you that sends energy to all parts of you.

C. Visualize a third triangle, within and about the width of six fingers smaller than the first. Again, the point at the bottom point represents willpower, at the right is wisdom, and at the left is action. Concentrate on them being unified and merging with your *mental* body, that part of you that controls all parts of you.

D. Visualize a fourth triangle, within and about the width of nine fingers smaller than the first. Again, the point at the bottom represents willpower, at the right nipple is wisdom, and at the left nipple is action. Concentrate on them being unified and merging with your *intellectual* body, that part of you that thinks and judges.

E. Now visualize a fifth triangle, within and about the width of twelve fingers smaller than the first triangle. Again, the point at the bottom represents willpower, at the right is wisdom, and at the left is action. Concentrate on them being unified and merging with your body of *bliss*, that part of you that gives you the bliss of knowing exactly who and what you are.

Step Two: In the center of the fifth triangle, visualize the Bindu, a small circle or dot that represents your very core. Now visualize your consciousness forming a beam of light and entering the Bindu, becoming one with yourself and one with everything. Allow everything to simply dissolve until only you remain, united with everything. Stay in this state for as long as you wish, then return to normal consciousness.

You will learn more about the five bodies, or sheaths, later in this book. You may wish to make an audio recording of this meditative ritual so you can play back the instructions.

Conclusion

The End of the Beginning

I am absolutely fascinated by the image of the Sri Yantra. Learning about this image is both a study and a passion. I hope this chapter has given you a glimpse of the power of this symbol, the experience of working with the image, and the desire to learn more.

But the truth is, reading books and buying or creating drawings or making 3-D images of the Sri Yantra can only take you so far. As you learn more about the Sri, you'll want to bring it inside of you. Or rather, you'll want to become aware of the energy paths and fields it sets up within you. Once again, Tantra is not something you do; Tantra is something you are. The same is true with the Sri Yantra.

Final Suggestion

If you don't have the time, desire, or ability to do a full, detailed worship of the Sri Yantra, yet you still want to work with it, there is a valuable but simple shortcut you can use. Look at the Sri Yantra and repeat ("do *japa*") the following simple mantra to the devi Tripura Sundari as an alternate to the one described earlier:

Om Aim Hreem Shreem
Sri Lalita Tripurasundari Padukam
Poojayami Namah!

SEVEN

Tools of Tantra

Virtually all spiritual traditions have a variety of tools. Among the tools of the Catholic Church are novena candles, holy water, and elaborate clothing for church leaders. In Islam, many followers will carry a special prayer rug. Jews have the scrolls of the Torah and a special holiday candle holder. Wiccans and Witches have altars with candles, chalices, cauldrons, and athames (ritual daggers). Spiritual traditions that aren't part of a religion have tools, too. The most common are the four elemental tools: the dagger, wand, cup, and pentacle.

Tantrics also have tools, but many are radically different from those Westerners most frequently have used. In this chapter I'd like to introduce you to some of the most important tools of Tantra. You can use some or all of them within the *Modern Tantra* system or adapt them to your own tradition or path.

Personally, I enjoy the use of ritual tools. Just holding them transports me into a mindset that is special and magickal. It takes me out of the ordinary and into the world of spirit and magick. If some of these tools have that effect on you, I would encourage you to use them. However, these physical tools can always be worked around. Don't avoid doing spiritual, ritual, or magickal work because you don't have a tool. The most important tool for Tantric work is the body/mind/spirit.

Tantric Tools for Personal Use

Mala

I have already discussed the basics of how to use the prayer beads known as a *mala*. The use of prayer beads is quite ancient. In fact, the word *bead* is in part derived from the Sanskrit word *buddh*, which relates to self-realization. For example, the word *buddha* means "a self-realized person." Some say, however, that *bead* comes from the Saxon word *bidden*, which means "to pray."

The use of the rosary by Roman Catholics is attributed to St. Dominic (1170–1221 CE). Supposedly, the Virgin Mary gave him the rosary beads and told him to teach their use to believers. They are called a "rosary" because they are like a string of roses, and using them is a metaphor for stringing together prayers that, like the flower, blossom forth.

There are two types of rosaries commonly used by Roman Catholics. The most common is made of fifteen sets of ten beads each. Each set is separated by a larger bead, and the beginning/end is usually set off by a cross or crucifix. The second type of rosary has only fifty beads, with each bead representing three prayers.

In Islam, a set of prayer beads known as a *tasbih* ("to glorify") is used. It has three sets of thirty-three beads, with each division set off by a different type of bead. This is also like the *ayat*, a round mark in the Quran where a reader may appropriately pause. A tassel is often included to ward off the evil eye.

The ninety-nine beads of the tasbih are said to represent the ninety-nine names of God in Islam. Sometimes there is a one hundredth bead for the ineffable (incapable of being expressed in words) name of God. There is also a version with only thirty-three beads, in which each bead, like the smaller Catholic rosary, represents three prayers.

The word *mala* literally translates as "garland of flowers." Smaller malas have 50 or 54 beads, the number of letters in the Sanskrit alphabet. The full-size ones with 108 beads may be worn around the neck or kept in a bag. Sometimes the bag has a special hole so you can reach inside and count the beads in private, even while you are in public.

The number 108 was not chosen at random. It is related specifically to the breath. The basis of this idea is that, on average, an adult takes one breath every four seconds. This means we take:

15 breaths per minute
900 breaths per hour
21,600 breaths per day

A half-day's worth of breaths would be 10,800, and 1/100 of that is 108. Therefore, repeating a mantra 108 times is symbolic of repeating the prayer during twelve daylight hours. Repeating a second round of 108 covers the twelve night hours.

This is an important concept. Not only is it a "shortcut" for doing a lot of mantra repetition, but it is focused on the importance of breath. Every movement of a bead on the mala is symbolic of a breath. It reminds practitioners that every breath they take, if understood and used properly, is a prayer to the Divine. That means everything a practitioner does is sacred. A Tantric will think about that concept when choosing to do anything. After all, every second of every day and every breath we take is a prayer and is sacred.

Some people use malas made of different materials for different purposes. For example, some people use malas made of the wood of a sacred basil bush known as *tulsi*. It is said to be good for general recitation of mantras, as it increases your spiritual level.

My personal favorite mala is made of sandalwood because I love its wonderful scent. Repeating mantras using a sandalwood mala is said to enhance your natural charisma.

Quartz crystal is a popular choice for malas because of its reasonable price and beauty. Repeating your mantras with one is said to increase peace of mind and spiritual strength. This may be related to the idea that quartz is associated with the earth element.

The delightful purple tones of a mala made of amethyst, when used with regular mantra repetition, are said to enhance your psychic abilities, including your natural insight and intuition.

The Dalai Lama uses a mala made of tiger's-eye. Another bead used by the Dalai Lama is the *rudraksha*. Rudra is a name of Shiva in the form of a storm deity and as god of the hunt. According to myth, Rudra/Shiva had spent a long period in deep meditation. When he awoke and opened his eyes (Sanskrit: *aksha*), he was so fulfilled and happy that he shed a tear. That tear became the rudraksha tree, a fast-growing evergreen with broad leaves.

The large seeds of the rudraksha have an outer shell that is blue. Inside, the seeds do something amazing. They are naturally green, but turn black with aging. More importantly, the seeds are highly textured and have grooves in them. These grooves divide the seed into from one to 108 *mukhi* ("faces"). Rudraksha seeds with only one face or above twenty-one faces are difficult to find and very expensive. Depending upon the number of faces, a rudraksha will have a meaning, a mantra, and correspondences. For example, a rudraksha with two faces represents the union of Shiva and the goddess Parvati. It is said to hold immense mystical power. Its ruling planet is the Moon. Its mantra is *Om Shiva Shakti-hih Namah-hah*. A rudraksha with eleven faces is said to hold immense spiritual power. It's good to have when on a spiritual quest. Its ruling planet is Jupiter, and its mantra is *Om Hreem Hum Namah*.

In your research, you may discover that the number 108 has become associated with numerous spiritual concepts in the East. The idea that it originally was associated with the breath makes the most sense to me. However, others give the following associations:

- 108 pilgrimage spots in India and Nepal
- 108 Upanishads (Indian holy books)
- 108 sacred Tantric places (*pithas*)
- 108 "auspicious illustrations" in the Buddha's footprint
- 108 *marmas* on the human body (points where three energy paths or nadis cross, the source for acupuncture)
- And perhaps most important of all to North Americans, there are exactly 108 stitches on a regulation Major League baseball!

Danda

The *danda* (Sanskrit for "stick"), sometimes called a "yoga staff," is a specialized object that looks like the top of a traditional crutch that has been cut off about a third of the way from the top. Besides being shorter, ranging from about eighteen to twenty-four inches in length, the danda has a crossbar at the top with a slight downward curve at the center. Mine is imported from India and is about nineteen inches in length (see photo), and appears to be made from a dowel turned on a lathe—perhaps originally intended to be part of the leg of a table or chair—beneath a curved crossbar resembling the top of a standard crutch.

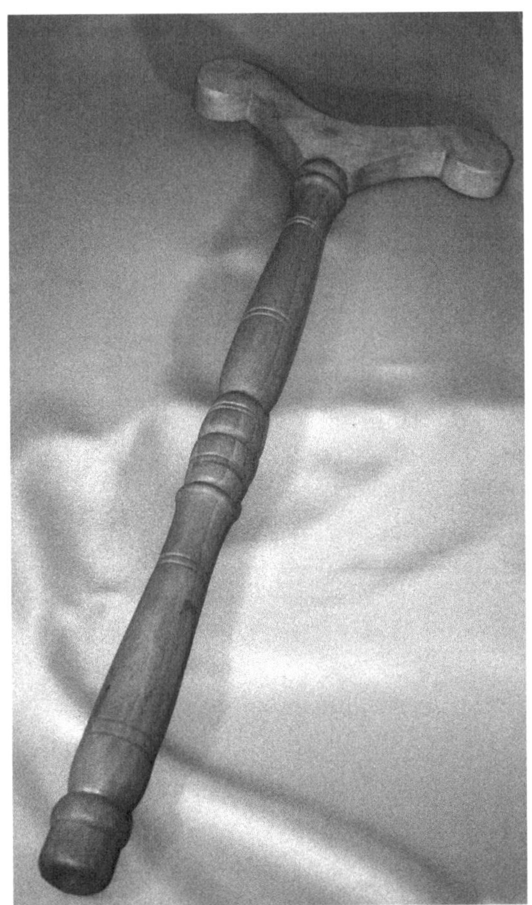

A Danda (from the Author's Collection)

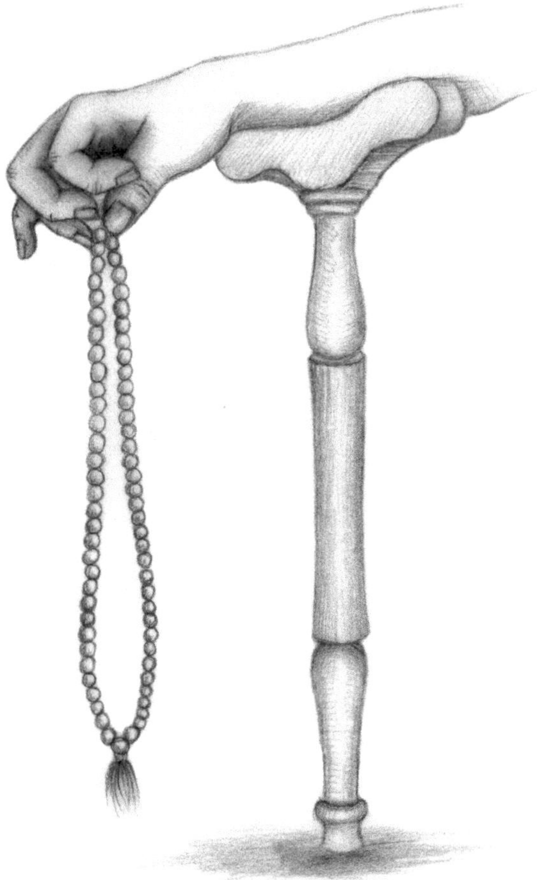

Supporting the Arm during Japa with a Danda

If you are making many rounds of a mantra using a mala—a process called *japa*—the arm holding the mala can tire. Some people use a danda placed in front of them while they are sitting on the floor to comfortably support the forearm while counting the mala beads. But that's not the most valuable use of this tool.

The danda is a powerful instrument for yogic breathwork. It is part of a Tantric technique known as *swara* ("flow of air") *yoga*, or brain breathing.

Although most people are unaware of it, we usually breathe more easily through one nostril at a time. Close off one nostril and breathe heavily through the nose. Repeat with the other nostril. You will find that one nostril is clearer. This is your primary nostril.

Your primary nostril changes about every ninety minutes. The period of balance and change, moving from one primary nostril to the other, normally takes up to four minutes.

Your nostrils are associated with the body's flow of energy. The left nostril is associated with the *Ida* ("Ee-dah") path and carries the lunar flow of energy. The right nostril is associated with the *Pingala* ("Ping-uh-luh") path and carries the solar flow of energy. When one nostril is clearer than the other, that energy is accentuated. When doing basic breathwork, a goal is often to balance the breathing and thus balance the flow of energy. Sometimes this is accomplished by breathing first through one nostril and then the other. I'll have more to share on the Ida and Pingala later.

Your nostrils are also associated with their opposite brain hemisphere. That is, your right nostril is associated with the left side of the brain. This is the side of the brain associated with logic and reason. Your left nostril is associated with the right side of the brain. This is the side of the brain associated creativity and artistry.

Forcing yourself to breathe through just one nostril, however, can have magickal effects. Spending twenty minutes four times a day for one month forcing breath through the right nostril (by closing the left) increases oxygen consumption. Left-nostril breathing can lower blood glucose levels. If you're taking a math test or working with spreadsheets, you can improve your results by forcing the breath, energy, and brain to work through the right nostril/left side of the brain. If you're writing a novel, making a sculpture, or composing music, you can improve your results by forcing the breath, energy, and brain to work through the left nostril/right side of the brain.

However, you'd look pretty goofy walking around or just sitting while talking with friends and holding onto your nose! The ancient Tantrics discovered an alternate solution.

It turns out that there are *marmas* (pressure points) that can change your primary nostril. These are located under your arms in the soft tissue of the armpits. Applying pressure on the armpit on the side of your body with the nostril that is clear will quickly open the opposing nostril.

You can do this with your thumb, but again, you will look pretty goofy walking around with your thumb stuck in your armpit. The solution is the danda.

When you are sitting or kneeling on the floor, simply put the danda under your arm and lean down on it. If the danda you obtain is too tall, you can either cut off the bottom or simply move the bottom of the danda out at an angle. If yours is too short, put the bottom on a book or flat stone. In a few minutes, the pressure on the underarm marma will result in a change of the nasal cycle. After it has changed, you no longer have to lean on the danda and may remove it.

Do you need to focus on legal matters, logic, or things that require analytical, deductive thinking? Make sure your nasal cycle has the right nostril (linked to the left side of the brain, which focuses on logical, deductive thinking) as the primary nostril. If that's not where you are, change the cycle.

If you need to be creative, break writer's block, do some art, or approach a problem from outside the box, make sure the left nostril (linked to the right side of the brain, which has a more artistic and inductive focus) is your primary nostril.

The technique of swara yoga has as its goal increased spirituality created by extending the period of balance that normally only appears for a brief time every ninety minutes. Use the danda briefly to keep both nostrils equally open. Place it under the arm that has the open nostril. This will open the other side. Once the flow of energy is balanced, you can cease leaning on the crutch.

If you look at the danda straight on, so that the arms extend to either side, the danda looks like the spine and shoulder blades. This should remind you that, when in meditation, your spine (called the *Meru Danda*) is metaphorically the center of the universe and the energy that rises up the spine, the *kundalini*, is the energy that is the creative power of the universe.

Tiger Skin

It is traditional for Tantrics to meditate while sitting on the skin of a tiger. I am strongly against this for three reasons. First, tigers in the wild are an endangered species. Buying a tiger skin is likely to encourage a trade in them and speed up the demise of the species. Second, it's illegal to buy them. Third, it's only symbolic anyway, so use a symbol of a tiger instead. Tibetans have done this for a long time.

I obtained a small rug that looks something like a tiger skin. It's cut to the shape of a small tiger skin, and the weaving of the fabric is designed to look sort of like a tiger skin. It's also thicker than a real tiger skin, making sitting on it (especially on top of a hard floor) when meditating more comfortable. I've also seen skins of cows that have been dyed to look like a tiger skin.

In traditional images of the Goddess as Shakti (pure energy), her "vehicle" (what she rides on) is a tiger. The symbolism of sitting on the skin of a tiger, then, is that you control the Shakti energy.

However, from a Tantric point of view, I don't think this is accurate. The goal of a Tantric isn't to control the Shakti energy. Rather, it is to latch onto it and direct it. You *ride* the energy. By mastering yourself with meditation (the place where you use a tiger skin), you and Shakti can become so attuned and aligned that your purposes and direction are united and you can function as one.

The problem I have with the term *control* in this context is that there is the implication that you have beaten Shakti into submission. Rather, the goal is through meditation and dedication, through self-control, self-development, and self-advancement, that you become spiritually awakened, resulting in a unity of purpose with the Goddess energy. If anything, what you want to do is submit to the will of your higher self, your purpose in life. In Western mystical terms, it is obtaining the Knowledge and Conversation of your Holy Guardian Angel. To those not as spiritually advanced, it may appear as if you control Shakti, but you know the truth.

A Shiva Statue (from the Author's Collection)

Similarly, it is said that the sinuous motion and power of a tiger represent lust, and by sitting on the skin of a tiger—even an imitation tiger rug—you have "conquered" lust. Again, I object to a term. In this instance, the term is *conquered.* The desire to conquer lust results in people who are severely psychologically scarred. It promotes the idea that you are wrong and should be punished for instincts that are natural and desirable.

When you are hungry, you should lust for nutritious, good-tasting foods in appropriate amounts. When you want to dance, you should lust for music to dance the way you want. When you are ill, you should lust for health. You should lust for a great day. You should lust for life. You should lust for freedom, wisdom, and knowledge. When tired, you should lust for sleep. And yes, you should lust for sex, too.

But you shouldn't lust for food when you're not hungry. You shouldn't lust for sleep when it's time to greet the day. You shouldn't lust for sex when you have other things that are important to do.

In short, you shouldn't conquer lust at all. Rather, you should *master* lust so you can call on it whenever it is needed. You should "ride" the tiger's skin, moving silently and gracefully through the forests of life. And when you are ready to appropriately experience the lusty power of the tiger, you can still ride as the animal leaps forth in harmony with your needs and desires. Lust can be mastered, but people who think they have conquered it often end up with severe mental, emotional, and even physical problems.

Working with the danda while sitting on the imitation tiger skin can help you in meditation when you balance your breathing in swara yoga.

Tantric Tools for the Devotional Altar

One of the first things I started to look at when studying traditional Tantra was the Tantric altar. There are a couple types of altars, one for devotional rituals and one for practical magick. I'll discuss the latter type in a moment.

Many Tantrics have altars with several deities, while others are focused on one deity (or both the deity and his or her consort), but some have separate altars for each of the deities they work with. Some have just one altar space and change it to fit the deity or deities they want to work with at any particular time.

One of the Author's Tantric Altars

Murthi of the Goddess Kali
(from the Author's Collection)

After looking at and working with Tantric altars for decades, I can now share the primary rule for setting up an altar devoted to a deity:

There are no rules!

I'm not joking. The key thing is to learn about a deity and include those things you think should be there. If there's not enough room on your altar for all the things you want to include, that's okay. Build or obtain a shelf so that you have a two-tiered or even three-tiered altar (more than that and it's difficult to physically balance things). The shelf or pedestal is known in Sanskrit as a *chowki*, and symbolically it elevates your deities to a higher plane.

That being said, there are some things you might want to include. Here is a selection of them.

Murthi

The *murthi* ("moo-r-tee") is an image of the deity. Most often it is in the form of a statue that expresses the spirit of the deity. Sometimes it is a drawing and sometimes it is the yantra of the deity. During a devotional ritual, the spirit of the Divine is called into the murthi ("seated"), where it can be honored and from which blessings can be received. Often there will be several murthis on an altar. For example, you might find Ganesh, Shiva, and Kali on an altar. A murthi is also known as a *vigraha*.

Shivaling

Often appearing on altars either as the main murthi or in addition to the other murthis is a *Shivaling* (or *Shiva lingam*). This is a representation of Shiva's phallus, and thus is a representation of Shiva and his energy. Although the focus of the description of the Shivaling is on the male, for an altar it is traditionally kept within the Shakti's yoni. I'll describe this in a moment.

There are two major types of Shivalings. The first is an oblong stone that comes from the Narmada River, an inlet of the Ganges River. These are beautiful, naturally polished stones with light and dark markings. The larger the stone and the more beautiful the markings, the more the stone is valued. I have seen some as small as under an inch long and others that are more than a meter long. The easiest way to have this on your altar is to fill a bowl with sand and stand your Shivaling upright in the bowl so that about one-half to two-thirds of it is showing above the sand. In this case, the bowl and sand function as the yoni of Shakti.

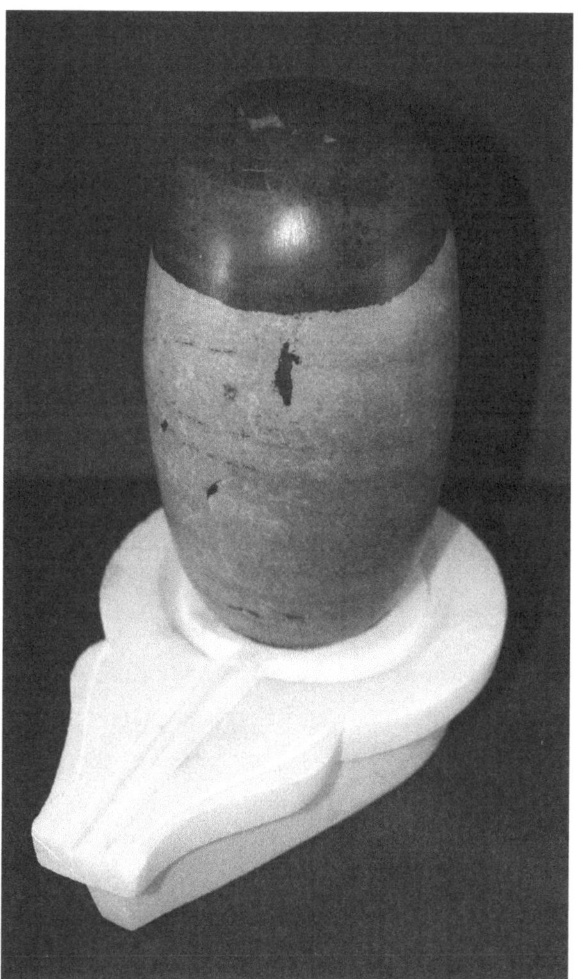

Eight-Inch Lingam from the Narada River Resting in Yoni Stone (from the Author's Collection)

Large Shiva Lingam Cemented into Yoni Stone (Although the small pillar on which it rests isn't traditional, it is a way to bring it up off the ground. Permanently in the author's yard, it has a light that shines on it at night.)

The second type of Shivaling is one that is handmade. They are cast from metals, ceramics, or other materials or carved from stone. Sometimes the lingam part will have one or more of the faces of Shiva carved into it or painted on it. The yoni stone in which it rests, called a *jaladhari,* is usually keyhole-shaped, and when seen from above it is obviously the Goddess's vulva with the God's lingam inserted. It is an image of the God and Goddess eternally joined in ecstatic Tantric bliss.

Sometimes a container in the shape of a *kalash* bowl (see illustration) hangs over the lingam. It comes to a point at the bottom where there is a tiny hole. During worship, Tantrics fill the container with water (or milk and water) that continuously washes and blesses the lingam in the form of a slender stream or drops of fluid.

Example of a Shiva Lingam with a Kalash Bowl Suspended Above (from the Author's Collection)

Shankh

This is a conch shell. It can be made into a horn by cutting off the end where the shell is thickest. To play it, you hold it by putting your fingers into the large natural opening with your thumb on the outside. If you purse your lips like a trumpet player (technically known as an *embouchure*) and blow through the cut-off end, it is possible to get a surprisingly loud and rich tone. It does take some practice to get it right. In my experience, blowing gently, rather than with great force, results in getting a good sound.

The shankh horn may be sounded at the beginning of rituals. It is a very delightful sound. It is said that the shankh produces the purest sound: the *Om*, or sound of creation. Sometimes gongs or small cymbals are used. If you decide to get one of these alternatives, try them out. Listen for a pleasant sound. The purpose is to welcome people and spirits. Musically this is known as a harmonious and sonorous quality. Many Tibetan gongs arc disharmonious and clangorous. Their purpose is to frighten away demons.

If you look at the large opening of a shankh, you can easily see why they are popular in Tantric rituals. The opening appears to be that of a yoni, right up to the beautiful pink color matching that found inside a woman's yoni. Thus, it is symbolic of Shakti and her energy. If you hold the shell with the opening up, the opening will be either on the left (most common) or the right. The right-handed shankh is considered to be the most auspicious.

A shankh, usually a smaller one, that has not been made into a horn can be used as a type of spoon that can be used to take fluids such as water to bathe the murthi during the process of waking it up.

Since the shankh is a shell, it is obvious to think that it will be found in areas associated with the ocean. While this is true, in many cases shankhs are found where ancient oceans once existed. One type is known as *Pahadi Shankh*, or "conch from the mountains," which has become fossilized and may have been decorated with embedded gems. I have two large shankhs, each costing me less than twenty dollars. Even a small fossilized, right-turning conch shell less than one-fifth the size of a large shankh horn can cost five or more times that price.

A Shankh Trumpet with the End Sawed Off (from the Author's Collection)

Traditionally, the shankh is associated with Lakshmi, goddess of wealth. Place the shankh on your altar so that the opening is down and the round end is pointing east. For better finances, you can chant Lakshmi's bija mantra *srim* ("shreem"). Just repeat it once per breath or rapidly, many times per breath. A slightly longer mantra for Lakshmi is *Om Gum Srim Maha Lakshmiyeh Svaha* ("Ah-oom Gahm Shreem Mah-hah Lahk-shmee-yeh S'vah-hah"). Keep one shankh in your home or place of work to improve business and prosperity. Students keep them to help sharpen the memory. Put one in the bedroom to help encourage love and harmony.

To purify your shankh before using, rinse it thoroughly with water. Then hold it just above your head and in front of you. Say the following:

At the mouth of this shell
is Chandra, Goddess of the Moon.
On the sides of this shell
is Varuna, God of Water.
On its back is Shiva in the form
of Prajapati, Lord of Animals.

And at its apex are the
Ganges, the Saraswati,
and all the other sacred
rivers of the three worlds in
which we make ablutions.
Glory to thee, sacred shell, blessed
by all the gods, born in the sea.
We adore thee and
meditate upon thee.
May we be filled with joy!

Incense Burner

The use of stick incense, commonly known as *joss sticks*, is the most common form of incense used by Tantrics, although any type of incense can be used. The incense burner can be very elaborate or just a bowl with sand in it. Joss sticks, unfortunately, are of wildly varying quality. Some are made with pure incense resins and high-quality oils. Others are made with pig or camel dung and artificial scents. Some are so thoughtlessly made that they are actually carcinogenic. If you burn one and it smells bad to you or makes you sneeze, gag, or cough, use a different brand. Their scent should be delightful and pleasant.

Tantrics keep the ash, spiritualized by the ritual, as *vibhuti*, or holy ash. It is used in ritual to mark the body in certain ways. Vibhuti found in stores is often primarily burned cow dung, perhaps mixed with purified butter (*ghee*) or milk. I've found that ash from incense works just fine.

Diya

This is simply a type of lamp. For ritual use, a diya will usually have a handle. It may have small indentations for holding what you intend to burn. Usually a diya burns one of three things. A wick is made of a small cotton ball that is twisted to a point on one side. This is dipped either in lamp oil or the traditional ghee. The ball is placed in the indentation and the twisted point is lit. A typical diya has one or more indentations, often three or five. Large ones are used for more public ceremonies.

Besides ghee and lamp oil, the third substance that can be burned does not require a wick. You use small blocks of pure camphor (Sanskrit: *kapoor*). If you opt for this, be very careful. Artificial camphor is very common and is not a good substitute for the real thing. Even the real thing can burn hot and fast and produce a lot of smoke, so you might limit its use to rituals held outside.

I have found that a candle or lantern, although not traditional, works well too.

Once lit, the diya is used for a part of rituals known as *aarti*. The diya is waved in a clockwise circle in front of each part of the murthi, and then around the entire image. Participants in the ritual follow this by holding their hands briefly over the flames. Then they touch their eyes (saying or thinking, "Bring me wisdom") and the top of their heads ("Bring me spirituality").

Diya Lamp (This diya, from the author's collection, has a handle with a serpent representing Shiva on it and wells for seven flames. At either end is an image of Ganesh.)

Bell Used as a Ghanta (from the Author's Collection)

Ghanta

The diya lamp is not used by itself. As the diya is held in the right hand and waved in front of the murthi, the left hand sounds a *ghanta* (Sanskrit for "bell"). The ghanta is what is commonly known as a hand bell. It is circular, with a wide mouth, and can rest on the open end. From the top comes a vertical handle. Inside is a clapper so when you shake the bell it rings.

If you remember the image of a teacher ringing a hand bell in front of a little red schoolhouse, you know the type of bell I mean. Although the handle could be of wood, it is often made of the same metal as the bell. It can be plain or decorated. My favorite one is a smallish bell with a trident—the *trishul*, a symbol of Shiva—at the top.

The tone of the bell should be full and rich, pleasing to humans and the deities they call and honor. The ghanta also functions as a type of noise filter. Its ringing drowns out irrelevant or inappropriate sounds, such as people talking, and keeps your attention on the ritual.

Kapala Bowl

In the introduction to this book I stated that I was not going to be dealing with Tantric traditions from Tibet. The kapala is an exception.

In Tantric symbolism, items related to death are typically metaphors for the death or destruction of those parts of us that are considered hindrances to spiritual development and evolution. An example of this symbolism is found in typical depictions of the goddess Kali, who is shown wearing a garland of sometimes bloody, decapitated heads and a belt of human arms.

This gory vision, upsetting to many Westerners, indicates that Kali will help destroy your ego (the false impression you may have of who you are). It also implies that she will cut away your attachments to material things—attachments that keep you from following a spiritual path—and your false belief that you have but one life. In some images of Kali, one of her hands holds a kapala bowl.

Although the symbolism of the kapala is found in Indian spiritual imagery, it is in Tibet, isolated from India to the south by the long climb up the Himalayas (the Tibetan plateau is surrounded by mountains and the land has been nicknamed the "Roof of the World" because of its elevation, averaging 16,000 feet), where the use of human bones as ritual items is not uncommon. In Tibetan Tantra, the use of the kapala in ritual is usually associated with the worship of Shiva as the great destroyer.

The kapala ("kah-pah-luh") bowl is a small bowl (so small that it is often referred to as a cup), used for libations, which is traditionally made from about the top one-quarter to one-third of a genuine human skull (I'll pause and let you think about that for a moment). The word *kapala* is actually Sanskrit for "skull."

Kapala Bowl
(This one, from the author's collection, is covered with a silvery metal. Note the skull imagery around the brim. Cover is at the right.)

The choice of a skull for use as a kapala is determined by several qualities, including its shape, color, marks on it, and how it "feels" (heavy or light compared to how it looks). The gender of the person is not relevant. If the skull is still attached to a corpse, you would need to take its position into account. For example, if it's bent forward, toward the chest, it is believed that using a kapala made from this skull will bring wealth. If it's bent back, as if looking up, it will bring power. Where the skull is found also is important, as well as the season and time it is found.

On the other hand, if the head is found separated from a body, using a kapala made from the skull is said to bring good luck, happiness, and freedom from enemies.

The preparation of the bowl from a corpse's skull is actually rather direct. You put the head in a hot spring for three days. This should remove all of the flesh. Then, using a bone saw, you saw off the top of the skull, wash it in alcohol, polish it, and anoint it with certain fragrant substances such as saffron. Then you add silver inlays, a stand, and a cover.

The kapala is said to be naturally possessed by both protective dakinis and evil spirits. It must be consecrated on an astrologically auspicious day and covered with incense to remove any evil. Then it is filled with positive things, such as precious gems and metals and the names of the ritualist's guru's lineage.

When called a "jewel bowl," a kapala may be worshiped directly. In some very secretive Tantric rituals, it is used as an offering vessel from which people drink nectar believed to give long life and spiritual wisdom. This nectar is made from red alcohol, representing menstrual blood, and white alcohol, representing sperm. However, considering the writings about some ancient mystics, the nectar may include actual substances rather than metaphoric substances. This will be discussed later.

Recorded uses for kapala bowls include it being a tool for prophecy, for use in evil magick, for exorcism and protective magick, and for visualizations concerning the nature of human life.

I do not know where the bowl I have was created. For me, it represents the concept of the impermanence of life and the conquering of the false ego, and it reminds the practitioner of the crown chakra. Kapalas also traditionally symbolize wisdom, bliss, self-sacrifice, impermanence, and the understanding that the Divine is beyond all concepts of duality.

Although you may be able to find kapalas from India—they are usually associated with Kali or a form of Durga—you are more likely to find ones from Tibet. Today, the use of human remains for religious artifacts is tightly controlled, and it is unlikely that you will easily find one actually made from a human skull. Those that are tend to be very expensive antiques, even the simplest of them often costing close to one thousand dollars or more. All of them tend to have ornate decorations, often in silver (or a silvery metal). Some are completely clad in silver and other decor. Since elaborate kapalas completely cover the skull with metallic decoration, some bright monk figured out that there was no real reason to have an actual human skull hidden by metals. As a result, if you find a kapala for sale today, it is likely that the "skull" under the metal is actually an artificial composite, although some have scrapings of a skull within the composite.

There are smaller kapalas that are made of monkey skulls rather than human skulls. However, most kapalas found today are composite or avoid the use of bone completely. The one I use has no bone whatsoever, but its powerful symbolism remains.

Often, an elaborate stand is made for the bowl (the curve of the inverted skull gives little stability when placed on a flat surface), and a cover is used to keep unwanted dust, dirt, and insects from partaking in the libation.

The use of the kapala in *Modern Tantra* is for making libations.

Lota Bowl (Kalash Bowl)

This small bowl is traditionally topped with five mango leaves and a coconut wrapped in red cloth. Its main purpose is simply to hold water used for a variety of ritual functions. A ritual spoon (Sanskrit: *uddharani*) used to give out water usually accompanies this bowl. The lota has a large belly, a small neck, and a brim that turns out from the bowl. A red or white thread is tied near the top and below the lip. It represents the love that binds together everything in creation. I own a small copper lota for my altar and a large one made of clay for group rituals.

The water used to fill a lota usually includes a few drops of *Ganga jal* (which I will discuss shortly). Alternatively, it may be filled with rice. When filled, the pot represents the idea that when we are filled with divine energy, we gain the strength to achieve our wishes.

Thali

The word *thali* is simply Sanskrit for "plate," as in a dinner plate. For your altar, this is usually a plate (commonly made of brass) with small containers on it. The containers are sometimes fixed in place.

The thali is used to hold several common items. First is a small spool of colored thread known as *mouli*. Traditionally this is colored red, but it is also common to have multicolored thread. A length is tied around the lota. A length is also tied around the wrists of ritual participants. Men tie it on their right wrists, and women on their left. Vedic Hindus—but usually not Tantrics—also wear a white thread called a *janeu*.

Another item for the thali is a selection of dried fruits and nuts. During the ritual they are given to the deities. Later, they are eaten by the participants.

In one of the containers on the thali is a special type of rice called *akshat*. This is a type of rice that will not germinate and has had its husk removed. Only perfect grains should be used. If you cannot obtain akshat, regular (but unbroken) rice works fine.

In another container on the thali is *kumkum* (or *sindoor*, Sanskrit for "vermillion"), a red paste traditionally made from dried, ground turmeric (Sanskrit: *haldi*). Haldi represents purified thoughts. Kumkum is used to mark the murthi when the deity is seated (brought into it). There are also traditions concerning the use of kumkum as a spot (*tilak* or *Bindu*) on the forehead worn by Vedic Hindus. It is said to be a symbol of good fortune.

You can purchase kumkum from Hindu religious supply stores and even some Indian groceries. Unfortunately, as with many uncontrolled substances, it is liable to contain adulterants, including forms of lead, which with repeated use can cause hair loss or even be toxic. Luckily, traditional kumkum is easy to make.

Simply take some ground, dried turmeric (it's yellow in color) and mix it with an equal amount of slaked lime (also known as hydrated lime, pickling lime, or calcium hydroxide). A white paste, slaked lime is available at Asian markets and other stores.

Large Ceramic Lota Bowl with Lid (from the Author's Collection)

Small Lota Bowl with Coconut by the Side

Mix the two together well. You may need to add a bit of water. Allow to dry for a couple of days. The result will turn the yellow of the turmeric to bright red. When ready to use, mix with some water to make a paste. If you don't want to go to that much trouble, I've found that dry, powdered red tempera paint works well too. I've used that for years.

Other items often found on the thali include incense, colored powders (*roli*), clove (*laung*), cardamom (*elaichi*), crystal sugar (*mishri*), and *Ganga jal* (see entry that follows).

A Flower Basket

This is just a small basket to hold colorful petals of flowers that are given to the deities. Floral wreaths, similar to Hawaiian leis, may be worn.

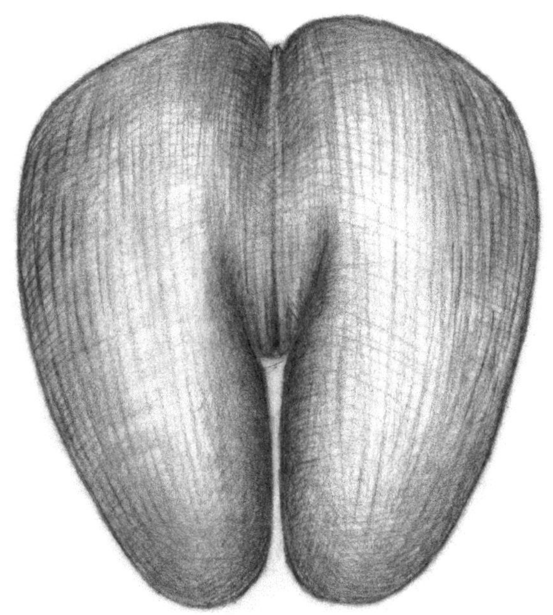

An Example of a Coco de Mer Seed

Coco de Mer

The seed of the coco de mer palm is the largest seed in the world, sometimes more than two feet long. It has two lobes and looks like a woman's buttocks, hips, and yoni. These are now protected and difficult to obtain, resulting in high prices. Not native to India, but native to the Seychelles islands in the Indian Ocean, they used to wash up on the Indian subcontinent, where Tantrics collected them and honored them as gifts from and representations of the Goddess. These seeds can be treated as murthis.

Ganga Jal

This is simply water from the Ganges (Sanskrit: *Ganga*) River. *Ganga jal* is not consumed. A few drops are added to the lota vase to spiritualize and sanctify the water.

If you don't have Ganga jal, use regular water in your lota. Use the same water for several rituals. Its use in sacred ritual space empowers the water so it can be used in the same way that Ganga jal is used. Store it and add a few drops to fresh water in each ritual.

I repeat: If you use actual Ganga jal, it should *not* be consumed. It is for external use only.

Do you need all of these items for your altar? No. Can you add more things, including items that are important to you? Absolutely. For example, several years ago I obtained some pieces of stained glass in the appropriate colors and shapes that are stylized versions of the chakras. They were called "chakra lenses," and I used them in healing and meditative work. If you can't find something that is exact, use something else.

Remember, the path of the Tantric is that of *Svecchachara*, the path of following your own will. What is given here is just a traditional outline. There is no right or wrong. Make your altars your own.

Tantric Tools for Magickal Rituals

The previous description is for an altar used for honoring the deities. There are other specific rituals that have unique requirements. For example, for the initiation ritual described in chapter 9, you will need a white or red powder, depending upon the gender of the person being initiated. I also like to use a wand for directing initiatory energy. If there are specific tools needed for rituals other than the tools already listed, I'll describe them with the ritual.

For general practical magick—making changes in your life and the lives of others, including healings, financial rituals, and others—there are a few tools that are important.

Havan Kund (and Sticks)

One of the most important events in human history was the mastery of fire. Fire was used to warm people when cold, cook food, purify sacred objects, and more. Fire rituals have been practiced all over the world.

Havans are age-old sacred fire rituals from India, and havan kunds are used as part of numerous rituals. They are used to invoke and propitiate various deities and spirits for the purpose of attaining desires and boons ranging from the materialistic to the spiritual.

If you attend a Pagan festival, you are highly likely to find people dancing around bonfires late into the night. People go into spontaneous trance as a result of the combination of fire, drumming, and dance. It is a powerful experience, revealing the fact that fire still has an enormous influence on our lives. The sacred fire acts as a link between a person's consciousness and the cosmic consciousness.

A havan rite can achieve a number of things, including:

- Cleansing of the atmosphere
- Cleansing of the physical and psychic bodies (*koshas*)
- Awakening of magickal and spiritual energies
- Enabling mystical experiences
- Invoking the grace of the Divine in our lives

A Large, Well-Used Copper Havan Kund and a Small Havan Kund
(Both are owned by the author and have spoons resting on them.
The larger one is used during public rituals and the smaller one is for personal use.)

When you have a permanent place for ritual, a space for a fire can be built permanently from bricks. As you may have guessed, the Vedic Hindus added an incredible list of specific rules for building such a fire pit. Since most people don't have the luxury of having such a space, an inexpensive copper havan kund is most frequently used. These range in size from very small for personal use up to two-feet square.

Naturally, you will also need some wood and kindling. You may want to get some ritual spoons (sticks) as well. These are also made of copper or another metal. For larger havan kunds, these spoons have long wooden handles. They are usually used to add one of two substances to the fire. The first is ghee, which is used to keep the fire going. The second is *samagri*, an incense made of powder and/or small chunks of sweet-smelling herbs.

Panchpatra (with Spoon) and Charanamrit

The *panchpatra* is simply a cup, usually made from metal such as copper or steel, which holds the *charanamrit*. This is a substance made of five elements: ghee, water, yogurt, honey, and sacred basil (*tulsi*). It is used as a sacred offering, and at the end of the ritual it is given in small amounts to the participants.

Garlands

It is common in rituals to see the use of garlands of flowers, similar to the Hawaiian *lei*. Two sizes are used, one for participants and smaller ones that are placed on the murthis. Sometimes full-sized garlands are used and wrapped around the small deity figures. Although traditionally garlands are made of flowers, these can be expensive to buy and time-consuming to make. As a result, some people use garlands made of paper or fabric. Garlands are signs of auspiciousness and may also be used to decorate doors.

These few items, along with the personal ones, are really all you need for Tantric ritual work. You may want to add robes, daggers, wands, and other items, but they're not necessary.

Bonus Section: How to Make Ghee

The simplest way to obtain ghee is to buy it at an Indian grocery. However, if there is not one near you and you don't want to order online, it is not too difficult to make.

1. Melt a pound of high-quality unsalted (preferably organic) butter in a saucepan over medium heat.
2. Watch the butter. It will begin to boil gently. It will also separate, with a white froth at the top and solids settling to the bottom. Do *not* stir.
3. You want to boil off all the water. After a time (about twenty minutes, depending upon the heat), several things will happen:
   a. The bubbling sound will decrease.
   b. The liquid under the froth at the top will turn transparent amber in color.
   c. The solids at the bottom will turn a golden brown (you can check by gently tilting the pan).
   d. The smell will change. Some have described this as the scent of freshly baked croissants.
4. Turn off the heat. If you wait too long, the butter will burn and be ruined.

5. Wait a half hour to allow your ghee to cool slightly. Adding ⅛ teaspoon of salt will help any floating particles to sink to the bottom.
6. Line a strainer with cheesecloth (you may need a few layers) and gently strain the liquefied and purified butter through it into sterilized jars. Discard the rest.

That's it. Congratulations, you've made ghee! As long as it's kept in a sealed jar, you can store it for up to a year without refrigeration. If you do refrigerate it, the ghee may last longer. However, when cold, it will turn hard and yellow. It will quickly melt when heated.

EIGHT

Repeated Rituals and Celebratory Festivals

A ritual is any repeated practice. For example, when you rise in the morning, if you regularly use the bathroom in a certain way, that is a ritual. When I get up, I wash my face, shave, take a shower, then brush my teeth. That is my morning ritual. If you follow a different pattern, that is your ritual.

Magicians have certain rituals, too. There are banishings, evocations, invocations, healings, and others. Each magician has his or her own unique pattern, although it may be based on some predefined tradition.

Followers of various religions have sets of rituals. Some are personal, such as private prayers. Others are public, such as regular religious services. Still others mark important events in either the history of the group (its myths) or the society at large. Those that represent important events to the group would include the Christian rituals of Christmas, Lent, and Ash Wednesday, the Jewish rituals of Hanukkah, Purim, and Passover, the Islamic Day of Ashura, certain Pagan sabbats, and many more. Those that represent the important events to the larger society would include the celebration of the new year, harvest festivals, solstice rituals, equinox rituals, and certain other Pagan sabbats.

In the Tantric tradition described in these pages, there are several types of rituals. Some, such as banishings and working with the Sri Yantra, have already been described.

Generally speaking, the rituals of *Modern Tantra* can be divided into three major categories. The first category is *magickal rituals*. In this book I've divided those into two sections based upon whether or not they use Tantric sexual practices as part of the technique. In order to understand these magickal methods, however, I'll need to share some more concepts. This information and appropriate techniques will be presented beginning with chapter 9.

The second major category I call *special occasion rituals*. These are rituals that are likely to occur only once or, at best, a few times during a person's life. Examples of this type of ritual include initiation into a Tantric order, a wedding, etc. You may participate many times in such rites as an observer or officiant, but you are usually the focus of such rituals only once. I'll be discussing and giving examples of these rituals in the next chapter.

In the present chapter I'll be sharing information and ideas concerning *repeated rituals and celebratory festivals*. These are those rites and fests that are held regularly each year.

In general, discussing Tantric rituals is quite challenging. Coming from ancient India where travel and communications were difficult, rituals were different from area to area, town to town, village to village, and even home to home. That's why books focused exclusively or partially on Tantric rituals are large in number, astoundingly complex, and often contradictory. The number of Tantric celebrations and repeated rituals is seemingly endless because of these differences based on location. No book could cover more than a few, let alone all. However, group rituals are important both as celebrations and for bonding among members of Tantric groups. That is why they are part of *Modern Tantra* and are included here.

....

In our modern world, new technologies develop that literally change everything. The telephone was one of these technologies, as was the personal computer. The CD replaced the phonograph record, and now Internet streaming is replacing the CD. Such technologies are called disruptive in that they disrupt established patterns that came before. Everything changes.

Tantra is disruptive, too. Part of the essence of various forms of Tantra is that the practice of its techniques and methods breaks down your personal boundaries and taboos, disrupting your "normal" life and opening you to astounding new possibilities. There are many spell books and magickal books that are filled with explicit directions for performing various rituals, spells, and techniques. Real Tantrics and followers of *Modern Tantra* laugh at that concept! How can you possibly explore new territory and new directions if all you do is copy what someone else, including me, puts in writing? That's called dogma. That's what the people of Agarthi-La would do, not the people of Ananda-La. When there is dogma, you will have priests and popes, not free thinkers, scientists, and experimenters. With dogma, you don't have Tantra.

So isn't everything I've shared in this book so far a type of dogma? That will depend upon how you approach it. If you read and think, "What's written there must be true because it's in the book," then yes, it's dogma. It's not a Tantric way of thinking. But if you examine the concepts thoroughly and find that some or most make sense to you, then it is not dogma; it is science and logic.

That means if something doesn't make sense, you either find out why and understand it better so it *does* make sense or you throw it out. And if meditating about what you've read changes the way you've thought about things before—if it's disruptive—then your thinking is definitely Tantric.

Please approach all of the rituals presented here from that Tantric—disruptive—point of view. I hope you will have tried out some of the rituals and ideas already presented. Do they work? If not, modify them or try something else. If they do work, you can add them to your magickal repertoire. Think like a scientist. Keep what works and discard what is useless. That's how to think like a Tantric. That's how to think as a Tantric. That's how to be a Tantric.

The following descriptions of rituals and festivals are intended as outlines, not strict instructions that must be followed on pain of death! There are no Tantric police who will come around and punish you if you do something more elaborately, add to the outline, simplify it, or modify what you read on the following pages. All I would ask is that you approach any changes or modifications from a Tantric point of view.

I am in favor of new interpretations of rituals and rites. I am in favor of evolution and change. However, I am *not* in favor of just throwing things in because you think it might be good. I have attended far too many rituals designed by people who thought that what they created would be good, but in practice the ritual was non-effective or, even worse, it was boring. Every change you make and idea you add should have a *practical* reason behind it, not just a philosophical reason. Every motion and action in a ritual should have a symbolic and/or energetic purpose. If what you want to add or change fits in with these things, try it! And if it doesn't actually work as you expected, discard it. Don't hold on to something because it's theoretically, philosophically, or traditionally right. Keep it if it works.

As an added bonus, this freedom gives members of your Tantric chakra, your Tantric work group, a chance to stretch their creativity. I would hope that your studies go far beyond this one book. What can you bring from other sources to your Tantric work?

One final note: Tantra should be a path of joy and laughter, of fun and smiles. This does not mean you cannot be 100 percent serious and devoted to this path. It means, as I like to say, "If it ain't fun, why bother?" Yes, make your rituals serious. Yes, make them thoughtful. Yes, make them meaningful and passionate. *But don't forget to have fun and smile, sing and dance, and enjoy the presence of Shiva and Shakti!*

Daily Ritual

Modern Tantra is more than a collection of ideas and practices. You can incorporate Tantric techniques and concepts into other spiritual traditions, but to actually *be* a Tantric, make them a part of your daily life. One aspect of this is to perform a simple ritual every morning.

1. Begin by purifying your body and mind. Do this by washing yourself and beginning the rite with a clear and positive mind frame.
2. Take the statue (murthi), framed drawing, or yantra of your regular deity (your Ishta Devata) or the deity you want to work with today, and put it on a large plate.
3. In a lota pot or other container, add a few drops of Ganga jal (if you have some), then fill the pot with fresh, cool water.

4. Using a small spoon, a leaf from a tree, or your fingers, sprinkle some water on the deity while chanting the deity's name or mantra. This brings the deity into the image. Move the statue, drawing, or yantra to your altar. This is called *seating the deity*.
5. Light an incense stick and wave it in three clockwise circles in front of the deity. Put the incense back in its holder.
6. Chant the deity's name or mantra 108 times using a mala to keep count.
7. Use ash from the incense to draw three horizontal lines (top, middle, bottom) across the forehead of the statue. Alternatively, put a dot of kumkum (or red powder) on the forehead, image, or center of the yantra.
8. Add a few grains of akshat (the special rice described in chapter 7) around the image.
9. Make an offering of dried fruits and nuts or hard candy to the deity.
10. From the special spool of red thread, take a piece and tie it around your wrist. Males do this on their right wrist, women on their left wrist.
11. Light your diya lamp and take it in your right hand. Take a bell in your left hand. Make three clockwise circles with the light in front of the deity as you ring the bell and focus on the deity. If you don't have this type of lamp, use a candle or other light. This part of the ritual is called *aarti*.
12. Practice sun-moon breathing (see the following section).
13. Leave the deity on the altar. Pick up the offering and give the candy, fruits, and nuts to friends and family.

....

This may seem like a lot of steps, but try it! You'll see that the ritual moves very quickly. Excluding step 1 (most of which you'd be doing anyway), this ritual should take perhaps 10–15 minutes at most.

In the section in chapter 7 on the danda, I described the practice of swara yoga, or brain breathing. There is another way to help balance the energy that is a great way to start any day. It's called *sun-moon breathing* and it's very easy to do.

1. Sit in a comfortable position. Place the index finger of your right hand on your third eye between the brows. Place your middle finger lightly against the left nostril and thumb against the right nostril.
2. Press with the thumb against the right nostril, closing it. Inhale deeply through the left nostril. Pause.
3. Release the thumb's pressure and use the middle finger to close the left nostril. Exhale slowly through the right nostril. Pause.
4. Inhale deeply through the right nostril. Close the right nostril with the thumb and release the middle finger's pressure on the left nostril. Exhale slowly through the left nostril.
5. Repeat steps 2–4 for three minutes. When you feel good about it, extend this practice by a few minutes at a time until you can do this for twenty minutes.

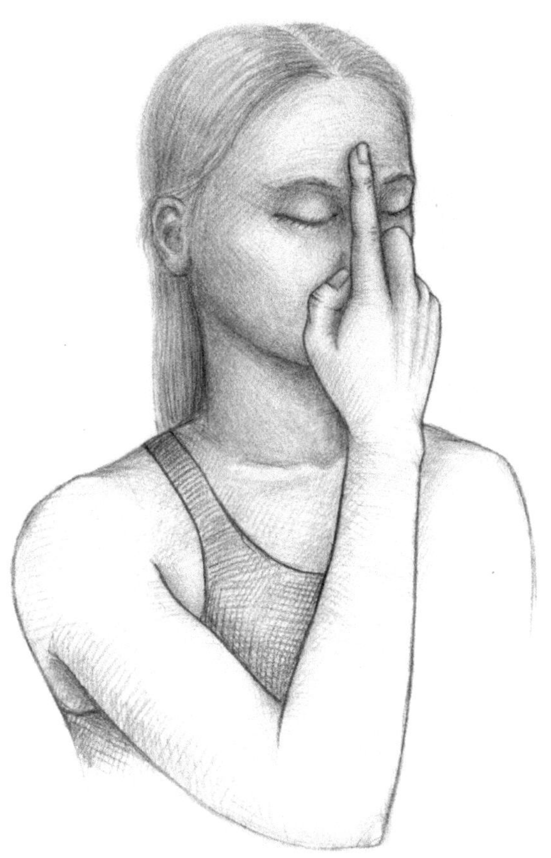

Sun-Moon Breathing

As you may remember, the Ida and Pingala nadis—the carriers of the solar and lunar energies, respectively—begin at the tip of the spine and conclude at the nostrils. This Tantric technique of sun-moon breathing will clear the solar and lunar currents of energy in your body, increasing your vitality and energy level (without coffee!). If you have any breathing issues (allergies, asthma, emphysema, etc.), begin this practice for a much shorter time, perhaps only fifteen seconds. Go gently. Don't be surprised, however, if you find your symptoms lessen and your need for medicines decreases. Do not change your prescriptions or dosages without consulting your physician.

Basic Group or Individual Ritual

As with Western traditions, there is a basic format for performing most Tantric rituals:

1. Banish
2. Create sacred space
3. Invite deities
4. Perform ritual work
5. Close sacred space
6. Banish

Here is the way this can be generally performed:

Banish

Banish using your favorite ritual. I really like using the Mahavidya banishing ritual given at the end of chapter 4. A more rapid technique is to use the thunderbolt mantra, *Phat!* Pronounced like "top hat" without the beginning "to-," it should explode from your mouth like thunder. Start at the east of your area. Shout *Phat!* while facing the east. Move to the south and shout *Phat!* while facing that direction. Repeat in the west and north and return to the east, completing a circle.

Move in a clockwise direction to the southeast and shout *Phat!* while facing in that direction. Move to the southwest and repeat. Do the same in the northwest and northeast. Complete this second circle by returning to the southeast. Move to the center of your space. Look up and shout *Phat!*, then look down and shout *Phat!* The banishing is complete.

You may also banish by going to the directions in the same order and striking a gong in each location, sounding a conch horn, or even just clapping your hands once or snapping your fingers.

If you don't have a lot of room, then instead of walking around in a circle, you can just pivot in place from a central point. I would add that with the directions marked out this way, it is very common for sacred space to be square or rectangular rather than circular, but it is still referred to as a *magickal chakra* (circle). The outer edge of the chakra is called the *Lakshmana Rekha* ("lahk-shma-nah rayk-ha"). This refers to a magickal limit that cannot be crossed without permission. (Note: A group of people getting together to work Tantric rituals is called a *Tantric chakra*. It equates to the idea of a Wiccan coven or ceremonial magick group. The magick circle may be called a magickal chakra or a KalaKakra. And, of course, there are also chakras associated with parts of the physical and non-physical body.)

Create Sacred Space

On the altar, have a pitcher or large bowl of fresh water (do *not* use Ganga jal in it) along with eight small bowls. From the pitcher or large bowl, partially fill each of the smaller bowls. Do this one at a time. Place each smaller bowl at the same locations where you banished: the cardinal directions and the cross-quarters. The larger bowl is placed at the center of the magickal chakra. If you have several people and lots of room, two or more participants may perform this part of the rite.

The ritual leader stands at the center of the room and faces east. This leader says:

Om!
I give honor and respect to
all Tantric brothers and
sisters, gurus and teachers.
Om!
I give honor and respect
to all the deities.
Om!
I caste this circle, aglow with the
spirit of innumerable Tantrics.
Om!
This chakra is now
formed and complete!
Om!
May the peace of Om-Shiva-Shakti
fill this sacred space.
Om!

If you are performing this ritual by yourself, continue. If you are working with others, it is now time for the rest of the participants to enter.

They may enter, one at a time, from any single direction as your space permits. As each person enters, place three horizontal lines of ash from incense across their forehead. If you do not have enough ash, make the three lines using a red powder on the males and a white powder on the females. For a more elaborate entry, also put the three horizontal lines on the upper arms and thighs. As your group increases in size, a woman should do this to the men and a man should do this to the women. You might also sprinkle the participants with water from a bowl that contains a few drops of Ganga jal.

Give each person a red thread long enough to tie around his or her wrist. Men put it on their right wrist and women on their left.

Invite Deities

Use the method described in the daily ritual earlier in this chapter. Before placing the incense in its holder, take it around the circle so each participant may wave it toward himself or herself to better smell the scent. After you do aarti with the lamp and bell, take the lamp around so that participants can briefly hold their hands over the flame to feel its warmth.

Perform Ritual Work

In rituals designed just for magick—where you do some sort of working to obtain a goal—this is where the actual work takes place. Typical techniques involve raising and generating magickal energy, as well as directing that energy toward achieving your goal. Several magickal techniques have already been explained and others will be described later in this book.

In the rituals described in this chapter, the goal is not primarily magickal work, but rather celebration. It is a time of enjoyment rather than exertion. However, that does not mean you cannot or should not perform goal-oriented magick during the rites and holidays described here. In fact, you are encouraged to do so, especially magick that seems appropriate to the purpose of the rite.

At the end of ritual work, you have time to relax, talk about the ritual, share the nuts, fruits, and candy of the offering, and so forth.

Close Sacred Space

Do this by collecting the bowls of water. Do so in the reverse order that they were put out. Pour the water back into the larger bowl or pitcher. This water has been made sacred and magickally empowered by its presence at the ritual. Pass the collected water around so participants may drink of it and splash it on their bodies.

Banish

Use your favorite banishing to close the ritual.

Do you have to follow this basic ritual to the letter? Absolutely not! If you want to modify this rite, go ahead. However, you should follow the basic concepts outlined here.

Digambara

The ancient Sanskrit word *digambara* means "clothed with the directions of space." It's the Tantric term for what Wiccans refer to as "skyclad." It indicates ritual nakedness. In the previous ritual, you will note that there is a part where ashes or colored powder may be placed on the upper arms and thighs. This would be hard to do if a person were fully clothed. Tantric rites are traditionally performed digambara.

There is a long history of nakedness in ritual in both Eastern and Western traditions. Unfortunately, some people are very repressed about such a practice. Some Western ceremonial magicians are incredibly repressed about nudity due to its association with sexuality and would never consider performing magick this way unless they were alone. Some people who practice a Western Pagan path—often having learned primarily from books—may still have personal issues over the way they feel about the appearance of their bodies or don't want to see the genitals of others. Some men are afraid they'd become embarrassed if they got an erection. There are even Eastern and Western spiritual traditions where people hate their bodies.

I understand these feelings. We've all been there in one way or another. But these attitudes are decidedly *not* Tantric.

Tantric rituals are not about you and your physical appearance. They're about working with energies and deities. Practicing digambara is about honoring your body (a gift from the gods!) however it looks… or, more accurately, however you may *think* it looks.

If you have issues about being digambara yourself or seeing others honoring the deities without clothes, you are attached to some limiting beliefs and ideas. This is a klesha pushed right into your face! Spend some time meditating on the foolishness of this attachment and free yourself from this klesha.

However, this Tantric attitude should *never*, under any circumstances, be used as a means to coerce someone into ritual nudity before that person is ready to work digambara. If someone is uncomfortable with this concept, they should work through their issues and attachments *before* working this way. Nor should a person's decision not to work digambara be treated in any way other than with respect and honor. If a person is ready to work this way, great. If they're not ready to work this way, that's great, too. They should be informed before a ritual whether it will be digambara, and they should be free to participate or not. Simply by knowing that to be part of full rituals requires being clothed with the directions of space may result in a person examining their issues as to why they want to be a part of your Tantric chakra yet not participate fully. Tantra may not be their path at this time, and this can be the issue that separates members from those who are not ready for membership at this time. They should be allowed to depart from your group in friendship and with respect.

Although *private* rituals are traditionally digambara, you may want to have participants remain clothed if you have public rituals that are not limited to the members of your chakra. Modify the rituals to meet the requirements of the situation.

Tantric Lunar (Full Moon) Celebrations

As with most Pagan traditions, Tantra includes rituals focused around the beauty of the Goddess as represented by the full moon. According to multiple sources, various ancient (and modern) Pagan cultures and traditions have names for each full moon. For example, the full moon in February was called the Budding Moon by the Chinese, Bony Moon by the Cherokee, Little Famine Moon by the Choctaw, Moon of the Raccoon by the Dakotah Sioux, Moon of Ice by the Celts, and Storm Moon by the people of medieval England. Some Neopagans refer to it as the Snow Moon.

The word for full moon in Sanskrit is *purnima* ("purr-nee-mah"), and each full moon has a term attached to that word. While the ancient months were more astrological in nature (the month of *Paush*, for example, began on the winter solstice, December 22, and ended on January 20), today we follow the familiar Western solar or Gregorian calendar, celebrating the full moon in the Western month named.

In terms of timing, naturally you will want to perform some sort of celebration or ritual on the day of the full moon itself or as close as possible to that date. But what is the ideal time of day to perform such a celebration? The simplest traditional answer is "during twilight." In Tantra, there are four daily twilights. The notion of twilight is that you are transitioning from one period of the day to another. The best-known twilight occurs at sunset, between the day and night. The second type of twilight occurs at sunrise, between night and day. The third Tantric twilight occurs at noon, the transition from morning to afternoon. The fourth Tantric twilight takes place at midnight, the transition from one day to the next, from the beginning and growth of darkness to the diminishing and end of darkness.

So which of the twilights is the best time to perform a Tantric rite? Any of them will work perfectly.

January: Paush Purnima

This is a festival for cleaning out of the old and making way for the new. Follow the basic group ritual given in this chapter. For ritual work, bring washcloths and warm water into the sacred space. Take turns bathing each other. As you are thoroughly cleansed, visualize all of the problems and issues of the old year being washed away as you prepare for the year. Also, there should be a bucket of water with a ladle so that after each person is washed, he or she may ladle water over the Shiva lingam, if you have one, on the altar.

February: Magh Purnima

This is a festival of remembrance. Everyone should be sure to take an extensive shower or bath before attending. Follow the basic group ritual. During the period for performing ritual work, each person should share stories of deceased loved ones, of heroes and heroines. What is meant by "hero" is up to each person to determine. Although preferably these stories should have taken place during the previous year, any story of heroes from any time and of any sort will work. At the end of your turn, become a hero yourself by announcing what charity you will give to—with money or work—before the next full moon.

March: Falgun Purnima (Holi)

This is the celebration of the holiday known as *Holi*, marking the victory over a demon. People throw colored powder or use squirt guns to shoot colored water at each other. If you come to the ritual in clothes that are not stained, expect to get clobbered! Work magick for fresh starts. After the ritual, dress in clean new clothes that you brought with you to the rite.

April: Hanuman Jayanti Purnima

As you may remember from chapter 3, Hanuman, the monkey god, is the strongest and best warrior. This is an ideal time for playing games, especially warlike games such as chess or Parcheesi, both of which began in ancient India. Play some of these games during the ritual work section. Keep in mind that concepts behind warfare can relate to business, friendships, and other relationships. What can you learn from playing these games and how can you apply this to your daily life?

May: Buddha Purnima

The root of the Sanskrit word Buddha, *Budh*, means "enlightened." A Buddha, then, is an enlightened person. Part of this full moon ritual includes each person sharing a spiritual truth with others. It should be one that they learned during the previous year.

June: Vat Purnima

This is a day for honoring nature and healing. During the day, find a tree that is especially meaningful to you. Clear and clean the area around it. Meditate on the tree. As part of your meditation, say, "I pray for the health and well-being of my family, my friends, my chakra, and my community." Tie a string around the tree. Burn incense for the tree and spread some beautiful flowers and uncooked rice around it. Finally, water the tree.

Next, go out and honor the first woman you meet. Compliment her in some way. Be sure your compliment is sincere.

Prepare some delicious food to share with the members of your chakra. Share it during the ritual work section of the ritual. Tell what you did for the tree and the woman you complimented. How do you think it made her feel? How did you feel?

July: Guru Purnima

This is the equivalent of a birthday party for your leader as a representative of all gurus, past, present, and future. Honor him or her with small gifts. If your chakra has a guru or leader, wash your guru's feet. During the ritual work section, honor the first guru of Tantrics, Shiva, by giving gifts (flowers, candy, burn incense, dried fruits, etc.) to the Shiva lingam. Also, pour water over the Shiva lingam.

The guru or leader should then give a special talk, granting the grace of knowledge. The guru giving a blessing to everyone in the chakra concludes this month's ritual work section.

August: Narali Purnima

This is a nice celebration, preferably with singing (perhaps some karaoke?) and dancing. Eat some tasty fish (some Tantrics, especially those who live on or near a coast, consider the day as honoring the sea god *Samudra*), and, since this is also known as Coconut Day, offer coconut to Shiva. Have some yourself, too. Some take their coconut to the sea and offer it to Samudra.

September: Bhadrapad Purnima

Before going to the ritual, spend time cleaning your home. Wash or paint some walls. Perhaps change or put up some new artwork.

Even though you're working, eat as little as possible or fast (if it's medically safe for you to do so) during the day. During your ritual work, meditate on whom you may have harmed in some way during the year and how best to make it up to them. Eat only bread and drink water during the ritual.

October: Sharad Purnima

Traditionally a harvest festival, it's also a time to worship Lakshmi as the goddess of wealth. If you don't have her murthi in your ritual space regularly, include it for this ritual. Give typical offerings (dried fruits, nuts, candy) and ask for her blessings. Eat rice cakes and drink milk.

November: Kartik Purnima

This is a very special time. Every few minutes during the ritual, light some more candles. Give small gifts to each other. Gambling for fun is encouraged. This is one of the days of the festival known as *Diwali*.

December: Margashirsha Purnima

Giving gifts to charity on this day is very auspicious. During the ritual, honor Lord Dattatreya, the founder of one of the leading Tantric traditions.

....

The regular cycle of the moon around the earth is shorter than any calendar month. As a result, every few years there are two full moons experienced in one month. There were two full moons in May 2007, December 2009, August 2012, and July 2015.

When two full moons occur during the same month, celebrate the first as just described. The second is considered *Dvitiya Purnima*, second full moon. Honor and give offerings to Shiva, Shakti, and the guru.

I want to reiterate that these are full moon *celebrations*. They're not about performing magickal work to achieve a goal. However, that doesn't mean you cannot perform magick, as described later in this book, during the ritual work section of these celebration rituals.

The Challenge of Tantric Solar Festivals

The calendar of Tantra is not the same as the current Western calendar. Rather, like the Jewish calendar and many Pagan calendars, it is lunar in nature. Events take place at times associated with the motions of the moon and do not occur yearly on the same dates of the Western solar calendar. Thus, as with holidays such as Easter (which is held on the first Sunday after the full moon following the spring equinox and can fall between March 22 and April 25), the dates of some holidays, as shown on a Western calendar, change from year to year. In Roman Catholic tradition, this is known as a *movable feast*.

Unfortunately, most Westerners don't seem to like holidays where you have to figure out the dates. They prefer to leave it to the church, the synagogue, or some other group to determine and give out the dates. Tantra, however, has no such single authority. As a result, the group described at the beginning of this book, NAMASTE, made compromises on establishing specific dates for yearly festivals. This may sound like taking the easy way out, appropriating an ancient tradition and modifying it to fit Western needs, but that's not the case. In 1957, India enacted a calendar reform, giving a unified calendar for civil use. Up to that time, there were thirty different calendars being used in India. Although things are changing, religious calendars from one tradition and in one district in India may not match those in the next. The same holiday was often celebrated on different days in various parts of the Indian subcontinent. By giving standardized dates for holidays, this book continues the methodology of the standardization that began in India over half a century ago.

Yes, this does make practicing and living a Tantric life easier and more compatible for Westerners. Thanks to the Internet, you can alternatively learn about the Indian calendars and figure out an appropriate date for a celebration each year. However, those are the dates that have been adopted as modern *Hindu* holidays. The dates that follow are associated with pre-Hindu Tantra and have been updated for the needs of people today. In fact, since these festivities are celebratory in nature, you could add to the revelry by following both these dates and the ones that change. Nevertheless, *Modern Tantra*–based chakras have their main celebration on the given dates.

....

Most Westerners involved with Paganism are familiar with the Celtic Wheel of the Year, the eight celebrations that include the two equinoxes, the two solstices, and the four days midway between them. Traditional Tantra, while definitely Pagan, does not have a matching wheel. I am told that NAMASTE tried to create one based on the traditional movable holidays, but the timing was so off that they went with the following, more appropriate, system.

So why was there not a Wheel of the Year? I can only speculate. India officially has four major meteorological periods each year. There is a long, brutally hot summer that begins in March or April and ends in June or July. Temperatures have reached as high as 122° F (50° C), with high humidity, making the heat even more challenging. So there are not going to be a lot of celebrations and festivities during this period. Sometimes summer is known as *pre-monsoon*, as it is followed by the monsoon season, with torrential rains and winds, again making the holding of festivities difficult. The post-monsoon season takes place from about October to December, and the weather is warm and humid, but pleasant. Finally, there is winter beginning in December or January and continuing to a brief spring before the return of summer. The weather in spring tends to be cool and very nice.

Of course, India is a huge landmass, and there are major weather variations from east to west and north to south, compounded by elevation and the influence of rivers, lakes, and oceans. However, from summer through the monsoon season, the number of festivals is limited. Thus, from the end of March (beginning of summer) to the time when the monsoons begin to decrease (middle of August), there are no festivals.

Again, this is only speculation on my part, but I feel it makes sense.

Finally, the solar celebrations I'm about to describe are festivals and are meant to be fun. In later Hindu traditions, there are often long and even multiday versions of these holidays with extensive rituals. For Tantrics, everything we do is a type of worship. Attending a fun festival is just as meaningful as participating in a traditional rite.

Yugadi—March 21

Also spelled *Ugadi*, this is the new year. As is typical in lunar calendars, it occurs on the first day of the Western astrological sign of Aries, the spring equinox. Publicly it is celebrated by exchanging greeting cards and decorating the outside of your home. By yourself (or with your family or Tantric chakra), you would perform your daily ritual, adding to it divinations and wishes for the coming year. Each person is also given two tasks:

- Make a donation to a charity.
- Do something that will make another person happy.

The second item could be anything from doing someone's chores for them or taking a friend to a movie, to something far more intimate and ecstatically joyful.

It is a tradition to eat a dish made of six tastes. These flavors, blended together, remind you to accept what comes and deal with it as necessary rather than dwell upon it and let it bother you for days, weeks, months, or longer. The tastes are:

Bitter: symbolizing sadness
Sweet: symbolizing happiness
Spicy hot: symbolizing anger
Salt: symbolizing fear
Sour: symbolizing disgust
Tangy: symbolizing surprise

Traditionally, the components of this dish include bitter flowers (from a fast-growing evergreen known as *neem*), ripe banana, hot peppers, salt, tamarind juice, and unripe mango, respectively. However, you may consider having a contest to see who can come up with the best dish of six tastes.

Rakhi—August 15

Also known as *Raksha Bandhan* (the bond of protection), this is specifically a family holiday. But unlike those family holidays that focus on relationships between parents and children, this is about renewing the bonds between brothers and sisters.

Sisters and brothers traditionally have deep bonds with each other. Brothers are expected to protect their sisters for their entire lives. Sisters are expected to love their brothers. In families, sisters tie the red thread (*rakhi*) around the right wrists of their brothers, saying:

As the sun spreads sunlight,
As the plant spreads its seeds,
I tie the sacred thread on your wrist.
O sacred thread, may you
Grant my brother long life,
And may he never stumble
In his protection of me.

In return, brothers present gifts to their sisters as a token of their love and affection.

Some people may see this as sexist. Indeed, in modern terms, it is. But remember, Tantric concepts are often written in *Sandhya Bhasha*, or twilight language. The concept of brother and sister, male and female, sun and moon, can just as easily relate to the energies of the body. Therefore, *all* are brothers and *all* are sisters within a Tantric chakra. Members of the group should treat each other that way, loving and honoring each other as brothers and sisters. Everyone should protect each other and the group. The Tantric chakra becomes as close as a family, perhaps closer, as you become a member by choice, not chance.

This is an ideal time to create rituals that will allow all members to dedicate themselves and all of their solar/lunar energies to each other and to the chakra. It is a renewal of the chakra's members to each other, to the leader, and to the chakra.

Ganesha Chaturthi—September 1

As implied by the name, this is the festival of Ganesh. If you're unfamiliar with Ganesh, go back to chapter 3 to read about him. He breaks down obstacles. His feet are the largest of any animal, allowing him to walk through anything, making him an ideal leader. Honor your statue of Ganesh with flowers, foods, incense, oil lamps, and chanting. You can chant his mantra, *Aum Gam Ganapatiye Namaha*.

The word *Chaturthi* has a special meaning. It's a special state of consciousness that is neither waking, nor dreaming, nor deep sleep. Rather, it is far deeper than all three states. This is a wonderful time to meditate deeply on the concept of Ganesh and how he can break through the obstacles in your life. As a group, you might want to have a guided meditation on this or even work with hypnosis (Sanskrit: *sammohan*).

Maha Navaratri—October 1

This is more than just a festival of nine (*nava*) nights (*ratri*). In modern India, this celebration of nine nights occurs five times a year, for an astounding forty-five days. Of all five solar festivals, this is considered the greatest (*maha*), so modern Tantrics celebrate this festival on this day.

It's no wonder that this festival is so popular. It's dedicated to Shakti, the primal energy, the Goddess who manifests as all the other goddesses, the energy that is in us all.

Also in India, there are many stories about the meaning of this festival. One of the traditions is dancing. Of course, there are dances that have become traditional. One is called the *Garba*, which comes from the Sanskrit word *Garbha*, meaning "womb." This is clearly a dance of and for the Goddess.

Place an image of the Goddess or an oil lamp (or a candle within a vase) in the center of your area. Draw three large concentric circles, with the image at their center. Play music and dance around the center. When you are in the ring closest to the center, think of the energy you are raising. In the middle ring, focus on the concept of love. In the outer ring, concentrate on your notion of deity. If you have the lamp or candle in a vase, consider that all humans have the light and energy of deity (lamp) within their bodies (vase). If you go into trance from the dancing, so much the better!

If you want to follow the idea of nine days (Maha Navaratri is on the last day), the first three days should honor Durga or Kali and you should focus on destroying or discarding all unwanted things in your life. The next three days are in honor of Lakshmi, the goddess of wealth. This includes spiritual wealth as well as material wealth. The final three days honor Saraswati, the goddess of wisdom. It ends with the celebratory dance.

Why is dance so important even in modern India? Think about it. As you dance and swirl about (the music should be up-tempo, not slow), your pulse increases and your breathing quickens. Your body produces hormones that accompany these changes. All of this is also indicative of the movement of Shakti energy within you. This festival is about the movement of the energy, so *get up and move!*

Diwali—October 31

Diwali is a beautiful festival intended for families. The name is a contraction of *Deepavali*, which means "row of lights." This festival is also dedicated to Lakshmi, the goddess of wealth.

Today, Diwali is celebrated in countries all over the world over a period of five days. Each day you light more small lamps and place them in front of your home. By the fifth day, this can be incredibly beautiful.

In combination with the lamps, people use colored powder to draw simple to elaborate geometric images, like yantras, on the ground. Today, these images, known as *rangoli*, are sometimes premade in plastic or metal and simply placed on the ground. Traditionally, the skill of drawing these figures was passed from grandmother to granddaughter.

As this holiday is associated with Lakshmi, it's an ideal time for some fun gambling. Children can also participate in the Halloween trick-or-treat as part of Diwali.

I have to draw attention to the practices and date of this festival. Clearly this is an ancient festival urging the sun to return through sympathetic magick—more candles, more sun. However, the similarities of Diwali to the later Jewish Chanukah are obvious. Both, in fact, are referred to as the "festival of lights," both include an increasing number of lamps, and both encourage gambling for fun.

As I mentioned earlier in this book, there is evidence of communication between India and the Middle East long before Chanukah became a minor (in the US, a major) Jewish holiday. Of course, merely having similarities and predating the later festival does not prove direct influence, but it is surprisingly suggestive.

Maha Shivaratri— New Moon in February

Although a lunar and not a solar festival, this celebration, a night dedicated to the great Tantric deity Shiva, is an incredible experience. On this night, people gather around the Shiva lingam and sing chants to him . . . all night. As I described earlier, I was at a Hindu temple in a Los Angeles suburb doing this, and at 2:00 AM, because we were chanting too loudly, the police busted us!

Also to honor Shiva, gifts are made to him by pouring them over the lingam. These can be gifts of flowers, water, milk, and plain yogurt.

Holi—Full Moon in March

This is another lunar festival, and since it takes place on the full moon, it was described in the previous section. It remains one of the most popular festivals in India, so it is listed again here. For celebration instructions, however, please see the previous entry.

NINE

Special Occasion Rituals

In the previous chapter, I described the rituals that take place every year. In this chapter, I'll be describing several rituals that most frequently happen only once in a lifetime.

Some people may also think that initiation can occur many times. While it is true that you may be initiated into several groups or organizations, or move through the degrees in such groups several times, the reality is that either the initiation into each of these events is successful or it is not. In this book, the example of initiation will be an initiation ritual into the *Modern Tantra* tradition. Two forms of it, a basic or essential version and a more elaborate version, are provided.

Although some of these rituals are quite complete (as with the rituals in the previous chapter), others are more outlines than fully described rituals. This is intended to allow you plenty of leeway in personalizing and adding to these rituals. However, this does not mean you should just throw in anything you happen to like at a particular moment. Rituals should be well thought out philosophically and practically, and, in some cases, theologically. The magickal rituals designed to achieve a specific end, described later in this book, are more complete.

Ritual for the Birth of a Child

According to one tradition I was initiated into, there are three great mysteries in the world: what comes before life, what comes after life, and the nature of life itself.

In this ritual, we celebrate the miracle of birth by presenting the child to the deities of the ten directions. This ritual also functions as a naming rite. It is meant to be celebratory and joyous! Have as many friends and family present as possible as you introduce your child to ten forms of the Goddess:

1. Perform a banishing of your choice. Honor Ganesh by saying, ***Om Gam Ganapataye Namaha!***
2. Take the baby to the east of your chakra. Say: **All honor to Chhinnamasta, goddess who resides in the east. This is [baby's name]. Watch over him/her and guide him/her to having satisfaction with all he/she does.**
   All say: *Om namah Shivaya!*
3. Take the baby to the south of your chakra. Say: **All honor to Kali, goddess who resides in the south. This is [baby's name]. Watch over him/her and guide him/her to evolve spiritually through his/her life.**
   All say: *Om namah Shivaya!*
4. Take the baby to the west of your chakra. Say: **All honor to Bhuvaneshvari, goddess who resides in the west. This is [baby's name]. Watch over him/her and guide him/her to develop independence and self-mastery.**
   All say: *Om namah Shivaya!*
5. Take the baby to the north of your chakra. Say: **All honor to Bagalamukhi, goddess who resides in the north. This is [baby's name]. Watch over him/her and guide him/her to develop superior communication skills.**
   All say: *Om namah Shivaya!*
6. Take the baby past the east to the southeast of your chakra. Say: **All honor to Dhumavati, goddess who resides in the southeast. This is [baby's name]. Watch over him/her and guide him/her to honoring the wisdom that comes with age.**
   All say: *Om namah Shivaya!*
7. Take the baby to the southwest of your chakra. Say: **All honor to Tripura Sundari, goddess who resides in the southwest. This is [baby's name]. Watch over him/her and guide to find beauty and bliss in this world.**
   All say: *Om namah Shivaya!*
8. Take the baby to the northwest of your chakra. Say: **All honor to Matangi, goddess who resides in the northwest. This is [baby's name]. Watch over him/her and guide him/her to discover the beauty of music.**
   All say: *Om namah Shivaya!*
9. Take the baby to the northeast of your chakra. Say: **All honor to Kamala, goddess who resides in the northeast. This is [baby's name]. Watch over him/her as her/his life unfolds in ways we can only guess.**
   All say: *Om namah Shivaya!*
10. Complete the second circling by returning to the southeast. Take the baby to the center of the chakra and raise him/her up. Say: **All honor to Tara, goddess who resides above us. This is [baby's name]. Watch over him/her and give him/her hope for the future and help when needed.**
    All say: *Om namah Shivaya!*
11. Put the baby on a mat on the floor. Say: **All honor to Bhairavi, goddess who resides below us. This is [baby's name]. Watch over him/her and give him/her strength of body and spirit.**
    All say: *Om namah Shivaya!*

12. Taking ash from incense or colored powder (red for a boy, white for a girl) and make three horizontal lines on the child's forehead. All say: ***Om namah Shivaya!***
13. Celebrate with food and drink. Each person attending should make a toast with a good wish for the future of the child.
14. When the celebration concludes, close with a banishing of your choice.

Tantric Ritual Upon Reaching Puberty

In ancient times, entering puberty was a sign of achieving adulthood. It wasn't uncommon for "adults" to marry in their early teens. Although there is evidence that puberty is now being reached earlier by males and especially by females (possibly due to hormone pollution in milk, foods, and drinking water), the time when people are considered adults seems to be reached later and later.

In *Modern Tantra*, we honor the achievement of puberty. It is at this age that a person can fully participate in all rituals (excluding those of a sexual nature) and even lead them if he or she takes training to do so. The age at which a child reaches puberty depends upon each child. However, this ritual may be delayed until a child's fifteenth birthday, whether physiological puberty has been reached or not. Some people will simply choose to do this on the fifteenth birthday no matter what. Others may choose to do this on the occasion of a young woman's *menarche*, her first menses. The decision to do this depends upon the maturity of the young person and the desires of both the young teen and his or her parents.

The child needs to do two things to perform this ritual. First, the child must select a spiritual name. Although the child, as the first act of adulthood, makes the choice, he or she should demonstrate maturity by making the decision with the guidance of his or her parents. In India to this day, where the retreats known as *ashrams*, run by a guru, remain popular, it was (and is) the guru who gives the spiritual name to the *chela* (student). The supposedly enlightened guru intuitively selects a name based on the needs, qualities, and aspirations of the student. For example, in AMOOKOS I was given the initiatory name *Shambhala Nath* (sometimes written as one word), meaning "Lord of Shambhala." Indeed, in your *Modern Tantra* chakra, the leader/guru may give another name to the student upon initiation into the chakra. The guru is believed to have spiritual insights others do not have.

In the West, however, deciding upon and taking a spiritual or magickal name has become a virtual rite of passage. Since authentic gurus are difficult to come by in the West, the *Modern Tantra* technique is to let the student decide. One way to do this is to get a list of Hindu baby names (many are available online) and find one that is meaningful.

Second, the parents should teach the child to perform an effective banishing. The child should also learn, but not necessarily memorize, the various gods and goddesses as described in *Modern Tantra* and other books.

This ritual follows the same format as that of the ritual for the birth of a child. That makes sense because in the previous ritual a child was born; in this ritual an adult is metaphorically born. In the previous ritual the child was introduced to ten forms of the nurturing Goddess by his or her parents. Here, the new adult introduces himself or herself, using the spiritual name, to ten forms of the strengthening God.

Tantra tends to focus on basic forms of the God and multiple forms of the Goddess. Therefore, the forms of God, and the names used here, are not used in most *Modern Tantra* rites. As part of preparation for this rite, it is up to the child to learn as much as possible about the gods named here. Parents, family, and adult friends may guide and direct the child in this, but they should *not* provide answers. Learning to accept personal responsibility and demonstrating self-reliance are indicators of adulthood. The child performs the following ritual with his or her parents, friends, and family observing. At the conclusion of the ritual, the child is accepted as an adult member of the *Modern Tantra* community.

Note that this is *not* an initiation into the *Modern Tantra* chakra. For that, the person must be of legal age in your local area. This ritual does give the person the right to study the spiritual system more fully.

1. The young person performs a banishing of his or her choice, then honors Ganesh by saying: ***Om Gam Ganapataye Namaha!***
2. The young person moves to the east of his/her chakra and says: **I honor Indra, thundering god who resides in the east. I am [young person's spiritual name]. Teach me the divine mantras, watch over me, and guide me on my path.**
   All say: ***Om namah Shivaya!***
3. The young person moves to the south of his/her chakra and says: **I honor Yama, the god who resides in the south. I am [young person's spiritual name]. Teach me to let go of that which is unneeded, watch over me, and guide me on my path.**
   All say: ***Om namah Shivaya!***
4. The young person moves to the west of his/her chakra and says: **I honor Varuña, the god who resides in the west. I am [young person's spiritual name]. Teach me the laws of karma and how to treat others fairly and justly. Watch over me and guide me on my path.**
   All say: ***Om namah Shivaya!***
5. The young person moves to the north of his/her chakra and says: **I honor Kubera, the god who resides in the north. I am [young person's spiritual name]. Teach me the skills to accumulate the wealth of the spirit and of the world. Watch over me and guide me on my path.**
   All say: ***Om namah Shivaya!***
6. The young person moves past the east to the southeast of his/her chakra and says: **I honor Agni, the god who resides in the southeast. I am [young person's spiritual name]. Teach me how to ignite the fires of the spirit and the body, and how to control them with my will. Watch over me and guide me on my path.**
   All say: ***Om namah Shivaya!***
7. The young person moves to the southwest of his/her chakra and says: **I honor Nir'rta, the god who resides in the southwest. I am [young person's spiritual name]. Teach me the ways to banish the unwanted. Watch over me and guide me on my path.**
   All say: ***Om namah Shivaya!***
8. The young person moves to the northwest of his/her chakra and says: **I honor Vayu, the god who resides in the northwest. I am [young person's spiritual name]. Teach me the secrets of the breath of life. Watch over me and guide me on my path.**
   All say: ***Om namah Shivaya!***
9. The young person moves to the northeast of his/her chakra and says: **I honor Ishana, the lord who resides in the northeast. I am [young person's spiritual name]. Teach me to be satisfied with what I have while giving me the knowledge of how to**

achieve even greater goals. Watch over me and guide me on my path.
All say: ***Om namah Shivaya!***

10. The young person completes the second circling by returning to the southeast, then moves to the center of the chakra, looks up, and says: **I honor Vishnu, the god who resides above me. I am [young person's spiritual name]. Teach me devotion to all that is sacred. Teach me to be free and to allow freedom to others. Watch over me and preserve me. Guide me on my path.**
All say: ***Om namah Shivaya!***

11. The young person looks down and says: **I honor Brahma, the god who resides below. I am [young person's spiritual name]. Teach me the rites and rituals. Teach me skills with language, watch over me, and give me strength of body and spirit. Guide me on my path.**
All say: ***Om namah Shivaya!***

The young person takes ash from incense or colored powder (red for a male, white for a female) and makes three horizontal lines on his/her forehead.
All say: ***Om namah Shivaya!***
The young person makes three horizontal lines on both of his/her upper arms.
All say: ***Om namah Shivaya!***
The young person makes three horizontal lines on the backs of both of his/her hands.
All say: ***Om namah Shivaya!***
The young person makes three horizontal lines on the tops of both of his/her feet.
All say: ***Om namah Shivaya!***

12. The parent(s) of the new adult say: **As a son becomes a man and a daughter becomes a woman, we (I) proudly acknowledge you as an adult in the eyes of our community. This gives you new opportunities to learn, grow, and interact with us while remaining obedient to the laws of the land. It also gives you new duties, making you responsible to the best of your ability for your health and safety, for your mental, emotional, and spiritual growth, and for making contributions to the community. You will always be our (my) son/daughter. You are now also an adult. Welcome!**

13. All: Cheers and applause.

14. Celebrate with food and drink. Each person attending should make a toast with a good wish for the future of the newly "born" adult.

15. The new adult performs his/her first ritual as an adult by closing with a banishing of his/her choice.

Initiation into a *Modern Tantra* Chakra

This ritual comes from several sources. First, some of the basic concepts are derived from the initiation ritual of AMOOKOS, the order described elsewhere in this book. Second, large parts of it have been taken, by permission, from NAMASTE's initiation ritual. There have been major changes, as NAMASTE is intended for both Tantrics and those following a Western sex magick path. It should also be noted that some of the aspects are very modern. If you wish to alter them for your chakra, you should do so.

1) Preparation

A. The candidate should bring a change of clothes and wear old clothes that can be sacrificed. In preparation, the sacrificial clothes are snipped with a scissors or they should have small tears at their hems. These are going to be torn away, representing the tearing away of unwanted outside beliefs and attitudes as well as inner limitations. The shock value of being stripped can help alter consciousness as part of the rite, too. The candidate should wear no shoes or stockings, but jewelry is okay.

B. Props:
   - A long strip of cloth, 1–2 feet wide and perhaps 20 or more feet long. It should be neatly laundered. Preferably, it should have the pattern of a starfield, but it may be white (for women), red (for men), or a rainbow of hues.
   - Blindfold
   - Soft, heavy ropes (red for male candidates, white for females)
   - Images of devas for the directions
   - Sri Yantra
   - One large bowl with water and eight smaller bowls for the quarters and cross-quarters
   - Incense
   - Candles or traditional small oil lamps
   - Vibhuti ash (from incense) or colored powders (again, red for male candidates, white for females)
   - Scented oils and waters (a few drops of oil in water)
   - Appropriate recorded music with a way to play it
   - Gong (or bell)

C. At the beginning of the ritual, the candidate is placed in a separate room or area where the ritual can be heard but not seen.

D. People present should be gender-balanced, or close to it. A minimum of three people plus the candidate should be present. Everyone comes into the circle fully dressed as his or her desires dictate.

E. Time: one of the dark twilights (sunset, midnight, or sunrise).

F. On a piece of paper, print the legal name of the candidate and a name selected by that person or by the head of the *Modern Tantra* chakra determined through an interview with the candidate. The meaning of the name should also be written. Be sure it can be read in dim light.

G. The candidate should have been interviewed previously to make sure he or she is appropriate to join the chakra and that the path of Tantra is appropriate for the candidate. The candidate should also assure the interviewer that he or she is not claustrophobic.

2) Introitus

Items for the ritual are assembled but not in place.

Main Officer (MO): **Greetings.**

ALL: **Greetings. Hello. Hiya.** Ad-lib.

MO: **It is time once again to enter our chakra.**

ALL: Cheers and applause.

2nd Officer (2nd): **Wait.**
There is business at hand.

ALL: **What? What do you mean?**
What's this about? Ad-lib.

MO: Holds up hand to silence group.
Yes. Tell us what this is about.

2nd: **A traveler in the world**
seeks to join us in our chakra.

3rd Officer (3rd): **Is he/she prepared?**

2nd: **Yes. He/She has passed through all the levels of the world and is ready to join us.**

ALL: Cheers and applause.

MO: Holds up hand to silence group.
Wait. No one is perfect. Are you telling me that he/she is ready at this moment?

2nd: Sadly: **I'm afraid not. He/She still wears the clothes of the outer world.**

MO: **Then it is time for a change. Let us prepare our chakra to break his/her connection to the past of mediocrity and conformity, fear and cowardice, so that she/he may be born anew into a greater world of freedom, creativity, and abundant, unending love.**

3) Aperi Laboritorium

ALL: Set up laboratory while chanting ***Om Namah Shivaya.*** Place Sri Yantra at center. From large bowl, fill smaller bowls and place them in eight directions. Place large bowl at center. Place the images in the proper directions derived from the group's study. Place incense, vibhuti, or colored powders on central altar. The Main Officer participates and assures everything is correct. When the chakra is ready to the MO's satisfaction, they continue.

MO: **Let the laboratory be banished.** People near each quarter banish it using the thunderbolt mantra, noisemakers (cymbals or drums), or claps, going east-south-west-north. This is followed by cross-quarters, starting at the southeast, then southwest, northwest, and northeast. Then above and below. Up to this time, all members are in street clothes.

MO: ***Svaha!*** **I salute the line of innumerable Tantrics and cast the circle of semen glow. May the circle be intact and the peace of Om Shiva Shakti dwell herein. Let us consecrate ourselves to the work.**

2nd: **All honor to the Lord**
and Lady residing in my heart.

ALL: Put hands on their hearts. **Om.**

3rd: **All honor to the Lord and Lady residing in the crown of my head.**

ALL: Put hands on the
crowns of their heads. **Om.**

2nd: **All honor to the Lord and Lady residing in the top of the forehead.**

ALL: Put hands on their hairlines. **Om.**

3rd: **All honor to the Lord and**
Lady residing in the armor.

ALL: Put hands on
their upper chests. **Om.**

2nd: **All honor to the Lord and Lady residing in the three eyes.**

ALL: Put hands on their eyes, also covering the third eye. **Om.**

3rd: **All honor to the Lord and Lady residing in the lingam and yoni.**

ALL: Put hands on their lingam or yoni. **Om.**

MO: **Now that we have again dedicated ourselves to the path, let us initiate a new member into our chakra of light, life, freedom, and love. *Svecchachara!***

The 2nd stands at the place where the candidate will enter while the 3rd goes out and returns with the candidate. The 3rd tells the candidate that he/she must answer from the heart and truthfully, without any perceived form of hesitation. This is stressed and repeated. When the candidate says that he/she understands and the 3rd believes this is so, they enter the room and the ritual chakra *backward*, looking at the old world, and the 2nd moves to where the candidate can see him/her.

2nd: **The time has come. Your old world must die!**

4) Initio—Section A: Old World

3rd: Turns the candidate around to face the circle. The candidate sees people for the first time.

ALL: **Jeers.**

MO: Disgusted. **Who do you think you are that you can come in here like that?**

CANDIDATE (CAND): **???**

MO: **What do you think gives you the right to join us?**

CAND: Says anything. The candidate is prodded by the 2nd officer to ***say something!*** if he/she says nothing.

MO: Says, no matter what answer is given: **That's not good enough.**

ALL: **Yeah! That's right** Ad-lib. They close in on the candidate and may even push him/her around, acting tough.

MO: **These men and women have struggled to overcome their fears and blockages and to release their inhibitions, limiting beliefs, and societal strangleholds in order to enter a new world and a new life. Before you can join us, you must be willing to die—to give up everything old in order to let in the new. Are you willing to do that?**

2nd: Breaking in, looking at the candidate. **Wait! Don't answer yet. This is not just about joining the chakra. This is about dying to the old and becoming something entirely new. Everything in your life will change. Are you sure you want to do this?**

3rd: With no pause and looking at the candidate. **Most of those who have joined have dropped by the wayside. After being reborn, they are not able to rejoin the old nor stay with the new. If you join us and fail, you may forever be alone and unhappy. I really don't think you should chance it.**

ALL: **Yeah. Go home. We don't need you.** Ad-lib.

MO: Raises hand and all are quiet. **My friends, just as each of you had to make this decision, so too must [candidate's full name] make his/her decision.**
To candidate: **If you start but choose not to complete the training, you may end up unhappy and alone. Most people who have made it this far either choose to quit now or do so within a short time. There will be no supernatural powers turned against you if you decide to leave, but I can guarantee that if you decide to go further now and drop out later, unhappiness will be your lot for years to come. If you stay the course, the changes, like going through death and rebirth, might be painful, but the possibilities are endless. The choice is yours.**

ALL: Circling so close that they are bumping into the candidate. All speak in loud stage whispers. **Decide. Decide. Make up your mind. Decide. Choose. Decide.** Ad-lib until...

MO: Raises hand and all stop moving and speaking. **Decide now. Either join us for endless possibilities or leave for your safety. You have ten seconds to decide.**

CAND: If the candidate does not answer within ten seconds or answers negatively, he/she is taken back to the waiting room and the chakra is closed (instructions to follow). If the candidate answers affirmatively... **Yes.**

MO: Surprised. **Are you sure?**

CAND: Any hesitation and she/he is taken out and the chakra is closed. If affirmative... **Yes.**

MO: **This is your last chance. Our path is not an easy one. There are those who would stop us because we offer freedom, and freedom is dangerous to authorities. Are you *really* sure you want to join us?**

CAND: Any hesitation and she/he is taken out and the chakra is closed. If affirmative... **Yes.**

MO: **Then it is time for you to die. Strip him/her of her/his past.**

ALL: Savagely reach out and rip off the candidate's clothes, making growling sounds.

5) Initio—Section B: Death

ALL: Circle the candidate, staring at her/him to make him/her uncomfortable. If the candidate is comfortable with being nude, stares should focus on his/her primary and secondary sex organs.

2nd: Reaches out and touches candidate's cheek. **She's/He's very cold.**

ALL (excluding MO): Briefly touch arms, face, or back of the candidate's body. **Cold as ice. Cold as a freezer. Cold as a Himalayan winter.** Ad-lib until...

3rd: Loudly enough to be heard over all: **Cold as death.**

ALL: **Cold as death. Cold as death. Cold as death.** Repeat, getting quieter and quieter until at the level of a loud stage whisper. Stop when...

MO: **Indeed. From your reports, she/he is dead. I saw his/her discomfort in the old world of her/his past. It must have been horrible being afraid of something as simple as the human body, terrified of the lingam and yoni. Oh, what a shame that such an ugly society could exist!**

ALL: **Shame. Shame. Shame. Shame.** Repeat until…

MO: **But she/he passed the threefold test and asked to be born anew. Let us honor him/her by treating him/her as if he/she were one of our own honored dead. Prepare her/his body for the coming passage. Wrap him/her for the journey to rebirth.**

6) Initio—Section C: The Funeral

ALL: Circling the candidate, moaning and keening. **Woe to the world. We have lost a daughter/son. We have lost a soul.** Ad-lib.

2nd: **Anoint her/him with oils and scented fluids that will preserve his/her mind so that in her/his next life she/he will remember the horrors of the shame-filled old world.** Done. A pitcher of scented water may drip down on the hair.

3rd: **Wrap her/him in the shroud that marks the end of his/her life in the old world.** Starting at the feet, the long piece of fabric is *loosely* wrapped up the candidate's body. A spring-loaded clip holds it together above his/her head.

ALL: **Om.** Quietly chant in reverence while the wrapping is done.

MO: **And now, she/he sleeps between the worlds.** Silence. Soft music. Together the ritualists gently lay the candidate on the floor. Lights are put out. Everyone quietly disrobes and all receive the marks of membership across their foreheads. Depending upon the number of people present, this should take 5–20 minutes.

7) Initio—Section D: Rebirth

A single candle or oil lamp is lit. From that one is lit another. From that another, until the room is filled with candlelight or oil lamps. The candidate is lifted to his/her feet.

MO: **Behold. Another child seeks to be born to a new world.**

2nd: Fearfully: **But birth is painful.**

3rd: Fearfully: **But birth can be dangerous.**

MO: **Yes, but as bringers of the light and shadow to those who wish to see, we have no choice. We must willingly accept pain and danger for a brief time so that more clarity can be brought to the world and so another can choose the path of life, love, and liberty.** Moans loudly, as if giving birth. **By the gods! It hurts so much!**

ALL: Everyone crowds against the standing candidate and undulates their bodies as if they are the muscles moving involuntarily, forcing a fetus down the birth canal. They all moan and cry out ad libitum.

MO: Excitedly: **Look! She's/He's crowning!**

ALL: **Aaaaaaaaahhhhhhhh** Start at a low pitch and slowly move up. Continue through …

MO: **Ungh! Look! She's/He's here!**

ALL: **Ohhhhh!** Quickly falling in pitch, all fall to the floor so that only tired panting can be heard.

8) Initio—Section E: Preparing for the New World

2nd: **Look. She/He is born with a caul.**

3rd: **The sign of a person who will have great spiritual power.**

MO: **Remove the caul, but forever be marked by it.** The long piece of cloth is removed.

ALL: **Ahhh.** Circle the candidate, staring, in joy and awe.

2nd: **She's/He's so beautiful.**

3rd: **What shall we name him/her?**

MO: **Wait, a name signifies identification. Before we identify her/him, we must make sure that he/she is fit to join us. Let her/him see no more until we are sure.**

2nd: Puts blindfold on the candidate's eyes. **This is the darkness of spirit from which you came.**

MO: **Movement in our society is only for the free. Bind him/her.**

3rd: Loosely but securely ties the candidate's wrists behind his/her back, then uses long rope to bind the wrists to the ankles. **These are the false bonds of ignorance, ego, repulsion, attachment, and clinging to life, which you experienced due to the illusory nature of the old world.**

9) Initio—Section F: Vows and Challenges

Each successful vow results in a marking.

MO: **This is your last chance to avoid being reborn into our new family. If you refuse to make any of the following vows to yourself, you will be dismissed and not permitted to join our chakra. To start, repeat after me. "I, state your name."**

CAND: **I, [candidate's name].**

MO: **Am an adult in the state of (name state or province).**

CAND: **Am an adult in the state of [candidate's state or province].**

MO: **And am of sound mind and body.**

CAND: **And am of sound mind and body.**

MO: **I hereby swear …**

CAND: **I hereby swear …**

MO: **That I will answer the following questions …**

CAND: **That I will answer the following questions …**

MO: **Without hesitation …**

CAND: **Without hesitation …**

MO: **Without equivocation …**

CAND: **Without equivocation …**

MO: **And without deception.**

CAND: **And without deception.**

MO: **You will now answer the following questions by saying yes or no. Do you accept nakedness as your symbol of freedom?**

CAND: **Yes/No.**

MO: **Then I consecrate your crown to divine wisdom.** MO marks the candidate's crown with three horizontal lines of vibhuti or appropriately colored powder. **Do you seek to sincerely study Tantra?**

CAND: **Yes/No.**

MO: **Then I consecrate your breasts to love's embrace.** MO marks the candidate's breasts. **Do you seek a magickal way of life?**

CAND: **Yes/No.**

MO: **Then I consecrate the genitals to the gods' enjoyment.** MO marks the candidate's genitals. **Will you renounce shame, shyness, and inhibition?**

CAND: **Yes/No.**

MO: **Then I consecrate your hands to eternal service.** MO marks the candidate's hands. **Will you renounce any forms of ignorance, even ours?**

CAND: **Yes/No.**

MO: **Then I consecrate your feet to walk our path.** MO marks the candidate's feet.

If the candidate says no to any of these questions, remove him/her and close the ritual. Otherwise, continue.

10) Initio—Section G: Freedom

MO: **You have passed all of the tests. You will now be made free to walk among us.** 3rd removes rope as gong sounds. **You will now be able to see the light, the dark, and all of the colors.** 2nd removes blindfold as gong sounds. **You will now receive our blessings.**

All touch the top of the candidate's head, bringing down energy and visualizing the moon.

MO: **May your thoughts be reflective.**

All: **Om.**

All touch the candidate's heart, bringing down energy and visualizing the sun.

MO: **May your heart be steady and warm.**

All: **Om.**

All touch the candidate's genitals, bringing down energy and visualizing elemental fire.

MO: **Let fire be your passion.**

All: **Om.**

11) Initio—Section H: The Charge of the Chakras

2nd: **He/She is not yet complete.**

3rd: **What can be done?**

2nd: **Incomplete, he/she cannot become part of our chakra.**

MO: **We must open the path of energy, for by opening the path, she/he will become free.**

ALL: All lean their faces into the candidate's coccyx and chant three times: **LAM.**

ALL: All lean their faces into the candidate's genitals and chant three times: **VAM.**

ALL: All lean their faces into the candidate's navel and chant three times: **RAM.**

ALL: All lean their faces into the candidate's heart and chant three times: **YAM.**

ALL: All lean their faces into the candidate's throat and chant three times: **HAM.**

ALL: All lean their faces into the candidate's head and chant three times: **Om.**

ALL: All hold their hands above the candidate's head and silently send energy.

MO: **The path is open. Now it is up to you, nameless one, to keep it open.**

12) Initio—Section I: Union

2nd: **Yes. He/She is nameless.**

3rd: **Without a name, how can we truly know him/her?**

2nd: **Without knowing him/her, he/she cannot become a part of our chakra and know us.**

3rd: **What can we do?**

ALL: Moans of sadness.

MO: Mo raises hands to stop moaning. **Because you have diligently worked through this introduction to us, and so that we will all know you, you are hereby given the name [spiritual name], which means [name's meaning].**

ALL: One by one: **Greetings, [candidate's new name], and welcome.** Kiss and full-body hug. If there are enough people, lift the initiate up and carry him/her around the room, repeating his/her new name. If there are not enough people, form a circle around the candidate and move him/her around the inside of the circle (the candidate puts arms by sides and keeps body straight) while chanting the new name. Eventually, all fall to floor, very close together, touching one another.

Optional Section

This section is optional. It was widely used by NAMASTE at one time, and although its use is permitted and acceptable, it is not considered necessary for the success of the initiation. Some *Modern Tantra* chakras may wish to use it, so it is included here. If so, all members, including the initiate, should be informed of this at least one week before the rite. Members not wishing to participate must make this clear before the ritual and should not attend. Neither favor nor disfavor can be earned in a *Modern Tantra* chakra by participating or not participating in this optional section.

MO: **Originally, the God and Goddess were one, known as *Ardharishvara*. For love's sake, for the chance of union, they**

divided into two, Shiva and Shakti. Reach out and let the power of the God and Goddess flow through us all as we take our will and fill of love where and with whom we will. Svecchachara!

ALL: **Union. Union. Union.** Repeated ad lib. All reach out, touching one another, including intimate parts. The ritual continues as it will, with eroticism increasing.

MO: Moves around the circle three times, extinguishing candles and lamps as he/she goes. When finished, he/she joins group. **Welcome to our family.** Erotic activity dedicated to Shiva and Shakti continues until it is played out, as determined by the MO.

End of Optional Section

MO: If not done in the optional part, the MO moves around the circle three times, then says: **Welcome to our family.**

13) Initio—Section J: Advice of the Goddess

If the lights are out due to the optional section, the 2nd and 3rd each light a candle.

MO: **The twilight ends and light/darkness** (depends on actual time of day) **comes. Remember, with the exception of the names of the members, the location of our meeting places, and the specifics of what is done there, you are *required* to share our information with any who ask. Further, not only are you *required* to make sure they understand what you share, but, when the information is practical and not merely philosophical, you must make sure that any person you teach knows how to put that information to use. Do you understand and accept these conditions and responsibilities?**

NEW INITIATE (NI): **Yes** (or similar).

MO: **Know, too, that although you are free to share information about the chakra, other than what is forbidden, you may not initiate into it. Is this clear?**

NI: **Yes** (or similar).

MO: **The time is fleeting before the twilight ends. But before we close this chakra, I ask that you hear the words of the goddess Jyotsñya.**

2nd or 3rd (a female, if possible): **Time moves on. The moon continues on her path. Soon it will be nighttime/the darkest part of night/the beginning of daylight** (depends upon the time) **and I must depart. In the coming weeks and months, you will have the opportunity to increase your knowledge and wisdom through a variety of resources and the ability to question those who have followed this path for a longer period of time. I urge you to expand upon that through other studies and personal work both within your mind and within your personal chakra or laboratory. Experiment with this new magickal way of life and the truths of Tantra will unfold. But be warned:**

Do not mistake common religion for authentic spirituality. Gong sounds.

Do not mistake written scriptures for divine wisdom. Gong sounds.

Do not mistake so-called civilization for human progress. Gong sounds.

Do not mistake mere endurance for real happiness. Gong sounds.

Do not mistake meek submission for actual acceptance. Gong sounds.

Do not mistake forced obedience for true freedom. Gong sounds.

Spiritual attainment, transcendental wisdom, and magickal power are the true objects of human life. All others are secondary. Seek real attainment, but don't permit it to be lost in a meaningless whirl of activity. Enjoyment is a magickal means but is not the goal. The true, spiritual, and magickal way of life is not to limit or frustrate, but to give life fullness and happiness. Surrender to the Goddess and both the old world and your old self will dissolve. A new and better life, woven together like the warp and woof of the finest silk cloth, must begin. You must do the work yourself. No one can do it for you. Tantra is a path of action, not dreams; doing, not fantasizing; achieving, not forever waiting. The grace of Shiva and Shakti, combined with your efforts, will lead you to success.

14) Clude Laboratorium

MO: **Between the dark and the light, and between the light and the dark, is the twilight wherein magic surrounds us and the gods smile on our work.**

2nd: **Behold, the sun is arising/ setting** (depends on actual time).

3rd: **It is the start of a new day/ night** (depends on actual time).

MO: **Then our time is up. Our work here is finished. It is time to spread the results of our work to the world so that the peace of Om Shiva Shakti can dwell within. Banish the chakra.**

Banishings are done as in part 2.

MO: **Now let us go out and enjoy life the way we were meant to do.**

ALL: **Om.**

MO: **Svecchachara!**

Clean area. Conclude with a party.

Essential Initiation into a *Modern Tantra* Chakra

Westerners tend to love rituals. They are a combination of theater, spirituality, and entertainment, and a means of personal transformation. Many of us are so used to the jump-cut, MTV-influenced, tranced-out lightshows found around us that we need an initiation ritual such as the previous one to help us change from outsider to insider, from uninitiated to initiated. The ritual, as presented, can really achieve that, especially if you have an area to perform it and enough people to do it.

Many of us, however, don't have the ability to perform such an elaborate ritual due to a lack of time or space or a minimal chakra membership. And, in truth, such an elaborate presentation may not be needed. Here is another version of the same rite, broken down to its essentials. It is especially appropriate for a person who may have a history of occult studies and experience.

Although this ritual is designed for at least three officers and a candidate, the Main Officer can do all of the parts, meaning the initiation can be performed by one person.

ALL: Everyone is digambara, with a set of three horizontal lines of vibhuti or colored powder on their foreheads. Set up the laboratory while chanting ***Om Namah Shivaya.*** Sri Yantra at center. From the large bowl, fill the smaller bowls and place them in the eight directions. Place the large bowl at center, with the images placed in the proper directions derived from your study. Place incense, vibhuti, or colored powders on the central altar. The Main Officer participates and assures everything is correct. When the chakra is ready to the Main Officer's satisfaction, perform a banishing.

MO: ***Svaha!* I salute the line of innumerable Tantrics and cast the circle of semen glow. May the circle be intact and the peace of Om Shiva Shakti dwell herein. Let us consecrate ourselves to the work.**

2nd: **All honor to the Lord and Lady residing in my heart.**

All: Put hands on their hearts. **Om.**

3rd: **All honor to the Lord and Lady residing in the crown of my head.**

All: Put hands on the crowns of their heads. **Om.**

2nd: **All honor to the Lord and Lady residing in the top of the forehead.**

All: Put hands on their hairlines. **Om.**

3rd: **All honor to the Lord and Lady residing in the armor.**

All: Put hands on their upper chests. **Om.**

2nd: **All honor to the Lord and Lady residing in the three eyes.**

All: Put hands on their eyes, also covering the third eye. **Om.**

3rd: **All honor to the Lord and Lady residing in the lingam and yoni.**

All: Put hands on their lingam or yoni.) **Om.**

MO: **Now that we have again dedicated ourselves to the path, let us initiate a new member into our chakra of light, life, freedom, and love. *Svecchachara!***

A member goes out to get the candidate. The candidate disrobes and is told he/she must answer all questions from the heart, truthfully and without any hesitation. This is stressed and repeated. When the candidate says that he/she understands, the candidate enters the room with the chakra and comes to the center.

MO: **If you start, but choose not to complete the training, you may end up unhappy and alone. Most people who have made it this far either choose to quit now or do so within a short time. There will be no supernatural powers turned against you if you decide to leave, but I can guarantee that if you decide to go further now and drop out later, unhappiness will be your lot for years to come. If you stay the course, the changes, like going through death and rebirth, might be painful, but the possibilities are endless. The choice is yours. Decide now. Either join us for**

endless possibilities or leave for your safety. You have ten seconds to decide.

CAND: If the candidate does not answer within ten seconds or answers negatively, he/she is taken back to the waiting room and the chakra is closed. If the candidate answers affirmatively … **Yes.**

2nd: Puts blindfold on the candidate's eyes. **This is the darkness of spirit from which you came.**

MO: **Movement in our society is only for the free. Bind him/her.**

3rd: Loosely but securely ties the candidate's wrists behind his/her back, then uses long rope to bind the wrists to the ankles. **These are the false bonds of ignorance, ego, repulsion, attachment, and clinging to life, which you experienced due to the illusory nature of the old world.**

MO: **Repeat after me. "I, state your name."**

CAND: **I, [candidate's name].**

MO: **Am an adult in the state of (name of candidate's state or province).**

CAND: **Am an adult in the state of [name of candidate's state or province].**

MO: **And am of sound mind and body.**

CAND: **And am of sound mind and body.**

MO: **You will now answer the following questions by saying yes or no. Do you accept nakedness as your symbol of freedom?**

CAND: **Yes/No.**

MO: **Then I consecrate your crown to divine wisdom.** MO marks the candidate's crown with three horizontal lines of vibhuti or appropriately colored powder. **Do you seek to sincerely study Tantra?**

CAND: **Yes/No.**

MO: **Then I consecrate your breasts to love's embrace.** MO marks candidate's breasts. **Do you seek a magickal way of life?**

CAND: **Yes/No.**

MO: **Then I consecrate the genitals to the gods' enjoyment.** MO marks candidate's genitals. **Will you renounce shame, shyness, and inhibition?**

CAND: **Yes/No.**

MO: **Then I consecrate your hands to eternal service.** MO marks candidate's hands, then says: **Will you renounce any forms of ignorance, even ours?**

CAND: **Yes/No.**

MO: **Then I consecrate your feet to walk our path.** MO marks candidate's feet.

If the candidate says no to any of these questions, remove him/her and close the ritual. Otherwise, continue.

MO: **You will now be made free to walk among us.** MO removes rope. **You will now be able to see the light, the dark, and all of the colors.** MO removes blindfold. **You will now receive our blessings.**

All touch the top of the candidate's head, bringing down energy and visualizing the moon.

MO: **May your thoughts be reflective.**

All: **Om.**

All touch the candidate's heart, bringing down energy and visualizing the sun.

MO: **May your heart be steady and warm.**

All: **Om.**

All touch the candidate's genitals, bringing down energy and visualizing elemental fire.

MO: **Let fire be your passion.**

All: **Om.**

MO: **You are hereby given the name [candidate's spiritual name], which means [name's meaning]. Welcome to our family.**

MO: **Remember, with the exception of the names of the members, the location of our meeting places, and the specifics of what is done there, you are *required* to share our information with any who ask. Further, not only are you *required* to make sure that they understand what you share, but, when the information is practical and not merely philosophical, you must make sure that any person you teach knows how to put that information to use. Do you understand and accept these conditions and responsibilities?**

NEW INITIATE (NI): **Yes** (or similar).

MO: **Know, too, that although you are free to share information about the chakra, other than what is forbidden, you may not initiate into it. Is this clear?**

NI: **Yes** (or similar).

MO: **But before we close this chakra, I ask that you hear the words of the goddess Jyotsñya.**

2nd or 3rd (a female, if possible): **Time moves on. The moon continues on her path. Soon it will be nighttime/the darkest part of night/the beginning of daylight** (depends upon the time) **and I must depart. In the coming weeks and months you will have the opportunity to increase your knowledge and wisdom through a variety of resources and the ability to question those who have followed this path for a longer period of time. I urge you to expand upon that through other studies and personal work both within your mind and within your personal chakra or laboratory. Experiment with this new magickal way of life and the truths of Tantra will unfold. But be warned:**

Do not mistake common religion for authentic spirituality.

Do not mistake written scriptures for divine wisdom.

Do not mistake so-called civilization for human progress.

Do not mistake mere endurance
for real happiness.

Do not mistake meek submission
for actual acceptance.

Do not mistake forced obedience
for true freedom.

Spiritual attainment, transcendental wisdom, and magickal power are the true objects of human life. All others are secondary. Seek real attainment, but don't permit it to be lost in a whirl of activity. Enjoyment is a magickal means but is not the goal. The true, spiritual, and magickal way of life is not to limit or frustrate, but to give life fullness and happiness. Surrender to the Goddess and both the old world and your old self will dissolve. A new and better life, woven together like the warp and woof of the finest silk cloth, must begin. You must do the work yourself. No one can do it for you. Tantra is a path of action, not dreams; doing, not fantasizing; achieving, not forever waiting. The grace of Shiva and Shakti, combined with your efforts, will lead you to success.

MO: **Our work here is finished. It is time to spread the results of our work to the world so that the peace of Om Shiva Shakti can dwell within.**

Banishings are done.

The *Modern Tantra* Wedding

This Tantric wedding is delightful, fun, and meaningful to the bride, groom, priest, bridesmaids and groomsmen, and attendees.

Some aspects of the ritual are described within the ritual itself rather than at the beginning. The purpose is to have you read through this ritual and consider everything carefully, including any changes you may want to make.

Priest: **Welcome to the wedding of [bride's full name] and [groom's full name]. You are all specially invited as family or close friends of the bride and groom. Thank you all for attending. I am [priest's name], an ordained minister** (omit if not true), **who will be performing this rite based on the ancient traditions found in India, a spiritual path that both [bride's full name] and [groom's full name] have come to appreciate and admire. Since most people in the West are unfamiliar with this, I'll be narrating the process as well as leading it.**

I stand here under the canopy that, in Sanskrit, the language of ancient India, is called a *mandap* (an open canopy about seven feet tall, covered with flowers). **We begin with the *baarat,* the wedding procession. First, please stand and welcome the bride and her entourage.** (Both the bride and groom and their entourages are not in the room.)

The bride leads her entourage through the crowd up to the priest. Her parents remain halfway up the path. The bride and the rest of the party come up to the right side of the mandap but do not enter.

Priest: **Now please welcome the groom.**

The groom enters with his entourage. They jokingly push him on while he pretends to resist. At the point where the bride's parents are standing, the bride's mother performs the traditional Indian welcome by performing the *aarti*, making three large clockwise circles with a lamp in front of the groom.

Priest: As mother does so: **The act of *aarti*, being performed by the bride's mother, is a traditional Indian greeting and blessing.**

The bride's mother uses incense ash from incense burning near the table that held the lamp or candle used for *aarti* to make three horizontal lines across the groom's forehead.

Bride's Father: **May your body, mind, and spirit join with that of our daughter.**

The groom and his party move to the *mandap*, left of the bride and her party, but do not enter. The bride's parents follow and move to the side with her party.

Priest: **The ancient faith of India has been described as monotheistic with thousands of gods and goddesses. They have many names, but are merely ways to better understand and relate to the ultimate divinity. I now call on all the gods and goddesses to be here now, overseeing this ritual of loving union. May they bless this couple today, tomorrow, and forever.**

Bride: **I welcome you to this rite with this gift from my heart.** She places a flower garland, like a Hawaiian lei, around the groom's neck.

Groom: **I welcome you to this rite with this gift from my heart.** He places a garland around the bride's neck.

Priest: **The next part of this rite is called *kanya danam*, the giving away of the bride. It begins with the father of the bride making a libation of sacred water imported from the Ganges River and known as *Ganga jal*.** The bride's father pours some water to earth from a small pot. The water contains a few drops of Ganga jal.

Priest: **Before the bride and groom may enter the mandap, the bride's father extracts vows from the groom.**

Bride's Father: **Before we agree to give my daughter to you, we must demand three vows from you.**

Groom: **I vow to support your daughter as she finds her path through life. I will not condemn or direct her, but I will support her in a lifetime adventure of self-discovery.**

Bride's Mother: **We accept your first vow. What is your second?**

Groom: **I vow to support her in finding her own unique individuality, including fame, wealth, and respect as she so desires.**

Bride's Father: **And the third vow?**

Groom: **I will remember that we are human. We will be happy or sad, angry or pleased, and all the various levels in between. And during all these ups and downs, I vow to always remember what is bringing us here today in front of our friends and loved ones: love. I vow to remember to love your daughter at all times.**

Bride's Parents, together:
We accept your vows.

Bride's Father: **Before this assemblage on [date], at [time], I, the father of [bride's full name], do, of my own free will and that of my daughter, hereby hand her to you in marriage.**

Groom: **I promise to protect her in all ways.**

Priest: **Will the bride and groom please enter the mandap? Members of the entourages may be seated.**

Done. The priest uses thread to tie the groom's right hand to the bride's left hand.

Priest: **We call on Ganesh, the breaker of obstacles, to destroy any and all barriers to the bride and groom's mental, physical, emotional, and spiritual happiness.**

Om gam ganapataye namaha!

The bride and groom will now please look at each other. Done. **Do you have a token of your love and symbols of this union?**

Bride and Groom: **Yes.**

Priest: **Will the ring bearer approach.**

The ring bearer brings up the rings. The groom puts a ring on the bride's finger. The bride puts a ring on the groom's finger. The priest lights fire in the *homa*/fire pit. Wood has previously been soaked in clarified butter (ghee), but lighter fluid is ready if needed.

Priest: **Fire has amazed humanity from the beginning of time. It heats and cooks and lights, but it can also destroy. As I light this ancient symbol of power, may it bring happiness, long life, and a lifelong relationship.**

The priest pours *samagree,*
a special incense, into fire.

Priest: **May these sweet scents bring the sweetness of the Divine's blessings to you both. And now comes the part of this rite known as *paanigrahana*, the holding of the hand.**

The groom faces west and takes the bride's other hand.

Groom: **O Saraswati, I beg that you give us that which you symbolize: knowledge, music, art, science, and the wisdom to forgive disagreements and remember the beauty of our union.**

Bride: **O Lakshmi, I beg that you give us that which you symbolize: wealth in all areas, including financial, spiritual, mental, and physical, along with the wisdom of how to use it.**

They release hands.

Priest: **Now comes *laya homa*, the oblation of parched grain.**

A previously chosen member of the bride's entourage, usually a sister, relative, or very close friend, comes forward and pours half of the grain she has into the bride's free hand. The bride offers some of it to the fire in the homa.

Bride: **This grain I spill. May it bring to me well-being and unite you to me. May Agni hear us.**

The grain bearer shakes the bride's hand so the rest of the grain goes into the fire.

Bride: **Blessings on my husband. May my relatives all be prosperous in all areas of their lives.** ***Svaha!***

Priest: **Next comes *agni parinaya*, the circumambulation of the fire.**

The bride and groom walk three times clockwise around the homa.

Bride and Groom together: **We ask for prosperity together, far more than we could ever have apart.**

The bride and groom walk three times around the fire again.

Bride and Groom together: **We ask that no matter what separates us—for a moment, hour, or longer—we are always brought together.**

The bride and groom again walk three times around the fire. They then put their free hand on each other's hearts.

Bride and Groom together: **We pray for the union of our hearts, minds, and spirits.**

The bride and groom walk three times around the fire. The bride gets the remaining grain from the grain bearer and pours it into the fire.

Bride: **To *Bhaga svaha!***

Priest: **Now comes the rite of *asmaarohana*, the mounting of the stone.**

Groom: **Come, beautiful one. Come step on the stone.**

The bride puts the toe of her right foot on a large stone that had been placed near the mandap.

Groom: **Be strong like a stone. Resist all enemies, known andunknown. Overcome any and all who might attack you.**

Priest: **Now comes the most important part of the ritual. Without *satapadi*, the seven steps, there is no marriage.**

Priest: **Take your first step together around the fire. Do you promise to nourish each other and look after each other's health? Will you be noble and respectful to one another?**

Step is taken. The bride and groom's response: **We do.**

Priest: **Take your second step. Do you promise to grow together in strength? Will you develop your physical, mental, and spiritual powers in order to live in a wonderful lifestyle? Will you be together in perfect love and perfect trust?**

Step is taken. The bride and groom's response: **We do.**

Priest: **Take your third step. Do you promise to work toward wealth in all areas of your lives, material, emotional, and spiritual? And will you do this**

**only by proper means that lead
to an increasingly spiritual life?**

Step is taken. The bride
and groom's response: **We do.**

Priest: **Take your fourth step. Do
you promise to share joys and sorrows?
Will you acquire knowledge, happiness,
and harmony by mutual love, respect,
understanding, and faith?**

Step is taken. The bride
and groom's response: **We do.**

Priest: **Take your fifth step.
Do you promise to encourage
each other's productive endeavors?**

Step is taken. The bride
and groom's response: **We do.**

Priest: **Take your sixth step. Do you
promise to be together forever?**

Step is taken. The bride
and groom's response: **We do.**

Priest: **Take your seventh step. Do you
promise to be lifelong friends? Will
you be true and loyal to each other?**

Step is taken. The bride
and groom's response: **We do.**

Priest: **Repeat after me:** (The bride
and groom repeat after each line.)

With seven steps we become friends.

Let me reach your friendship.

**Let me not be severed
from your friendship**

**Let your friendship
not be severed from me.**

Priest: **Let the bride and
groom bow their heads.**

Done. The priest places one
hand on each of their heads.

Priest: **I now confer this blessing:**

**May this couple be blessed with an
abundance of resources and comforts and
be helpful to each another in all ways.**

**May this couple be strong and
complement one another.**

**May this couple be blessed with
prosperity and riches on all levels.**

May this couple be eternally happy.

May this couple live in perfect harmony.

**May this couple always be true to their
personal values and their joint promises.**

**May this couple always
be the best of friends.**

Priest: **The perfect halves thus make the
perfect whole. By the power vested in me,
both spiritually and under the laws of
the [name of legal jurisdiction] and the
country of [name of country], I hereby
declare you to be married. The groom
and bride may now seal their vows
and end this rite with a kiss.** Done.

**Priest: Will everyone please
welcome this newly married couple!**

The priest starts the applause.

The *Modern Tantra* Funeral

To Tantrics, death, and what awaits beyond, is not seen as an end. Rather, it is simply the final initiation and ultimate enlightenment (*maha samadhi*) during any single life. Although there are traditional Tantric beliefs about the continuation of the spirit after the change known as death, each person should develop their own ideas based on their experience, observation, and an analysis of possibilities.

As already explained, the concept of time in traditional Tantra is not the linear focus that most Westerners have, with a beginning, middle, and end. Rather, it is seen as a massive loop, taking hundreds of thousands of years to complete and restart. Individuals are seen as microcosms of that macrocosm, reincarnating to the wonders of the narrow vision we call "life" in order to enjoy the miracle and bliss of Tantric existence.

Unlike those who see life as a one-way trip or an endless loop (with a goal of escaping from the loop), those of us in *Modern Tantra* see life as a spiral, looping around, yes, but ever increasing. Each incarnation gives us the pleasure of new understandings, new knowledge, new wisdom, new enjoyment, and new bliss. Death is neither feared nor encouraged. Just as people enjoy new births, passing into adulthood, initiation, and the rite of marriage, so too should death be treated as the beginning of a new adventure, an adventure that should be taken only when the current lessons are complete, the current adventures finished, and the body ready to return to its original chemical form.

Therefore, the *Modern Tantra* funeral is a celebration, more of a joyous wake than a sad event. It deals with the spirit of the deceased, so it need not take place near the body or the home of the departed. Instead, it can occur at the normal chakra meeting place. There should be a photo of the departed along with many fragrant flowers. There should also be a person who can really sound the *shankh* (conch trumpet) and who blows it where the word *shankh* appears in the ritual. There may be multiple shankh players.

1. Shankh. Perform a banishing of your choice. Shankh.
2. Main Officer (MO): The MO honors Ganesh by saying: **Om Gam Ganapataye Namaha! Ganesh, breaker of obstacles, see to it that our brother/sister [name of deceased] moves smoothly and quickly to return to us, ready to face new challenges, learn new and greater things, and have more bliss while bringing bliss into our lives.** Shankh.
3. 2nd Officer (2nd): **Yama, ruler of *Naraka*, a place where spirits go for rest and purification before rebirth, be merciful in your divine justice. Allow our brother/sister to understand and evolve, learn and improve, and prepare for a new life of new discoveries and new bliss. Wrap him/her in a garland of letters so that he/she will utter mantras with great beauty, meaning, and joy.** Shankh.
4. 3rd Officer (3rd): **Indra, great ruler of *Svarga*, the place where the souls of great spirits go for rest and bliss, if [name of deceased] appears before you, treat him/her with honor and love. Allow him/her rest and bliss as he/she recovers from the life he's/she's left and prepares for the life to come.** Shankh.
5. MO: **Shiva, great transformer of the universe, we are saddened by the loss of our friend and brother/sister [name of deceased] yet are overjoyed at the thought that he/she will be refreshed and renewed**

through your love and guidance. Make sure she/he is prepared for his/her next life, a life, we pray, that will be filled with wisdom, joy, friendship, wealth, and love. Shankh.

6. A large chalice is filled with water and a few drops of Ganga jal. The cup is passed from person to person. Each person takes turns doing the following:
    a. Recounts a memory of the deceased and the feelings associated with that memory.
    b. Provides wishes for peace, recovery, and a rapid return to life in a new incarnation.
    c. Spills a few drops of fluid from the chalice to honor the gods and the deceased.
    d. Passes the chalice to the next person.
7. When the chalice reaches the MO, he/she recounts a memory, provides wishes, and spills the remaining water/Ganga jal mixture in honor of the gods and the deceased. Then he/she picks up a flower and places it in front of the picture of the deceased. All members of the chakra also present flowers to the photo in memory of the deceased. The shankh is sounded as the flowers are presented.
8. MO: **May the good wishes and good memories fill us with love for he/she who has left so that he/she will never be forgotten. [Name of deceased] will always remain in our hearts. As long as he/she is there, he/she will always be here, in our circle of friends. Om.**
9. All: **Om.** Then all stay in silence. Shankh.
10. When ready, banish as before. Each person should take a flower home and place it on their altar.

TEN

Tantric Astrology for Magick

The long history of Tantra has allowed practitioners to develop several systems of divination that can help a Tantric learn from unknown or not fully understood past events, predict the future to give guidance and direction, and, perhaps most importantly, understand the present to a greater depth than would otherwise be possible. Initially I was going to cover several Tantric divinatory systems. Unfortunately, that simply would have been too lengthy for one book. Each system would require a complete book, or even several books, just to fully introduce their concepts and methods. These systems include such things as drawing one of a bunch of banana tree leaves on which the diviner has written oracular ideas. This technique is similar to the divinatory use of the *I Ching*, or rune sticks, and it's close to the Chinese divinatory system known as *Kau Chim* or *Chien Tung*, commonly known as Chinese fortune sticks. Another system involves finding an astrology chart on the palm of the hand. Palmistry, too, is a popular Tantric divinatory system. One variation looks exclusively at the thumb. The creation of Tantric divinatory systems has not ceased. Recently a card deck that has similarities to the tarot but is Tantrically focused, called *The Tantric Dakini Oracle* (previously titled *The Secret Dakini Oracle*), was released by Nik Douglas and Penny Slinger.

The system I'm going to discuss briefly in this chapter is Tantric astrology. To really learn it, or any of the systems mentioned, requires study and practice. To learn more, consult some of the books listed in the bibliography. For this book I wanted to provide you with concepts that are unique and practical, traditional, and yet not commonly known in the West, and explain how you can apply them to enhance your magick within or outside of a Tantric format.

Tropical and Sidereal Zodiacs

Even if you don't know much about astrology, you're probably familiar with the little predictions that appear in daily newspapers. You also probably know your "sign," such as whether you're a Capricorn, a Scorpio, or one of the other ten signs. Technically, your sign is actually your *Sun sign*, the zodiac sign the Sun was in when you were born. This leads us to the first major difference between the Western astrology you may know and Tantric astrology.

Modern Western astrology is based on something known as the *tropical zodiac*. Tantric astrology is based on the *sidereal zodiac*. This difference changes everything.

Both zodiacal systems focus on the *ecliptic*. This is the path the Sun appears to follow across the sky. When I was younger, I couldn't understand where to look for the constellations that make up the zodiac. When it was explained to me that they're all along the ecliptic, they became much easier to find and identify in the night sky. All I had to do was look at the path the Sun had followed during the day to see the zodiacal constellations at night.

In Western (tropical) astrology, the beginning of the year is based on the positions of stars that are believed to be unmoving, or *fixed*. As a result, the spring equinox is always on the same date. Each sign of the zodiac always begins on the same date. But there's a problem with this.

The fixed stars aren't really fixed. It's just that from our perspective it takes a long time for us to see that, in relation to our position, they appear to move. This slow movement is due to the wobble of Earth on its axis. This wobble causes small changes known as the *precession of the equinoxes*.

The dates and appearances of the zodiac signs are no longer where they once were. The wobble induces a slow change that takes about 26,000 years to bring us back to the same perspective we have at any moment. That means every 2,150 years or so, we move backward through a full astrological sign.

From about 4,200 years ago to about 2,100 years ago, we were in the Age of Aries. We experienced events and mental states that were associated with that age. About 2,100 years ago, we exited the Age of Aries. That is, at the spring equinox, Aries was already fully up in the sky. The sign of Pisces was beginning to rise on the spring equinox, as we were at the dawning of the eon of Pisces, including all of the events and mental states associated with that age.

Today we are entering the Age of Aquarius. If you look for the constellation of Pisces to be just rising in the sky at the spring equinox, you won't find it. Nor will you find the first sign of the Western zodiac, Aries, just rising, either. They're both already up in the sky. Instead, you'll find Aquarius beginning to rise.

Tantric astrology, which is based on the sidereal zodiac, recognizes this change. It looks at where the constellations actually are rather than where they theoretically are. The astrological houses and signs are aligned rather than different.

So why is it that Western astrology uses the relative positions of stars and planets and not the actual positions? It may actually be due to one book: *Tetrabiblos* by Ptolemy.

Claudius Ptolemy (c. 90–c. 168 CE) lived in Egypt, but his actual lineage is a question mark. The name Claudius indicates he was Roman, and he lived in Egypt during the time of Roman rule. It appears that he was granted Roman citizenship later in his life. At least one author (albeit 700 years later) claimed he was a member of Egypt's royalty. His last name (actually *Ptolemaeus*) indicates a Greek (probably Macedonian) background. Whatever Ptolemy's genetic background, there is no doubt that he was a genius.

Ptolemy was known as a mathematician, a geographer, a poet, an astronomer, and an astrologer. Astronomy, it should be remembered, was originally a subset of astrology. You needed to be able to tell where the planets were in order to do the important part: make and interpret an astrological chart.

Ptolemy's book, known as the *Tetrabiblos*, gives an explanation of basic astrology. It was based on earlier sources and focused on drawing the horoscope (the positions of the planets and constellations in relation to time and place of birth) and horoscope interpretation. During the Dark Ages (generally given as 476–1000 CE), most astrological knowledge (as with most knowledge in the West) was lost or forgotten. As Western civilization crawled out of that period, the past was rediscovered. *Tetrabiblos* was translated from Arabic into Latin in 1138, making it available to educated Westerners. That one book became the source for Western astrology. And an unlikely coincidence may have resulted in the split between the tropical and sidereal zodiacs.

When Ptolemy wrote his book, both the sidereal and tropical zodiacs coincided. Ptolemy wrote that Aries began with the vernal equinox, and he was right... during his time. One thousand years later, that was no longer correct, but the astrologers went by the book rather than looking at the skies. (Sadly, I have met few astrologers who can go out at night and point out the planets and constellations.) Thus, tropical astrology became the favored astrological system of the West.

When I explain this to some Western astrologers, they get upset. "Are you saying that all of my charts are wrong?" No, I'm not saying that at all. Astrological charts are actually about relationships. If Venus has a certain relationship to Mars—perhaps they are at a 90-degree angle, or *square*, to each other—they'll still have that same relationship. The major change between tropical and sidereal astrology consists of the planets in relation to the constellations or zodiac signs and houses. We could use any circle of twelve signs and relate it to the relative positions of the planets. Each circle and the planets located on it could be referred to as a paradigm or model. Tropical astrology can be perfectly accurate within its paradigm, just as Tantric astrology is perfectly accurate within its sidereal zodiac paradigm.

If that's true, and both versions of astrology are valid, what difference does it make? Today, most Western astrologers focus on psychological issues. Most Tantric astrologers focus on practical, physical-plane issues. A Western astrologer might tell you in a general way how to best get along with the person you are about to marry or what to look for in a business partner. A Tantric astrologer would tell you the best day and time to marry or start a business, what specific mantra to chant for happiness or success, your good luck numbers and colors, and the gem you should wear for good luck.

This is something that has always bothered me about several divination systems, including the tarot. They may give you great information about yourself, such as what attitudes you need to develop to enhance the relationship with your spouse. Or they might tell you to beware of someone who is not being honest.

"That's great. But how, *specifically*, do I do that? What, *specifically*, can I do to overcome this problem?" This, in my opinion, is a great stumbling block. While it is certainly possible to provide solutions through the exclusive use of information from tropical astrology charts, many Western astrologers don't do this. Wise Western astrologers may give you some advice that can answer questions such as these based not on astrology, but rather on their own experience and training in areas that are often outside of the astrological realm. This can include the use of psychism, intuitive insights, knowledge of psychology or life coaching, and just plain common sense. In questions of finances, the advice may come from the astrologer's own understanding of economics rather than just the astrological evidence. Even the personal ethics and politics of an astrologer, tarot reader, or other diviner may come into play.

Perhaps the most valuable source of advice of this type comes from the astrologer's life experience. Again, this is not because the information isn't available from the charts, but simply because most Western astrologers are not trained to find it. Most Western astrologers don't think that's the way astrology should work.

But, then, why should they think in any other way? Most books for people looking up their own charts don't include it. Most books that train in astrology don't stress it or even include it. Most clients who come to professional astrologers don't seem to be seeking it, or are at least willing to accept the lack of specific solutions or *remedies* from astrological data that would help ensure what is desired or overcome what is undesired.[14]

Tantric astrologers, on the other hand, do just the opposite. They will use the chart to tell you the best date and time to have the wedding; yantras you should have in your home to ensure health, wealth, and harmony; gems to wear for health, luck, and prosperity; mantras to chant, etc. Frankly, I think one of the reasons for this is that Indian astrologers will often offer to sell clients appropriate astrological remedies for their problems. Charged yantras or appropriate planetary gems can be very expensive. It's an additional income stream that is not generally found among Western astrologers. Some people might refer to these remedies as magickal solutions to problems. These *explicit* types of remedies are not common in Western astrology, but form a major aspect of Tantric astrology, or *jyotish* astrology.[15]

Here, then, is a list of the dates used in Tantric astrology to determine your astrological sign, or *rashi* (see chart). I'm including the Western names of the signs for familiarity and ease.

Does this surprise you? I was born on March 28 and always knew myself to be an Aries. According

14 There are always exceptions to this generalization. *Astrocartography,* developed by the late Jim Lewis, gives advice on specific places for an individual to live, work, etc. Llewellyn's *Moon Sign Book* gives good dates for general tasks, such as the best times to get a haircut, plant crops, or go fishing. These are based on the energies of the Moon. However, most Western astrologers don't focus on such predictive dates unless specifically asked to do so, and few are trained in these skills. Nor do most sell remedies for problems.

15 Calling Tantric or Indian astrology *Vedic astrology* only dates back to the 1980s. Calling it *Hindu astrology* only dates from the 1800s, and at that time anything from India would have been called "Hindu." Therefore, I reject the terms Hindu astrology and Vedic astrology as inaccurate neologisms.

to Tantric astrology, I'm a Pisces. That's a big change. However, this is still just the Sun sign and only gives one part of the entire picture. A complete horoscope, Western or Tantric, will look at all of the planets and their relation to the constellations and to each other. Just looking at one position, albeit a very important one, doesn't give a thorough understanding of a horoscope's astrological information. To go into the meanings of just these Sun sign shifts would fill at least another book. What I want to focus on is how to use this information practically—that is, how to use astrological information for magick.

Date	Sign	Sanskrit Name
January 14–February 11	Capricorn	Makara
February 12–March 13	Aquarius	Kumbha
March 14–April 12	Pisces	Meena
April 13–May 13	Aries	Mesha
May 14–June 14	Taurus	Vrishabha
June 15–July 15	Gemini	Mithuna
July 16–August 15	Cancer	Karka
August 16–September 15	Leo	Simha
September 16–October 16	Virgo	Kanya
October 17–November 15	Libra	Tula
November 16–December 14	Scorpio	Vrishchika
December 15–January 13	Sagittarius	Dhanu

Determining Your Astrological Sign, or Rashi

Sign	Lucky Numbers	Lucky Colors
Capricorn	6, 8, 9	White, Red, Blue (avoid Yellow, Cream)
Aquarius	2, 3, 7, 9	Yellow, Red, White, Cream
Pisces	1, 3, 9 (avoid 8)	Yellow, Orange, Red, Rose (avoid Blue, White, Cream, Green)
Aries	6, 8, 9	Blue
Taurus	5, 6, 8	Pink, Green, White
Gemini	3, 4	Green, Yellow
Cancer	2, 7, 9 (avoid 5, 8)	White, Cream, Red, Yellow (avoid Blue, Green)

Numbers and Colors of the Signs

Sign	Lucky Numbers	Lucky Colors
Leo	1, 4, 5, 6, 7 (avoid 2, 7, 8)	Orange, Red, White
Virgo	2, 3, 5, 6, 7	Green, White, Yellow
Libra	1, 2, 4, 7 (5 = loss; 6 = opponent's success)	Orange, White
Scorpio	3, 9, 4, 1, 2, 7 (in this order) (avoid 5, 6, 8)	Yellow, Red, Orange
Sagittarius	3, 5, 6, 8 (avoid 2, 7, 9)	White, Cream, Green, Orange, Light Blue (avoid Red, Pearl)

Numbers and Colors of the Signs (continued)

Day	Planet	Influence	Color
Monday	Moon	Mind	Pearl White
Tuesday	Mars	Strength	Coral Red
Wednesday	Mercury	Communications	Green
Thursday	Jupiter	Knowledge	Yellow
Friday	Venus	Potency	White or Multicolor
Saturday	Saturn	Grief	Blue
Sunday	Sun	Spirit	Ruby Red

Influence and Colors of the Days and Their Associated Planets

Gemstones and Astrology

The associations between "gems" and planets have a long tradition in Tantric astrology. I put quotes around *gems* because some of the associations are not with what we consider gems—stones mined from the earth—at all.

If your chart indicates a lack or excess of some planetary energy, one of the remedies is for you to wear a gem that will appropriately increase or counter the energy as needed. There are supposed minimum sizes, but as a general rule, the larger the gem and the higher the quality, the better. Further, you are supposed to wear the stones against your skin. Therefore, you need a special ring or pendant that is open in the back. A higher-quality setting—that is, a more expensive setting—is supposedly better.

Personally, I think this general rule is primarily a way for an Indian astrologer to extract extra money from you! They often also sell gems and appropriate jewelry, or may have a friend or family member who sells them.

People of all economic classes in India use jyotish and work with the gem remedies. Some people want to use the gems but can't afford anything more than a mere chip, and a low-quality one at that. These seem to work perfectly. Rather than wear them, you can place them in a glass of water and leave them over night. In the morning, drink the water to obtain the gem's influence. Be careful not to swallow the gem! This practice can be repeated nightly. You can also make combinations of gem powers.

Here is a description of the planets and their "gems." Names of the planets and gems are given in English followed by their Sanskrit names in parentheses.

Planet: Mercury *(Budh)*

Gem: Green Emerald *(Panna)*

Planetary Influences: Investments and exchange of money for goods; education; verbal and written forms of communication; sense of humor; nervousness and feelings of insecurity; diseases of the lungs, nervous system, and intestines.

Comments: Emeralds come in a wide variety of shades and levels of transparency. The best ones as a planetary gem are dark green and translucent, with no flaws or occlusions. If the planet Mercury is strong in your chart, use this to increase the energies of Mercury and overcome energies that counter those of the planet.

Wearing a planetary gem of Mercury is also said to be good to improve the eyesight, calm the nerves, and enhance focus. It is supposedly good for asthma if worn in a gold ring on the third finger on Wednesdays. This can be amplified by wearing a yellow sapphire in a gold ring worn on Thursday on the third finger. It is also good for gallstones and mental problems.

Primary Alternatives: Green Jade, Peridot, Aquamarine, Green Tourmaline

Secondary Alternatives: Green Zircon, Turquoise that is primarily green

Planet: Venus *(Shukra)*

Gem: Diamond (*Heera*)

Planetary Influences: Beauty, grace, charm, romance, and good taste. Also important for the immune system and reproductive organs.

Comments: The idea that diamonds are of great value due to their rarity is a myth. One company has obtained a virtual monopoly over the international distribution of diamonds and artificially created high price points through a combination of limiting their availability and advertising heavily to create false needs. Diamond engagement rings, for example, are not part of some ancient tradition. They only became popular due to an extensive advertising campaign that began in 1947 using the slogan "Diamonds are forever." In 1999 those three words were selected as the best advertising slogan of the century by *Advertising Age* magazine.

I have never been especially attracted to diamonds. But this isn't about whether we like their looks; it's about the power they exert. For this purpose, the best diamonds are completely clear or have a blue tint. Well, unless you're a political leader, in which case a red or yellow diamond is best for you.

Wear a diamond if Venus plays an important role in your chart. Diamonds can also help to enhance marital happiness, encourage fearlessness and patience, and help increase wealth. They are also said to help relationships with loved ones and artistic pursuits. They are associated with diseases of the reproductive organs.

Primary Alternatives: White Topaz, White Sapphire, Zircon

Planet: Mars (*Mangal*)

Gem: Red Coral (*Moonga*)

Planetary Influences: Drive and energy, completing what you start, independence, masculine energy. Mars also governs the blood and circulatory system.

Comments: Here is the first planetary "gem" that is not a stone. Coral is actually the exoskeleton of a living creature. It has been considered so precious that it has been imitated by using bone, horn, or ivory and then staining it with a red dye made from cinnabar.

Unlike emerald or diamond, red coral should be opaque and, as the name says, red in color—not pink or orange or another color. There is a story that it warns of a coming health problem by changing its color. It's also supposed to give courage, prevent nightmares, and protect from evil spirits.

If your chart shows you are ruled by Mars, wearing a red coral gem is beneficial. However, Mars is so energetic that it can indicate problems when it appears in various astrological houses. If this is true for you, don't wear this gem.

Red coral is said to be a male aphrodisiac. Wear it and see. It can help you with decisiveness, money issues, and overcoming opponents. It supposedly cures arthritis. Red coral is traditionally a cure for breast cancer or lung cancer and a help for hernias, kidney problems, and kidney issues. It may help strengthen leadership characteristics and overcome anger issues. It is associated with diseases of blood and bile.

Primary Alternatives: Bloodstone, Carnelian, Red Agate

Planet: Jupiter (*Guru*)

Gem: Yellow Sapphire (*Pukhraj*)

Planetary Influences: Improved physical health. Enhances joy.

Comments: Yellow sapphire is traditionally believed to be good for a woman who is seeking marriage but is having trouble finding a suitable partner. It's also said that a person wearing this will be blessed with children. But beware! If the stone has blemishes, it can disturb your sense of balance and result in increased anxiety. So wear this gem if you are interested in maximizing the effects of Jupiterian energy. It is also said to help with normalizing blood pressure. It is supposedly good for appendicitis and anemia if worn in a gold ring on Thursdays on the third finger of the right hand. To amplify this, wear a red coral in a copper ring on Tuesdays on the same finger.

This gem may help with issues of career and the development of a sense of optimism and piety. It is associated with diseases of the liver and fat.

Primary Alternatives: Yellow or Golden Topaz, Citrine, Beryl, Yellow Tourmaline, Pearls that are yellow.

Planet: Moon (*Chandra*)

Gem: Pearl (*Moti*)

Planetary Influences: Love, increased intimacy, friendship.

Comments: Here is the second "gem" that does not come from the earth. The saltwater pearl, or *moti*, comes from an oyster, and the ideal is a perfect sphere that is shiny and glossy. It doesn't matter if it is natural or cultured, but if it is chipped, get rid of it, as it could result in you losing your job or source of money.

As usual, wear it if the Moon is strong in your birth chart. Traditionally, Cancers can wear it in a silver ring on the pinky of the right hand during the waxing of the Moon.

It is believed that wearing a pearl can increase your compassion and feelings of love for others. It can calm your mind, improve finances, increase popularity, and lead to good health. It may strengthen a woman's reproductive system and enhance fertility.

Primary Alternatives: Moonstone, Freshwater Pearls from a mussel.

Secondary Alternatives: White Sapphire, White Agate

Planet: Saturn (*Shani*)

Gem: Blue Sapphire (*Neelam*)

Planetary Influences: Order and stability. Success and magnanimity. It can also bring a desire to find solitude and become detached from the world in order to achieve self-realization. Good for recovery from chronic diseases, phobias, and depression.

Comments: Wear this gem if Saturn is strong in your chart. If Saturn is indicative of a weakness in your chart, wear a blue sapphire to strengthen the energy. Have it set in a gold ring for the middle finger of your right hand and wear it every Saturday. The setting should be open in the back so the gem touches your skin.

Primary Alternatives: Lapis Lazuli, Blue Topaz, Amethyst

Secondary Alternatives: Blue Spinel, Cordierite, Blue Zoisite, Star of India

Planet: North or Ascending Lunar Node (*Rahu*)

Gem: Hessonite (*Gomedha*)

Planetary Influences: Heightened self-awareness, discrimination, fearlessness. May also help in the recovery from skin diseases.

Comments: Just as some of the gems are not really stones, *Rahu* is not what Westerners normally consider a planet. In Tantric astrology, both Rahu and its partner, *Ketu*, are described as *chhaya grahas* (shadow planets).

As already mentioned, the zodiacal constellations are associated with the ecliptic. The Moon, in its monthly orbit, also follows the ecliptic. However, instead of tracing a straight line, it ranges above and below the invisible ecliptic. Where it crosses the line going up, it is called *Rahu*, the ascending Lunar Node. Where it crosses the line going down, it is called *Ketu*, the descending Lunar Node. So instead of actually being a planet, the Nodes are points where the Moon intersects the plane of the ecliptic.

Hessonite is a type of garnet that is yellowish in color. The best ones are also transparent and lustrous. Rahu does not rule any zodiac sign. The stone is worn for safety and protection. However, it's a bit more complex than this. Look at the natal chart and find the house that Rahu is in. If it's in a house that has a planet that is *auspicious* (is considered positive in that sign), wear a hessonite. Otherwise, leave it alone. Rahu is associated with both lethargy and insatiable desires. It's linked to drug addiction, spirit possession, and suicidal tendencies, but it also helps remove fear and develop insight.

Primary Alternatives: Orange Zircon, Orange Garnet

Secondary Alternatives: Spessartite, Agate

Planet: South or Descending Lunar Node (*Ketu*)

Gem: Cat's Eye (*Lashsunia*)

Planetary Influences: The energies of this shadow planet aid in the cultivation of spirituality and generally govern wisdom.

Comment: Lots of stones are called cat's eyes, but the gem associated with Ketu is the chrysoberyl. The best ones for Ketu energy are golden yellow in color with straight white fibers that are said to "gleam."

This gem is said to give protection from hidden enemies and eliminate nightmares. It can also help in recovering from wounds and especially in getting over the pain from wounds. Wearing a cat's eye can aid a person in overcoming obsessive, compulsive, or even addictive behaviors. It will also enhance psychic abilities. Diseases associated with Ketu include those of the joints and associated nerves.

Primary Alternatives: Beryl, Fibrolite, and Tourmaline Cat's Eye

Secondary Alternatives: Tiger's-Eye, Reddish Turquoise

Planet: Sun (*Surya*)

Gem: Ruby (*Manik*)

Planetary Influences: The Sun influences such things as strength of will, self-confidence, assertiveness, and independence.

Comment: The ideal ruby is large and deep red, and shoots out red rays in the sun. It should almost glow in the dark. Wearing one is great for improving willpower and spirit. It's also generally protective.

Wear a ruby if your Sun sign is ruled by the Sun. Have it set in a gold ring and wear it on the right hand's ring finger on Sundays. This will maximize the ruby's power and solar influence.

Besides obtaining optimism, willpower, and determination to achieve one's goals, wearing a ruby brings political power and freedom from liver disease and promotes good health. It can also protect you from false friendships.

Primary Alternatives: Red Garnet, Red Tourmaline, Red Spinel

Secondary Alternatives: Star Ruby, Sunstone

The Navaratna

If you don't know much about astrology, or just want a great general positive charm, I can suggest nothing better than a *nava* (nine) *ratna* (gems). If you wear a single gem, it will focus on the specific energies of the planet with which the gem is associated. Instead, wear all nine of the gems: a *navaratna*. Most commonly this is done in the form of a ring or pendant (see illustration) on a necklace.

As a general-purpose good luck talisman, a navaratna brings the positive energies of all the planets—prosperity, health, better communication, happiness, spiritual development, love, passion, and composure. It wards off all negative energies.

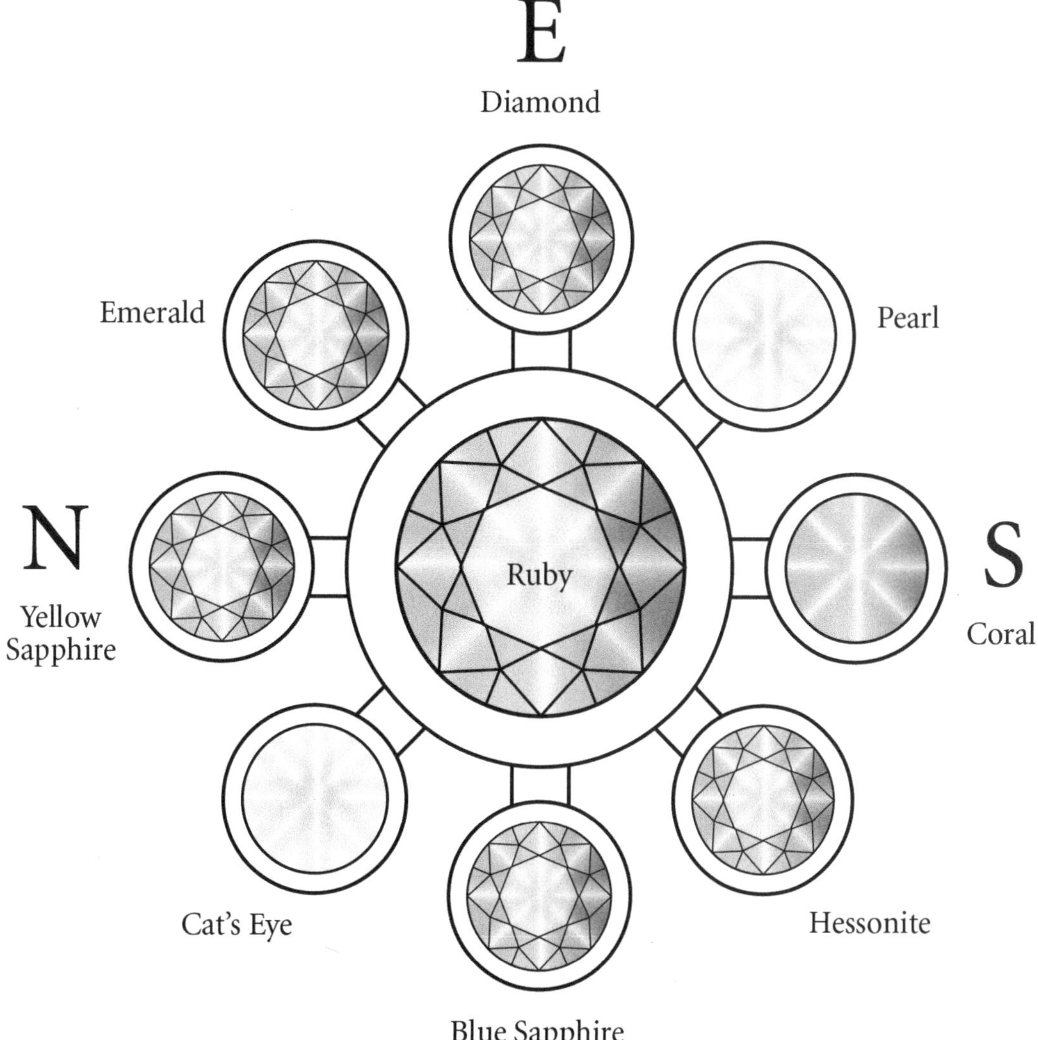

A Navaratna Pendant

I suggest getting a navaratna with equal-sized gems. You can get the gems listed here or their primary or even secondary alternatives. To cleanse it, obtain an old-fashioned horseshoe magnet, the most powerful one you can find. Every two to four weeks, hold the magnet about five to eight centimeters (two to three inches) above the navaratna for a minute.

Nakshatras

There are two concepts known in Tantric astrology as the *nakshatras* ("nahk-shah-trahs"). The first concept is a way to further interpret horoscope charts. Just as there are 12 signs and 12 houses, the nakshatras give 27 (some authorities give 28) divisions of the year. These are associated with astronomy in two ways. First, they are associated with the Moon and are known in the West as the *lunar mansions*. Second, they are each associated with a different set of stars and are known as *asterisms* ("pattern of stars"). When doing a typical Tantric horoscope interpretation, you would interpret the position of a planet not only in a sign or house, but also in a nakshatra.

For our purposes, however, there is another concept, again based on the division of the year into twenty-seven sections. You may be wondering, why this number? It takes the Moon a little less than 27⅓ days to orbit the Earth (27 days, 7 hours, 43 minutes, and 11.6 seconds, to be exact). This forms a *sidereal month*. Some of you reading this may be thinking, "Wait, isn't a lunar month about 29½ days?" If you go by the phases of the Moon—new, waxing, full, waning—it does, indeed, take that long to have a lunar month. That's technically known as a *synodic month* and is defined as the time between two new Moons. As you can see, the synodic and sidereal lunar months differ in duration. For our purpose in Tantric astrology, we use the sidereal month to determine the length of the nakshatras because of the astronomy and because of the mysticism of the number.

How is 27 a mystical number? Go back to chapter 7 and reread the section on the meaning of the number 108. When you multiply 27 by 4, you get exactly 108. Therefore, 27 can be seen as a symbolic representation of 108.

Starting at the beginning of the sidereal zodiac, we divide the year into 27 sections, each lasting about 13 days. These sections of the year are also called the nakshatras.

Each nakshatra has a set of correspondences. Here is a list showing some of their correspondences. Note that because the sidereal month has more than a third of a day over 27 days in its cycle, there are some overlaps in the dates:

Name: *Ashvini* ("Ahsh-vee-nee")
Date: April 13–26
Astrological Ruler: South Lunar Node
Symbol: The Head of a Horse
Color: Blood Red
Purpose: To get things started. Good for business and leadership.

Name: *Bharani* ("Bar-ah-nee")
Date: April 27–May 10
Astrological Ruler: Venus
Symbol: Yoni
Color: Blood Red
Purpose: To obtain justice and truth. Endurance. For creativity and overcoming anger or pride.

Name: *Krittika* ("Krit-tih-kuh")
Date: May 11–23
Astrological Ruler: Sun
Symbol: A cutting instrument, such as a razor, knife, or spear

Color: White

Purpose: To obtain monumental, outstanding accomplishments. Good for the arts, but also for computers and other technology.

Name: *Rohini* ("Roh-hee-nee")

Date: May 24–June 6

Astrological Ruler: Moon

Symbol: Chariot

Color: White

Purpose: To obtain love and spark desire. To develop grace and write poetry.

Name: *Mrigashira* ("Mree-guh-shee-rah")

Date: June 7–21

Astrological Ruler: Mars

Symbol: Head of a Deer

Color: Silver Gray

Purpose: To obtain great beauty, especially for a woman. To improve perceptive abilities and speaking skills.

Name: *Ardra* ("Ahr-drah")

Date: June 22–July 5

Astrological Ruler: North Lunar Node

Symbol: Human head

Color: Green

Purpose: To develop empathy, the ability to forgive, and compassion. However, this is not weakness. It still encourages passionate and fierce action.

Name: *Punarvasu* ("Poo-nahr-vah-soo")

Date: July 6–19

Astrological Ruler: Jupiter

Symbol: Bow and Quiver

Color: Lead

Purpose: To obtain energy, especially for renewal. Also for intelligence and gaining intellectual and spiritual wisdom.

Name: *Pushya* ("Poosh-yuh")

Date: July 20–August 2

Astrological Ruler: Saturn

Symbol: Lotus, Arrow

Color: Black mixed with Red

Purpose: To obtain auspicious new beginnings after reaching spiritual maturity.

Name: *Ashlesha* ("Ah-shleh-shuh")

Date: August 3–16

Astrological Ruler: Mercury

Symbol: Serpent

Color: Black mixed with Red

Purpose: To obtain secrets, especially esoteric wisdom. Also for sexual desire. Perfect for developing a hypnotic gaze and enhancing communication skills.

Name: *Magha* ("Mahg-hah")

Date: August 16–29

Astrological Ruler: South Lunar Node

Symbol: Throne

Color: Ivory

Purpose: To attain nobility. Gives tremendous personal power but can be fearsome.

Name: *Purvah Phalguni* ("Purr-vuh Pahl-goo-nee")

Date: August 29–September 12

Astrological Ruler: Venus

Symbol: Fireplace

Color: Light Brown

Purpose: To obtain material wealth honestly. Great for performers and teachers and for experiencing joy and play.

Name: *Uttara Phalguni* ("Oo-tahr-uh Pahl-goo-nee")

Date: September 13–26

Astrological Ruler: Sun

Symbol: A Small Bed

Color: Bright Blue

Purpose: To be able to provide financial assistance to others. Humanitarianism.

Name: *Hasta* ("Hah-stuh")

Date: September 27–October 10

Astrological Ruler: Moon

Symbol: Hand, Fist

Color: Deep Green

Purpose: To consolidate bothersome issues. To get things under control. To improve speaking, writing, and memory.

Name: *Chitra* ("Chee-trah")

Date: October 10–23

Astrological Ruler: Mars

Symbol: Jewel, Pearl

Color: Black

Purpose: To obtain beauty through both fine arts and practical arts such as fashion design. Helps you develop charisma.

Name: *Svati* ("Svah-tee")

Date: October 23–November 4

Astrological Ruler: North Lunar Node

Symbol: Coral

Color: Black

Purpose: To encourage freedom, self-reliance, logic, adaptability, and independence. May result in anxiety or restlessness.

Name: *Visaka* ("Vih-sah-kuh")

Date: November 5–18

Astrological Ruler: Jupiter

Symbol: Potter's Wheel

Color: Gold

Purpose: To obtain desires by any means. Also good for pure research and science.

Name: *Anuradha* ("Ahn-ur-ahd-uh")

Date: November 19–December 1

Astrological Ruler: Saturn

Symbol: Lotus

Color: Reddish Brown

Purpose: To obtain friendship and the benefits of association. Good for becoming a leader.

Name: *Jyeshtha* ("Jyesh-tuh"

Date: December 2–15

Astrological Ruler: Mercury

Symbol: Earring

Color: Cream

Purpose: To obtain power and fame, especially through hard work and seniority.

Name: *Mula* ("Moo-luh")

Date: December 15–28

Astrological Ruler: South Lunar Node

Symbol: Lion's Tail

Color: Brownish Yellow

Purpose: To obtain wisdom in all branches of education, including the sciences, philosophy, and so forth. Great for performing rituals for those wanting to be teachers. Helps you to keep your head during a crisis.

Name: *Purva Ashadha* ("Purr-vuh Ahsh-ahd-uh")

Date: December 29–January 10

Astrological Ruler: Venus

Symbol: Elephant Tusk

Color: Black

Purpose: To obtain protection for friends and loved ones. Also for courage, popularity, and leadership.

Name: *Uttara Ashadha* ("Ooh-tahr-uh Ahsh-ahd-uh")

Date: January 10–23

Astrological Ruler: Sun

Symbol: A Small Cot

Color: Copper

Purpose: To establish rapport with others. Allows you to more easily absorb everything, from the emotions and feeling of others to energies in the environment. Lets you change society.

Name: *Shravana* ("Shrah-vahn-uh")

Date: January 23–February 4

Astrological Ruler: Moon

Symbol: Ear

Color: Light Blue

Purpose: To obtain the ability to consider the ideas of others without dismissing them. This is the period to focus on meditation and scholarly pursuits. Promote health.

Name: *Dhanishta* ("Dahn-eesh-tuh")

Date: February 5–18

Astrological Ruler: Mars

Symbol: Drum

Color: Silver Gray

Purpose: To become strongly altruistic. Also, to become more artistic and musical and even achieve fame.

Name: *Shatabhisha* ("Shah-tahb-hee-shuh")

Date: February 18–March 3

Astrological Ruler: North Lunar Node

Symbol: Empty Circle

Color: Aquamarine

Purpose: To obtain protection. Also for healing others, especially children. Creativity.

Name: *Purva Bhadrapada* ("Purr-vuh Bhad-rah-pahd-uh")

Date: March 3–16

Astrological Ruler: Jupiter

Symbol: Swords

Color: Silver Gray

Purpose: To help others become more contrite and seek atonement for their actions. Mysticism and creativity.

Name: *Uttara Bhadrapada* ("Oo-tahr-uh Bhad-rah-pahd-uh")

Date: March 17–30

Astrological Ruler: Saturn

Symbol: Snake in Water

Color: Purple

Purpose: To develop the ability to endure the unwanted actions of others even as you restrain their activities. Also for developing a quick mind and psychic abilities.

Name: *Revati* ("Reh-vah-tee")

Date: March 31–April 12

Astrological Ruler: Mercury

Symbol: Fish

Color: Brown

Purpose: To become a protector of others. Also to develop as a guru who nurtures and assists others on the spiritual and physical journey in this lifetime.

Magick

I have stated several times that magick is part and parcel of Tantra. Some of you reading this will be familiar with real magick. Others will not. So I'd like to discuss it a bit.

Real magick is not Harry Potter. You can't just wave a wand and mumble a word or two of bad Latin and have miracles occur. That's just movies and novels.

So what is magick? The following is adapted from my book *Modern Magick*:

According to the famous occultist Aleister Crowley, magick is "the Science and Art of causing Change to occur in conformity with Will." Crowley was a member of the famous Hermetic Order of the Golden Dawn. Another member of the Golden Dawn was Dion Fortune. Her definition of magick was the same as Crowley's except that she considered the "change" to be a change in consciousness.

But what exactly do these definitions mean? Let's say that you do a magickal ritual to get fifty dollars. It, therefore, is your "will" to get the money. You go out for a walk, and although when walking it is your habit to turn right at a particular street corner, something makes you decide to turn to the left. A block down this street you meet an old friend who returns the fifty dollars you loaned him several months ago.

What made you turn left? According to Crowley's definition, your magickal ritual would have caused some change in the physical world that resulted in your turning in an unusual direction. Perhaps it was a smell, or a telepathic message from your friend or from a higher entity telling you to "turn left!" If you subscribe to Dion Fortune's definition, then you would say that your ritual made a change in your consciousness that gave you the insight to turn to the left instead of the right.

In either case, three things are apparent:

1. No matter which definition you use, the actual result is the same.
2. The result functions *as if* there had been a change in the physical world, regardless of whether there had been a change in the physical world or just a change in your consciousness.
3. Magick works.

Unfortunately, either definition is still too broad. If you cause a change in conformity with Will and call it "magick," then almost anything you do is a magickal act. If it is your will to open a door, and you turn the knob and open the door, then according to the previous definitions you have done a magickal act. In fact, Crowley (his name rhymes with *holy*, not with *howdy*) wrote that "every intentional act is a Magickal Act." If you follow his line of reasoning, then opening the door is a magickal act indeed. While moving everything you do to the level of being part of your will, and therefore magickal, has value, that idea is not what we are seeking at this time. For the purposes of this book, we need to make the definition of magick a bit longer:

Magick is the science and art
of causing change
(in consciousness) to occur
in conformity with will,
using means not currently understood
by traditional Western science.

We have added the idea that the magick is accomplished by some means not known by modern science. A ritual that causes something to occur does not make sense to current Western scientific thought. Therefore, "scientists" are inclined to think that real magick, since it doesn't fit into their worldview, is nothing more than supernatural hokum. But, *magick is not supernatural.*

Whether our entire universe came about either as the creation of an intelligent being or beings, or merely as the result of chance events, we still must come to the same conclusion: *everything in the universe is natural.* Some ancient cultures considered the apparent rise and fall of the Sun to be a supernatural event. As time passed, it was discovered that the apparent rise and fall of the Sun is, in fact, a natural event caused by the rotation of the Earth.

Similarly, I am firmly convinced that magick will one day be understood in Western scientific terms. History proves this. Reading, writing, mathematics, astronomy, chemistry, medicine, physics, and more were all at one time deep occult secrets. Today, many of these things are taught to children before they begin school. The occultism of the past becomes the science of the future. Arthur C. Clarke, the famous science fiction writer and author of *2001: A Space Odyssey*, wrote, "Any sufficiently advanced technology is indistinguishable from magick." Decades earlier, Crowley wrote something similar: "In one sense, Magick may be defined as the name given to Science by the vulgar."

We now have a definition of magick that is far more specific than either Crowley's or Fortune's. Since the results are the same, by the way, I drop Fortune's "in consciousness" from the definition.

....

Virtually every spiritual system has involved magick. Judaism has Moses and Aaron in front of Pharaoh, casting a rod and having it change into a snake. Jesus walks on water. Muhammad's great miracle is the Quran itself. Later, as spirituality and mysticism devolve into static religions, magick becomes part of the past and is forbidden so that current leaders can have temporal control over followers. After all, if you can perform magick and communicate directly with deity, why would you need priests or imams or rabbis?

You do not have to do magick to practice *Modern Tantra*, but magick is a part of it. I will be sharing specifically Tantric magickal methods later in this book. In the meantime, if you are familiar with any form of magick, feel free to take the concepts presented in this chapter and add them to your practices.

ELEVEN

The Bodies, Nadis, and Chakras

For thousands of years, Tantrics have observed humans. They learned much about the physical and non-physical nature of humans. They determined that a human is composed of five *koshas,* or sheaths. These became known as "bodies" and were adopted by the Theosophists, which led to them becoming part of Western spirituality.

Within these bodies is a system of energy paths. When fully studied—something far more than can be covered here—these paths are incredibly complicated. When the discovery of these energy paths spread to China, they were originally considered paths of "wind." Later, it became understood that they were paths of energy and were called *meridians,* a basic part of traditional Chinese medicine, including acupuncture and acupressure.

Among Tantrics these paths are called *nadis.*

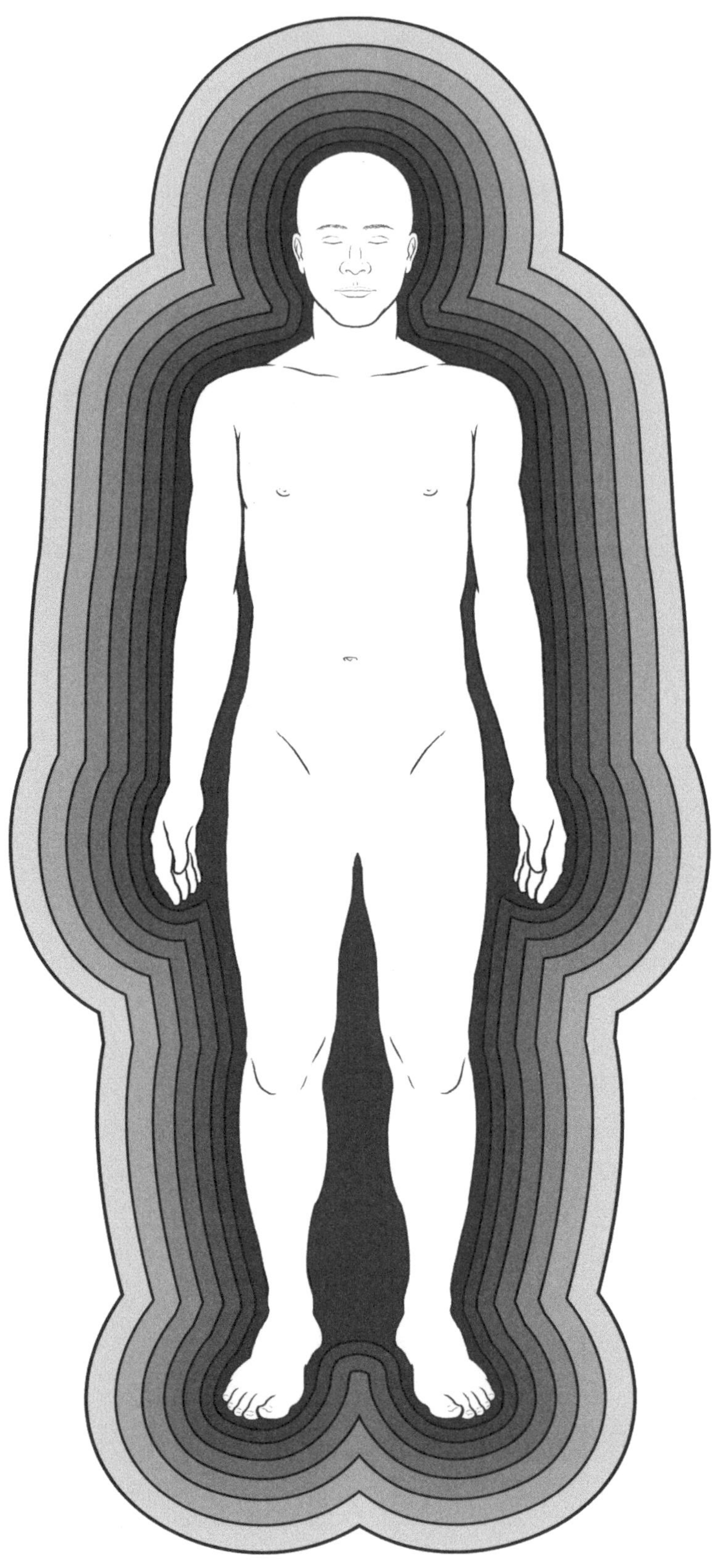

The Five Koshas

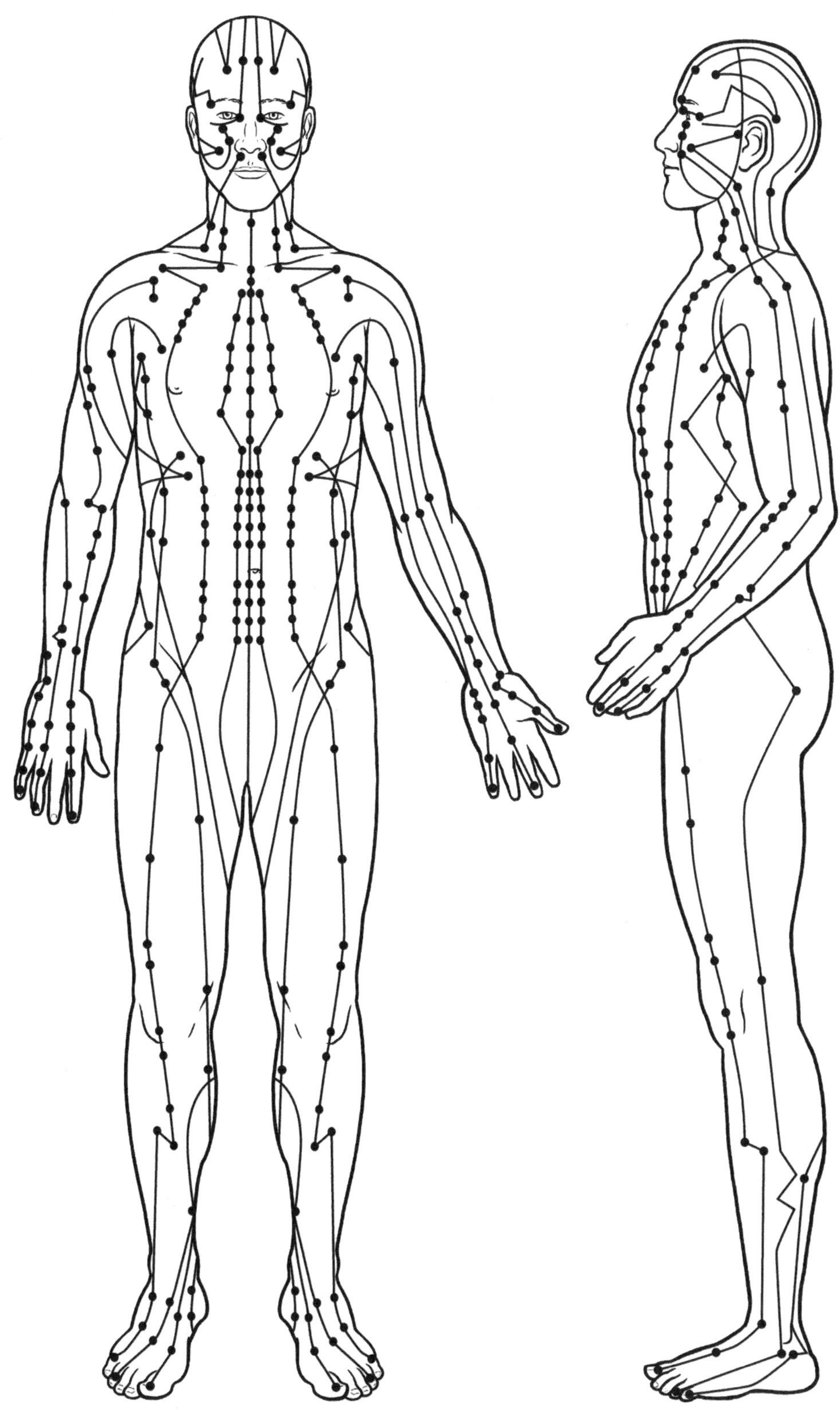

The Nadis

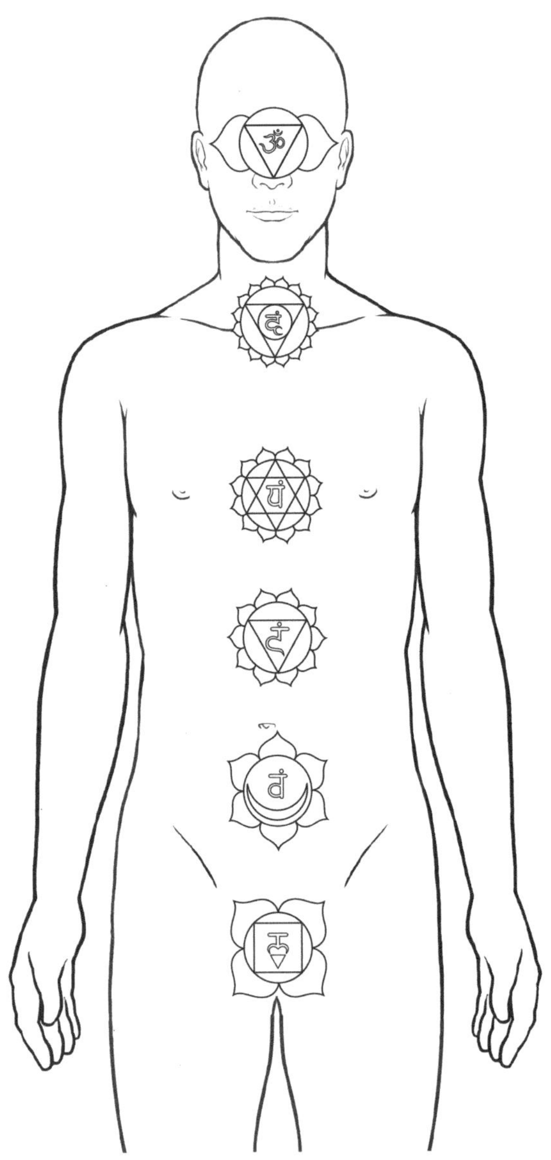

The Six Major Chakras

Where these energy paths cross there is a vortex that allows the transfer of energy between the bodies. Each vortex or power center is known as a wheel or *chakra*. Although the seven famous chakras associated with the spine are well known, there are numerous other chakras throughout the body.

Imagine, if you will, a brilliant lightbulb representing your higher self. In Sanskrit, this higher self, the source of the stuff of which your soul is made, is called the *Atman* ("Aht-mahn"). Although we may not recognize it or be aware of it, the Atman is always united with the Divine, the ultimate source of all, known as *Brahman* ("Brah-mahn" or "Brach-mahn," not to be confused with Brahma, the Hindu god of creation).

The First Sheath: The Body of Bliss

The first manifestation of the Atman is the body known as the *anandamaya kosha* ("uh-nahn-duh-mai-yuh koh-sha"). This is the level of what has been called "God consciousness." The term is generally translated as the "sheath of bliss." It is that part of us that evolves through evolution and reincarnation, leading us to experience unity with the Divine. When your conscious and unconscious function together in perfect harmony from within this sheath or body, you are constantly in a state of bliss. One of the signs of this is that you will have no attachments to any objects or desires.

Some people misunderstand this concept. It does *not* mean that you won't have desires. When people try to get rid of their desires, they become frustrated, angry, and unhappy. It's a natural part of the human experience to have desires. However, what you can do is not become so attached to your desires that they control you.

For example, let's say you'd love to have a particular new car. Or perhaps your desire is for a romance, a certain amount of money in the bank, a trip around the world, etc. It's fine and normal to have desires. But do the desires control you? Are you unhappy because you don't have that car or romance or money or trip *now?* Are you desperate to have the goal of your desire? Is that desperation controlling you?

We always have desires. Even if you obtain a desire, there will always be more. Therefore, the idea is to acknowledge the desire but not have it control you. You can go to sleep tonight and not be upset that you don't have it. When you awaken, you can be thrilled about a new day, work to achieve your desire, and not be concerned about whether you have it or not.

Some people who teach magick describe being totally focused on achieving your goal. But that doesn't mean you have to be so attached to it that it controls you. Aleister Crowley described this in *The Book of the Law* as doing the magickal work without "lust of result":

> *For pure will,*
> *unassuaged of purpose,*
> *delivered from the lust of result,*
> *is every way perfect.*
>
> —*Liber Al*, I:44

This is the sheath where the original vibration, pulsation, or throb of life enters and flows into all the sheaths. When we operate from this sheath, the feelings of erotic pleasure are permanent. And, contrary to what the "experts" say, these feelings are independent of effort or stimulation. You don't have to do something to feel the erotic bliss of unity with all; you simply are that way. This is the very essence of spiritual sex.

Even though this perfectly blissful state is where we're entitled to be, few people are there. That's why it is viewed as a sheath or covering. It is actually separated from the Divine as a result of our focus on desires and on our illusion (*maya*) of the self as being separate from everything else. Although this is the highest level we can achieve before becoming one with the Divine, it is still separated from the Divine. It's as if we have placed a lampshade around the lamp, dimming the light of the Divine. At best, it is but a dim reflection of the Atman. Cut off from direct experience of the Divine, we become convinced that the only thing that is real is the fifth and most distant body from the godhead, our physical body. It becomes our only reality. Sex is only physical and not spiritual. This can lead to the consciousness loop of increasing the physical and decreasing the spiritual until the physical is all that matters.

Some people may fear they will "lose themselves" if they allow a merger between their essence, Atman, and the godhead, Brahman. Our human logic seems to imply that this would be so. In fact, however, just the opposite is true. We do not lose ourselves; we grow to what our conscious thinking would call an impossibly larger universe. We don't become lost; we become complete.

It is sometimes possible to get hints of the amazing potential of this sheath during trance and dreams, but we don't usually experience it during our wakeful hours. The *anandamaya kosha* is associated with the use of the life force energy.

The Second Sheath: The Body of the Intellect

The second body is called the *vijnanamaya kosha* ("veen-yah-nuh-mai-yuh koh-sha"). It is the intellectual or knowledge sheath. It is less close to the Atman, but is still very ethereal. Even so, it combines our intellect with the five sense organs. It identifies "us" with the physical world and what will be our physical sheath or body. If, with our intellect, we are able to see through the lampshade of what most people consider physical reality, it can lead to the serenity and spiritual bliss of the first body.

The intensity of knowledge, here, is extreme. It is derived from both current-life experience and past-life experience.

The two major functions of the vijnanamaya kosha, functions we can tap into at any time, are discrimination (here that means the ability to tell the difference between relative truth and absolute truth) and non-attachment. Because people reading this may have skipped other parts of this book, I feel it is necessary to repeat that non-attachment does *not* mean being cold or reserved or trying to escape from the world. Rather, it means that we *embrace* the universe as it truly is: everything is a vibratory, energetic manifestation of spirit. And that means everything is Divine. When we accept this concept, it changes the way we approach life every day. How can we want to pollute the environment when it's sacred? How can we put junk food into our bodies when they're sacred? When we go beyond merely thinking about the sacredness of all things to accepting it on all levels, the way we approach ourselves and the world changes.

When we see the universe as it truly is and accept it, we come to realize that everything is composed of pure energy. That energy vibrates at different frequencies, so, in my experience, the energy in each sheath has its own "flavor." With practice, we can identify it. We can work with this energy, but we cannot possess or own it. Understanding this leads to living in the world, loving what we have access to, striving to increase access when desired, but realizing we cannot permanently possess or own energy. Therefore, there is no reason to be attached to it.

Again, this body is like another lampshade added, taking us further from our highest self. The vijnanamaya kosha is associated with the functions of the mind. Note that the mind is not the brain. The brain is a physical organ, while the mind is non-physical. They are associated but not the same.

The Third Sheath: The Body of the Mind

The third body is called the *manomaya kosha* ("mahn-oh-mai-yuh koh-sha"), or the mental or mind sheath. Like the previous sheath, it is associated with the mind. However, this sheath is the source of rational, sequential thought (*manas*) and the ability to discriminate after you have knowledge of something: the removal of ignorance (*buddhi*). There are various yoga practices (*pratyahara*) that have the goal of controlling the senses. Doing this will allow you to discover the nature of this body.

This is also the body that "houses" the subconscious, including memory, rationality, dreaming, and experiences of pleasure or pain as a result of our reactions to our actions in the past. Here are our fantasies and desires, our joys and hopes, our jealousies, angers, and sorrows. The manomaya kosha is also associated with the nervous system.

Note that this body and the previous one are both associated with what we commonly call the mind. The second sheath deals more with what some people might call the "higher" aspects of the mind, such as the intellect and inductive reasoning, neither of which require external input or verification. The third sheath described here deals more with the way the mind deals with and interacts with the exterior world. It's also associated with the subconscious. Therefore, beside rationality and discrimination, it also is the house of the memory (including the memory of pleasure and pain based on past experience) and dreaming.

The manomaya kosha is unique in that it holds the concepts by which we identify and attribute a socially agreed-upon meaning to the events and sensations that occur in the two sheaths that follow. Here is where fantasies, desires, joys, jealousies, angers, hopes, and sorrows reside to be shared with those whom we trust.

The Fourth Sheath: The Body of Energy

So far, then, we have our higher self, our intellect, and our mind including the subconscious. Something has to supply energy for all of this, and that comes in the next sheath, the *pranamaya kosha* ("prawn-yah-mai-yuh koh-sha"). This is the sheath or body that is energized through "vital breath" (*prana*), the life force of vital spirit. Within this sheath the energy is triggered by the breath and charges all of the other koshas, including our physical and mental activity. Note that because of the importance of the breath, some people believe that the energy is actually in the air. This is not accurate. Breath and breathwork *trigger* the movement of the energy that flows through channels known as *nadis* ("nah-dees").

The three most famous, and most important, of the nadis are the *Sushumna* ("Soo-shoom-nuh"), *Ida* ("Eee-dah"), and *Pingala* ("Ping-uh-luh"), which go through the center of the spine and on either side (see illustration). The seven famous chakras are vortices, whorls of energy that are connected to these nadis and send energy through the five bodies. That is why the major chakras are so important. The pranamaya kosha is associated with the respiratory system, circulatory system, and endocrine system.

This fourth kosha and the following one, the physical body, are the most dense and material form of sheaths. They operate together to produce that delightful blend of physical and emotional warmth. They produce our hormonal rhythms. They also are the basis for the concept of pure sensuality.

The Fifth Sheath: The Physical Body

The energy that comes from the fourth sheath operates with the fifth sheath, the body furthest from the Atman known as the *annamaya kosha* ("ahn-uh-mai-yuh kosha"), or physical sheath. Technically, the name indicates that this is the sheath of food, as food is necessary for the physical body to exist. When we look at the physical body, we often see separate systems that control all of the bodily functions. From a Tantric viewpoint, these functions are the result of the interaction of energy and consciousness.

Some spiritual traditions downplay the importance of this fifth kosha. They say we are just souls temporarily residing in bodies and that the goal is to die and go to heaven and live with God or that we need to die and live repeatedly in a world of suffering and pain until we learn enough that we don't have to reincarnate anymore. Tantra takes the view that the physical body is every bit as valuable as the other bodies. It is through the physical body that we can experience life. And when we harmonize our bodies, instead of life being painful, it becomes beautiful. The annamaya kosha, the body of food, is naturally associated with the digestive system.

Of course, being the fifth "lampshade," this sheath is furthest from our highest self. But the goal, according to *Modern Tantra*, is not to get rid of the lampshades, but to harmonize them and enable them to work together. This sheath is also important because it is where we experience the universe and matter.

If you want to see a true miracle, you need look no further than the human body. It is composed of the five elements and yet, with the addition of energy and consciousness, it is a synergy that is far more than the mere sum of its parts.

....

The study of the koshas is a complete science in itself. But we don't have time to focus on them, nor do we need to. There are vortexes—vortices—of energy that move between them. These are the *chakras*. And that's the next thing we need to look at.[16]

16 The preceding paragraphs were taken in part from my blog post "The Five Tantric Bodies," which originally appeared on the Llewellyn.com website.

The Chakras

The chakras are vortices where energy can pass between the koshas. They occur wherever two nadis cross. Contrary to popular belief, the locations, functions, and appearance of the chakras are not universally accepted. David Gordon White, in his book *Kiss of the Yogini*, reveals that there is no single agreed-upon interpretation of the chakras. He writes that each tradition or school—in fact, sometimes different teachers in the *same* school—teach their own system.

In addition to the major chakras I'm about to discuss, there are also secondary and minor chakras in places such as the back of the head, the palms of the hands, and the soles of the feet. When I was first initiated into a Tantric tradition, my teacher revealed that originally there were only three chakras that were considered important: the genital, heart, and crown chakras (see illustration). Some schools teach that there are seven chakras, some teach five or six, and others teach eight or more. In *Soul Searchers: The Hidden Mysteries of Kundalini*, the author describes the purposes of 547 chakras.

Thomas Ashley-Farrand, one of the Western world's foremost experts on mantras, told me that the chakras on the soles absorb energy. If you went to a temple in India, he said, and sat with your legs extended toward the front where the priest was leading a ritual, it is likely that you would be asked to either cross your legs or leave. Otherwise, you would be sucking the energy from the temple's leader.

Some people look at the chakras as forming a 3-1-3:

- The three lower chakras exchange energy dealing with the physical world.
- The three upper chakras exchange energy dealing with the spiritual world.
- The chakra at the middle, the heart chakra, allows the blending of energy and issues between the physical and spiritual worlds.

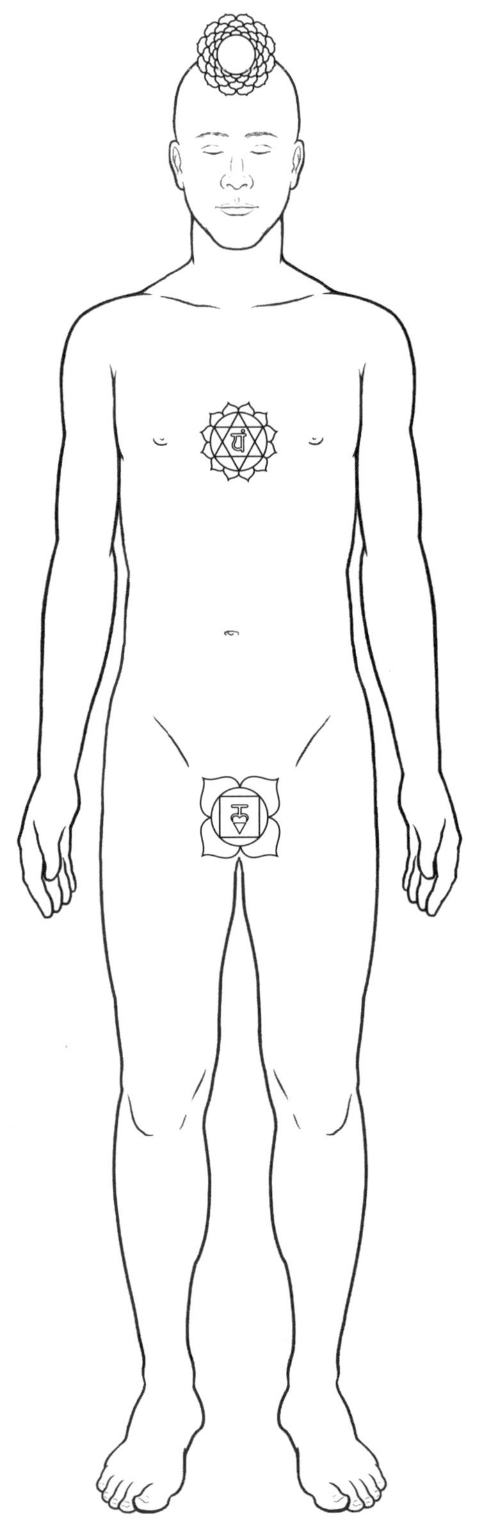

The Original Three Chakras: Genital, Heart, Crown

This 3-1-3 concept has a lot going for it and makes a good paradigm for understanding the chakras. You have the physical chakras, the spiritual chakras, and a place where they blend. This approach is good for understanding the chakras, but ultimately it is divisive. It mirrors the concept that the body and mind are separate entities, something foreign to *Modern Tantra*. In the *Modern Tantra* tradition, although we can discuss body and mind separately (just as we can discuss the koshas separately), the reality is that it is the unity and totality of the body/mind/spirit that makes each of us unique.

If you had been born in a different body—if your appearance were different, if your skin color were different, if your gender were different—the blending of consciousness and body would result in you being a far different person than you are. Contrary to the popular belief found in many spiritual systems, traditional Tantrics believe we are not merely a soul temporarily housed in a body. It is the unity of the body, mind, and spirit that makes us who we are.

I prefer to describe the major chakras as being 6 + 1. The six are the lower six chakras as they relate to the physical and mental/non-physical. The + 1 is the crown chakra, which is actually above the head. It has significantly different qualities than the others. For example, each chakra has a special one-syllable mantra. The mantra for the crown chakra is… silence. The crown chakra allows divine energy in. The other chakras disseminate this divine energy throughout the koshas.

Besides the 6 + 1 major chakras and the secondary chakras, there are also "secret" chakras. I'll be revealing information about one or two of these later because they're important to Tantra, kundalini energy, and spirituality. But first, here are a few correspondences and important concepts associated with each chakra.

Root Chakra

Element: Earth

Location: Base of spine; perineum

Physical: Coccyx, anus, large intestines, back, legs, feet, bones

Issues: Grounding, safety, survival, shelter, trust, nourishment, self-esteem, boundaries, physical health

Scents: Sandalwood, bergamot, vetiver

Food: Protein

Sanskrit Name: Muladhara ("home of the root")

Planetary Ruler: Mars

Memory Cue: "I am"

The first chakra is associated with our basic animal instincts of survival and self-preservation—food, shelter, health, and security. It is the very foundation of our being and our identity. Linked to the physical body at the base of the spine, it sends energy between the five bodies, to the physical world exterior to our bodies, and to the ground below.

As the chakra related to excretion, the root chakra is also closely associated with your relationship to your physical body. Often, we hold on to things we don't need, a sort of "spiritual constipation" preventing our mental and mystical growth. Meditating on this chakra can help you eliminate beliefs that are obsolete in your life.

Foods that support this chakra include proteins such as meats, soy, tofu, nuts, and legumes. Consuming them can help "ground" you; like gravity, they can bring you down to earth. This is valuable for when you feel as if you cannot link to other people and the world.

Using the chakras for healing works on two levels, the energetic/physical and the spiritual. For the energetic/physical level, sending energy (described later in this chapter) to this chakra can increase vitality and energy. It can also help with colon issues, tension (especially in the spine), and constipation. On a spiritual level, sending energy to this chakra is good for grounding, enhancing feelings of security, increasing courage, developing patience, and overcoming greed, anger, and the fear of death.

The root chakra is associated with the element of earth, so magickally it is associated with money, jobs, promotions, business, investments, material objects, fertility, agriculture, health foods, ecology, conservation, the stock market, antiques, old age, museums, buildings, construction, progress, the home, the physical world, and daily necessities such as food.

Popular First-Chakra Stones

Black Tourmaline: For protection

Hematite: For setting boundaries

Black and Snowflake Obsidian: For clarity in determining what to let go

Smoky Quartz: For blending first-chakra and seventh-chakra energies

Tiger's-Eye: For physical security

Genital Chakra

Element: Water

Location: Genitals, lower back, lower abdomen

Physical: Sexual organs, hips, lower back, bladder, kidneys, stomach, bodily fluids

Issues: Intimacy, confidence, creativity, sexuality, sensuality, emotions, warmth, pleasure, relationships, desire, imagination

Scents: Rose, jasmine, ylang-ylang

Food: Liquids

Sanskrit Name: Svadisthana ("one's own support")

Planetary Ruler: Sun

Memory Cue: "I feel"

The second chakra is the focal point of our emotions, sexuality, and creativity. It governs our sense of self-worth, how we relate to others (both sexually and nonsexually), and the confidence we have in our own creativity. This chakra concerns flow: feelings, fluidity, openness. The essence of this chakra is that of water, always flowing, never static. It represents grace and acceptance, and the ability to go with the flow.

There is also a long Tantric tradition of using bodily fluids—tears, urine, blood, semen, lubricating fluids, ejaculation, menstrual fluids—for healing and magick. As I briefly mentioned earlier, Mohandas Gandhi, famed as a supporter of nonviolence and given the title *Mahatma* (*Maha* = great, *Atma* = soul), helped lead India to independence from England. One of his practices was to drink his own urine for spiritual purification. Many Westerners cringe at the concept, but if you are healthy, your urine is sterile. I am not an advocate of this practice, known as *Rasa Tantra.*

The consumption of sexual fluids and menstrual fluids has a long tradition in magick. The Barbelo Gnostics of the first century CE and before included the consumption of sperm as part of their eucharist. Among more contemporary authors, Aleister Crowley and Kenneth Grant have discussed the magickal potency of consuming sexual fluids, Crowley from an alchemical perspective and Grant from a more Tantric perspective. I also discuss it in both *Modern Magick* and *Modern Sex Magick.*

Of course, if just consuming sexual fluids gave you magickal or healing power, everyone who performed any kind of oral sex would be a powerful and healthy magician, and observation shows that isn't true. The bodily fluids need to be energized through various magickal practices.

For the physical aspects of healing, sending energy to the genital chakra can help with issues associated with the ovaries, testicles, prostate, womb, and bladder. It can help with issues of impotence and overcoming the inevitable results of physical excesses. Spiritually, it can help you deal with issues of being able to give and receive, balancing the emotions so you are not over-emotional or under-emotional, being able to accept and give pleasure, and becoming mentally open to your sexuality and sexual potential. It can also help you learn to deal with change, become a more tolerant person, surrender to spiritual impulses, become more able to work and play with others, and overcome purposelessness and jealousy.

The genital chakra is associated with the element of water, so magickally it is associated with higher forms of love and the deeper emotions such as compassion, faith, loyalty, and devotion. Working magick with this chakra will also help you improve friendships, partnerships, meditation, and spirituality. It can help heal mental and spiritual wounds and restore spiritual growth. Working with this chakra can help with childbirth and children, the home, receptivity, the family, swimming, diving, fishing, ancestors, medicine, hospitals, compassion, doctors and nurses, and clairvoyance.

Popular Second-Chakra Stones

Bloodstone: For energy stimulation

Carnelian: For creativity and decisiveness

Red Garnet: For patience

Ruby: For passion and increased intensity of the senses

Solar Plexus Chakra

Element: Fire

Location: Abdomen (solar plexus)

Physical: Stomach, liver, gallbladder, spleen, adrenal glands

Issues: Personal power, ego, self-esteem, vitality, forcefulness, perception, insight, will and willpower, discipline, personality

Scents: Peppermint, ginger

Food: Complex carbohydrates

Sanskrit Name: Manipura ("filled with gems")

Planetary Ruler: Venus

Memory Cue: "I do"

The third chakra is associated with identity and self-esteem. Known as the "power center," this is the area of assertiveness, intuition, and inner drive. It controls digestion and the metabolic systems, processing energy and giving us the spark we need to overcome inertia and apathy. It allows us to assert our personal power, follow our gut instincts, take risks, and make decisions.

The foods to eat to improve the functioning of this chakra are complex carbohydrates such as whole grains and beans. Avoid processed foods that destroy the natural benefits of these edibles.

For our physical bodies, sending energy to this chakra aids in healing or improving the pancreas, adrenals, stomach, liver, gallbladder, nervous system, muscles, metabolism, and digestion. Spiritually, sending energy to this chakra can enhance the will, personal power, authority, self-control, charisma, and sense of humor. It can help you overcome anger, fear, and hate.

The solar plexus chakra is associated with the element of fire, so working with it can be helpful for magick associated with success, sex, banishing some illnesses, the military, conflicts, protection, courts, law, police and sheriff's agencies, contests, competitions, and private detectives. It's also good for improving dowsing, treasure hunting, gambling, athletics, strength, and general good health. Magick with this chakra is associated with overcoming or initiating war and terrorism. On a more personal level, work with this chakra for anything related to the Freudian *id,* the lower emotions of absurd desire and lust (that is, too much desire or lust), and for overcoming anger and violent emotions. The third chakra is also associated with things having speed.

Popular Third-Chakra Stones

Aragonite: For calmness

Citrine: For abundance and magick

Golden Calcite: For integration of new energies, ideas, and beliefs

Rutilated Quartz: For creative dreaming

Heart Chakra

Element: Air

Location: Center of the chest

Physical: Heart, lungs, diaphragm, chest, thymus, circulatory system, shoulders, arms, hands

Issues: Love, healing, compassion, kindness, relationships, self-acceptance, forgiveness, hope, sympathy, empathy

Scents: Rose, neroli

Food: Green vegetables

Sanskrit Name: Anahata ("unstruck")

Planetary Ruler: Mercury

Memory Cue: "I love"

The fourth chakra is linked to the heart center. As I described earlier, this chakra may be thought of as the balance point between the three lower, physical chakras and the three higher, spiritual chakras. The heart chakra is the location of true compassion, kindheartedness, selfless love, emotional well-being, and devotion. It's where we process and store emotional experiences. It speaks of "we" instead of "me."

When it comes to foods, consuming green, leafy vegetables charges this chakra. As a general rule, the darker the green, the better it is.

Sending energy to this chakra can help heal physical issues dealing with the circulatory system, including the blood and the heart. Spiritually, sending energy to this chakra can help you become more open to giving and receiving unconditional love, forgiveness, compassion, understanding, balance, harmony, contentment, and acceptance. It can help you overcome the fear of love, emotional instability, or feeling out of balance.

The heart chakra is associated with the element of air. Therefore, work magick with this chakra to enhance schooling, memory, intellectual abilities, teaching, and test-taking ability. It's also good for working with organizations and groups of all kinds, theorizing, and overcoming drug addiction.

Popular Fourth-Chakra Stones

Aventurine: For physical health

Emerald: For the spiritual aspects of love

Green Calcite: For eliminating limiting beliefs

Green Tourmaline: For adding love to creative efforts

Lepidolite: For stress relief

Pink Calcite: For eliminating limiting behaviors and patterns

Rose Quartz: For total self-acceptance

Throat Chakra

Element: Ether

Location: Throat, neck

Physical: Throat, neck, jaw, mouth, teeth, gums, tongue, thyroid gland

Issues: Communication, creativity, expression, humility, manifesting ideas

Scents: Orange, rosemary
Food: Fruit
Sanskrit Name: Vishuddha ("perfectly pure")
Planetary Ruler: Moon
Memory Cue: "I communicate"

The fifth chakra is associated with sound and has to do with creative self-expression, speech, and communication. The ability to speak honestly, to receive, process, and assimilate information, and to connect and speak our inner truth all relate to this chakra.

One of the challenges most people face is the ability to express anger. Not expressing it or holding it in can manifest as diseases such as high blood pressure and diabetes. Letting it explode without thought, seemingly the essence of many TV and radio shows today, not only can result in isolation but may also be ineffective as a means of communicating anger and releasing the energy of that emotion. This can result in further explosions later.

Common symptoms of having energy blocked in this chakra include binge eating and drinking. When your mouth is filled with food and drink, it prevents you from needing to actually communicate what you're feeling! Meditating on this chakra and freeing its ability to transfer energy within the five bodies will result in the development of constructive ways of releasing both the cause of the anger and the emotions associated with it.

Although all fruit will help energize this chakra, it is especially berries that are good for it.

On the physical level, sending energy to this chakra can help with problems of the thyroid, parathyroid, hypothalamus, throat, mouth, and voice. Spiritually, sending energy to this chakra can help with creativity, communication, knowledge, truth, wisdom, loyalty, honesty, reliability, gentleness, and kindness.

The throat chakra is associated with the element of akasha (aka ether or spirit). So working magick with this chakra is good for all forms of white magick (linking with the Divine), bringing in spiritual energy, inspiration, intuition, self-healing, evocation (especially of various elemental spirits), divination, and reincarnation.

Popular Fifth-Chakra Stones

Angelite: For evocations
Aquamarine: For peaceful communication
Blue Lace Agate: For logical communication
Chrysocolla: For confidence when communicating
Larimar: For being able to express your deepest feelings and beliefs
Turquoise: For gaining the support of others

Brow Chakra

Element: Light
Location: Between the eyebrows
Physical: Eyes, brain, pituitary gland, pineal body, lymphatic system, endocrine system
Issues: Intuition, clairvoyance, telepathy, inner wisdom, connection to the higher self, imagination, dreams, ideas, reasoning
Scents: Clary sage, lavender, lemon
Food: Air
Sanskrit Name: Ajña ("overseer")
Planetary Ruler: Saturn
Memory Cue: "I see"

Because this chakra is also known as the third eye, I originally labeled this section the third-eye chakra. The problem with this is that some people focus on the idea that it is between and *above* the eyes, toward the middle of the forehead, forming a sort of triangle with the eyes. Its position is actually associated with a location that is lower on the forehead.

Draw an imaginary horizontal line connecting the eyebrows. The point in the center of this line, directly above the vertical mid-line of the nose, is associated with the position of this chakra.

The brow chakra is associated with sight and seeing, both intuitively and physically. It is related to the energies of clear vision, intuition, light, and spirit. It is through this chakra that we may tune in to the higher self in order to seek and receive inner guidance.

When energy is blocked in this chakra and not freely flowing, it can result in a lack of foresight and imagination. It results in dull dreams and bizarre ideas that can suddenly take over your life. Spiritually, blockages here result in fear of the unknown. Physically, it can result in fear of others, ranging from agoraphobia to xenophobia. Symptoms also include insomnia, feelings of anxiety, and headaches that either last a long time or fade away only to rapidly return.

Foods that charge this chakra include items that use a lot of air, especially greens (possibly due to their chlorophyll content), green drinks (not, I regret to say, including absinthe), and teas.

On a physical level, sending energy to this chakra can help in healing issues related to the pituitary gland, left eye, nose, ears, headaches, general eye problems, bad dreams, and detachment from the world. Spiritually, sending energy to this chakra can help enhance imagination, intuition, insight, clairvoyance, peace of mind, wisdom, and devotion, while overcoming fear and cynicism.

The element associated with the brow chakra is not found in traditional Western forms of magick. It is the element of light. Working magick with this chakra can help you accept energy and divine wisdom, give up your ego, and surrender to your inner will: the highest good. It can help you become a tool of the Divine. It's also good for works of shapeshifting, spiritual strength, and rites intended to lead to enlightenment.

Popular Sixth-Chakra Stones

Amethyst: For peaceful dreams and overcoming insomnia

Azurite: For the elimination of ideas we've kept after we've found that the source of the beliefs is no long meaningful

Charoite: For eliminating fears of the known and unknown

Kyanite: For accepting personal responsibility and discriminating between reality and mere belief

Lapis: For uncovering hidden beliefs that may help or hinder

Sodalite: For regaining balance, especially after becoming upset

Moss Agate: For balance of the energies flowing between the brain hemispheres

Sugilite: For releasing anger, rage, resentment, and guilt

Crown Chakra

Element: Energy

Location: Top of the head

Physical: Head (especially the fontanel), the brain

Issues: Higher wisdom, oneness, intuitive knowing, humanitarianism, connection to the Divine, selflessness, higher consciousness, yoga

Scents: Frankincense, sandalwood

Food: Fasting

Sanskrit Name: Sahasrara ("thousandfold")

Planetary Ruler: Jupiter

Memory Cue: "I understand"

When looking at a drawing of the chakras in front of the body, you can't help but be struck by this chakra's location. The other six are directly in front of the body. The crown chakra is above it. This is why I refer to this chakra paradigm as "6 + 1."

The seventh chakra is symbolic of pure spirituality. It is our highest energy center, both in terms of physical location and rate of vibration. It represents liberation, great knowledge of the Divine, deep metaphysical understanding of the universe and ourselves, inner wisdom, and a connection to the highest state of enlightenment and spiritual growth. It represents union of the higher self with both the cosmos and the Divine.

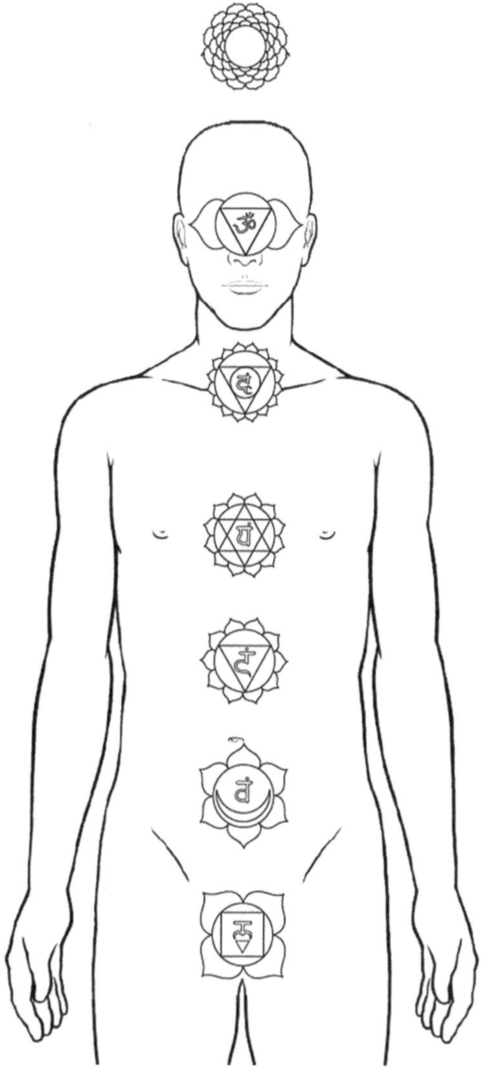

The Seven Major Chakras

Later, I'll be describing the concept of kundalini energy. When it rises up the Sushumna nadi and energizes the crown chakra, a person is said to have achieved *samadhi*, or enlightenment.

To enhance this chakra's energy, you should fast. If you want to try fasting, do so only if you are healthy enough to do it. Check with your doctor *first* if you have any questions or concerns. Then, do short fasts, perhaps just half a day. Increase to a day and slowly move to longer periods. Be careful to stay hydrated. Fasting (avoiding food) does *not* mean you shouldn't drink water. Some people believe that pure fruit and vegetable juices are okay on fasts. If your doctor says it's okay for you to fast, I'd suggest trying different styles of fasting to see which is the most tolerable and most effective for you.

On a physical level, sending energy to this chakra can help with healing the pineal gland, brain, and right eye. It can help you overcome the experience of confusion and improve decision making, overcoming hesitation. On a spiritual level, sending energy to the crown chakra brings oneness with the infinite, inspiration, unity, idealism, divine wisdom, and understanding. It can help you understand personal survival and reincarnation as well as overcome depression, alienation, and the mental aspects of senility.

The element associated with the crown chakra, once again, is not one found among the typical magickal elements of Western traditions. Just as this chakra is different from the other six major chakras, the element associated with it is different. This element doesn't have a simple name, but it is the element I call *ETW*: Energy, Thought, and Will. Magick linked to this chakra can help you find your "true will," the essence of who you are when you are aligned with the Divine. This essence is you without the trappings of the superficial ego layered upon it. Magick associated with this chakra is also valuable for actually doing your will after you discover what it is. As Crowley wrote in *The Book of the Law* (I: 42–43):

> "Thou hast no right but to do thy will.
> Do that, and no other shall say nay."

Magick with this chakra is also great for improving your personal mental, physical, emotional, and spiritual strength.

Popular Seventh-Chakra Stones

Diamond or Moldavite:
Stimulate the crown chakra

Amber: Although often treated as a stone, amber is actually fossilized tree resin (resin is actually a secretion of certain plants and trees, such as the pine, and is not sap) and has functions like diamond and moldavite.

The Chakras and Sound: The Bija Mantras

If you go back to the first chapter, you'll see how fundamental the concept of vibration is. This is true not just in *Modern Tantra*, but in virtually all traditional Tantric systems I've ever worked with or studied. Thousands of years ago, Tantrics knew that the universe was made of energetic vibration, something that Western science has only recently accepted.

In Tantra, the science of vibration in the audible range—sounds you can make and hear—is known as *mantra vidya*. Chances are you're familiar with some concept of mantras. I've given numerous mantras earlier in this book for you to work with. I've also revealed the translations and meanings of these mantras. But there's more to mantras than that.

Mantras are not merely nice sentiments or a way of honoring the gods. They're more than prayers to be repeated in order to gain something, such as forgiveness, as is practiced with the prayers known in the Roman Catholic Church as the "Ave Maria" ("Hail Mary") and the "Pater Noster" ("Our Father").

Mantra **is** *the God or Goddess in vibratory (sound) form.*

I don't mean a metaphor for the Deity, or a symbol of the Goddess or God, or something that triggers the Deity, or just his or her name or title. Just as a yantra is the Goddess or God in two dimensions, mantra, *the sound itself,* ***is*** the God or Goddess in vibratory form. As evidence of this I would remind you that the symbols that represent sounds, the letters of *Devanagari*, the Sanskrit alphabet, are called *matrikas* ("little goddesses").

The meanings of mantras are of value to your conscious mind. But it is the sound itself, the vibration you make when you repeat the mantras (Sanskrit: *japa*), that has a powerful effect within your five bodies and throughout the universe. This is a powerful aspect of Tantric magick and practice. Audible vibration (and even silent vibration within our minds) can initiate changes within us and outside of us.

Each of the first six major chakras has a special sound that is important in Tantra. They are called the *bija*, or seed, mantras. Each has just one syllable. It is the sound and vibration of the bija mantras that is important.

- **Bija mantras have *NO* translation.**
- **They have *NO* meaning.**
- **They are *NOT* metaphors.**
- **They are *NOT* symbolic of anything.**
- **They may be combined to form more complex mantras.**

As I wrote previously, each of the six lower major chakras has a bija mantra. The highest chakra, the crown chakra, also has a bija mantra, and it is the most sublime of all sounds: it is silence. How does one vibrate silence? That is a mystery of the crown chakra.

The bija mantras are Lam, Vam, Ram, Yam, Ham, Om, and silence. Memorizing all of the bija mantras, in order, can be accomplished easily using this mnemonic: *Lover, You Home?*

LoVeR, You HOMe?

If you simply repeat the mnemonic a few times, with feeling, you'll always remember the bija mantras and their order.

Chakra	Name	Location	Bija Mantra	Pronunciation
7	*Sahasrara*	Crown	—	Silence
6	*Ajña*	Brow	Om	Ah-
5	*Vishuddha*	Throat	Ham	Hahm
4	*Anahata*	Heart	Yam	Yahm
3	*Manipura*	Solar Plexus	Ram	Rahm
2	*Svadisthana*	Genitals	Vam	Vahm
1	*Muladhara*	Root	Lam	Lahm

The Chakras as Bija (Seed) Mantras

Bija Mantras

Charging the Chakras Using the Bija Mantras

There are several ways to charge the chakras. You'll learn about raising kundalini energy through them later. However, each chakra is attuned to a bija mantra. The relationship is shown in the illustration. Putting this into action is easy.

Although most of the time the easiest way to practice something is by oneself, the easiest way to learn how to work energetically with the bija mantras is by working with another person. Here's the technique:

1. To begin, you and your partner should take showers or baths. You want to be very clean for this practice.
2. Although this practice is traditionally done digambara, you may do it wearing robes or light clothes.
3. One person should banish the area being used for this practice. You may use any of the banishings presented in this book or your favorite banishing.
4. One person should be the sender of the energy. The other person may sit in a chair

or lie on his/her side. This sender leans in close to the part of the body where the appropriate chakra is linked. The first chakra is at the tip of the tailbone, usually an inch or two below the beginning of the separation of the buttocks. The sender should be between one and three inches from the area. Then the sender chants the bija mantra for the first chakra, ***Lam***, ten times. This should take no more than sixty seconds. As the sender does this, both people should visualize the chakra that is there and allow the sound vibrations to energize it, causing it to brighten and spin faster. Since this is practice, the sender might want to experiment with the speed, high or low pitch, volume, and tonal quality to see which works the best. The receiver can comment on this.

5. Repeat this with the other chakras:

   In front of the genitals, repeat **Vam.**

   In front of the solar plexus, repeat **Ram.**

   In front of the heart, repeat **Yam.**

   In front of the throat, repeat **Ham.**

   In front of and between the brows, repeat **Om.**

   Just above the head, repeat **silence.**
6. If you like, reverse positions. The sender becomes the receiver and vice versa.
7. Banish again.
8. Discuss the experience. What worked? What didn't work? What could be better?

The more you practice this and the more people you work with, the better at it you will become. At the beginning, charge all of the chakras as described. After you've practiced this several times, try charging just one or two chakras with the appropriate bija mantra. Try charging from the crown chakra to the root. How are the effects different?

The goal at this point is simply to become familiar with the technique.

The Chakras and Color

Traditionally, there are multiple colors associated with each chakra. For example, the second (genital) chakra in some traditions is said to be a black lotus with red petals. Inside of that is a white crescent moon. So which color should be associated with this chakra: black, red, or white? Or do we need to focus on all of them when working with colors?

I posed this question to a true Tantric master, Dr. Jonn Mumford. He told me that the importance was not the specific color, but that you were focusing on the chakras.

At first I liked this answer, but then I had a problem with it. By this thinking, you could simply focus on a chakra and not use any specific color at all.

Then I had a realization that there was more to it and that color was important. Sound has a certain range of frequencies. Color is also a vibration, but at a different range of frequencies. So while focusing on the chakras can have an impact, adding the vibration at the higher frequencies of visual color is also of value. The colors would have to be related to the chakras and in a vibratory relationship with each other for this to work. Luckily, there is such a set of colors.

These colors are not the ancient Indian colors, but they have been accepted by many people today in India. Because of all the people focusing on these colors, they have been linked to the chakras. But they are not the ancient complex system. They are a simpler system associated with … Sir Isaac Newton.

Newton (1643–1727) is known primarily for his scientific research. His analysis of physics provided the basic rules that are still taught to millions of students. They also revolutionized warfare, by allowing accurate predictions of the trajectory of projectiles, and helped plan such things as the manned landing on the moon.

What isn't commonly known is that Newton wrote far more on occultism and spirituality than on science. His heirs, however, didn't want his nonscientific studies made public. His book on alchemy, for example, was not published until the 1980s, some 250 years after his death.

Newton became fascinated with crystal prisms. He was the first person to prove that they broke the light into component parts rather than changing or adding colors. You probably know what a prism looks like and how it breaks a white light into component parts.

If you look at the colors generated by sending a beam of white light through a prism—or the colors of a rainbow—you'll see that they blend from one into another. There are literally thousands of detectable colors. Newton wanted to list them, but how?

Thinking of his occult studies, he remembered that the number seven was special:

- Seven days of creation
- Seven heavens
- Seven visible planets
- Seven Christian archangels
- Seven notes in the Western musical scales
- Seven days in a week
- Seven Wonders of the World

A Simple Mnemonic for the Seven Colors in the Spectrum

So Newton decided that there were seven colors in the spectrum, for no known reason other than their spiritual value. These colors are red (with the longest wavelength and lowest frequency), orange, yellow, green, blue, indigo, and violet (with the shortest wavelength and highest frequency).

That's a lot of colors, but luckily, a man named Roy G. Biv[17] came up with a way to memorize them and their order quickly (see illustration). As with the bija mantras, it's a simple mnemonic. In this case, it's his name:

17 Okay, there's no real person named Roy G. Biv. I just wanted to make it a bit easier to remember. So if you were wondering, "Is there *really* some guy named Roy G. Biv?," it worked.

Again, as with the bija mantras, repeat this mnemonic name a few times, with feeling, and you'll always remember the chakra colors and their order. Since color is simply a vibration of energy, it follows that you can use color to charge the chakras, too.

Charging the Chakras with Color

This practice for charging the chakras is similar to the bija mantra technique. However, you can do this by yourself, too.

1. To begin, you and your partner should take showers or baths. You want to be very clean for this practice.
2. Although this practice is traditionally done digambara, you may do it wearing robes or loose clothes.
3. One person should banish the area being used for this practice. You may use any of the banishings presented in this book or your favorite banishing.
4. One person should be the sender of the energy. The other person should sit in a chair. This sender stands or sits so he or she can directly view the area associated with the chakra being charged.

   The first chakra is at the tip of the tailbone, usually an inch or two below the beginning of the separation of the buttocks. At this point the sender can do one of two things:

   a. The sender visualizes a sphere of pure white light between his/her hands. Using just the imagination and will, the sender changes the color to *red.* When the sphere is seething with red energy, the sender pushes, throws, or sends it toward the location of the root chakra.
   b. The sender visualizes a beam of powerful *red* light coming from his/her eyes and hands and directs it at the location associated with the chakra.

   Once the sending of the red energy is established, allow the energy to flow for no more than sixty seconds. As the sender does this, he or she should visualize the chakra that is there and allow the color vibrations to energize it, causing it to brighten and spin faster. Since this is practice, the sender might want to experiment with the shade of color and its intensity, transparency, light or darkness, etc., to see what works best. The receiver can comment on this.
5. Repeat this with the other chakras:

   In front of the genitals, use the color *orange.*

   In front of the solar plexus, use the color *yellow.*

   In front of the heart, use the color *green.*

   In front of the throat, use the color *blue.*

   In front of and between the brows, use the color *indigo.*

   Just above the head, use the color *violet.*
6. If you like, reverse positions. The sender becomes the receiver and vice versa.
7. Banish again.
8. Discuss the experience. What worked? What didn't work? What could be better?

The more you practice this and the more people you work with, the better at it you will become. At the beginning, charge all of the chakras as described. After you've practiced this several times, try charging just one or two chakras with the appropriate colors. Try charging from the crown chakra to the root. How are these effects different?

The goal at this point is simply to become familiar with the technique.

Charging the Chakras with Sound *and* Color

Now let's combine the two previous techniques.

In front of the root chakra, use the sound **Lam** and the color *red.*

In front of the genitals, use the sound **Vam** and the color *orange.*

In front of the solar plexus, use the sound **Ram** and the color *yellow.*

In front of the heart, use the sound **Yam** and the color *green.*

In front of the throat, use the sound **Ham** and the color *blue.*

In front of and between the brows, use the sound **Om** and the color *indigo.*

Just above the head, use **silence** and the color *violet.*

6. If you'd like, reverse positions. The sender becomes the receiver and vice versa.
7. Banish again.
8. Discuss the experience. What worked? What didn't work? What could be better?

As described with the previous two exercises, the more you practice this and the more people you work with, the better at it you will become. At the beginning, charge all of the chakras as described. After you've practiced this several times, try charging just one or two chakras with the appropriate color and bija mantra. Try charging from the crown chakra to the root. How are these different?

The goal at this point is simply to become familiar with the technique.

The Nadis, Kundalini, and the Tantric Secret of the Chakras

I want to go back for a moment and discuss the energy paths called the *nadis.* Some sources claim there are 35 million of these energy paths. Others say there are 72,000. Traditionally, just 108 are important. Of those, three are of special interest.

The *Ida* ("Ee-dah") goes from the root chakra, up the left side of the body, to the left nostril. It is white, feminine, and cold, and carries lunar energy.

The *Pingala* ("Ping-uh-luh") also begins at the root chakra but goes up the right side of the body and ends at the right nostril. It is red, masculine, and hot, and carries solar energy.

Many versions of the chakras and Ida and Pingala show the energy paths winding back and forth around the chakras. This was probably a complexity that was added to the original understanding.

The *Sushumna* ("Soo-shoom-nuh") is the energy path that runs up the center of the body, through the spine. It also begins at the root chakra (some say just below it) but goes all the way to the crown chakra. It is a pinkish color (red and white) and temperate.

This mighty central path does not carry solar or lunar energy, although those energies may amplify or be amplified by the energy it does carry. This energy is called *kundalini.* This energy is said to be a serpent that rests in three-and-a-half coils around the root chakra, ready to rise up the central nadi.

Obviously, this is a metaphor. There's no snake curled up in your body. If you happen to find one, please see your doctor immediately!

The concept of the kundalini serpent being coiled at the base of the spine is symbolic of *potential energy*—it's a snake filled with energy and ready to spring! This energy can be enlivened through such things as visualization, breathwork, a gift from the Goddess, a gift from your guru, or sexual activity.

When the serpent is aroused, it rises through the Sushumna and the chakras. When it reaches the crown chakra, it supposedly produces enlightenment. I have heard lots of people talk about this, but not many seem to have actually experienced it. Frankly, most of those who claim to have done so certainly don't manifest being enlightened! In fact, they tend to use their experience as a way of lording their supposed spiritual superiority over others.

I'm sorry, but the truth is that in most of these instances it's a matter of ego, not enlightenment. It's literally a klesha staring the person right in the face, but he or she doesn't have the training or knowledge to realize it. The person instead uses it to brag, "I'm more enlightened than you!" Maybe, but your attitude and false ego don't indicate it.

There is more to the process than most tell you. However, it's not dangerous, as some would claim, saying that you could develop something called "kundalini psychosis" as a result of trying to send the energy through the nadis and chakras before they are open. Nonsense!

One way to understand this system is to compare the nadis to a set of pipes and the chakras to valves in the pipes. What happens when one of the water valves on your pipes at home is closed? The water doesn't flow. And that's it. You don't get "water pressure psychosis." The water simply stays in the pipe until you open the valve. The same is true with kundalini energy. There is no reason to be terrified of it, as some people seem to be. If your chakra valves are open, the energy will flow when triggered. If one of the valves is closed, the energy will flow up to that valve and stop. If the valve is only partially open, the water/energy will trickle through.

And that's it. Sorry, no psychosis. However, remember that the chakras are also ways of passing energy between the bodies. If these *spiritual wormholes* (like the predicted wormholes in the universe that are so often used in science fiction stories and movies) aren't open, communication fueled by kundalini energy can't take place. This lack of communication can cause various mental, physical, and emotional issues. Such issues are not caused by trying to send kundalini energy before the chakras are open.

I've already discussed a few methods for opening the chakras, including the use of color and vibration. What I haven't discussed is the nature of the "pipes between the valves," the *nadis*, and it's important that you understand a bit about them. Nadis are ethereal. They're not physical. *Inside* the Sushumna nadi is another nadi known as the *Brahma* nadi. It's even more ethereal than the more famous nadis. Its purpose is to allow the free flow of knowledge to occur between yourself and the Divine. Unfortunately, it's usually blocked.

When the kundalini rises to the crown chakra, that chakra inverts. You may have seen images of this where instead of looking like it's floating above the head, the chakra covers the head like a skullcap (see illustration). When it's inverted, it sends energy back down to two chakras that are linked to each other. These two chakras are located in the center of the head, at the point where a line from the brow chakra going straight back meets a line drawn straight down from the crown chakra (see illustration).

These two chakras are even more ethereal and subtle than the 6 + 1 chakras already covered. The first is called the *vhirkuti* ("veer-koo-tee") chakra. When enlivened, it allows you to *have* spiritual understanding.

The second is called the *trikuti* ("tree-koo-tee") chakra. When enlivened, it allows for the *opening* of spiritual understanding.

Combined, these two chakras are the beginning and advanced aspects of the *kailasa*, or *guru*, chakra (*gu* means "darkness" and *ru* means "remover"). First you must have the understanding, then you must become open to it and accept it.

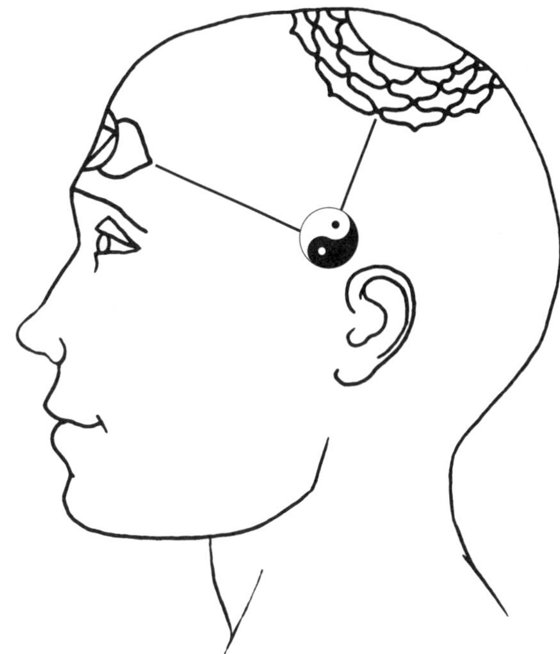

Location of the Guru Chakra

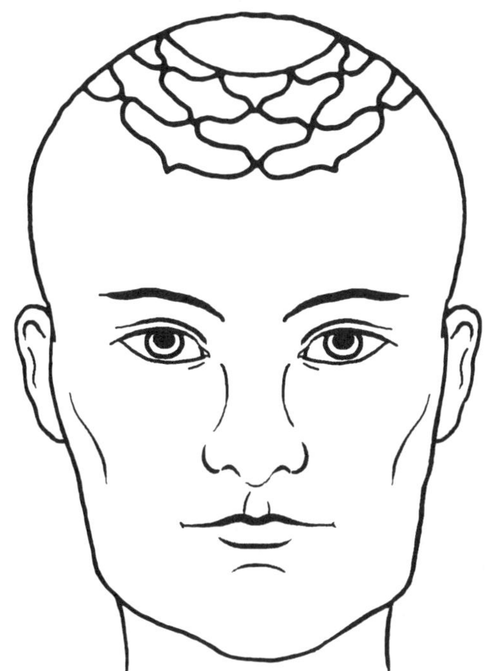

The Crown Chakra, Inverted and Appearing Like a Skullcap

So the inversion of the crown chakra as a result of the movement of the kundalini up the spine results in the triggering of the guru chakra, which allows you to open to and understand spiritual wisdom. That's as good an explanation of the concept of enlightenment as any.

The inversion of the crown chakra also produces another phenomenon. It releases a substance known as *amrita.* (Note: Neo-Tantrics use this term to describe female ejaculatory fluid. They do not use it with the traditional meaning.)

Amrita being released feels like warm, delicious oil being poured over you. It may be that the concept of anointing with oil is derived from this experience. This experience, the release of amrita, is *not* merely subjective, psychological, or imaginary. It has a physical effect on the body. Specifically, it will make all of your bodily fluids—perspiration, saliva, tears, sexual lubrication fluids, female ejaculate, male sperm, and even urine—briefly have a delightfully *sweet* taste and scent. In my experience, it reminds me of drinking the nectar from a freshly picked honeysuckle flower.

This is physical proof of the spiritual experience of *samadhi*, enlightenment, unity with the universe and the godhead. Unfortunately, I can't describe this because for each person it is different. I've seen people sob with tears or break into outrageous laughter or even experience intense orgasms. All I can say is, like being hit over the head with a two-by-four, when it happens, you'll know it!

TWELVE

HEALTH AND HEALING

Earlier in this book, I described how some Neo-Tantrics and some traditional Tantrics often do not agree with one another. Those Neo-Tantrics believe that the key element of Tantra is movement of a special form of the body's energy, kundalini. Along with traditional Tantrics, they believe that this energy can be caused to move up the Sushumna nadi through visualization, breathwork, ritual behaviors, sexual arousal, or a combination of these methods. They believe traditional Tantrics waste their studies and practices on relatively useless things such as spiritual aspects, religious rituals, deities, mantra, yantra, and other concepts.

Some of the traditional Tantrics, on the other hand, claim that by focusing primarily on the movement of the kundalini, the Neo-Tantrics miss out on the essence of Tantra. They also believe that Neo-Tantrics oversimplify and misrepresent Tantric concepts and techniques. To them, it's as if the Neo-Tantrics think the fuel pump is the only important part of a car, while to them there is so much more.

Practitioners of *Modern Tantra* believe that both the Neo-Tantrics and traditional Tantrics have much to share. We want to take from both sides and not eliminate anything that is practical and good.

To begin this chapter, I'm going to look at the technology used by so many Neo-Tantrics for healing and maintaining health. These techniques are closely related to a subject from the previous chapter, the chakras.

Symptoms of Ill Health Associated with the Chakras

The chakras are not physical things; they are pathways for energy to move between the five koshas. As pathways, they cannot become diseased, as some have claimed. They can, however, become partially or completely blocked. Later I'll describe ways to unblock them. But first I'm going to share a chart listing the chakras and issues associated with blocked chakras.

Chakra	Location	Physiology	Physical	Non-Physical
1	Coccyx	Base of spine, legs, feet, ankles, rectum, back, perineum, excretory system, skin, immune system	Sciatica, rectal tumor or cancer, diseases of the immune system, malfunctions resulting in depression, bloating, general physical health	Grounding, family issues, safety, survival, self-esteem, trusting, social skills
2	Genitals	Large intestine, lower vertebrae, pelvis, lower stomach, kidneys, appendix, bladder, reproductive system, genitals, bodily fluids excluding blood	Gynecological problems, pelvic and lower back pain, painful sex, erectile dysfunction, anorgasmia, potency, urinary issues, prostate, childbirth	Guilt, power and control, creativity, ethics, honor, blame, going with the flow, openness, giving and receiving, impotence, tolerance, dealing with change, jealousy, devotion, spirituality
3	Solar Plexus	Stomach and abdomen, small intestine, gallbladder, liver, kidney, pancreas, adrenals, spleen, mid-spine, muscles	Arthritis, ulcers, pancreatitis, indigestion, eating disorders, liver problems, adrenal problems, diabetes, energy and drive	Fear, intimidation, confidence, self-care, decision making, defensiveness, risk taking, assertiveness, having "guts", charisma, humor, anger

Chakras and Related Issues

Chakra	Location	Physiology	Physical	Non-Physical
4	Heart	Circulatory system, respiratory system, heart, lungs, blood, diaphragm, shoulders, arms, wrists, hands, ribs, chest and breasts, thymus	All heart problems, all lung problems, upper back, shoulders, breast cancer	Ability to love and be loved, resentment, grief, anger, bitterness, loneliness, forgiveness, hope, hate, compassion, balance, acceptance
5	Throat	Throat, neck, jaw, tongue, trachea, mouth, teeth, gums, esophagus, thyroid, parathyroid, hypothalamus	All mouth and throat issues, swollen glands, thyroid problems, joint problems, scoliosis, vocal problems	Communication issues, humility, expressing anger, binge eating and drinking, understanding new information, bringing in spiritual energy, self-healing
6	Mid-Brow	Lower brain functions, nervous system, eyes, ears, nose, pituitary, pineal body, lymphatic system, endocrine system	Brain problems including tumors, stroke, neurological disturbances, hemorrhage, headache, blindness (especially of the left eye), deafness, learning challenges, seizures, nose issues, insomnia, anxiety	Uncovering truth, intellect, accepting others' ideas, learning abilities, intuition, fear of the unknown, imagination, accepting spiritual energy, surrender to higher will
7	Crown	Higher brain functions, head, muscular system, skeletal system	Sensitivity to sound or light, chronic exhaustion, depression, energy disorders, pineal gland problems, eye problems (especially the right eye)	Values, ethics, selflessness, seeing the bigger picture, spirituality, inspiration, liberation, confusion, hesitancy, unity, finding "true will"

Chakras and Related Issues

The first column in the chart is the number usually associated with the chakra, and the second column gives the chakra's location. The third column reveals the organs, body parts, and other physiological aspects of the body associated with the chakra. The fourth column is a brief listing of potential physical issues associated with each chakra. The final column includes mental, emotional, and spiritual issues associated with each chakra.

You will notice that, on occasion, some of the physical and non-physical issues described for each chakra overlap. In such a brief chart, there is not room for an in-depth description of these issues. In fact, since this book is not centered on the chakras, you will want to do further research for a more in-depth explanation. However, if you take a look at the listed issues and relate them to the broad associations of the chakras, you should be able to develop a more complete understanding of these listings.

Chakra Healing Methods

Let's assume that a person is suffering from asthma. Asthma is a challenging problem. Not being able to breathe due to constricted airways can be terrifying and life-threatening.

Very often, asthma is either caused by or triggered by psychological issues. Treatment is usually limited to drugs classified as bronchodilators, short-acting beta agonists, corticosteroids, etc. Sometimes a sharp doctor, realizing that these drugs are only masking the asthmatic problems and that the illness is a symptom of something else, will send a person to a psychologist. After a long term of therapy, they may discover the cause, and that cause may be related to fourth-chakra non-physical issues such as unresolved grief or anger.

Remember, however, that the bodies, or koshas, are not really separate. They interweave and are interconnected through the chakras. Release the psychological cause of the physical issue and that physical issue will decrease or be eliminated. Overcome the physical symptoms by clearing the energy and the original psychological issue will fade away. In this example, the feelings of grief or anger will dissipate.

The key to the healing, then, without spending months or years in therapy, can be the opening of the appropriate chakra. Blocked as the chakra is, and unable to allow energy to easily pass from kosha to kosha, body to body, the result on the physical plane, the manifestation of the problem in your physical body, is asthma.

Open the chakra and allow the energy to pass through easily, and the physical problem may quickly dissolve.

Unfortunately, I had to use the word "may" in order to be completely truthful. The idea that there is only one cause and the problem is only affecting one chakra is simplistic. Usually there are multiple causes, and several chakras, to a greater or lesser degree, are blocked.

Even so, working with the primary problem area can often have a cascade effect, opening all of the other constricted chakras and nadis.

Method One: Color Visualization and Breathwork

Color healing has a long Tantric history. Using a combination of breathwork and color visualization, sending color-filtered energy to the area of the chakra, can result in a dramatic change.

Method Two: Using Physical Color

Although in some traditions burning a candle of a specific color is seen to energize a ritual or spell with an appropriate color, the candle flame's color remains the same and is not altered by differences in the candle's color. In a completely dark room, no matter what color candle you light, the light—and the light's energy—remains the same.

You can easily obtain glass votive candle holders in a variety of colors. Burning a small candle in the colored glass will fill the room with light that is the color of the glass. In my experience, the more lights used, the more powerful the effect. As an alternative, you can use colored light bulbs or lights that have colored "gels" or lenses in front of them.

Method Three: Chakra Lenses

I previously mentioned that some time ago I obtained a set of stained-glass items called *chakra lenses*. These were cut to resemble the traditional shapes ascribed to the chakras, and the colored glass matches the colors assigned to the appropriate chakras. I have found that shining a bright light, such as a powerful flashlight beam, through the lens, so that the light falls directly on the area of the chakra, can have powerful results. The advantage over method two is that you don't have to fill the room with ambient colored light just to treat one area.

Unfortunately, the glass used to make the chakra lenses was very fragile, and several of them broke. I no longer have them and have never seen chakra lenses advertised since I purchased my set. I see no reason why you could not use a piece of appropriately colored glass, perhaps a disc a few inches in diameter, in the same way. You could even use colored "gels," as used in theaters and in light shows, directly in front of the bright flashlight.

Method Four: Vibration

As described in the previous chapter, you can vibrate the appropriate bija mantra directly in the area of the chakra. Allow the person being treated to breathe deeply, visualizing his or her breath going directly to the area of the chakra in question. This is also a very good technique for group work. With several people chanting the mantra together, the result is intensified.

The Neo-Tantric Solution to Healing

Neo-Tantrics realize two things. First, simply working with a single chakra may not be enough to help a person. The chakras are connected to the nadis, or energy paths, and they're all contained within the koshas, or bodies. To give a complete healing, and to keep healthy, the entire system needs to be opened so that energy can flow through it. And second, as you may recall, an important focus of Neo-Tantra is kundalini, the sexual energy. Thus, as part of this chakra-opening process, stimulating the energy with sexual activity can be healing. This technique has several steps.

Step One: Honoring

Begin the healing by honoring yourself. Both the healer and the person being healed should take time to honor their own bodies with purifying baths. Dress to honor yourself, your sensuality, and your sexuality, and to entice your partner. As you do this, give yourself positive affirmations. If you are seeking healing, you might say, "I deserve healing. I am a beautiful person. I am open to change." If you are acting as a healer, you might say, "I can help this person heal. I am a powerful, beautiful person."

Come together in a room designed for beauty, tranquility, eroticism, a healthy attitude toward sexuality, and overall health. Be sure there is water to drink. Take some time to discuss how you feel. If there are any concerns or issues you have, share them. Get them out into the open and resolve them.

When you both feel good about the healing about to take place, honor the person you are with. Tell that person that he or she is beautiful, deserves to be healed and healthy, etc. Be honest! Don't make up things and say them if you don't believe them to be completely true.

Step Two: Align the Chakras

Lie on your sides, face to face. Begin breathwork. On the inhalation, feel the energy and breath go down the body to the pit of your stomach. As you exhale, feel the energy and breath go up the spine, over the head, and out through the mouth and nose. Each time you exhale, make sure to sound the exhalation, saying, "Ahhhhhhhhhh..." Continue as you look your partner in the eyes.

Still on your sides, looking into each other's eyes, pull yourselves ever more tightly together. You will notice that the flow of energy naturally expands to include your partner. Soon you will sense that the cycling energy is combined with all of your bodies.

If you have not yet removed your clothes, now is the time to do so. Continue with the visualization, breathwork, and loud exhalations.

It is time to make the chakras receptive to the energy that is about to flood them. Use the bija mantras from the last chapter. Repeat each bija mantra until you feel that the appropriate chakras in both of you are stimulated, perhaps even pulsing. If you find there is a natural urge to kiss, caress, fondle, and erotically stimulate each other, allow yourselves to do so. If you haven't done this by the time the crown chakra is pulsing, it is time to do so.

Step Three: Let the Kundalini Rise

Sexual activity will automatically cause the kundalini energy to rise through the chakras. Begin intercourse, but don't focus on trying to achieve orgasm. Instead, surrender to the goddess Kundalini. Visualize her as a serpent of energy, uncoiling from the bottom of the spine and starting to rise toward the crown. You can encourage her with breathwork and visualization and by using the bija mantras.

There is no magick spell. Just sense the energy rising. Allow it to do so. If it becomes "stuck" at a chakra, that's okay. Work with the bija mantra and color visualization of that chakra until it opens to the power of the kundalini.

When the kundalini reaches the crown chakra, don't stop. Continue the breathwork and let whatever happens, happen. Keep up the breathing pattern. Eventually there will come a time to allow the energy to return. It may be a few moments later, or it may be hours later.

Repeating these steps will eventually clear the problem. Continuing this practice will help you obtain optimum health and avoid a return of the issues.

Traditional Tantric Healing

Method One: Herbalism

The practice of using herbs for healing has been popular all over the world. There have been two basic forms of this system. The first is based on the magickal "law" of similarities: You can have an effect on *B* though the use of *A*, which in some way is similar to *B*.

Thus, an herb's shape, color, taste, etc., can be used to help with an ailment that has some relation to those qualities of the herb. For example, if a person has a fever, using an herb that grows in winter and has a blue color can be of help.

Remember, however, that the Tantrics were spiritual scientists. They would observe the results of using those herbs, then continue using what worked and abandon what didn't. As a result, there was a large pharmacopeia of herbs used effectively for healing in India over two and a half millennia ago. (There was also an extensive practice of surgery, and the ancient Indian physicians performed such things as plastic surgery, cataract removal, and oral surgery. They identified eight branches of surgical practice.)

Unfortunately, many of the herbs used are indigenous to India and not easy to find elsewhere. Therefore, rather than provide a limited introduction using a few of the herbs available in the West—and giving you an incomplete overview of the system—I respectfully suggest that you consider exploring Western herbalism. Be sure to note the difference between herbs that have been observed as having an effect and those that, due to following the law of similarity, only supposedly have an effect.

And, of course, remember that in the West, herbalism is primarily a complementary form of healing. Don't stop following your doctor's instructions. Use herbs to aid the effectiveness of medicines and techniques used by your doctor, as well as to maintain health.

One last point: some people think that because herbs are natural (whatever that may mean to you), they won't have any side effects. This is definitely *not* true. Some can have extremely dangerous side effects. In fact, some herbs can counteract the effects of expensive drugs prescribed by your physician. For example, flaxseed and green tea can delay the absorption of drugs. Garlic and ginkgo biloba can increase the effects of blood thinners to a dangerous level. Ginseng can dangerously increase the effects of stimulants. Licorice root can result in a loss of potassium. St. John's wort can negatively interact with antidepressants and legal narcotics. Valerian can increase the effects of sedatives. Brewer's yeast can interfere with MAO inhibitors.

Right now, the herbal industry in the West is primarily self-regulating. As a result, there is often no way to tell the dosage of an herb you are taking. I'm not sharing this to scare you away from taking herbs! Rather, I'm suggesting that if you are taking any herbs, inform your physician. Do research. Herbs can be incredibly powerful drugs and should be treated as such.

I know this from experience. When I lived in San Diego, a friend of mine had to be rushed to the hospital because he was taking handfuls of various Chinese herbs. He was in the hospital for several days.

My own experience was more positive. As a result of a blood test, my doctor determined that my kidneys were not working properly. When another blood test a few weeks later showed increasing problems, I was sent for an ultrasound. The diagnosis was that I had "lots" of small kidney stones. If they didn't pass, I'd have to experience even more painful and possibly invasive measures.

I went online and started looking for herbs that would supposedly help with the problem. I finally found a formula that seemed to have a lot of clinical studies backing its ingredients' effectiveness. I started taking it. About ten days later, I had another blood test. Two days later, my doctor called. She asked how I was feeling. "Fine," I said. She told me that she was unhappy with the test results and asked if I was well enough to get my blood tested again right away. "Sure," I said. "Where would you like me to go?" She said I should go to the emergency room of a nearby hospital.

I drove there, and after waiting for hours, they finally admitted me and gave me a blood test to check on my kidney function. My only actual symptoms were mild low back pain and not having much of an appetite. I was on a bed when my doctor came in to see me. I sat up and said hello. She turned pale looking at me.

It turns out that my previous blood test had shown that my kidneys had actually shut down. She thought I would need dialysis or a kidney transplant. The test at the hospital, however, showed that my kidney function had returned to about 50 percent. They kept me in the hospital for three days for observation, but gave me no treatment for my kidneys. When I left, my kidneys were working at 90 percent. Today they're functioning at 98 percent.

While I was in the hospital, I had an ultrasound. Before I was discharged, I asked my doctor what the results were. How many kidney stones did I have left? To my surprise, she very quietly answered, "None."

"How could so many kidney stones have vanished so quickly?" I asked. She hemmed and hawed. She didn't know. Maybe the first ultrasound had been inaccurate. She refused to believe it was due to the herbs I had taken. In fact, she even thought the herbs might have *caused* the kidney problems. I pointed out that the problems had been there for weeks before I took the herbs. She maintained her belief that the herbs were responsible.

My feeling is that people can get very upset if your magick works better than their magick. Herbs can be very powerful. They can be beneficial if you're knowledgeable and careful, or dangerous if you are neither.

Method Two: Cupping

Cupping is an ancient healing technique. In chapter 5, I briefly described the *marmas* as points where three nadis intersect. Medically, they are also specific points where nerves, bones, tendons, veins, and arteries may cross or connect. A medically valuable feature of marmas is that they tend to be near the surface of the skin, allowing direct stimulation as a powerful healing tool.

In the past, one or more small glass or ceramic cups was used in cupping. The inside was doused in alcohol and set on fire. The alcohol would quickly burn up and the cup was then placed, mouth down, on a marma point.

Another method was to burn a piece of tissue held in the cup. Because of the use of fire, these methods were also referred to as *fire cupping.*

The heat in the cup would cause the air to expand. When placed over the skin, the result was a vacuum, drawing the skin up and into the cup. The result was a powerful stimulation of the marma, changing the flow of energy through the nadis and resulting in healing. Cupping was also used to help maintain general health and vitality.

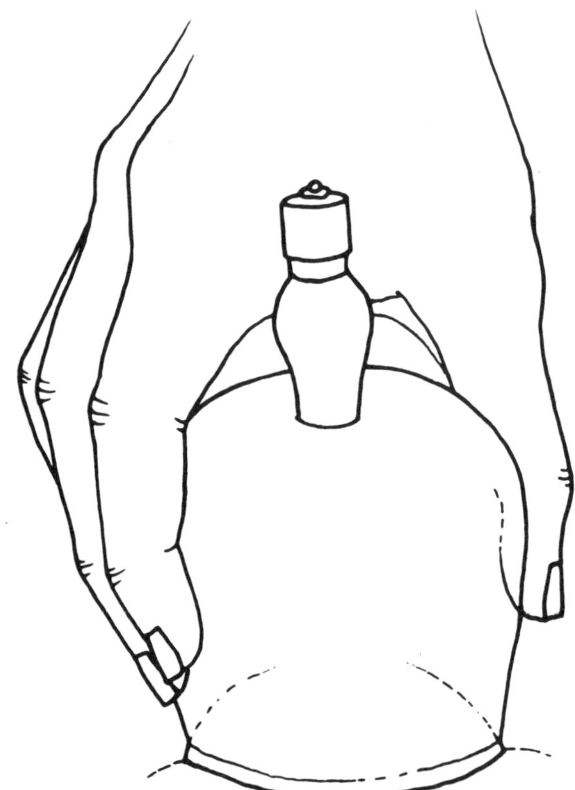

A Vacuum Cup Being Applied to a Person's Back

Today, cupping remains very popular in China. As a result, modern cupping sets come from China and are available very inexpensively. You can get a very nice set for fifty dollars or less. Modern sets are made of very strong plastic rather than glass or ceramic, and they use a vacuum pump instead of fire. Some of the cups have a magnetized piece of metal that comes to a slight point in the center of the cup. As a result, when vacuum is applied, the skin is sucked up into the cup and pressure is applied directly on the marma by the metal.

Unfortunately, there is only one book on this powerful technique that is currently available and that I would recommend. It's *Traditional Chinese Medicine Cupping Therapy* by Ilkay Z. Chirali, and its retail price is over sixty dollars. As the title indicates, it is based on traditional Chinese medicine rather than Indian medicine. However, cupping seems to have been brought to China from India, so you can get the concepts. I hope that more books on the subject will appear in the future. In the meantime, many acupuncture points equate to marmas, so books on acupuncture and acupressure can give you an introduction to this healing technique.

There is one even more extreme method of cupping. Known as *wet cupping*, it's a combination of cupping and medical exsanguination, or "bleeding." Using a sharp razor or knife, a cut is made over the marma. Cupping is applied, drawing both blood and skin into the cup. This is said to be very efficacious for some treatments. I have not worked with this.

Method Three: Massage and Acupuncture

When the ancient systems of Tantric healing arrived in China from India, they grew and evolved. Although massage and marma puncture began in India, they became major aspects of traditional Chinese medicine. Although there are books on Indian massage, learning Chinese acupressure massage, also known as *shiatsu*, and even acupuncture can be highly appropriate and beneficial in the study and practice of Tantric healing.

I had been studying and helping teach acupressure with my teacher, Dr. Turk, for about a year when the book *Do-It-Yourself Shiatsu* by Wataru Ohashi was first published. At the time, there were no good beginning books on the subject, and this quickly became our textbook. If you want to learn this skill, I highly recommend this book. The acupressure points are similar to the marmas.

The Knowledge of Life

The previous techniques have all been focused on general forms and styles of healing. Their purpose has been to direct you in your further studies. Any one of these methodologies could be expanded into a book. Some of the topics are covered in many books.

The real key to health, of course, is not to become ill in the first place! With the exception of the results of accidents, whose treatment we can leave to doctors who are great at helping in such cases, illness, in many instances, can be prevented.

As described at the beginning of the previous chapter, for thousands of years Tantrics have observed humans. They learned much about health and healing. The healing system that developed is known as the Knowledge of Life, or *Ayurveda*. It is considered by many scholars to be the oldest healing science, and has been recorded as being practiced in India for at least 5,000 years. It is certainly much older than that.

Many books have been written about Ayurveda. They go deeply into the subject and total many thousands of pages. However, even a basic understanding of this system can help you keep healthy, and that's what will be presented here.

As with everything in the universe, we begin with the elements that formed the universe, the five elements of nature. Since they form everything, it is inevitable that they form us, our bodies, too.

However, observation showed that the five-element system didn't accurately indicate our makeup. It turns out that there were three controlling factors, called *doshas*, that channeled or directed these energies. Air and ether formed the dosha known as *Vata*. Fire and water became *Pitta*. Water and earth became *Kapha*.

The basic qualities of the doshas are as follows:

- **Vata**—This is the controlling factor of bodily *motion*, so think of it in terms of controlling the circulatory system and the lungs. It also controls small movements such as eye blinks. When the energy controlled by Vata is balanced, a person is filled with vitality and creativity. If it is out of balance, it can manifest as anxiety or fear.
- **Pitta**—This is the controlling factor of the body's *metabolism*, so think of it in terms of controlling nutrition. This includes all of the systems from digestion through absorption of nutrients. One of the things that is created with metabolic energy is heat, so Pitta is also a controlling factor of body temperature. When the energy controlled by Pitta is balanced, you will naturally have a feeling of balance and peace. You will be able to easily tap into your intuition and your intelligence. If it is out of balance, it can manifest as being short-tempered and filled with anger. In health terms, anger can cause all sorts of problems, from ulcers to a lack of healing of body wounds.
- **Kapha**—This is the controlling factor of the body's *growth*. Fluid is necessary for things to grow, so the energy controlled by the Kapha dosha is involved with spreading moisture to all parts of the body. It moisturizes the skin and lubricates the joints. It's also important for maintaining the immune system, as you need fluid to flush out many signs of illness and "dis-ease," including excess mucus, phlegm, and white blood cells. When the energy controlled by Kapha is balanced, you will feel a sense of being cared for and a desire to care for others: true unconditional love. This also allows you to forgive others and yourself for real or perceived slights. Some people doubt the value of forgiveness, but it's quite important. Forgiveness does nothing to the person you forgive, but it allows you to release your negative feelings and return to a position of personal power and control. If the energy controlled by Kapha is out of balance, the result can be feelings of insecurity, paranoia, envy, etc.

Your Constitution

Your health constitution, or *prakruti*, is with you from birth. It comes from your karma and your genes, the health of your parents, and your development within your mother. It's also influenced by the time and location of your birth, as indicated by your astrological natal chart. Your constitution does not change. However, by knowing what is there, you can overcome its negative effects and enhance its positive aspects.

Air Aether Fire Water Earth

Vata Pitta Kapha

The Three Doshas

The major interpretation of your constitution is the ruling dosha. Please note that the following descriptions of the doshas as parts of your constitution are *generalities*. Nobody is purely of one dosha, and they can change from day to day or even minute to minute. Some people are so strongly blended that we can see in them blended types: Vata-Pitta, Pitta-Kapha, Vata-Kapha, and Vata-Pitta-Kapha. However, it is rare that people are quite so balanced. Usually one dosha will predominate and other aspects will be minor or only be associated with certain characteristics. So if someone is primarily Vata but has some Kapha characteristics, don't become confused. In this case, helping the person obtain and maintain health may be based on determining the relative strengths of the major and minor doshas and seeing if they need your external assistance.

		Vata	**Pitta**	**Kapha**
1	**Body Type**	Ectomorph	Mesomorph	Endomorph
2	**Skin Character**	Dry	Medium	Oily
3	**Eye Qualities**	Dull, dark	Green to gray	Blue
4	**Mouth Size**	Small	Average	Large
5	**Lip Character**	Small, thin	Average	Full
6	**Teeth**	Crooked or protruding	Small and yellowish	Strong and white
7	**Personal Qualities**	• Little perspiration • Poor long-term memory • Good short-term memory • Moves quickly • Dislikes cold • High energy for short periods • Nervous • Small appetite • Imaginative	• Light sleeper • Heavy perspiration • Assertive • Self-confident • Passionate • Good memory • Competitive • Good manager • Good communicator • Likes intense flavors • Dislikes heat	• Easygoing • Slow • Graceful • Deliberate thought processes • Deep sleeper • Large appetite • Resistance to disease • Business-oriented • Loves food • Dislikes cold and damp

Qualities of the Doshas

		Vata	Pitta	Kapha
8	**Health Issues**	• Depression • Hypertension • Dry cough • Arrhythmia • Digestive issues • Sexual dysfunction • Cramps	• Stubbornness • Opinionated • Pushy • Skin inflammation • Heartburn • Eye problems • Anemia • Jaundice	• Obesity • Depression • Respiratory problems • Atherosclerosis • Hay fever • Allergies • Colds
9	**Seasons**	Fall and early winter	Late spring and summer	Late winter and early spring
10	**Tastes**	Bitter, astringent (pungent)	Salty, sour (pungent)	Sweet, sour (salty)
11	**Mental Strengths**	Creativity, spirituality, peacefulness	Intelligence, good memory, discrimination, acuity	Nurturing, patience, compassion
12	**Mental Challenges**	Anxiety, fear, stress, forgetfulness	Anger, quick temper, controlling	Greed, envy, inability to forgive
13	**Physical Strengths**	Circulatory and nervous systems, physically dealing with emotions and reactions to situations	Metabolic and digestive systems, skin, clear eyes, sharp brain function	Reproductive and musculature systems, natural control of internal bodily fluids
14	**Physical Challenges**	Constipation and flatulence, dry skin, osteoporosis, PMS, hyperactivity	High blood pressure, acne, migraines, heartburn, GERD (acid reflux)	Obesity, congestion, allergies and sinusitis, tiredness or laziness
15	**Healing Pets**	Dog, guinea pig	Cats	Birds, large dogs

Qualities of the Doshas (continued)

Notes

Rows 1–8: Allow you to determine prakruti doshas through observation.

Rows 9–10: Both qualities enjoyed by a person of a particular dosha and qualities of a dosha itself.

Rows 11–14: Strengths and challenges of a person ruled by each dosha even though they may not currently be evident.

Row 15: If a person has a particular dosha imbalance, these pets will help bring balance to the energy.

Body Type

Ectomorph: Ethereal, thin, and petite, like Audrey Hepburn.

Mesomorph: Strong and tight, like Bruce Lee.

Endomorph: Strong and large, ranging from Russell Crowe to John Goodman.

Using the previous chart, you can determine the dosha(s) that form a person's constitution (prakruti). For example, if a person is petite and doesn't perspire, he or she is Vata. If the person has a strong, medium build with small teeth, the person is probably Pitta. If a person is overweight with breathing problems, he or she is probably Kapha.

If a person has an average-sized mouth with green eyes and loves to eat, that person is Pitta-Kapha. If a person is very thin, with white teeth and a large mouth, and has lots of allergies, the person is probably Vata-Kapha.

The following chart has three purposes. First, after you determine your primary dosha, it lists the types of foods that will best fit your constitution and enhance your natural skills and abilities. That doesn't mean you should eat only these foods. Second, if you have an ailment, it shows what foods to focus on to counter the influence of a dosha. Thus, if you are experiencing skin inflammations (symptomatic of excessive Pitta), you could help yourself by eating foods that counter the influence of that dosha. Finally, the chart lists the foods that enhance and counter the controlling factors of the respective doshas.

	Vata	Pitta	Kapha
Vegetables to Enhance	These should be cooked, not raw: beets, carrots, garlic, green beans, onions, asparagus, turnip, sweet potato, radish. Small amounts of leafy greens.	Asparagus, broccoli, zucchini, cabbage, squash, green beans, celery, cauliflower, lettuce, okra, peas, bell pepper, Brussels sprouts	Spinach, radish, potato, asparagus, broccoli, beets, cabbage, carrots, celery, eggplant, garlic, leafy greens, peppers, peas, onions, okra, cauliflower, mushroom
Vegetables to Counter	Zucchini, mushroom, eggplant, broccoli, tomato, peas, celery, Brussels sprouts, potato, bell peppers, cauliflower, cabbage	Tomato, hot peppers, beets, carrots, radish, spinach, garlic, eggplant	Zucchini, sweet potato, tomato, cucumber, and other vegetables that are juicy and sweet

Doshas and Foods

	Vata	Pitta	Kapha
Fruits to Enhance	Apricots, plums, figs, grapefruit, peaches, avocado, coconut, lemon, grapes, bananas, oranges, cherries, pineapple. They should be fresh and ripe.	Apples, raisins, prunes, avocados, cherries, pineapple, pears, coconuts, figs, red grapes, melons, mango, oranges. All should be sweet and ripe.	Dried fruits, especially pomegranates, pears, mango, berries, apples, apricots, figs
Fruits to Counter	Dried fruits. Fruits that aren't ripe, especially green bananas. Apples, pears, cranberries, and pomegranate, unless they are cooked.	Fruits that are sour. Fruits that aren't ripe. Examples: persimmon, banana, sour cherries, papaya, apricots, cranberries, grapefruit.	Fruits that are sweet, sour, or really juicy, including plums, bananas, coconut, pineapple, papaya, dates, melons, grapes, grapefruit, avocado
Grains to Enhance	Wheat, oatmeal, rice	Barley, wheat, white rice, oats	Corn, rye, millet, buckwheat, rice
Grains to Counter	Millet, rye, buckwheat, barley, corn	Corn, rye, brown rice, millet	Wheat, oats
Dairy to Enhance	All okay	Ghee, butter, milk, egg whites	Boiled eggs, warm fat-free milk, small amounts of whole milk
Dairy to Counter	None	Cheese, sour cream, egg yolk, yogurt, buttermilk	Anything other than above
Meat, Fish, Fowl to Enhance	Chicken, turkey, fish	Turkey, chicken, shrimp	Turkey, shrimp, chicken
Meat, Fish, Fowl to Counter	Red meat	Red meat and fish	Red meat and fish
Beans to Enhance	Lentils, chickpeas, mung beans, tofu	Mung beans, tofu, soybean, chickpeas	All legumes excluding tofu and kidney beans
Beans to Counter	Anything other than above	Lentils	Anything other than above
Oils to Enhance	All	Soy, sunflower, olive, coconut	Minor amounts of sunflower, safflower, almond, or corn

Doshas and Foods (continued)

	Vata	Pitta	Kapha
Oils to Counter	None	Corn, safflower, almond, sesame	Anything other than above
Nuts and Seeds to Enhance	All, especially almonds	Sunflower seeds, coconut, pumpkin seeds	Pumpkin seeds, sunflower seeds
Nuts and Seeds to Counter	None	Anything other than above	Anything other than above

Doshas and Foods (continued)

Living in Harmony with Your Natural Constitution

If you are primarily Vata, you can enhance your life with a few basic practices:

- Keep a regular routine.
- Meditate for calmness and balance.
- Before taking a shower, massage yourself with warm oil.

If you are primarily Pitta, try these practices to enhance your life:

- Practice breathing exercises regularly. This will help keep your system cool.
- Do physical exercise in air conditioning or during the coolest part of the day.
- Meditate regularly on compassion for others and for peace.

If you are primarily Kapha, here are some practices to enhance your life:

- Get up early and do some exercises.
- Vary your routine.
- Stay active.

For optimum health, you can follow, to the best of your ability, a lifestyle that is in harmony with the rules of this Tantric Knowledge of Life.

Mudras for Healing

I'd like to discuss one more aspect of traditional Tantric healing: *mudras*. The Sanskrit is usually translated to mean "gesture" or "seal" (in the sense of completing or "sealing" an electrical circuit to power a device). The word is also commonly translated as "symbol" or "attitude." An important Tantric book, the *Kularnava Tantra*, says the word *mudra* comes from the root *mud*, which means "delight" or "pleasure," and *dravay*, a form of the word *dru*, which means "to draw forth."

In the book *Sexual Secrets*, co-author Nik Douglas says that mudras are "mystic hand gestures used to focus subtle energy, transmit teachings through symbols, and confer psychic protection."

Mudras have always been shown in various paintings and statues of deities and spiritual personages. Buddhist and Christian imagery frequently features people with their hands in the positions of mudras.

Normally, the energy paths (nadis) and minor chakras in the hands and palms constantly radiate energy from the body into the environment. Mudras redirect the energy. In some instances, once the dissipation of this energy (prana) is changed through the practice of mudras, the mind becomes focused inward, resulting in the withdrawal of the senses from an outward focus followed by deep concentration. These are two aspects of traditional meditation.

How, specifically, does this work? When the fingers touch the palm, other fingers, or the thumb, a new circuit is produced that allows pranic energy (which would normally be squandered by being released into the environment) to cycle back into the body and up to the brain, the physical link between your body and mind.

Mudras can also be valuable for rousing the kundalini energy. Some mudras are performed while you sit and rest your hands on your knees. There is a pranic energy channel known as the "hidden path" (*gupta nadi*) that extends from both knees, up the insides of the thighs, and into the perineum. Mudra work with your hands on your knees arouses the flow of energy in this nadi and stimulates the potential kundalini energy in the root chakra.

It is by altering common energy paths that mudras can change the flow of energy, thus awakening innate therapeutic and magickal abilities that flow through the hands. Through regular practice of mudras, the minor chakras in the palms and fingertips are activated to their optimal level. This practice permits the free flow, in and out, of pranic energy, which you can use for magickal or healing purposes. When you have this mastered, a mere touch may induce trance, result in intense fascination, or heal someone who needs such help, including yourself.

After the previous complete explanation, it may be easier to simply say that the energy that flows through the fingertips is rearranged by a mudra and directed to achieve a desired goal. This energy is generally looked at in the following three ways.

Elemental Associations

First, the fingers can be associated with the magickal/alchemical/Tantric elements of air, earth, water, fire, and mind or spirit. Normally, the energy just flows off the fingers. However, if you blend fire and air by holding the tip of the index finger against the tip of the thumb, (with the remaining fingers extended), you are charging the spirituality of air with the energy of fire, making this an ideal position for meditation.

Chakra Associations

The next set of correspondences is with the chakras. If you put the tips of the pinky, ring finger, and thumb together, you are connecting the energies of the first (root), second (genital), and third (solar plexus) chakras. This is an extremely powerful position for generating energy, so it is naturally known as the energy gesture, or *prana mudra.*

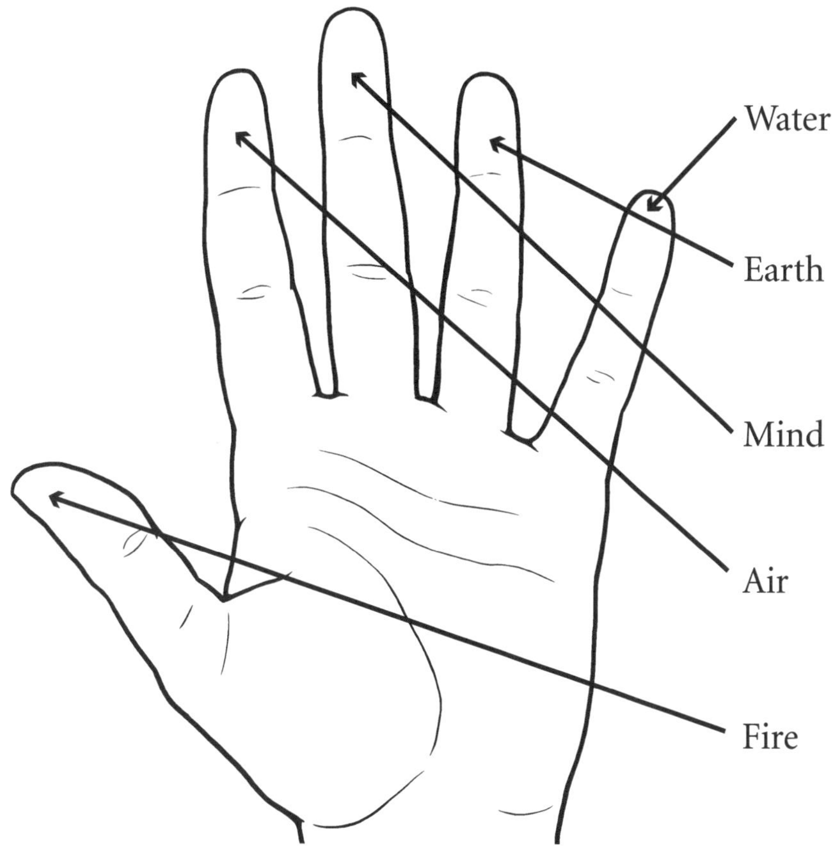

Elemental Associations

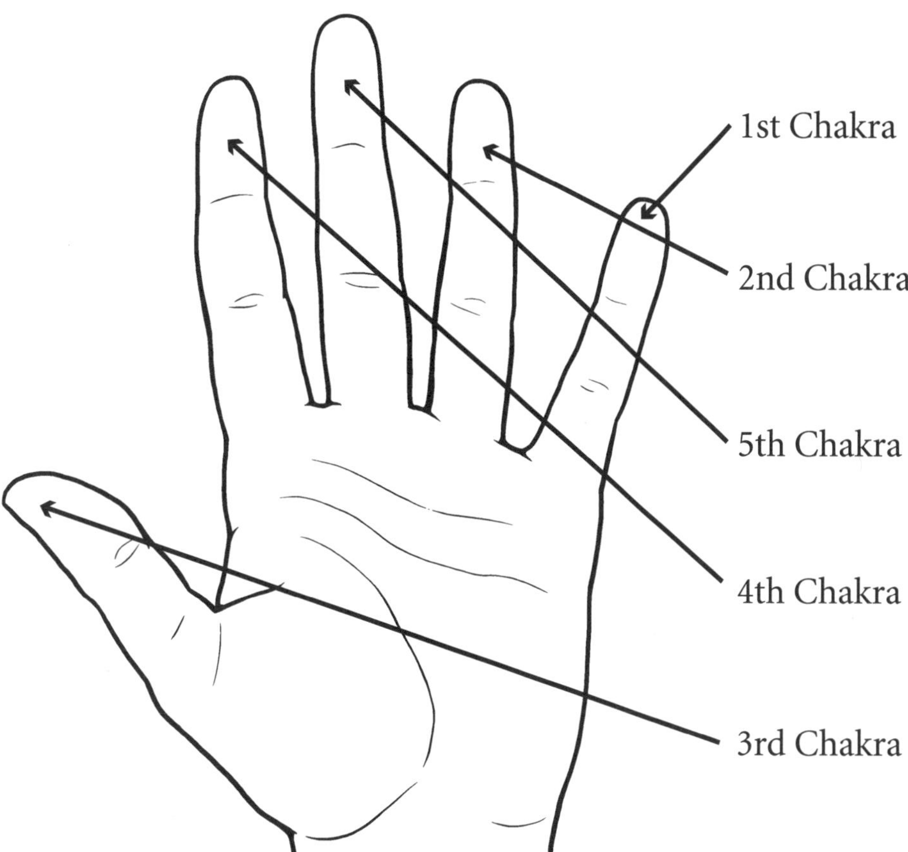

Chakra Associations

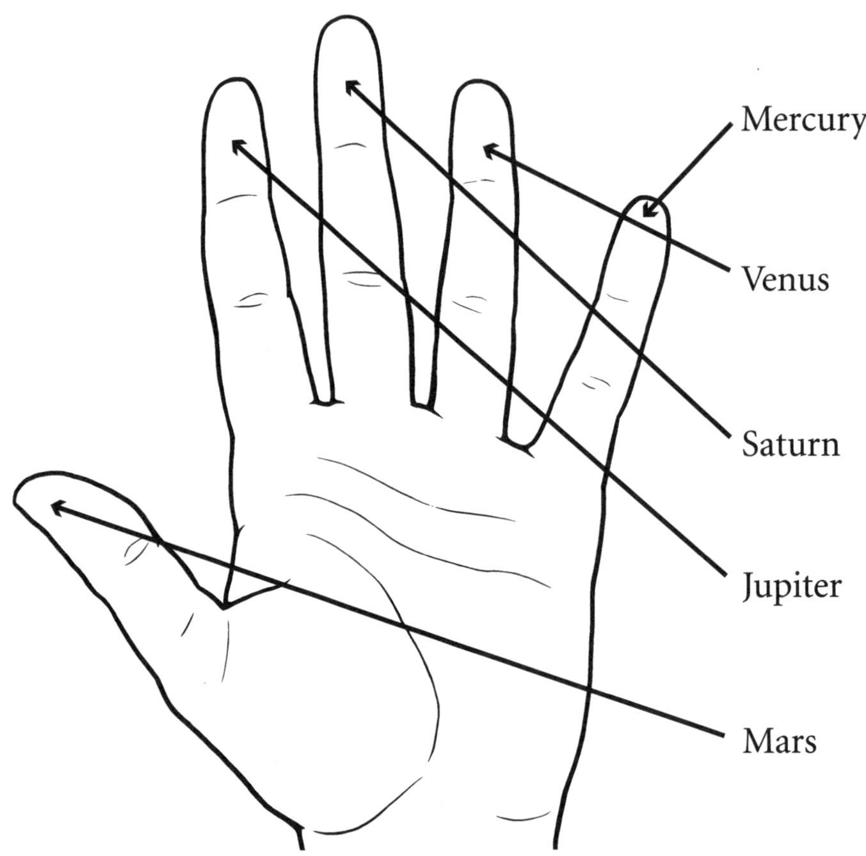

Planetary Associations

Planetary Associations

The third set of correspondences links the fingers with their planetary counterparts. By taking the energy that starts things (Mars) and linking it to responsibility (Saturn) and affection (Venus), you have a powerful position for magickally empowering your desires to achieve and maintain something. Known as the *Apana mudra*, it's brilliant in terms of health for getting rid of what isn't needed in order to start something new. It supports elimination (Saturn) and stimulates the liver and gallbladder.

With meditative practice, you will eventually be able to experience the energy flows of the mudras. For balance, they link your individual energy to the cosmic forces that fill the universe. Mudras can balance the energy within your bodies (koshas) and enable the redirection of the energy.

What follows are examples of healing mudras you can use. Please note, however, that simply holding your hands in any position will do little. Practicing the mudras while using breathwork and visualization of the movement of the energy will bring success. And, of course, I need to repeat that these techniques do not replace the work of your doctor and you should not discontinue taking any prescriptions without consulting with him or her first. As a general rule, hold these mudras for three to fifteen minutes.

Yoni Mudra

The word *yoni* means "womb" or "source." The Yoni mudra functions to balance the flows of masculine/feminine or solar/lunar energies. It invokes the primal energy inherent in the womb or source of creation.

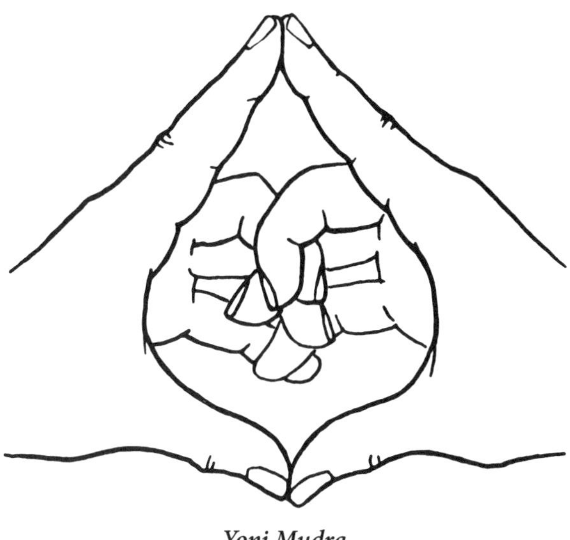

Yoni Mudra

Use this mudra when you're having difficulty concentrating or when you need to focus on physical or mental awareness. It's also good for relaxing, both physically and mentally.

To form this mudra, begin by finding a comfortable meditative position. This can be as simple as relaxing into a chair with your spine upright.

A. Put the palms of your hands together with the fingers pointing away from your body. The thumbs and index fingers should form as large of an "L" shape as possible, with the thumbs pointing up.

B. Turn the middle, ring, and little fingers inward and interweave them.

C. Spread the palms and allow the thumb and index fingers to separate so only their tips touch.

As a variation, you can do this without turning the fingers inward. The thumbs may be crossed or have their pads touch.[18]

18 I describe a different type of Yoni mudra in *Modern Magick*. It has a different focus and turns the attention inward by using the hands to close the eyes, ears, nose, and mouth. One of the challenges in understanding Tantric writings is that, depending upon the context, the same word or expression, such as Yoni mudra, may have different meanings.

Hridaya Mudra

Hridaya is a Sanskrit word for heart, so this mudra is known as the heart gesture.

Physically, this mudra is good for heart ailments of all kinds. Mentally, it helps you unburden your heart by releasing pent-up emotions. It is very good for bringing calm during emotional conflicts, even strong ones, that happen between you and others, or just occur within yourself.

The Hridaya mudra diverts the flow of universal pranic energy from the hands (which would normally merely discharge into the environment) to the heart. Thus, it can also help increase the vitality of your heart.

To form this mudra, begin by finding a comfortable meditative posture. Rest both hands in your lap, palms up.

A. Curl your index fingers so they touch where the thumb meets the palm.

B. Touch the tips of the middle and ring fingers to the tips of your thumb.

C. Allow the pinky to remain outstretched.

The middle and ring fingers relate to energy paths that are associated with the heart. Touching them to the tip of the thumb closes or completes a pranic circuit, which is why this mudra is a heart energizer. It diverts the flow of pranic energy from the environment to nadis associated with the heart.

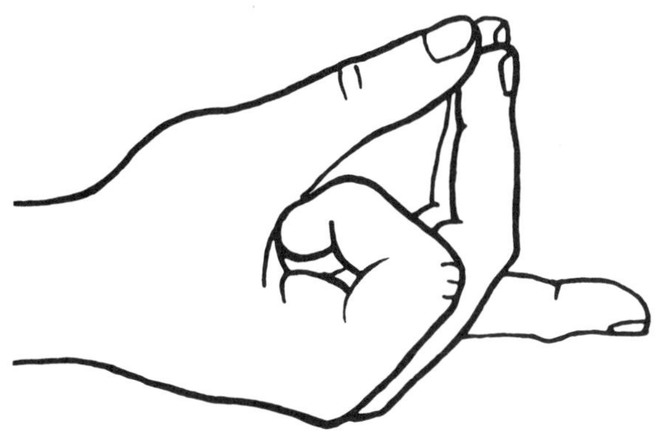

Hridaya Mudra

Ganesh Mudra

Ganesh, of course, is the elephant-headed deity who helps you to overcome obstacles. This mudra will help stimulate your heart activity and strengthen the heart and the muscles associated with the heart. It can also help open the bronchial tubes.

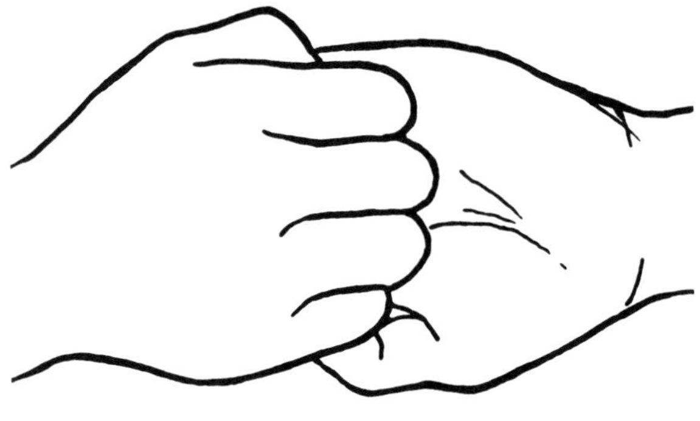

Ganesh Mudra

This mudra can be formed while sitting in a meditative position or while standing.

A. Hold your left hand in front of your chest. Your thumb should be pointing down and your palm will naturally face outward. Bend the fingers so the tips are pointed toward your wrist.

B. Position your right hand with the thumb up, the palm toward you, and the fingers pointing toward the wrist.

C. Now grasp the curled fingers of the left hand with those of the right hand. If your hands have dropped, move them back to the level of the heart, directly in front of the chest.

D. While exhaling, use your strength to vigorously attempt to pull the hands apart but *without* releasing the grip. This will tense the muscles of the upper arms and chest area. Hold in this tensed position for as long as it is comfortable.

E. While inhaling, let go of all the tension. Feel your arms, chest, and shoulders relax.

F. Repeat six times and then, still holding your hands in this relaxed position, place both hands on the sternum, the breast bone between the ribs. While in this position, focus on the feelings you get in this part of your body.

G. Repeat this mudra but with the hand positions inverted: your right palm now faces outward with the thumb down and the left palm faced inward with the thumb up.

H. As in step F, repeat the exercise six times in this position, then move your hands to rest on the sternum.

I. Remain in silence for a while. Working with this mudra once a day is enough.

Using the Ganesh mudra can open your heart chakra, allowing you to be more available to accepting and sharing love and caring. Many people think of love and caring as a weakness. However, to be loving and caring means you have enough confidence and inner strength to let down your guard. This mudra can enhance your courage, confidence, and openness toward others. It's an excellent Tantric remedy to overcome shyness.

Pushan Mudra

Pushan means "nourisher" and is a title of the solar deity Surya. Without the power of the sun, plants would not grow and we would have little to eat. So Surya is, indeed, the deity of nourishment, as well as the sun.

The Pushan mudra has the hands separated and holding different positions:

Pushan Mudra (Right Hand)

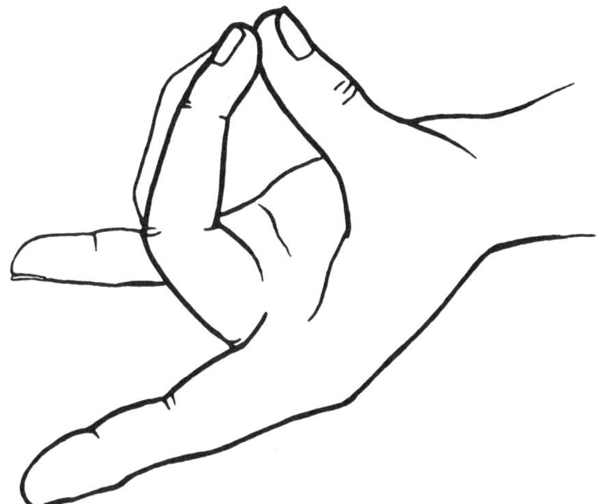

Pushan Mudra (Left Hand)

A. Begin by assuming a comfortable meditative position.

B. The right hand may rest on the knee.

C. The tips of the right thumb, index finger, and middle finger meet.

D. The right ring finger and pinkyremain extended.

E. An alternative is for the right hand to assume the Prana mudra (see upcoming section) wherein the tips of the thumb, ring finger, and little finger touch at the tips while the index and middle fingers are extended.

F. The left hand may rest on your other knee.

G. The tips of the left thumb, middle finger, and ring finger touch each other.

H. The tips of the left index and pinky remain extended. This, by itself, is called the Apana mudra (see upcoming section).

The Pushan mudra enhances the energy currents that are responsible for absorbing and utilizing the nutrients in your food. It can also help in the elimination of wastes. Without oxygen, the nutrition in food is meaningless, so this mudra also helps with breathing, breathwork, increased absorption of oxygen, and the effective release of carbon dioxide from the lungs.

This multipurpose mudra also has a relaxing effect on the solar plexus, including such organs as the stomach, liver, spleen, and gallbladder. I like to refer to this as the "biofeedback mudra," as it regulates energies in the autonomic nervous system, a process that, until the acceptance of the viability of biofeedback, most scientists thought was impossible.

Being a mudra that helps with nutrition, the Pushan mudra can also counter responses that harm nutrition. Thus, it is great for relieving mild or acute nausea, motion sickness, flatulence, and that sensation of being overly full that you may feel after consuming a large meal. Needless to say, this is an ideal mudra to practice after a Thanksgiving feast with relatives.

This mudra has been called a "general energy pump," as it will help stimulate functions of the brain such as concentration, memory, logic, enthusiasm, etc., with increased nutrition.

Finally, the position of the right hand activates energy in the pelvic floor while the left hand directs it upward. Do this up to four times per day, but only five minutes each practice. However, in a crisis (such as when you feel nauseated), use when needed.

Bronchial Mudra

Breathwork is important for Tantra and yoga, so having mudras that help open the breathing passages are logical. Curiously, I've not found the Sanskrit name for the Bronchial mudra, so it may be a modern technique. Even so, I've found it works quite well.

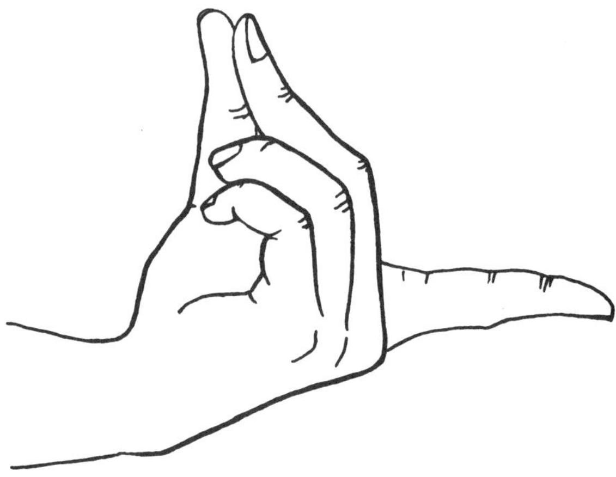

Bronchial Mudra

To form the Bronchial mudra, again begin by finding a comfortable meditative position. Keep your hands about four inches in front of your body. When your arms get tired—and trust me, they will—place your hands on your thighs and bring your focus to your pelvic area well below the lungs.

A. Place the little finger of each hand at the base of the thumb.

B. Place the ring finger of each hand on the upper thumb joint.

C. Place the middle finger of each hand on the pad of the thumb.

D. Extend the index fingers.

Thus, the pinky, ring, and middle fingers of each hand form a line up the thumb of that hand, while the index fingers are extended. For an acute attack of asthma, in addition to any prescriptions you have, begin by using this mudra for four to six minutes followed by the next mudra (the Asthma mudra), and hold the mudra until breathing normalizes. If you have chronic asthma, practice this mudra for five minutes, five times a day.

When I was very young, I had acute attacks of asthma and had to be rushed to the hospital for injections of adrenaline several times. Often, physical problems have psychological causes. I came to realize much later in life that my asthma had been caused by feelings of anger and abandonment by the death of my father when I was six. Some people with respiratory problems also suffer from feelings of inner loneliness, isolation, sexual problems, and sadness. These feelings may be successfully played down (and thus ignored) with humor. Using this mudra can help people keep their sense of humor but become aware of and face their issues.

Another indicator of such feelings is shallow breathing. When you run or exercise, you have to exert your strength, and without proper respiration, you can't develop a healthy pool of inner strength. When breathing is limited, weakness also occurs in the emotional body. Fear, sadness, discontentment, and exaggerated sensitivity are the consequences. Again, using this mudra opens the breathing passages and allows a person to understand these issues, confront them, and become victorious over them.

When you practice the Bronchial mudra, breathe slowly. Allow the air to fill you from the bottom up. Pause between inhalations and exhalations for as long as it is comfortable. Don't strain. Most people, when doing breathwork, focus on making the inhalation as long as possible. Don't worry about that! Instead, focus on extending the exhalation for as long as is comfortably possible.

Asthma Mudra

This is a companion to the previous mudra. Although you can do it by itself, it is most effective when used following the Bronchial mudra. Use the Asthma mudra to calm down your breathing.

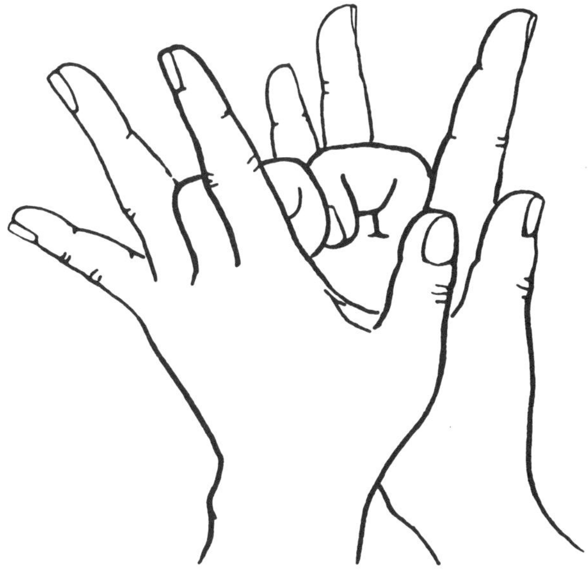

Asthma Mudra

Begin by finding a comfortable meditative position. Perform the Bronchial mudra for four to six minutes, as just described.

A. Hold your hands in front of you, about two inches apart, with the thumbs toward you.

B. Curl the middle fingers inward.

C. Press the fingernails and upper knuckles of the middle fingers together.

D. Keep other fingers and thumbs extended.

Even if your breathing has not calmed down and your bronchial passages opened from using the previous mudra, it will have started the energy moving properly. After no more than six minutes of the Bronchial mudra, move to the Asthma mudra. Stay in this position and focus on your breathing, as described for the Bronchial mudra, until your breathing is calm and the sense of fear and desperation has fled.

Prana Mudra

Also known as the Pran or Life mudra, the Prana mudra activates the root chakra, the locus of the source of the kundalini. It also increases general vitality, reduces fatigue and nervousness, and improves vision.

The Prana mudra is also practiced using both hands. Begin by sitting in a comfortable meditative posture.

A. Place the tips of the thumb, ring finger, and little finger together. Note that this is not the pads, it's the tips. To do so requires you to curl your fingers and thumbs.

B. The index and middle fingers remain extended.

The Prana mudra increases your endurance and assertiveness. It gives courage to start new projects and the strength to see things through. It may also be used against eye diseases. Clear eyes are often a sign of having a mental outlook that emphasizes a clear mind. This implies having clearly structured thoughts and ideas.

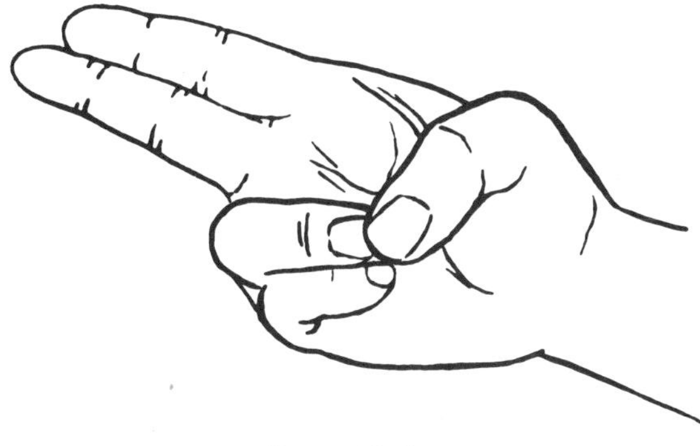

Prana Mudra

For an alternative form of this mudra, put your thumb onto the *fingernails* of the other two fingers instead of on their tips. This has the effect of causing both hemispheres of the brain to function equally, become active, and complement each other.

Either form of the Prana mudra—combined with a conscious, slow, and gentle way of breathing, as described earlier—has the effect of being as stabilizing, calming, and secure as a boat anchor. This is perfect for any form of meditation.

Apana Mudra

I already discussed the Apana mudra (also known as the Apan mudra) a bit in the previous section on planetary associations, as it can be combined with another mudra to form the Pushan mudra. Here, both hands take the position.

As usual, begin by sitting in a comfortable meditative position.

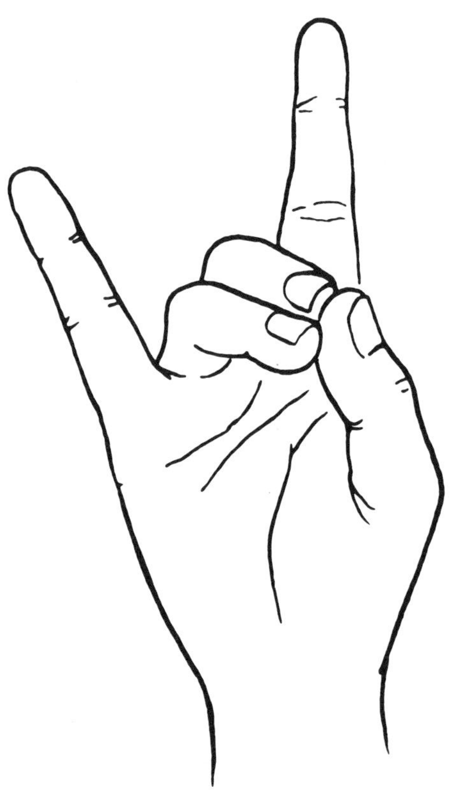

Apana Mudra

A. On both hands, place the pads of the thumbs, middle fingers, and ring fingers together.

B. Extend the pinkies and index fingers.

This mudra supports the removal of waste materials and toxins from the body and eliminates urinary problems. It stimulates the energy of the liver and gallbladder. When needed, practice this mudra for five to forty-five minutes once a day, or use it three times a day for fifteen minutes each.

On a mental level, the practice of this mudra creates the ability to develop vision. That makes this an ideal mudra to use in preparation for any method of divination, such as astrology or palmistry. It's also good for preparing yourself to face new challenges.

Shankh Mudra

As described in chapter 7, the *shankh* is the Sanskrit name for a conch shell. So this mudra is also known as the Shell mudra. It helps to eliminate chronic or acute problems in the throat. There is also something very calming about it.

When preparing to work with the Shankh mudra, find a comfortable sitting position.

A. Hold the left hand with the fingers forward and the thumb upright, so the index finger and thumb form an "L" shape.

B. Encircle your left thumb with the four fingers of your right hand.

C. Your right thumb rests on top of the right index finger.

D. Pivot all of the extended fingers of the left hand up and touch the pad of the right thumb to the pad of the middle finger of your left hand.

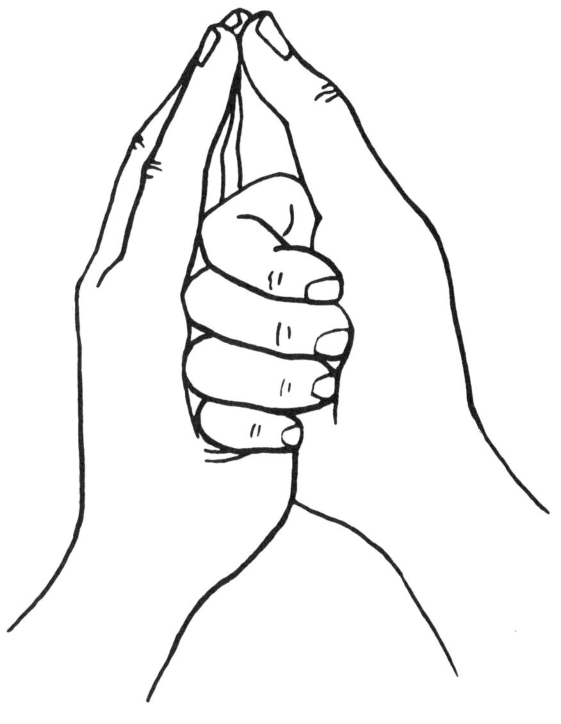

Shankh Mudra

Together, the two hands look like a conch shell. Hold your hands a few inches in front of your sternum. Do this as often and as long as you want, or use it three times daily for fifteen minutes each practice.

When you perform this mudra, chant *Om* several times. Take a deep breath and chant slowly and clearly on the exhalation. After your last chant, listen to the silence within yourself for several minutes.

As I described in chapter 9, the actual conch trumpet (shankh) may be sounded as part of the opening of rituals. With this mudra, the same is true of your inner temple, the temple through which the divine light may shine. Using the Shankh mudra opens your inner spiritual temple just as sounding the shankh opens the physical temple.

....

These are just a few of many mudras that can help you with healing. There are so many mudras available that an entire book could be written. Indeed, my favorite book on this topic is *Healing Hands* by Acharya Keshav Dev and Acharya Vikrmaditya.

THIRTEEN

Tantric Magick

As described earlier, even in India, home of so many spiritual traditions and known for being accepting of other deities and religious paths, most people think of Tantra as being either "that sex stuff" or the practice of "black magic." This can be understood, if not forgiven, as most of the rich tradition of Tantric spirituality has been denounced by invaders and mauled over, watered down, and subsumed into Vedic Hinduism. This is comparable to the way the long history of Western Paganism was absorbed into Christianity even as the Christian leadership mocked and later ruthlessly attacked Pagans and their beliefs.

Part of any complete spiritual system, such as *Modern Tantra*, consists of techniques that manipulate the underlying strings that tie together the fabric of the universe. From time to time, people come up with theories as to what those strings are, providing untestable theories as to how they function. Most practitioners, however, are quite content to simply manipulate the strings and get the desired results. For people into technology, this is known as *black boxing:* we don't know what goes on in the black box of silicon and software we call a computer, but we do know that when we do certain things and click on certain buttons, we get the desired results.

In spiritual systems, when someone performs a certain task, allows it to go into a metaphorical black box where *something* happens, and gets a desired result, the process is named *magick.*

In previous chapters I've shared techniques, rituals, and concepts underlying those rituals. You may choose to use just what has been shared, or you can move on to understand that if you have been doing what has been described so far, you have been preparing mentally, physically, emotionally, and spiritually for the practice of an inner core of Tantric magick.

In chapter 10, I also gave my definition of magick from *Modern Magick:*

> *Magick is the science and art*
> *of causing change to occur*
> *in conformity with will,*
> *using means not currently understood*
> *by traditional Western science.*

In *Modern Sex Magick*, I used a different approach to explaining magick. What follows is an abbreviated version of the set of theorems of magick that appear there.

Some of you, familiar with my previous focus on magick, may wonder why I am repeating this. The reason is that it is my hope that many people reading this will be coming from other areas, including Neo-Tantrics, who are interested in finding greater depth. I hope everyone has achieved this so far with this book. My purpose here is to give a more practical understanding of how magick can be a part of your daily life.

Theorem One

All actions have magickal reactions.

This means that everything you do, whether you are conscious of it or not, has a magickal reaction. Many people fail with magick because they do a brief ritual to achieve a desired result and then spend hours bemoaning their lack in that area. That negative attitude and the negative energy and accompanying actions create magickal results that are the opposite of what was intended.

This theorem implies that everything you do is magick and that everyone is a magician. Observation shows this is not true. So there is a bit more to this.

Corollary: Only a willed action is a magickal action.

Because every action has a magickal result, it is hard for non-magicians to deal with the seemingly unknowable reality of the universe. They blame their problems on fate, bad luck, kismet, or something similar. By not being able to tell what will happen as a result of their actions, they are spun around helplessly by the results of those actions. Life is a mess.

By doing as little as possible—leading an austere and isolated life such as that of a renunciate monk—it is possible to live a somewhat peaceful life: no actions, no magickal reactions. But for such a person, there is also little freedom and no adventure.

Magicians understand this theorem and its corollary and act accordingly. They accept and deal with any problems that are created. This is the essence of personal responsibility and is a hallmark of Tantric magicians: Svecchachara! You're free to do what you want and create your future, but you're responsible for everything you do.

Magicians go beyond merely accepting responsibility for their actions. By realizing that actions have magickal results, they can perform acts—rituals—that will successfully achieve desired outcomes and overcome the presence of unwanted or unexpected responses to actions.

Here's an analogy: A non-magician is like a man falling from a great height. The effects of wind and gravity control his fall, and he believes there is no way to avoid his inevitable fate. A magician can also fall from a great height, and knows that wind and gravity will buffet and pull him down. But the magician's magick is like flying in a plane: controlling the fall, moving up and down, and landing safely. Magicians don't fight gravity and wind; they work in harmony with natural forces to achieve desired goals.

Theorem Two

Magick is not something you do.
Magick is something you are.

The idea that you can pick up a book, mumble some Latin (poorly), wave a stick in the air, and have real magick happen only occurs in novels, comic books, TV, and movies. Real magick is more than just something you do.

With study and practice (as with the study and practice of any learned skill), magick becomes a part of you. It is something you are. With the skills of a magician, you can correctly use a book of magick and obtain desired results. Further, by understanding that everything you do has magickal results, you can literally *design your own rituals.*

Theorem Three

Magick requires the following:

1. The ability to generate or raise magickal energy.
2. The ability to manipulate that energy to an appropriate frequency for a goal.
3. The ability to direct that energy to achieve a desired goal.

A magician, as the result of months or years of practice, can do these three things almost automatically. Most magicians begin the process of developing these abilities with the help of tools such as wands and talismans, but with practice, although such devices may be used, no props are required.

Note: There are some fairly recent schools of magick that follow a different magickal paradigm: they deny the concept of magickal energy. Here, however, I'm sharing the classical approach. Since Tantrics work with specialized energies (prana, kundalini, etc.), it is appropriate to use the more classical paradigm here.

Corollary: The nature of magickal energy is threefold.

I refer to this as the psycho/sexual/spiritual nature of magickal energy. The "psycho" (as in "psychological") aspect of this energy indicates that magickal energy is controlled by the mind. It can be strengthened with the help of the emotions. For example, being happy or sad, angry or loving, affects how well you can manipulate the energy.

Part of this is that for magick to be controlled, you need to have a positive attitude about your success. This does *not* mean magick is all mental, just that a positive mental attitude will have an impact on your magick. Consider what might happen if you spent hours directing all of your energy in a negative, unhappy, failure-focused way toward your magick. You would literally be controlling the magickal energy with negativity toward achieving your goal. The practice of meditation and breathwork can help you develop an attitude of balance and equipoise.

The second part of this is the energy raised with the help of the body. It is sexual in the very broadest sense, that of male/female, yin/yang, magnetic/electric, or the anode and cathode of a battery. This is not about physical gender; it's about the movement of the energy in cycles. You'll learn more about this in chapters 14 and 15.

Finally, this energy transcends your physical body and your mind. It's also spiritual. It is linked to the Divine, the godhead. Thus, the energy is spiritual, mental, and physical.

This does not mean you can only do Tantric rituals for goals that are not oriented toward the physical world. Rather, this is associated with the Tantric concept of *Svecchachara*, the path of doing one's will. This involves finding your true purpose in life and doing what is required to achieve it. You may need money, food, housing, love, partners, safety, etc., to achieve your ultimate goal that, by its very nature, is in harmony with the Divine and with nature.

Theorem Four

Creation on the spiritual planes results in creation on the physical plane.

Since natural forces created the universe, the concept of magick being supernatural doesn't make sense. Everything is natural. We may think of something as not being natural simply because we are uncomfortable with it.

We do not have non-physical *koshas*, or sheaths, because our physical body was born. Rather, the physical body is the inevitable end result of our spiritual sheath being created on its associated planes.

Therefore, if we create something on the spiritual planes, eventually *it must manifest, via natural means, on the physical plane*. Of course, this only remains true as long as we do not, knowingly or unknowingly, create magick that counters our spiritual creation.

Theorem Five

A ritual's success is inversely proportional to time.

I credit this theorem to chaos magician Peter Carroll. As a comparison, if you're doing some sort of divination, the further in the future you're looking at, the less likely is the divination's accuracy. This is because unknown and unplanned actions (the result of free-will activities by you and others) between now and the distant outcome you're considering may send unplanned and/or unconscious magickal energy to what was the focus of the divination. Things change. If the event being divined is to take place soon, it is much more likely to occur as predicted when compared to something in the distant future.

Similarly, when magick is performed, results desired to have a rapid manifestation are more likely to be obtained than those planned for years from now. For something in the distant future, events not anticipated by the magician may creep into his or her life, and thoughts (these events are called *noise*) and pull the magician away from focusing on the magick. Other interests may simply pull the magician away from his or her conscious desires. Other people may work, knowingly or unknowingly, to counter your own work. In fact, your interests may change so much that you end up consciously working against your original magick.

Therefore, rather than focusing on grand magickal experiments with goals intended to take place years from now, I suggest that you have a series of intermediate goals that you do magick for and that occur between now and the ultimate goal. For example, if your ultimate goal is to become a schoolteacher, your intermediate goals might be something like this:

1. Get good grades at school
2. Graduate with a great GPA
3. Get accepted into a good college
4. Get good grades at college, with a degree leading toward teaching
5. Get accepted into a teaching program
6. Do a great job as a student teacher
7. Get a degree in teaching
8. Get accepted to teach the subjects you want at the school you want

Using magick to help you achieve all eight goals, one at a time and in the appropriate order, will tend to be more effective than just doing magick to become a schoolteacher.

Theorem Six

Let go and let the magick work.

As I have repeatedly told magicians of all kinds, *just do the work*. Do the best you can. Don't focus on whether you did something perfectly, whether you mispronounced something, or whether it will really work. All of that sort of mental focus will send magickal energy away from achieving your goal and toward your doubts. This does not mean you shouldn't strive to do everything as accurately and passionately as possible. Rather, it means that once you've completed the magick, don't obsess about it.

Keep a record of your magickal work, including all of the variables, such as location, time, your feelings and attitudes, etc. Look back at your records later. You'll see any patterns that encouraged success or failure.

If your goal will take place in many months, you might want to occasionally repeat your ritual, not with the intent of "fixing" what you did wrong, but rather, to amplify and add to the original rite.

Theorem Seven

Magick is magick.

Nobody talks about good or bad electricity; there is just electricity. It may be used to light up the night or kill someone. Similarly, the notion of black, white, gray, pink, puce, or green magick may be good for theoretical or philosophical classification of the results, but the methodologies are still the same.

Magick is magick. I suggest performing a divination before doing an actual ritual. When doing the divination, don't ask, "Should I do this ritual?" That places the responsibility on your divinatory tool rather than on you. Instead, ask, "What will be the result if I do this magick?" When you learn the result, you can adjust the magick if necessary to avoid any problems and enhance potential success. This empowers the magician and helps prevent the person from doing anything stupid that might harm the magician or someone else.

Corollary: An effective magician may choose to be "stupid."

Real magicians don't need to do magick to harm others. In fact, they won't do magick to harm others because the karmic response to such an action would be to harm oneself, and that would be stupid.

In some circumstances, however, a magician may consciously choose to do something "stupid," something that will harm him or her, because the situation warrants it. For example, a magician I know used magick to stop a rapist who was attacking women in his neighborhood. Within a week, the alleged rapist was in a serious auto accident and the police were able to catch him. A month later, the magician was laid off at work. He believes it was a karmic response to his actions (working the magick) that resulted in another person being harmed.

To this day, he doesn't care about losing his job. To him, it was a conscious effort to stop a person who was harming people around him. He performed more magick to obtain a better job, and a short time later he obtained a position that paid him much more than his previous job.

Theorem Eight

Magick is a science and an art.

This means that some people may have a natural ability to do magick. But don't let that bother you! If you study and practice, you can become as good or better than even the most naturally skilled person who doesn't continue to study or practice.

Theorem Nine

Magick is synergistic.

Synergy is the concept that the total is greater than the sum of its parts. Saying magick is synergistic means that the amount of energy raised during a group (two people or more) ritual is greater than the amount of energy that can be raised by each person working individually.

However, remember the old saying that a chain is only as strong as its weakest link. One experienced, well-trained magician may be far more successful than a group of untrained people or a group of people who simply do not work well together or are not synchronized on the magickal goal of the work. To enhance the magickal energy, help the weakest person of a pair or the weakest members of a group become better at magick.

....

I hope these nine theorems have given you some ideas to consider. There is something else I now need to share. It's related to theorem seven.

When we come to magickal methodology, there are two major divisions. The first is natural or folk magick (also known as Pagan magick or low magick). Various forms of natural magick occur all over the world. Typical types of natural magick that are performed by Tantrics include working with gems and with simple spells (the latter mistakenly called *mantra* magick, when it's more accurately *japa* magick).

The other division of magick in the West is ceremonial or ritual magick (also known as high magick). The ritualism of this kind of magick can be far more complex. Some Tantrics really like the ritual aspect of this kind of magick. That is another reason why there were two versions of the initiation ritual given in chapter 9.

Many forms of magick cannot be clearly placed in either division. Tantric sex magick, for example, can be done in a variety of ways, ranging from very simple to very elaborate.

For the remainder of this chapter, I'd like to share two approaches to magick that seem to be exclusively Tantric in nature, although you may find similarities in other magickal traditions.

The Background, Version 1

The following is based on a 2011 Llewellyn blog post I wrote, at www.llewellyn.com/blog/2011/8/magick-101-4-true-meditation.

Meditation

I've mentioned meditation many times in this book, although I haven't yet fully explained it and let you work with your current idea of it. For most people, meditation means a type of relaxation or inner focus, or a type of extreme concentration. True meditation, however, is far more than that. True meditation has as its goal the ability to transcend your sense of individuality and separateness for a brief time, allowing you to experience your *Atman*, your higher self, and its unity with the universe. Meditation has three stages:

Stage One: Relaxation

The first stage of meditation is relaxation of the mind and body. Relaxation of the mind begins by eliminating those things that bother you. This usually involves two things:

- Accepting a set of ethics based on honesty and personal responsibility.
- Learning to focus on the present rather than dwelling on the past (which can't be changed) or worrying about the future (which is guessing about what might happen). An important part of this is simply learning to breath such as I've already described: slow and steady breath, with a focus on comfortably extending the exhalation.

Relaxing the body traditionally involved practices such as hatha yoga, what most Westerners consider to be the extent of "yoga." While hatha yoga is great (and yes, it originated with the ancient Tantrics, as newspaper articles in 2012 made clear), but for many Westerners the learning of hatha yoga may either take too long or not be something in which they are interested.

Luckily, there is something you can do to deeply relax your physical body. It is called *progressive relaxation* or progressive muscle relaxation. This system is often used as a beginning step in hypnotic inductions. Briefly, you simply "talk" to each part of your body and tell it to relax. When leading others in the practice of progressive relaxation, I like to begin this way:

"Get comfortable where you are, seated or lying on your back. Uncross your arms and legs and breathe normally. Now imagine a sphere of brilliant golden light, surrounding your feet. As you focus on your feet and that golden glow, all of the muscles in your ankles, feet, and toes just let go and totally, deeply relax. You don't have to do anything. When the sphere is there, the muscles just relax and any tension fades away. If you notice any tightness or stress, just breathe and allow it to fade away.

"Next, the golden glow moves up to your calves. The muscles of the calves simply become loose and totally relax. You don't have to do anything; just let go. If you notice any tightness or stress in either of your calves, just breathe and allow it to fade away..."

Continue this way up your legs, torso, arms, neck, and head. Alternatively, you can start at the head and work down to the toes. When you are deeply relaxed using this system, spend a few minutes just breathing using the methods previously described.

When you combine the mental focus and physical practices of relaxation, you take your attention away from the world and turn it inward. In Sanskrit, this is known as *pratyahara*, the withdrawal of the senses and the normal attention we pay to our environment.

Stage Two: Contemplation

The second stage of meditation involves the intense focus of your mind on a single thing. This can be any object, picture, sound, activity, etc. Traditional examples of this include a mantra or yantra. Up to this point, you may have merely been looking at a yantra. Here, we'll take it up a notch to true Tantric intensity.

Method One

Fix your gaze on an image. Do not take your eyes off it. Try to keep your eyes open as long as possible between blinks. If your eyes water, that is fine. Let them.

When you have the image burned into your mind, close your eyes and visualize or imagine the yantra. Make it as clear and complete as possible. Don't be concerned if it's not perfect. You will develop better visualization skills with practice.

When you have visualized the yantra to the best of your ability, imagine or visualize the yantra growing until it is enormous in size. When it is huge, imagine or visualize yourself stepping into the yantra, becoming one with it. Alternatively, see the yantra as a type of door and go through it.

If you're not comfortable focusing on the entire yantra at one time, divide the yantra in your mind into several horizontal strips, perhaps ten or more. Moving from right to left (or left to right), focus on just the top strip of the yantra. Repeat this for the next strip. Do this until you have spent some time with each of the strips. Then close your eyes and do this completely with visualization.

Again, don't worry if you're not perfect at this. Skill will develop with practice.

This extreme single focus, the second stage of real meditation, is known as *dharana*.

Stage Three: Negation

Leading to what is known as *dhyana* or *samadhi* in Sanskrit—the true meditative state—is the stage I call "negation." After you have the incredible and intense focus on the visualized yantra, allow it to dissolve. Let it just fade away. Alternatively, you may wish to peel away each of the strips just described. Continue until the entire image is gone.

At this point, a very interesting phenomenon will occur. By the time the yantra is gone from your visualization, your consciousness—which has been caught up in the act of intense focus—will also be "gone" (actually it will just be silent). The constant monologue in your head that is always going on while you are awake will be stopped. This will give your higher self, your link to the Divine, a chance to communicate with you and give you potentially important messages and information. The result is a wonderful state of bliss known as samadhi, nirvana, or cosmic consciousness. It is a sensation of being at one with the universe, and there is nothing else like it. It is a state of perfect balance and control, including control of the energies that run through the universe and your bodies.

When you first try this, it is common for this state to last for only a brief moment. Then the inner voice returns and asks something like, "Did I do this right?" As soon as the voice comes back, the meditation is over.

With regular practice, you will be able to make that instant last a minute, five minutes, or more. As this state stretches out in length, you will have a new feeling come over you, a feeling of being in total harmony with the universe, including being able to manifest and direct magickal prana.

The Background, Version 2

The following is based on a 2011 Llewellyn blog post I wrote, at www.llewellyn.com/blog/2011/7/magick-101-2-baseball-breath-and-magick.

Breathwork

There are some teachers who will tell you that you're breathing the "wrong" way. My advice: forget about them. While there are different levels of breath, each type is valuable for different reasons. What is of value is learning to use the different levels of breathing and being able to access them when appropriate.

High Breathing

Imagine you're a soldier and told to stand at attention.

Stand up straight!
Stomach in!
Shoulders back!
Chest out!

Now try to breathe. It's hard to do! You have to breathe by expanding and contracting the rib cage. This is done using the small intercostal muscles between the ribs. They weren't designed to do that.

This technique is called high breathing. It limits the amount of air you intake because it only uses the upper part of the lungs. Chronic high breathing may cause digestive problems and is common among people with asthma and people who wear tight clothes or belts at their waists. High breathing is a natural response to frights and shocks and may trigger the production of hormones necessary for the fight-or-flight response. Not having access to high breathing could result in not being able to handle dangerous situations.

Middle Breathing

Middle breathing is not as clearly defined as high breathing because you have to go through the upper part of the lungs to get to the middle. It will also partially fill the lower part of the lungs. However, middle breathing essentially fills the central part of the lungs. It gives a fuller breath than high breathing but is still not complete. A further difference is the movement of the ribs. With high breathing, because the body is held so rigid, the ribs tend to expand upward and forward. With middle breathing, they also expand out to the sides.

Because you get more air with middle breathing than with high breathing, middle breathing can be better for you, especially when sitting in a chair. The added breath and oxygen can give you more energy and enhance your concentration abilities.

Low Breathing

This is often described as "belly breathing" and, according to some teachers, is superior to high and middle breathing. It certainly does have some advantages:

- Low breathing uses the deepest part of the lungs, filling and allowing them to naturally clean themselves.
- It massages the organs of the stomach.
- More air is taken in.
- It has a positive effect on the nerves of the solar plexus.
- It can provide calmness and courage.

This is the style of breathing used by singers and martial artists. It is the most natural form of breathing (watch an infant on its back to see what low breathing looks like). Here's how it works:

The largest muscle in the body, the diaphragm, separates the upper organs from the stomach organs. When the diaphragm moves down, it creates a bit of a vacuum, causing the lungs to expand and fill with air. When it moves back up, it increases pressure and forces the air out of the lungs. To bring the diaphragm down, imagine your stomach expanding. In fact, let it expand forward. To push the diaphragm up, contract your stomach.

Okay, I know sticking your belly out isn't the modern Western visual ideal, but concentrate on what you're doing rather than how you look.

When is low breathing not a "better" form of breathing? Try each of these types of breathing and you'll see that low breathing takes a lot of time. When you are exercising in a way that raises your pulse and respiration rate, you can't breathe fast enough using low breathing. It's not ideal in all situations. It can be used to help calm the mind and spirit.

Complete Breathing

This type of breath puts it all together and is primarily used only during breathwork. It combines high, middle, and low breathing.

Find a comfortable position. Inhale through your nose for a high breath, expanding your chest up and out. Continue by allowing more breath into your lungs, expanding your chest and ribs to the side. Complete the breath by allowing your stomach to expand, pulling down the diaphragm and filling the lungs completely. Hold the inhalation for a few moments. Don't strain. Feel comfortable.

Now exhale sloooooowly through the mouth and nose. Focus on all your muscles and the air leaving you. As you exhale, do not allow your rib cage to relax. Keep it expanded. Focus on the exhalation, not the inhalation.

Repeat this a few times before you allow yourself to return to normal breathing. With each breath, fill your lungs with a smooth movement of air through high, middle, and low breaths. Try to lengthen the time it takes you to exhale with each breath. Don't strain. Go easy. Even a little longer is positive.

If you are dissatisfied with the depth and quality of your breathing, there are several devices that can help you improve your breathing capacity. They have a mouthpiece similar to that of a snorkel used for swimming, and a control for limiting how much air can come through the mouthpiece into your lungs. You have to inhale more strongly and exhale with greater force. The devices have names like "PowerLung," "Ultrabreathe," or "Expand-a-Lung." All of them can be useful (and they may help people with asthma, COPD, high blood pressure, heart disease, emphysema, cystic fibrosis, and other issues with lung involvement), but be aware that they can be scary at first because it will feel like you can't get a breath. Relax. Take it easy. Start slowly and take time to build up your lung capacity.

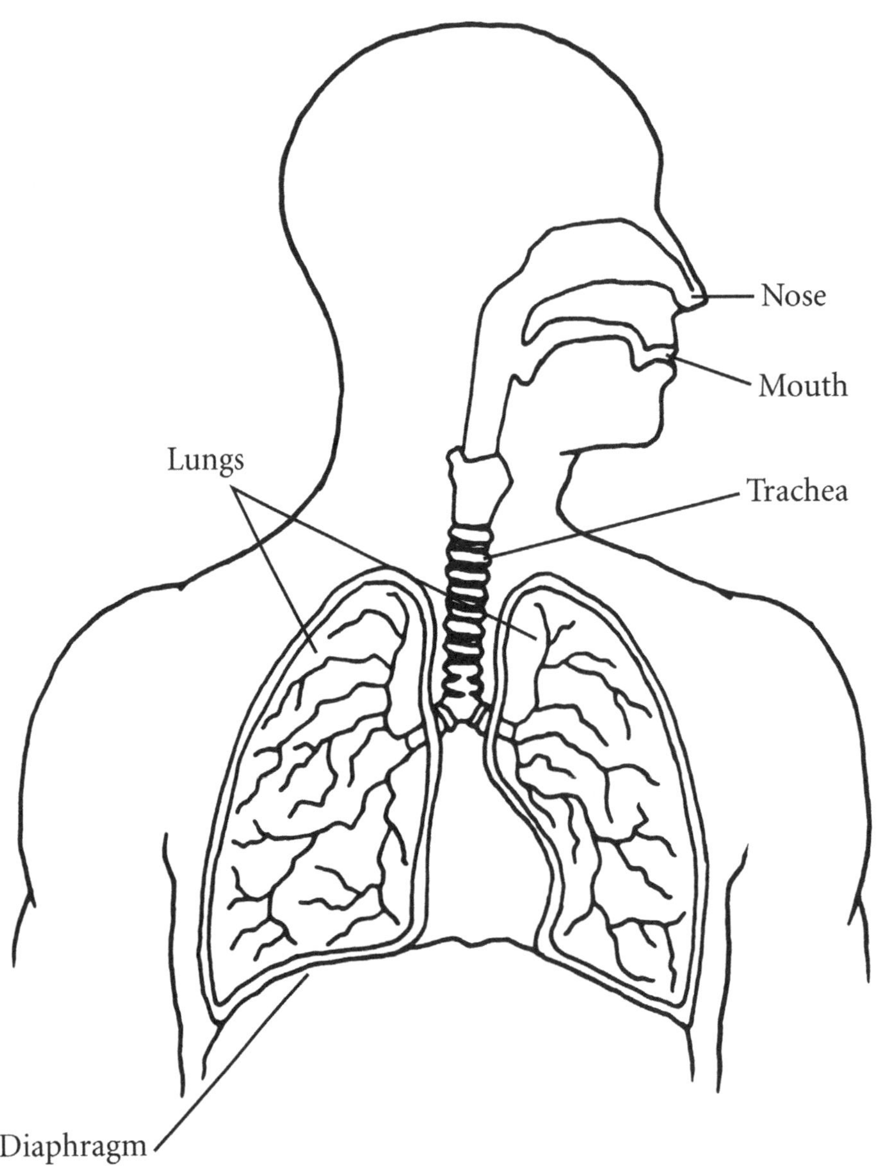

Respiratory System

The Technology

Projection and Absorption

When I studied martial arts, one of the things that was stressed was that weapons were to be thought of as extensions of the body. The sword extended your arms by a less than a meter. The staff extended your arms by a couple of meters. But they were still basically part of you. Further, they could be used to help you extend your energy beyond your normal reach.

Once you can extend your energy, you might not even need physical weapons. The ultimate form of this is a very secretive technique known in China as *dim mak*. Depending upon the time of day and the location of the body's energy, a master of dim mak could direct energy to an enemy by a slight touch to an acupressure point (marma) or by sending energy and not even touching the foe at all. This action would disrupt the victim's energetic system, and days or even weeks later, the person would sicken and die.

In this description, the point I want to make clear is that you do not need a variety of magickal tools or "weapons." They are, after all, merely extensions of who you are. They don't function on their own. They have no superpowers. They just help you.

You, your mind, your ability to move universal energy (prana) modified by the elements and the gunas (active, passive, balanced)—that is really all you need to perform powerful Tantric magick. You may choose to use tools of your choice, but they are not required, nor are they necessary.

Pictured here is an image from the chapter on the Sri Yantra. It shows the Tantric as being one with the 3-D version of the Sri. The Sri is also representative of the creation of all things from the Goddess, past her manifestations, beyond the play (*lila*) of maya, to the physical world. We can also move from our position in the physical world back through the Sri toward the Divine.

Sri Yantra in 3-D Projected on the Body

It is this concept—that we *are* the Sri Yantra, that we *are* the microcosm of the greater universe (macrocosm), and therefore, we need nothing other than ourselves to work incredibly powerful magick—that is at the heart of Tantric magick.

Using gems, yantras, color, visualization, breathwork, etc., can all be potent magickal techniques. But when combined with the following techniques, their power is amplified as they become extensions of our bodies.

The first technique is called *projection*. The technology is something you have been learning. Using breathwork and visualization, combined with the energies of the appropriate element(s) and guna(s), the energy is projected from the center of your being (the Bindu of the Sri Yantra) out toward the temporal and physical goal of the magick.

The second technique is called *absorption*. Here, again using breathwork and visualization, you take energies that are outside of you and bring them into your center.

Projection is the technique you use for making magick that will affect anything in your environment, including others. Absorption is the technique you use for making magick that is designed to change you.

The Method

Tantric Magickal Ritual

1. Clean the area where you will perform the ritual. Take a bath or shower. This ritual is performed digambara. Banish with your favorite method, such as through the use of the Dasa Mahavidyas or the thunderbolt mantra, as described earlier.
2. From a large bowl or pitcher of water, fill eight smaller bowls, one at a time, and place them at the eight directions of your chakra laboratory. Place the large bowl at center. If, from your research, you have images of the deities for the directions (or their yantras), place them at their proper location. Place incense, vibhuti, or colored powders on the central altar.
3. Stand in the center of your chakra and face east. Say:

   ***Svaha!* I salute the line of innumerable Tantrics and cast the circle of semen glow. May the circle be intact and the peace of Om Shiva Shakti dwell herein.**

4a. Put your hands on your heart. Say:

   I honor the Lord and Lady in my heart. Om.

   Use the vibhuti or colored powder (red if you're male, white if you're female) to make three short horizontal lines over your heart.

4b. Put your hands on the crown of your head. Say:

   I honor the Lord and Lady in the crown of my head. Om.

   Use the vibhuti or powder to make three short horizontal lines on the top of your head.

4c. Put your hands on your hairline. Say:

   I honor the Lord and Lady in the top of my forehead. Om.

   Use the vibhuti or powder to make three short horizontal lines on your forehead.

4d. Put your hands on your upper chest. Say:

   I honor the Lord and Lady in the armor. Om.

Use the vibhuti or powder to make three short horizontal lines over your upper chest.

4e. Put your hands on your eyes, also covering the third-eye chakra. Say:

I honor the Lord and Lady residing in the three eyes. Om.

Use the vibhuti or powder to make three short horizontal lines between your brows.

4f. Put your hands on your lingam or yoni. Say:

I honor the Lord and Lady in the lingam (or yoni). Om.

Use the vibhuti or powder to make three short horizontal lines over your genitals.

5. Sit in the center of your chakra, facing east. Visualize or imagine that you are sitting on a two-dimensional Sri Yantra. When the image is as strong as you can make it (and it will get better with practice), imagine it growing into a 3-D version of the Sri Yantra. It is all around you and encompassing you. Become one with it.
6. Understand that the outer edges represent the play (lila) of illusion (maya) in the physical world. As you move more toward your center and more toward the uppermost peak of the Sri Yantra (at the crown chakra), you leave the physical world and move into the spiritual world.
7. Follow previous directions for charging the chakras with colors and bija mantras (see chapter 11). Breathe using the complete breath. Notice the sensation of the kundalini rising.
8. When you become aware of the amrita descending, begin focusing on your magickal goal. Slowly chant **Om.**
9. To project all of this combined work, stress the vowel of the sound: **OOOOOOOOOOOOmmm.**
10. To absorb all of this combined work, stress the consonant of the sound: **oooMMMMMMMMMMMM.**
11. When the energy, focus, visualization, sound—*everything*—reaches its highest level, shout: ***SVECCHACHARA! IT IS MY WILL!*** You may find that you jump up, pump your fists in the air, or something similar in excitement. This is fine.
12. When the energy and excitement of the work retreats, collect the water from the smaller bowls in reverse order, pouring it into the larger bowl or pitcher. Banish as before.

Addendum One: Enhancing the Tantric Magickal Ritual

Just as there are no rules as to what may or may not be on your regular altar, there are no rules as to what you may include or exclude from the altar you assemble to perform this ritual.

Is there a deity associated with the goal of the ritual? Include that deity's picture, statue, or yantra. During the ritual, make time to honor the deity by performing aarti with a lamp or candle, while ringing a bell.

Include the elements. You can assemble five small bowls for your altar. Put water (with Ganga jal) in one to represent the element of water. Put a lamp or candle in another to represent fire. Put soil in a third to represent earth. Put a hand fan in another to represent air. Burn incense in the fifth as a symbol of spirit/akasha.

Use your hand (the chakra in the palm) or a tool such as a wand or dagger to direct the energy you're raising toward the element associated with the magickal goal of the ritual. Are you trying to increase that element's energy, decrease it, or balance it? Follow the directions for swara yoga (included with the description of the danda, or yoga staff) for changing the energy you're channeling to solar, lunar, or balanced. This is a way to work with the gunas.

What else can you do? Use your imagination! Modify this ritual until it fits you. Remember, the path of *Modern Tantra* is that of Svecchachara—the path of doing *your* will, not my will or the will of any particular group.

Addendum Two: Magickal Mantras

I have already discussed the incredible power of vibration. It is only natural that some people have worked with energy in motion to achieve magickal results. Personally, I am not a big fan of magickal mantras, but I have found some to be incredibly useful. For example, the Ganesh mantra, *Om Gam Ganapataye Namaha*, is highly useful for eliminating blockages on your path and opening unexpected opportunities.

Here are a few other mantras. Although there are some very long ones, I've selected ones that are both effective and relatively brief. I suggest that you do them in rounds of 108. Make a vow to your personal deity (Ishta Devata) how many rounds a day or month you will perform. Describe what you will do or give up when you receive the results of your magick. Be sure to follow through on all your promises!

For wealth in all things:
Om Namaha Dhandaye Svaha

For victory (especially in political issues) and to win lawsuits:
Om Hring Bagalamukhi Namah

For good luck:
Om aim hreem shreem Sri
Lalita Tripurasundari padukam
poojayami namah

For protection from non-physical entities such as ghosts, unwanted spirits, etc.:
Om namo bhagavate ru ru
bhairvaye bhoot pret shay kuru
kuru hum fat svaha

For energy and power, and also to eliminate fears:
Om Bhairavi Soaham

To gain magickal power:
Om Shrim Hreem Hreem Aim Vajra
Vairochaniye Shrim Hreem Hreem
Phat Svaha

For material success combined with spiritual advancement:
Dum dum dhumavati tha tha

For peace and harmonious living:
Om Preeang Preeng Prong
Sa Shange Namah

For luck in taking risks such as gambling, speculation, etc.:
Om shri mahalakyamaya namah

The Tantric I.O.B.: A Modern Tantric Method for Personal Development and Ending Psychic Attacks

One of the most popular sections of my book *Modern Magick* is my description of the I.O.B.

technique. This is a method for dealing with our inner demons as well as for dealing with something we experience as a psychic attack. The I.O.B. technique isn't new, but it is a new interpretation of traditional Western magickal and medieval techniques that in some cases were used as an early form of counseling. The magickal techniques include the formulation of *telesmatic images* and certain banishing methods. By considering some aspects of the I.O.B. a type of medieval counseling system, I am, of course, also giving a psychological interpretation of what was commonly called "exorcism."

Ever since the 1973 movie *The Exorcist*, people have become familiar with the idea of exorcism, or at least an exaggerated and fictionalized idea of the process. It is commonly thought of as a way to get rid of demons or devils (if they exist) that are supposedly "possessing" a person. Such demons seem to be fairly rare these days, but in medieval literature they seemed to be surprisingly common. We must assume that such demons have ceased to bother people or never existed, or that we interpret them differently today. Well, there is no reason to believe that the demons said to possess people in the Middle Ages have changed, and with all the reports of exorcisms during that period, there is little reason to assume that all those reports were imaginary. Therefore, we may assume that the "demons" are being handled today in a different manner. If you look at the actual reports of the exorcisms from that time, you will be struck by the similarity between the descriptions of the "possessed" people and symptoms of people who today would be described as having certain physical or mental issues, or a combination of both. So even if we are to assume that some exorcisms did deal with demon possession, it seems that many functioned as a sort of early form of psychotherapy in the tradition of what is known today as "psychodrama." Whatever the cause, reports show that in many cases the exorcisms worked.[19]

The magickal technique of creating telesmatic images is based on a complex system of visualization methods. We need not be that complex. Instead, we can use the basic idea of creating an image of something that is devoid of form. Thus, "justice" could be made to have a specific image. So could "freedom" become a particular angel or archangel. "Intolerance" could be visualized as an imagined demon, as could the sensations of a psychic attack. Any quality, good or bad, can be given form. It is this idea, along with the concept that in some or most instances exorcism was an early technology for dealing with unwanted psychological issues, that is the basis of the I.O.B. technique as described and used here.

A word of warning: It may be that going to a positive, growth-oriented psychotherapist who is not against occult studies may be better for you than attempting the I.O.B. technique to deal with your "inner demons." If you opt to attempt this technique and find yourself scared, physically ill, or feeling confused or lost, *stop immediately!* The unconscious mind works to safeguard the body and the conscious mind. The unconscious mind may have a reason for preventing us from learning the innermost truths about ourselves until we are ready to accept them. If you try out this system, go slow, be gentle, and be kind to yourself.

---

19 I'm not including the modern trend by some Evangelical Christian groups to brand virtually everything they don't like—from poverty and chronic illness to overeating, alcoholism, and genetic diseases—with the label "demon possession." The exorcisms they claim to do seem to be more about establishing or maintaining the power of a group or individual, as well as their associated hierarchy and leadership, rather than helping an "afflicted" person. I have seen no records of the long-term success of such rituals.

The technique may sound simple, but it is surprisingly powerful.

The "I" in I.O.B. stands for **Identify.** Your first and perhaps most challenging task in this technique is to identify aspects of yourself that you no longer wish to possess. Are you hardheaded? Egotistical? Self-centered? Insecure? Indecisive? Whatever it is, your first task is to identify it. Now, at the beginning this is quite safe, although it might not be that easy to admit to those things that you consider to be your faults. Later, it will become easier to admit your faults on a conscious level, but your unconscious may resist your conscious. This will be the time to go easy on yourself. Do not force something if it will not come easily. Work on one thing at a time. If you are applying this technique to deal with a psychic attack, try to determine why the attack is taking place. Don't come only from your point of view; also try to imagine the point of view of your attacker that triggered the assault in the first place. Be as objective as possible and see all sides. Is there a third way of looking at this, something that is not your interpretation or that of the supposed attacker? Also, see if you can identify the direction from which the attack is coming. If you don't know, use your emotions and guess.

The "O" in I.O.B. stands for **Objectify.** This second step is the easiest and most fun. The idea here is to build up an image that represents what you have identified. This can be any form, although it should preferably be capable of life. Thus, a rock would not be as good for this technique as would an elf, or a dog, or the imagined image of a monstrous demon.

Let's assume you have determined that one of the things you wish to rid yourself of is hardheadedness, the inability to change. In this step, we want to objectify this hardheadedness, make it into a thing. We can make up any image, but for our purpose here, let us give it a somewhat human appearance. Its face must have firmly chiseled features, and he (let's make it male) wears an army helmet. His eyes are steel gray. He is tall and strong, but the joints of his legs and hips do not work, so his strength is useless. He is wearing a metallic jumpsuit, and beneath it are seen hard muscles that can never relax. In fact, in some places the muscles look like nuts and bolts. Although this aspect is hidden, it is possible to sense that he feels great pain because he can never relax, must always be hard. There is a fear of not being right. In this way, an image of hardheadedness is built up. All of these things are objectifications of the archetype of hardheadedness. If it so happens that this is an aspect of yourself you wish to work on, you can start with what I have given and continue. What color is his skin and hair? (Don't be limited by standard skin tones.) Is he holding anything? Doing anything?

If you are using the I.O.B. to deal with a psychic attack, come up with an image of the *nature* of the attack, not of whom you suspect the attacker to be. We can end the attack without harming the attacker. This is important because most psychic attacks are the result of our own imagination, not some wizard working against you, and you wouldn't want to harm yourself. The image could be an animal, a plant, an unknown person, or even some imaginary monster. Spend some time making this as real as possible. What does it look like, smell like, sound like, and so forth? How does it make you feel? Spend time with this.

Lastly, name this creation. You can use any name as long as it is not the name of someone you know or know of. Again, it does not have to be standard. "I-gis" (hard "g") is short and applicable. "Grelflexor" is an interesting and perfectly acceptable appellation.

Spend some time making this image in your mind as concrete as possible. You may wish to draw it or perhaps make a statue, if you have some artistic abilities. If it's some sort of creature, you might even consider buying a small toy version of it. The time you spend doing this is important because you are literally giving life to it, and you can't stop something—end its life in a metaphorical sense—if it is not alive.

***The "B" in I.O.B. stands for* Banish.** This is the magickal equivalent of exorcism. However, this process of banishment—though based on the Banishing by the Mahavidyas (see the end of chapter 4)—is a little tricky because we are banishing an unwanted part of ourselves or something linked to ourselves. When doing the I.O.B. because you feel you are under psychic attack, it separates the attacker(s) from you, ending the attack, and allows you to set up a barrier to prevent further attacks. Let's go through this step by step.

Step One. Perform the Banishing by the Mahavidyas (see the end of chapter 4). If you have not done this before, do it at least twice a day for a minimum of one week, preferably two weeks, so you are sure it is effective. The best times to do this are at one of the four Tantric "twilights": sunrise, noon, sunset, or midnight. If you cannot practice at those exact times, do so when you can, but practice at least twice daily. Make the visualizations of the goddesses as real as possible. Study information on the goddesses from this book and from other sources. If you have a picture or sculpture of your objectification, bring it with you into the area you are going to banish.

Step Two. After the banishing, if you have a picture or sculpture of your objectification, look at it for a few minutes. Focus on it until it seems alive. Then put the physical image away and work it up in your imagination even more. If you have no physical image, simply mock it up in your imagination. Make it as real as you possibly can. What does it smell like, sound like, feel like? Does it have an energy that you can sense? Make it real.

Now *slowly* turn in a circle and see if you can sense where your objectified image belongs (or where the attack is coming from) outside the protective square you created with the banishing. If you don't know which direction, ask yourself, "If I knew where it belonged, where would it be?" and go with your first immediate feeling. Visualize your objectified image there.

Step Three. When your objectified image is as real as possible, notice that there is an energy link between you and this "thing." It may be a wispy trail or something more solid. On your side it may be attached to one or more of your chakras. The most likely primary points of connection will be at the top of the head, between the brows, at the heart, at the solar plexus, or at the genitals. Just note where this link is. On the creature's side it should be connected to its solar plexus, heart, or head.

By the way, your visualization needs to be only as good as you can make it. It does not have to be perfect. In fact, if you are not good at seeing things you are attempting to visualize, simply know (not think or believe or hope or wish, but *know beyond any doubt*) that it is there and that if your psychic vision were better you would be able to see it.

Step Four. In your hand, visualize one of the typical weapons of Durga or Kali, such as a sword or scissors. With the weapon, sever the connection between you and the objectified form. Be careful! You may experience some slight pain with this due to the shock of severing something that has been part of you for so long. Simply acknowledge it and you will find that any pain or other sensation will quickly dissipate. The important thing to remember about this step is that it should be both physical (you should do an action) and mental (you should visualize the cutting of the cord).

Step Five. When you are sure the link has been severed, *immediately* repeat steps 2–12 of the Banishing by the Mahavidyas. When this has been completed, make sure the figure you visualized is completely *outside* of your protective area. The ideal is to make sure that there is no trace of the severed cord that existed between you and the figure. In practice, a small vestigial piece of it may remain. That's okay, but anything attached to you should be completely within your part of the banished area, while anything attached to the figure must not enter the banished area at all.

Step Six. With the visualized tool you used to cut the link, and while staying inside your banished area, visualize yourself slicing the image into tiny bits. Do this with authority! Laughing at it is appropriate, too. Feel fantastic about what you've done. If you have something to say about how you no longer want it in your life, how it no longer has any power over you, how you are completely through with it, etc., tell it that as you destroy it. Speak from your heart. Tell it how you feel. Also, be sure to describe how wonderful things will be for you now that this thing can never bother or intimidate you again.

Step Seven. Now take a comfortable position (lying down, sitting, or standing) and simply breathe. Focus on your exhalations. Make them long, continuous, and slow. This will have the effect of increasing your personal energy (prana).

Step Eight. Become highly aware of the ten goddesses as they surround and protect you. Allow this image to slowly fade from your conscious attention, but know that they are still invisibly there.

Step Nine. Although this breaking of the link need only be done once, be sure to continue practicing the banishing at least twice a day for the week that follows. This will prevent any attempt by your unconscious mind or a known or unknown source to reestablish the link and again manifest the undesired behavior, belief, or attack. Practicing the banishing during each of the four twilights would be even more thorough.

....

I must point out that a chef learning to cook does not always have his or her food come out perfectly the first time, and your I.O.B. technique may not be perfect at first, either. With your first attempts, you may need to repeat the technique several times in order for it to completely succeed. You should wait at least three days between repetitions of this rite, although you should still perform the banishings at least twice daily. If you have created (or purchased) an artistic version of your visualization, it should be totally destroyed after doing the I.O.B. Eventually you will become very effective with the Tantric I.O.B.

FOURTEEN

TANTRIC SEXUALITY

One of the great mysteries of the universe is that of sexuality. What causes arousal? Since only a small percentage of sexual experiences result in reproduction, why is sexuality so incredibly enjoyable? The thousands of years of study of sexuality by Tantrics has resulted in a huge body of literature and unwritten lore. Some of that has become the basis of Neo-Tantra.

However, much of what has been described in the books comes down to just a few basic concepts.

Theories of Tantric Sexuality

First, Tantric sexuality is not about love and relationships, although it can enhance love and relationships. Remember, Tantra isn't something you do, Tantra is something you are. You don't become a Tantric by following certain sexual practices. Instead, you become a Tantric by following the spiritual and practical techniques of Tantra such as those described in this book. Tantric sexual practices are a natural outcome of learning those concepts. When you become a Tantric, the practice of Tantric sexuality will be as natural as sleeping when you're tired.

Second, Tantric sexuality is a combination of mental and physical techniques. There are some who tend to focus on either the mental or the physical. This inevitably leads to a lack of balance and either disappointment or living in a world of ego and unreality.

Third, Tantric sexuality is about raising and manipulating energy. Both of these are done through a combination of physical and mental techniques. Before moving on to the how and why of partnered methods of Tantric sexuality, however, I need to talk a bit about yoga.

Yoga, as already mentioned, means "union." The implication is union with the Divine. Although there are many forms of yoga, the best-known form in the West is hatha yoga. There are schools all over that teach the various postures, or *asanas*. A few teach some basic philosophy that is rooted in the post-Tantric Vedic tradition. Some eschew even that, focusing on the positive benefits of the stretching of the body.

But why is it that so few people ever talk about how simple and complex stretches are supposed to help you find union with the godhead? I mean, isn't it silly to assume that some of those postures are going to make you more spiritual? In fact, some people think that because they can do complex asanas, they are spiritual. That's like thinking that because you can say the words of a prayer, you are suddenly more spiritual than other people. Sadly, experience shows that some of the people who pray the most are not very spiritual at all.

Both hatha yoga and Tantric sexuality have physical, mental, and energetic aspects. You can enjoy hatha yoga for just the physical stretching. You can also enjoy Tantric sexuality for just the physical pleasure. But there is so much more if you involve all aspects.

To explain this a bit more, let's look once again at the major chakras. In the illustration here, you can see the locations of the chakras relative to their positions associated with the physical body. They form a vertical line. (Some illustrations show them slightly out of vertical, but to understand the concept, seeing them as a straight line is fine.) The second chakra is above the first, the third is above the second, and so forth.

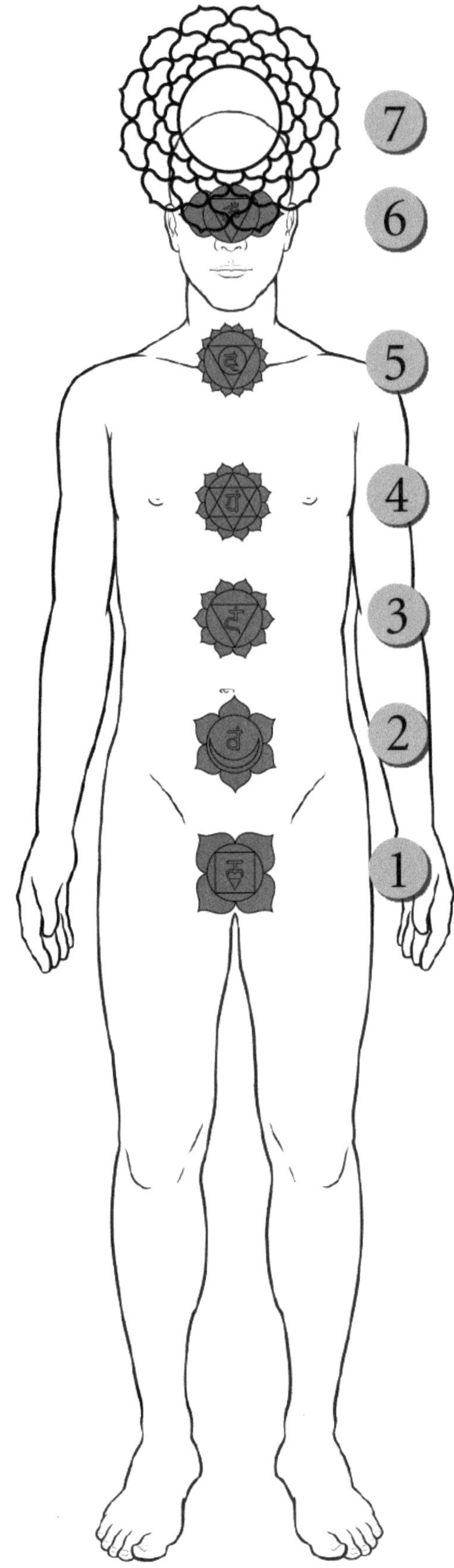

The Seven Chakras

But what about the energy flows? When you are sitting in meditation, you are urged to sit with your back straight so the energy can flow freely. This is not a subjective experience. Try sitting with your shoulders hunched forward and down. Depending upon your level of core strength, you will end up tiring far more quickly, and even find yourself in pain, when compared to how you feel when sitting with your back straight.

Part of this, certainly, has to do with physical structure. But another part of this is because the slumping and slouching prevent the easy motion of pranic energy. Many people will even find seeing a person sitting upright to be more attractive than seeing the same person slouching.

But what happens to the energy flows if you consciously decide to change those flows? Let's look at a popular hatha yoga asana known as Downward Dog (or Downward Facing Dog). On just the physical level, the supposed benefits of the stretching for this asana include the following:

- Lengthening the spine, resulting in the release of tension.
- Stretching the muscles and connective tissues around the shoulder blades.
- Stretching the hamstrings at the rear of the thighs, giving increased flexibility and reducing stress.
- Stretching the gastrocnemius muscles in the calves, giving flexibility and reducing stress.
- Strengthening several parts of the body, including the ankles, thighs, shoulders, arms, wrists, and the muscles that are called the "core."

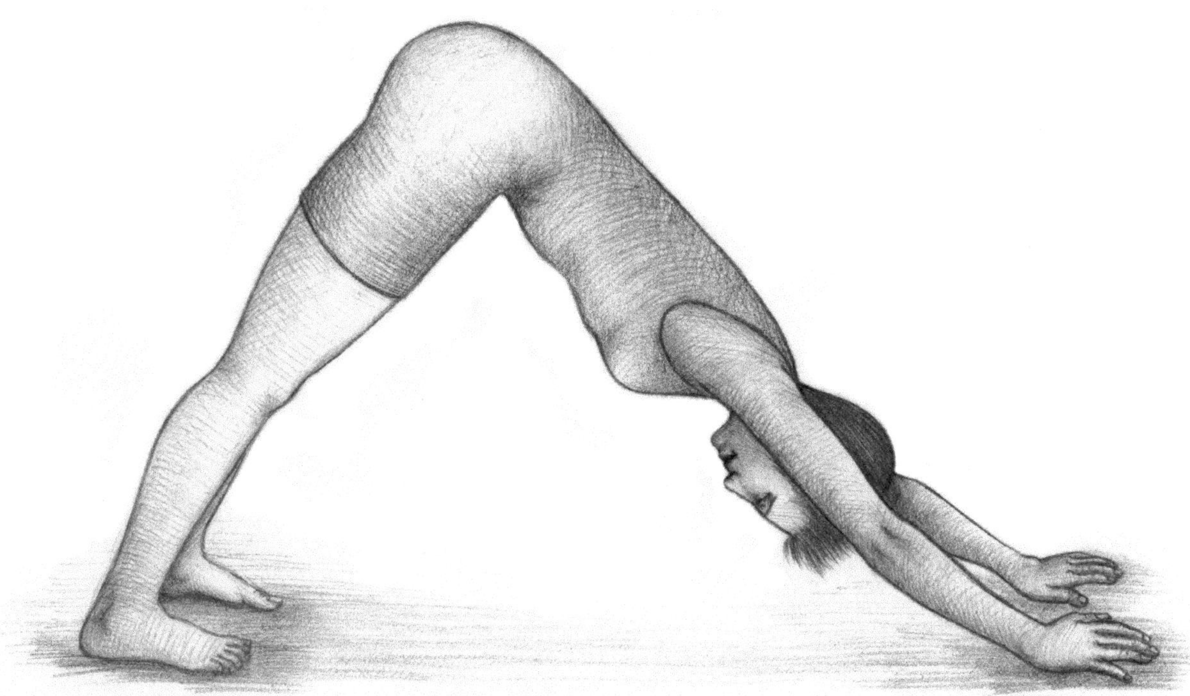

Downward Dog

Because of the stretching and reduction in tension and stress in Downward Dog, there is even data showing that this yoga position can help relieve back pain, improve digestion, lessen fatigue, and have a general calming effect.

Look, however, at what happens to the chakras in this pose. The topmost crown chakra is now below the rest of the chakras. The line of energy forms a chevron with one point up ^. The first chakra is now at the top instead of at the bottom.

The (root) chakra that is now at the top is associated with your instincts of self-preservation and survival, as well as your mental relationship to your physical body. It can help you eliminate what is obsolete in your life. All of the other chakras literally "look up" at it. The entire chakra structure, as well as the paths of the nadis, are inverted.

The koshas extend beyond the physical body. Consider what would happen if another person entered your sheaths with their sheaths. Have you ever met someone you were instantly attracted to? Have you ever met someone who left you feeling instantly repelled? This is simply because your sheaths, including the aura, are either in harmony or in disharmony with that person. It's the combination of the physical and the spiritual/mental.

Let's take it a step further and consider what happens when you make love with another person. All of your energies, nadis, koshas, and chakras interact. In a position where one partner is on top of the other, face to face, the energy from chakra to chakra goes straight across. But think about the interplay in other positions. How do the chakras and energies change their flow when you are both head to genitals or one partner is behind the other? The potential is almost endless. Is it any wonder that the ancient proto-Tantrics in the city of Khajuraho covered some of their temples with scenes of amazing eroticism?

There is a tremendous number of books that go into excruciatingly long explanations of the basics of Tantric sexuality, but it all comes down to exactly what you have been learning in *Modern Tantra*. There's a spiritual understanding that is bereft of practical value without the physical and energetic aspects. Omit any aspect and you'll be doing a mere fraction of what you could be accomplishing. So now that you have the background, the next step is the practice.

Practical Tantric Sexual Exercises for One

In these exercises, you will accomplish several valuable tasks:

- Improve breathing
- Enhance physical endurance
- Improve visualization skills
- Amplify second-chakra energy using physical, mental, and emotional abilities
- Trigger movement of kundalini energy

First Exercise

1. Lie on the ground with your knees up and your feet flat on the floor (see Position One in the illustration).
2. Inhale deeply, bringing the air down to the stomach.
3. Exhale quickly and thoroughly through the mouth, shouting **HAAA!**, letting all the air out.

3a. As you exhale, *thrust* your hips upward (see Position Two in the illustration). Do this upward thrusting with great speed and vigor.

4. Slowly inhale deeply.

4a. As you inhale, allow your hips to gently relax and rest back on the floor, as in Position One.

5. Repeat steps 3–4a five times.

Note: *Make no mistake, this is exercise!* If you are not used to doing this, you will feel sore in your core, including the hips, stomach, thighs, diaphragm, and glutes. If you find yourself sore, especially the day following this exercise, wait another day before repeating this. After a few times through this exercise day–relaxation day pattern, the soreness should decrease or cease. Then slowly increase the repetitions and frequency until you can do this for at least twenty repetitions daily.

Second Exercise

Once you are regularly able to do the first exercise a minimum of twenty times daily, it's time to add visualization of the energy to the exercise.

1. As you inhale (step 2 and then step 4 from the first exercise), visualize or imagine yourself bringing in the pranic energy through your nose. However, this energy goes beyond the stomach all the way to the first chakra.
2. Hold your breath for as long as it is comfortable before exhaling, as in the first exercise. As you do, allow the energy at the root to increase in strength and seethe until it has to explode out along with your breathe.

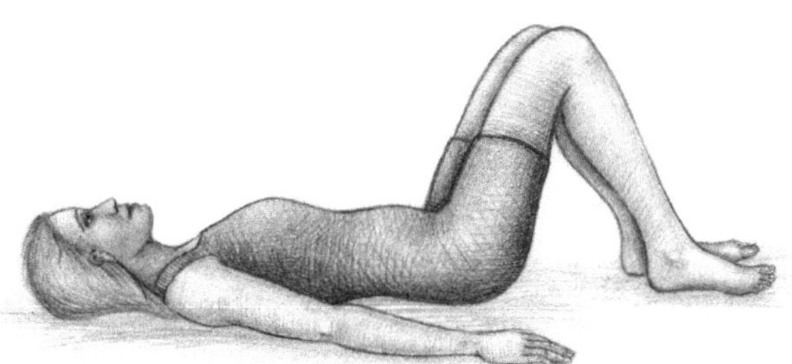

Position One

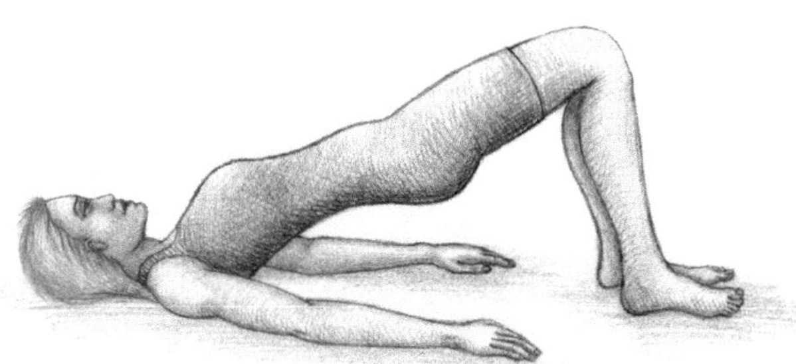

Position Two

Hips Up

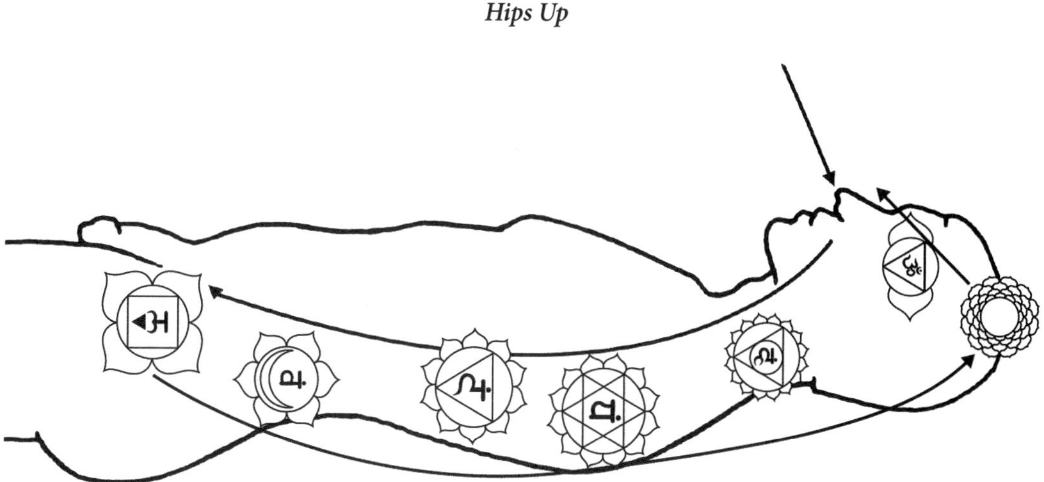

Visualized Energy

3. As you exhale and thrust your hips upward (steps 3 and 3a from the first exercise), visualize or imagine the energy exploding up your spine and moving all the way up to the top of your head.
4. Hold your hips up as you stay with your breath exhaled for as long as it is comfortable.

4a. During this pause, allow the energy to stay at the top of the head, and then complete the cycle by exiting through your nose and eyes.

5. Repeat.

Note: At first, because the energy and the breath are not completely the same, it may be a bit confusing to get them synchronized. Repeat until it feels completely natural and you can perform this exercise for a minimum of twenty repetitions daily.

Third Exercise

1. Assume a comfortable sitting position. This can be the famous lotus position, a simple cross-legged position, or sitting in a chair with a straight back. The two important features are that you are comfortable and that your back is straight.
2. Repeat the second exercise without the hip thrusts. However, still follow the breathing pattern and visualizations. Put all of your emotions and sensations into it. You want to have the same feelings and experiences as when you do the second exercise.

Note: The challenge for this exercise is to keep up the intensity. When you can keep up the intensity *and* the movement of the energy for twenty repetitions daily, you will have mastered this exercise.

Practical Tantric Sexual Exercises for Two

First Exercise

This exercise is designed for people who have mastered the third exercise just given. Each partner should be able to do the exercise completely.

1. Sit back to back. This can be done on the floor in the classic lotus position or with the legs simply crossed, while sitting on stools or with the help of chairs. The important thing is that the backs should have as much contact as possible. Each person is supporting the back of the other person, as shown in the illustration.
2. Now repeat the third exercise (just given) for one person. You should be able to detect your partner's breath as a result of the physical contact.
3. Repeat until you can do this exercise in perfect synchronization for twenty repetitions.

Note: There are two major goals for this exercise. The first is to become familiar with your partner's breathing patterns and energy work while maintaining synchronization with your energy and breath. The second is to expand your own ability to work with energy by maintaining your intensity and focus. As a side benefit, you should notice an increase in the energy flows.

Back to Back

Second Exercise

Repeat the first exercise (for two people) but with one major difference: breathe alternately to your partner. That is, as you inhale, your partner exhales. As you exhale, your partner inhales. Again, the challenge is to maintain focus and intensity with this opposite breathing pattern.

Third Exercise

This traditional Tantric technique will greatly amplify the energy. The key here is the concept of energy. This can be done with people of different genders, of the same gender, or even with a non-physical (i.e., angelic, deific, etc.) partner. However, this exercise involves cycling. So for this exercise, one person takes on the outgoing energy and will be called male, while the other person will be called female. There is no sexism here, as this can be reversed if desired.

The two partners stand and face each other. Look into each other's eyes.

2. Begin alternate breathing, as mastered previously. However, now there is a difference:

2a. As the male strongly exhales, he visualizes the breath and energy exiting through his genitals and going into his partner's genitals.

2b. As the female inhales, she visualizes the breath and energy coming in through her genitals, moving up her spine, and settling in her head.

2c. As the female exhales, she visualizes the breath and energy leaving through her eyes, nose, and mouth and going into those organs of the male.

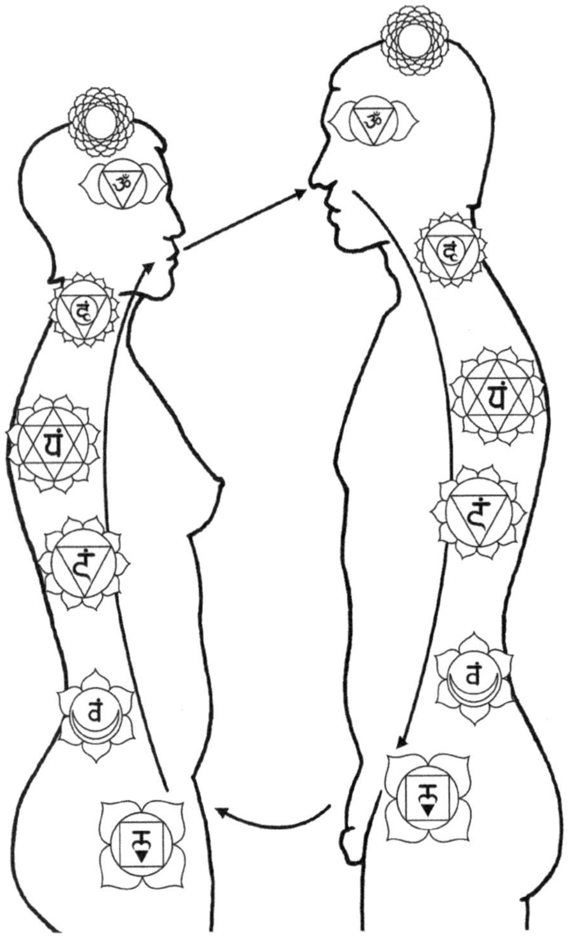

Female
Inhale
In Genitals
and up Spine
Exhale
Out Mouth

Male
Inhale
Through Nose
and down Spine
Exhale
Out Genitals

Energy Flow Pair

2d. As the male inhales, he visualizes the breath and energy coming in through his eyes, nose, and mouth, then moving down his spine and settling into the second (genital) chakra.

3. Repeat this until you can achieve a minimum of twenty successful repetitions.

Note: The focus and intensity need to remain high. Consider your partner to be the God or Goddess, and do your best to please and honor him or her.

Variations

You should spend some time mastering this last exercise. It is one of the most important ones in preparation for basic Tantric sexual practice. Become very comfortable with it. Try some variations. Instead of standing, try this lying on your sides. As an alternative, try it sitting in chairs, face to face, with knees touching. As another variation, do this ritual kneeling, with your knees touching.

Another very powerful variation is to "short-circuit" the energy path. If you remember the discussion of mudras, I mentioned how the energy usually discharges off the fingers. The mudras recycle the energy in different and powerful ways.

In this simple variation, all you have to do is place your right hand over your partner's heart. Although this seems like a simple change, the effect can be profound. The energy cycles from the second chakras (genitals) through the fourth chakras (heart). Being closer, the energy can actually move faster and with more intensity.

Let the energy build until it seems as though you will explode, then put your arms down. The energy, no longer being short-circuited, flows up to the crown chakra, charging it as never before.

As a variation on this version, you can also place your left hand on top of your partner's right hand, which is resting on your heart.

The Full Tantric Sexual Experience

In Neo-Tantra, the goals of sexuality tend to involve the use of various techniques (what one of my friends refers to as "Tantric technology") to activate natural functions, resulting in incredible sexual experiences, often combined with totally mind-blowing orgasms that transcend what is found in the vast majority of healthy sexual experiences. As a side benefit, Neo-Tantric sexual experiences tend to increase the feelings of love you have for your partner and give you feelings of unity with your partner and the universe. They can also improve your health, advance your well-being, and even enhance your sense of the spiritual and the Divine. *I'm 100 percent in favor of all that and more!*

With all these benefits, it's no wonder that so many people are entranced by the concept of Neo-Tantric sexual practices. In fact, you can use the exercises and techniques given in this book to achieve those results. In my experience, many of the people who are unaware of the potentials of Neo-Tantric sexuality are the ones who most deeply need it.

The goals of traditional Tantric sexuality, and the goals of sexuality for practitioners of *Modern Tantra*, run parallel to and are in harmony with the goals of Neo-Tantra. They are not, however, the same.

As I've stated before, Neo-Tantra is a small (but highly valuable) subset of traditional Tantra. All of the goals of Neo-Tantric sexual techniques are considered side benefits of the Tantric sexuality of *Modern Tantra*.

In traditional Tantric sexuality, the first and primary goal is to experience and thus realize that you and your higher self, your Atman, are one and the same. In fact, all of the koshas, the various bodies, are one and the same. Your mind, body, and spirit are one and the same.

Incredible sexual experiences and totally mind-blowing orgasms pale in significance to the traditional Tantric sexual experience.

And this isn't the ultimate goal; it's just a path to the goal of traditional Tantric sexuality.

In order to achieve this and more, in order to strive to achieve the goals, you have to do the one thing that terrifies most Westerners: give up.

You return to a completely natural existence, if only for a brief time, surrendering to the greater reality that is not hidden by the delicious illusions found in the sensual dance of Maya. But you don't defy her; you surrender to her. You surrender to the Goddess and let her have her way with you. You dance with her along the superstrings of the multidimensions of the universe.

For women, this often results in riding wave after wave of orgasmic bliss. You don't have a mind-blowing orgasm; you become orgasm itself. This is so far beyond the concept of "having" an orgasm (or multiple orgasms) that the very concept becomes meaningless.

For men, surrendering to eternal copulation with the Goddess means you are focusing on her/you and where you can go together. You go beyond what is usually called orgasm, surrendering to the experience, such that the very idea of having an orgasm becomes meaningless. The practice of Tantric sexuality means you will never have to fight off ejaculating what you or your partner consider to be too early because the practice of sex will take you far beyond the idea of orgasm and ejaculation to existing in a state of total bliss. Orgasm? Why waste your time focusing on it when there is so much more?

And what is that "more"? By surrendering to the Goddess, you will return to naturalness and the state of balance and equipoise in which you were always meant to live. You will realize that the Goddess is the godhead, Brahman is the godhead, your higher self is the godhead, and all are one.

Does this mean you are God? Westerners, brought up in de facto Christian cultures, consider this blasphemous. It's more like this. A drop of ocean water partakes of all aspects of the ocean, and yet it is not the ocean. Likewise, you can partake in all aspects of the Divine without being the Divine. Through traditional Tantric sexual practices, you can spread out through all of the universes and experience unity with them all.

Some people think, "Wow! Having sex for hours using Tantra—that sounds incredible." Well, for them, I guess it is. But why limit it to hours when you can experience this constant state of bliss for eons? And when you've experienced this state and realize that the world is wonderful and not a "veil of tears," why not be in the world and transcend it at the same time?

Yes, I know, what I have written here sort of wanders about without being very specific. But how can you describe the color red to someone who has never seen it? How can you describe an orgasm to someone who has never had one? I feel at a loss. My words are so subjective that they become meaningless and sound like I'm crazy.

So rather than try to describe it any further, I'll say this: *Don't take my word for it. Try it yourself and see what happens.*

1. Discuss what you aim to do. Make sure that if you wish to make any limitations, you should both agree to them before you start.
2. Prepare the place where you're going to practice. Make it beautiful! Be sure to have plenty of cool water and perhaps some finger foods. You should also have plenty of high-quality sexual lubricants available. If your agreements include the use of condoms or other barrier methods, have them available.
3. Make yourselves beautiful. Bathe. Cleanse yourself. Shave if need be. Add scented oils if you desire.
4. Come together in your sacred room. Sit and talk with each other—not about the petty cares of the day, which will be forgotten in a day, week, or month, and not about the world and its silly and temporal cares. There will always be time to discuss these things. Instead, talk about each other. Share your hopes and dreams. Reveal your goals. If your partner reveals his or her fears, comfort him or her. Tell your partner how much you love him or her and how much you care.
5. When it is natural to do so, begin to caress and kiss your partner. Surrender. That does not mean giving up your freedom. Rather, it means opening to a vastly greater freedom. Nothing is forbidden. Everything is sacred and beautiful.
6. Increase the intimacy of the touching, kissing, licking, etc., until you are both very aroused.
7. Assume the position for your Tantric experience. Traditionally, this is the yab-yum position (see illustration). The male

sits cross-legged or in the lotus position. The female sits on top of his lap, helping him to insert his lingam into her yoni.[20]

8. Use the alternate breathing and visualization of energy between the two of you as described earlier. Look into each other's eyes. Smile. Think of how lucky you are to be here. Feel the transcendent universal love.

   Note: You may have noticed it is hard—in fact, virtually impossible—to start making the typical thrusting movements used by most Westerners when you're in this position. That's the idea. Using the close physical contact and the raised energy and visualization enhanced by breathwork takes you beyond standard Western practices. Continue in this position for as long as you like.

   There are indicators that things are going correctly. You may feel a need to moan with your exhalations. Your body may have involuntary shaking. This is known as *shaktipat* and means that the kundalini energy is moving through you. Your partner may change in appearance. Your sensation of time and space may change. You may laugh or cry.

   Continue breathing. Continue focusing on what you're doing. Surrender to the experience. Surrender to the God/dess you are with. This is natural and the way sex is actually supposed to be. Feel the energy flow through you and your partner.

   Eventually the experience will end on its own, beautifully, organically. You may wish to share the experience. Do so as best you can, but you should both understand that some things are *ineffable* (impossible to describe).

The yab-yum position can be challenging for some people for many possible reasons. You can use pillows to help support you and ground chairs such as the BackJack (also known as a "meditation chair"). Alternatively, you can modify the position. For example, the male can extend his legs. Or you can use a standard chair that has no arms.

Modify. Experiment. Sacralize. Find balance. Become natural. Extend your limitations. Experience transcendence.

Love.

Yab-Yum

20 Remember, we are each the Goddess and the God. A person of any physical gender can participate as a male or female. This is dealing with energy, not physiological organs!

FIFTEEN

Tantric Sex Rituals

Now that you understand the ideas of Tantric sexuality, we can go on to the structure of some Tantric sex rituals. Although, as I stated earlier, the definition of *ritual* is simply "a repeated action or set of actions," the type of Tantric ritual I'll describe in this chapter involves more than mere repetition. It moves on to having a focus or direction for the performance of such rituals.

In the previous chapter, I briefly described the focus of Tantric sexuality. You may have noticed that it is spiritually and not magickally focused. That is, the goal of Tantric sexuality is spiritual evolution, not merely manifesting a partner, some money, or a trip to Barbados. In my *Modern Magick*, I defined the type of magick for spiritual evolution that helps unite you with the Divine as "white magick." However, this was only to make classification easy. In reality, it's challenging to find strict demarcations between supposedly different kinds of magick, especially since the actual magickal techniques are often the same.

So you could say that Tantric sex rituals are focused toward white magick. Personally, I don't like to describe these rituals that way because when we use the term *magick*, most people think of creating some sort of change in our physical world. Such methods are far more common in Western magickal traditions, although some of the Western practitioners—usually untrained other than through reading books presenting the errors of their authors—often inaccurately attribute such a focus to Tantra. There *may be* common sources, as described in the beginning of this book;

however, any specifics remain conjecture. If you are interested in creating exterior changes using sex magick techniques, my *Modern Sex Magick* may be to your liking. I trace everything back to Western sources and show how it evolved separate from Tantra, although, I repeat, there may be some common sources at the beginning.

So if Tantric sex rituals are not focused on magickal external changes, what are they for? Remember, the traditional Tantra of *Modern Tantra* is based on a legitimately ancient Pagan tradition. Pagan deities that are transcendent and beyond our comprehension are all-powerful. Most of the deities Pagans deal with, though, are not of the transcendent form. The so-called *immanent* deities manifest, communicate with us, and meet us. They are more powerful than us humans, but they are not all-powerful.

The most common form of Wicca today is solitary: people practice by themselves. The most common form of practicing the Wiccan Great Rite, where the God and Goddess make love, is symbolic, not actual. The symbolic Great Rite has become very common and is part of many Wiccan rites.

When I was first brought into Wicca, it was most common to be involved with a group called a coven. The Great Rite was a solemn and special aspect of the liturgy. The high priest and high priestess would perform it on certain special occasions. It was also included as part of an advanced initiation ritual. Some couples would use it for magick. At that time, the symbolic Great Right was even more rarely used than the actual Great Rite.

But why perform the Great Rite at all? The answer comes down to the notion that deities who are non-transcendent have limitations. One such limitation is that they are not physical. That means they can never experience the ecstasy of physical sexuality. By allowing the God and Goddess to temporarily inhabit the bodies of ritualists (through the ritual known as Drawing Down the Moon) who then have spiritualized sexual relations, we humans are giving the gods a great gift that is usually outside of their realm of possibility. In exchange, it is hoped that they will return this great favor with gifts of blessings, favor, good health, well-being, or more specific magickal goals. This was not intended as a payment-for-services bribe. The sharing of pleasure and physical energy with the deities was seen as a free-will offering, a gesture of honoring, and a form of worship of the gods.

In fact, Tantric sex rituals are usually directed toward the worship of deity. This brings up an important concept. In order to worship in other traditions, you do not have to be in love with your robes or candles or prayer shawl. Likewise, you do not have to be in love with your partner to perform Tantric sex rituals. This doesn't mean you shouldn't be or can't be in love with fellow participants, only that it's not necessary.

In later versions of Tantra, as I described in *Modern Magick*, it was illegal to have sex with someone other than your spouse. Therefore, I included a brief section revealing what some later Tantrics did: they performed a temporary marriage ceremony that was both legal and in force for one night. The earlier Tantrics, not limited to the moralisms of later Indian society, didn't worry about this.

The first ritual that I will describe in this chapter traditionally involved choosing partners by chance. If you decide to follow the traditional formula and work in a group that extends beyond your regular partners, I strongly urge you to talk with your regular partner about the nature of the ritual *before* participating. Sexual activity, especially in Western society, has become equated with love, and having sex outside of a monogamous relationship may seriously bother people. Make sure everyone involved is okay with this: and I don't mean someone gritting their teeth and agreeing to it for fear of losing their partner!

In what follows, I'll be sharing two sets of rituals that involve Tantric sexuality. The first, perhaps the best known of Tantric sex rituals (or at least the most discussed), is the *Ritual of the Panchamakara*, the Five Ms. The second section includes multiple forms of rituals that are focused around the worship of Shakti, the primordial goddess who manifests in the form of a woman, as well as of her yoni, the source of all creation. They are called the *Rituals of the Yoni Tantra*.

Note: Some of the following material appeared in a different form in *Modern Magick*.

The Panchamakara (Rite of the Five Ms)

Background

The Sanskrit word *Panchamakara* literally means "five letters" (*Panch* is a form of the word meaning "five," and *makara* means "letter" or "sound"). In this case, the five letters refer to the first letter "M" in five different words. The five Ms in question are as follows:

- Madya (wine)
- Mamsa (meat)
- Matsya (fish)
- Mudra (gesture or parched grain)
- Maithuna (Tantric sexual intercourse)

All five of these items are to be consumed during the ritual. To the best of my knowledge, no authority has ever denied the existence of this ritual. However, the interpretations, meaning, and performance of the ritual vary wildly.

The first interpretation of this ritual is the easiest. Those who practice *Vamamarg* Tantra, the Tantra of the left-hand path, consume these things literally. Right-hand Tantrics, those who follow *Dakshinamarg* Tantra, see these items as symbols and do not take them literally. But in this instance, what are they and why are they important?

These are supposedly five different items that are taboo, or at least taboo under certain conditions. For example, Vedic Hindus are traditionally vegetarian, and consuming wine, meat, and fish are religious taboos. Similarly, sexual activity outside of marriage is a religious taboo. But what about mudra, the making of certain gestures or the consumption of parched grain? Neither of these is religiously taboo.

According to some authorities, madya is a code (using *Sandhya Bhasha*, or twilight language) for the ultimate nectar, *amrita*. Mamsa is our animal nature. During this ritual, we sacrifice our animal nature with the intent of living a more spiritual life. Matsya is universal energy, prana. Mudra is the false ego that should be devoured and thus destroyed. And finally, maithuna is the union of opposites, Shiva and Shakti, male and female energies, manifested within us.

Personally, I think that's sort of stretching to avoid the reality of Tantra being the path of the fall, the understanding that anything can become holy if spiritualized.

Here are some other concepts that have become associated with the five Ms.

Meditation

This right-hand-path interpretation holds that the entire ritual is a form of meditation. Madya is the amrita that results from a special meditative position called the *Khechari mudra*. This involves curling your tongue backward so that the tip touches the soft palate of the top of the mouth. Some people stretch out the muscle under the tongue (or sever it) so the tongue can be inserted up into the nasopharynx. Mamsa is simply the meat or flesh that makes up the tongue. Another interpretation sees this as representing the control of speech, especially the inner talk that continually goes on in our heads. Matsya is not one fish, but two, the Ida and Pingala nadis. Mudra represents hand positions to help the flow of kundalini energy. Another version has the mudras forming a type of sanctuary wherein you keep good, spiritual people and avoid negative people. In this case, it's referring to positive spiritual thoughts as opposed to focusing on negativity. And finally, maithuna is simply the union of kundalini Shakti (female) energy with the physical body of Shiva (masculine energy). So the entire rite is just a form of meditation. Alternatively, it is the linking of your mind with that of the godhead so you can realize your Atman, or higher self.

Ayurveda

The entire discussion of traditional Tantric healing, including Ayurveda, is far too complex to be covered in this book. One of the theoretical principles that I chose to omit was that of the *dhatus*, the seven fundamental principles that support the body. There is no direct association with groupings like them in Western science. For example, one grouping incorporates some of the body's "fluids," including muscles, bones and bone marrow, and fat. Since there are only five Ms and there are seven dhatus, some of the dhatus have two per M, while others are singular. This makes the entire ritual nothing more than a metaphor concerning the body's health. It seems to me like the creators of this interpretation were overreaching the evidence to support their predetermined ideas.

Five Elements

In this interpretation, each M represents one of the five elements. Madya (wine) can excite you, so it is the element of fire. This elemental fire brings joy and dispels all the sorrows of humanity. Mamsa (meat) can nourish and bring strength. The energy that brings strength is prana, which can be triggered by breathwork, so this is representative of the element of air. Matsya (fish), of course, represents water. Mudra, using the meaning that it is grain, represents the element of earth. Finally, maithuna, spiritualized sexuality, is the source of creation and is therefore the element of ether. This, in my opinion, is an interpretation of the ritual based on developing spirituality through knowledge and understanding.

The Tattvas

While I feel it is important to understand that a concept of *Modern Tantra* is to move beyond constant study and the memorization of correspondences, that doesn't mean you should ignore them. Rather, it means that they should be understood on a deep level and internalized so you can actually forget about lists and work with the concepts. Traditional Tantra is a path of action and experience, not just philosophy and theorizing.

Still, some people find it easier to go from observing everything and then breaking it down through experience into its component parts, while others prefer having an intellectual understanding of the parts first. From there, they move on to get the big picture. To those of the latter type, this next set of correspondences is designed to offer guidance.

Although I have not seen lists other than the ones given here, it seems obvious to me that the five Ms can easily be associated with other fivefold concepts, one of which would be the tattvas, discussed earlier.

The Koshas

The second of these two lists of correspondences is that of the five bodies, or koshas.

In the *Mahanirvana Tantra*, the classic Tantric text, it states that without the practice of the Panchamakara ritual, worship of Shakti is impossible. According to translator and commentator Sir John Woodroffe, this is because in this ritual she is worshiped in her most primal form, as the creatrix or Great Mother of all, and as the universe itself. That is the way she should be honored.

Preparation

Traditionally, the ritual is planned to start at midnight, the twilight between one day and the next. The area for the ritual is cleaned, then festooned around the edges with beautiful pillows, candles, tables, incense, oils, etc., leaving the center of the chakra open. Remember, make this sacred temple as beautiful as possible. In the east of the chakra, set up a Tantric altar. Having music playing can also help set the mood. You may want to assign someone to run your music system. If possible, have a small fire in a havan kund either in the center of the room or near the altar.

M	Translation	Element	Tattva	Symbol
Madya	Wine	Fire	Tejas	Red Triangle
Mamsa	Meat	Air	Vayu	Blue Circle
Matsya	Fish	Water	Apas	Silver Crescent
Mudra	Gesture	Earth	Prithivi	Yellow Square
Maithuna	Intercourse	Ether	Akasha	Black Egg

The Tattvas

M	Translation	Element	Kosha	Body of...
Madya	Wine	Fire	Manomaya	Mind
Mamsa	Meat	Air	Vijnamaya	Intellect
Matsya	Fish	Water	Pranamaya	Energy
Mudra	Gesture	Earth	Annamaya	Physicality
Maithuna	Intercourse	Ether	Anandamaya	Bliss

The Koshas

In a separate room, make food preparations. Although it was traditional for the women to prepare foods, I find this attitude quite outdated. Everyone should participate in the cleaning, the layout of the chakra, and the preparation of foods.

The preparation of the foods should contain two types of items: ritual foods and foods for energy and sustenance. The energy foods should include fruits, vegetables, crackers, cheese, candy, etc., all cut into small pieces. There should also be carafes of cool, fresh water and tea. Include what your group thinks is appropriate.

The ritual foods are outlined in two places. First, if you go back to other sections of this book, you will see a description of foods that are appropriate to offer to the deities on the altar. Second would be the foods of the ritual: wine, meat and fish. Although you could use precooked meat such as smoked ham or turkey, and prepared fish such as smoked salmon, I have found that the work you do preparing for the ritual can be as spiritually valuable as any part of the ritual. So grilling or roasting your fish and meat is appropriate. Cut them into bite-size pieces.

Be sure to have enough wine for all participants. I would suggest having either plastic or, preferably, metal wine glasses available for drinking. Accidentally dropped glass or ceramic can easily break and lead to cut feet.

Once everything is ready, the men and women separate into two different rooms or areas. The number of men and women is traditionally equal.[21] However, you should adapt the ritual to fit your particular situation.

Separately, the men and women should shower or bathe, shave, brush teeth, etc., then return to their preparation room to prepare for the ritual. There are two options at this point. First, it is, of course, common for Tantrics to participate in rituals digambara. In this case, the only things they would wear would be makeup, jewelry, body paints, subtle perfumes or oils, and perhaps some scarves. All of the women would wear simple, soft-soled shoes that can be easily identified.[22] Alternatively, everyone could wear loose and appropriate items. For example, the men could wear large peasant shirts and drawstring pants, while the women could wear belly-dance-style clothes. If desired, the clothes can be transparent or sheer.

At the stroke of midnight, the ritual begins. The people come in and are marked on their arms and foreheads with ash or colored powder, as described previously. Then the opening of the ritual begins.

The Ritual

Leader: **Let the laboratory be banished.**

People near each quarter banish it using the thunderbolt mantra, noisemakers (cymbals or drums) or claps, going east-south-west-north. This is followed by the cross-quarters, starting at the southeast, then southwest, northwest, and northeast. Then above and below. Up until this time, all members are in street clothes.

Leader: ***Svaha!* I salute the line of innumerable Tantrics and cast the circle of semen glow. May the circle be intact and the peace of Om Shiva Shakti dwell herein. Let us consecrate ourselves to the work.**

Leader: **All honor to the Lord and Lady residing in my heart.**

All: Put hands on their hearts and say: **Om.**

21 Although this is written from the historical heterosexual (or "heteronormative") viewpoint, please remember that everyone has both the Goddess and the God within. This ritual can—and should!—be modified to fit pair-bonded couples, polyamorous people, gays, lesbians, or bisexual groups. *Modern Tantra* is about personal spiritual development, not dated rules set in stone thousands of years ago.

22 Traditionally, this could instead be a type of short shirt or vest called a *choli,* but among Westerners, shoes are going to be much easier to obtain.

Leader: **All honor to the Lord and Lady residing in the crown of my head.**

All: Put hands on the crowns of their heads and say: **Om.**

Leader: **All honor to the Lord and Lady residing in the top of the forehead.**

All: Put hands on their hairlines and say: **Om.**

Leader: **All honor to the Lord and Lady residing in the armor.**

All: Put hands on their upper chests and say: **Om.**

Leader: **All honor to the Lord and Lady residing in the three eyes.**

All: Put hands on their eyes, also covering the third eye, and say: **Om.**

Leader: **All honor to the Lord and Lady residing in the lingam and yoni.**

All: Put hands on their lingam or yoni and say: **Om.**

Leader: **Now that we have again dedicated ourselves to the path, let us honor the God and Goddess in our chakra of light, life, freedom, and love.** ***Svecchachara!***

All: *Svecchachara!*

With the leader beginning, each person comes up to the main altar and performs aarti with the flame and bell, making three large clockwise circles in front of the deities on the altar as they ring the bell. Each person may also recite prayers and give appropriate gifts to the deities.

When each person finishes at the altar, the men should sit near the rim of the circle. The women should walk or dance in a clockwise manner around the circle. They may laugh, talk, sing, or whatever they desire. The men may not use their hands in any way. The women may feed the men candy or fruit, kiss them, caress them, give them water to drink, but the men may not use their hands. This usually leads to much laughter and frivolity, a pleasant gift of the gods of Tantra. The women should not stay too long with any one man. Teaming up is fine.

This can last for as long as you like, although the smaller the number of participants, the shorter it will be. Usually there is a minimum of a half hour. Then each woman should remove one of her shoes and place it in the center of the area. Other articles may be used; however, each woman should be able to easily identify it as her own, and all of the women should put in the same type of object—i.e., one should not put in a shoe if all the others are going to put in earrings. When doing this, the women should form a small circle about their collection of items so the men will have difficulty seeing which woman put in what. Then all the items should be mixed. When finished, the women should find places to sit by the edge of the circle while the men get up.

Now that the women have had their fun, it is the men's turn. They also go around the circle feeding the women and giving them kisses and caresses or water to drink. When this is finished, the men go to the center of the circle and face out while holding hands. One woman claps her hands while the men walk in a circle clockwise around the items left by the women. When the clapping stops, each man reaches behind himself and without looking grabs one item from the collection.

Next, the men again go around the circle. This time their goal is to determine whose item they possess. The women may playfully try to hide the fact that an item belongs to them, and the men may playfully try to discover if an item belongs to a particular woman. This can be especially fun if the item is a woman's bra or panties. But there should be no force or violence. Finally, when the man discovers whom the item belongs to, he should sit to her right.

Thus are the couples formed. They should now, as pairs, feed each other, talk, joke and laugh, and eventually kiss gently and lovingly, though not very passionately.

Eventually, the passion of the kisses and caresses (and use of erotic toys, if desired) may increase. If still wearing clothes, they may gradually come off until all are digambara.

Stare into each other's eyes and synchronize your breathing. You are God/dess. Your partner is God/dess. All are God/dess.

Each woman gets up and takes some of the pieces of ritual meat from the altar and charges it by making a circle around it three times with a flame or a stick of incense. Then she puts some into the fire, shouting ***Svaha!*** She returns to her partner, sits at his left, and feeds both of them some meat.

Each man gets up and takes some of the wine into a cup and charges it by making a circle around it three times with a flame or a stick of incense. Then he puts some into the fire, shouting ***Svaha!*** He returns to his partner, sits at her right, and gives both of them some wine to drink.

Each woman gets up and takes some of the pieces of ritual fish from the altar and charges it by making a circle around it three times with a flame or a stick of incense. Then she puts some into the fire, shouting ***Svaha!*** She returns to her partner, sits at his left, and feeds both of them some fish.

Each man gets up and takes some of the parched grain in his hand and charges it by making a circle around it three times with a flame or a stick of incense. Then he puts some into the fire, shouting ***Svaha!*** He returns to his partner, sits at her right, and feeds both of them some grain.

Recalling the associations given previously, consider that the food and wine, including ones that are not traditionally consumed, have become sanctified by the rite. They are also representative of the elements, indicating that within each of you are all the powers of creation, as well as those of Shiva and Shakti, the God and Goddess.

Or rather, you have everything within you except the uniting of your energies. Focus on how, more than anything in the universe, you want—*need!*—to combine those energies. Attune your breathing. Share your partner's need for you. Touch, caress, kiss, stimulate; allow the energy to rise. There is nothing specific you have to do. It's all completely natural.

The activities should become increasingly erotic until *maithuna*, ritualized intercourse, becomes inevitable. Each couple should take a comfortable position. Although the yab-yum is traditional, it is not required.

Once intercourse has begun, do not thrust. Instead, kiss and caress. Use your PC muscle to make the lingam throb or the yoni repeatedly clutch the lingam. Feel your energy merge. Use alternate breathing, as previously described, continuing until a change of consciousness occurs. At that point, the couple should do as the gods direct.

When finished, each couple may sleep or rest together. If appropriate, they may assist other couples. When the first light of dawn is seen, the chakra is banished again. Then everyone should return to the dressing rooms, prepare for the external world, and return to their homes.

Notes on This ritual

1. It should start at midnight and end at daybreak.
2. If you pick someone who is not your regular partner for the rite, you should *not* seek them out for future sexual encounters outside of ritual unless (a) you are both unattached or (b) you are both completely honest with your regular partners and they freely give you permission to have a relationship of that kind.
3. Traditionally, there may be extra women in the circle. They may guide things (one of them may be the woman who claps to keep time for the men) and also aid the couples by bringing them food, drink, and erotic toys. They may also caress and kiss the couples while the couples are engaged in intercourse. At the beginning of the ritual they are treated like the other women as the men go around the circle, feeding the women and playing with them. Non-traditionally, I see no reason why men cannot do this if there are more men than women available for the ritual.
4. The method of picking partners given here is a traditional one. Another way is to have the women form a circle inside the circle formed by the men. Then one woman claps while the circles move in opposite directions—the women move clockwise and the men move counterclockwise, or vice versa. When the clapping stops, each person becomes a couple with the member of the opposite sex nearest him or her. Obviously, this can be adjusted for rituals where members are not exclusively heterosexual.
5. Although this is based on an ancient Tantric ritual, not all Tantrics practice it. Similarly, most Protestants don't worship in the same way Catholics do. So if someone tells you that they are a Tantric and they don't do that sort of ritual, it may be true. But… find out the Tantric tradition they belong to and who initiated them into Tantra. Chances are they speak with little knowledge.
6. There are many other traditions that your research may lead you to adopt. Besides this simplified description, there are other orders of ritual actions and the potential of other ritual anointings as well as gifting each other with garlands of red and orange flowers. The ritual described here is not set in stone. It is designed to be modified as you and your partners see fit.
7. Worshiping and honoring Shiva and Shakti does *not* require transmission of disease. People should discuss safer sex practices that will be used *before* the ritual begins. Anyone with any type of communicable disease, even a minor cold, should inform everyone before the beginning of the ritual to give members the opportunity to determine if they wish to work with that person. Transparency and honesty are vital within *Modern Tantra* practices.

The Rituals of the Yoni Tantra

Background

The *Yoni Tantra* is a startlingly explicit Tantric text. It dates back to the sixteenth century. Remember, however, that Tantra has always been an oral tradition, so this date is only that of the first *written* version of this short document. It, or its sources, is probably much older. It first appeared in writing in the area called Bengal in the northeast area of the Indian subcontinent.

The text has several aspects. It loosely describes the nature of a ritual, or puja, dedicated to the honoring of the Goddess who manifests as a woman's yoni. While this may seem odd to modern Westerners, the image of the yoni, sometimes called a *vesica piscis*, is common in Western mystical iconography.

It may simply be that artists throughout history have been attracted to the shape, or perhaps they felt that the joining of male and female, represented by two overlapping circles, would result in a shape indicating balance and harmony. The white area in the image here shows how this could develop. But I find this speculative at best and highly unlikely.

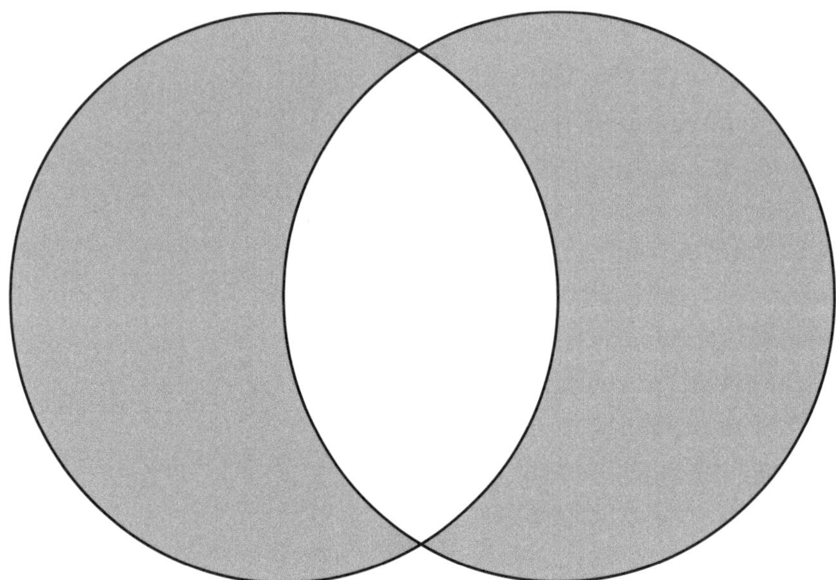

The Vesica Piscis, Formed by Two Overlapping Circles

There are all sorts of rules given for this ritual. For example, the woman can be of any age, from first menstruation to sixty years of age. While when this was written it was not uncommon for women to marry by first menstruation, and today young women are menstruating at earlier ages, it is the policy of NAMASTE and of the *Modern Tantra* tradition not to perform any of this work with any man or woman under the legal age of adulthood in the local jurisdiction. Further, even if they are legally of age, if it is the judgment of the leaders of the local chakra that they are not mature adults, they are not allowed to participate.

Other rules include that there should never be an incestuous maithuna. Women of high and low classes can participate. They may be married or unmarried, indicating acceptance of extramarital sex. This is remarkable considering that Hindu laws of this period heavily punished a woman for doing this, again showing how transgressive Tantra was … and is.

But perhaps the most radical, disruptive, and transgressive aspect of the *Yoni Tantra* is something called the *yoni tattva*. The yoni tattva was a Eucharistic substance, the most important ingredients being menstrual blood and semen.

In his informed introduction to his translation of the *Yoni Tantra*, Michael Magee reports that the yoni tattva was first mentioned in the West by Arthur Avalon (Sir John Woodroffe) in *Hymn to Kali* (1913). However, he considered this so sensitive that he didn't translate that section. It's also hinted at by Elizabeth Sharpe in her strange book that is part fact, part fiction, *The Secrets of a Kaula Circle* (1936). In that book, by the way, she gives a bizarre and highly slanted interpretation of a thinly disguised ritual led by Aleister Crowley and negatively compares it to actual Tantric rites.

HH Shri Paramahamsha Mahendranath (Dadaji) wrote an article in the 1970s for a now-defunct magazine in India, *Values* (vol. XIX, no. 5), called "The Occult World of a Tantrik Guru." In it, he discusses the yoni tattva quite plainly. This is one of the first real discussions of it. In 1973, Kenneth Grant also described it in his book *Aleister Crowley and the Hidden God*.

Although we live in an age in which oral sex has become popular and the consumption of sperm is not uncommon, the consumption of menstrual blood seems to retain an ick factor. And yet certain groups use the practice of giving oral sex to a menstruating woman as a rite of passage. These are usually groups trying to show their macho manliness, such as circles within the military, and among those who are trying to show how they are outside of the norm. An example of this is the practice by members of the Hells Angels Motorcycle Club as reported by Hunter S. Thompson. They call it "earning your red wings."

The *Yoni Tantra* makes very clear that worshipers should mix sperm with menstrual blood in water and then "sip" this amrita. This is said to be nourishing. Note, however, that it does not say *how much* sperm and blood should be in the water. As a comparison, the cakes of light used as Eucharistic wafers in Thelemic masses used to include menstrual blood and sperm in their recipe. I say "used to," as I have heard conflicting reports as to whether this practice is continued today, ranging from "no," to "just a drop of each," to "of course it is." It's possible, then, that just a drop of sperm and blood could be used in a large container of water or wine. Although the physical properties of these fluids could become so diluted as to be practically nonexistent, the energetic properties would infuse the water with their spiritual power.

The *Yoni Tantra* seems to be an addition to the *Panchamakara*, stating that doing the work of the five Ms is very important. The blood and sperm of the yoni tattva can be added in small amounts to the wine of the five Ms. This implies a Panchamakara practice that is far less structured than described previously.

NAMASTE created some rituals based on the *Yoni Tantra*, and they were incorporated into the practices of *Modern Tantra*. The *Yoni Tantra* itself does not have a step-by-step format for the ritual it describes, so the creation of more formal rituals based on the concepts presented in the *Yoni Tantra* is reasonable for modern Western practitioners. The following are versions of those rituals. Again, these are not unchanging laws! If you feel that something should be added or altered, try it out.

The Basic Yoni Puja for Couples

Unlike the Panchamakara rite (see chapter 15), this ritual requires one of the participants to be a physical woman. Prepare for the ritual as with the Panchamakara. Clean and adorn the area and yourselves. The only difference is that there should be a chair in the center of the area. Also, from the beginning, both celebrants should be digambara.

Enter the ritual area and purify yourselves with the traditional markings of ash or colored powder. Worship the deities of the chakra using fire and vibration (aarti).

The woman begins by honoring the man (or other woman), first as a manifestation of Shiva, then as Shiva himself. Having images of Shiva within the chakra—paintings, drawings, murthis, etc.—can help her transfer the image to her partner. As he becomes Shiva to her, she says:[23]

Salutations to Shiva!
Lord of all beings and gods,
From whose head is born the
waves of the Ganga[24]
And who wears the silvery
crescent of the moon as a crown,
Shiva, who is the eternally
benevolent one.

Salutations to Shiva!
Whose clothes are the deep blue
color of the precious lotus,
Showing how we all may rise
to the thousand-petaled wheel.[25]
You ride on Nandi, the bull,[26]
as you travel,
Revealing your inexorable,
inevitable strength.
Shiva, who loves to dance,[27] and
who grants favors when he does.

Salutations to Shiva!
With the sun, the moon,
and fire in your eyes.[28]
You dispel darkness[29] and defeat
oppressors[30] at every turn.
Your energy shines blindingly,
like the brightest gem.
You wear the translucent hood
crowning you king of all serpents.[31]
Shiva, who holds the keys to
magick in his hands.

Salutations to Shiva!
The amrita flows from your hands.[32]
Your devotees drink and it destroys
all sorrows.
You share your mastery of Tantra
and of the sun and moon[33]
So that all may achieve yoga[34] with you.
Shiva, who is the ultimate teacher,
grant me your love.

She kneels in front of Shiva and kisses both of his feet. Shiva helps her to rise and guides her to the chair where she sits. Then Shiva begins by honoring her, first as a manifestation of Shakti, then as Shakti herself. As she becomes Shakti to his Shiva, he says:

Salutations to Shakti!
You who are the ultimate source of all.[35]
From you flow the yugas[36]
and the kalas.[37]
From you flow the energies
that underlie existence.[38]
Without you I am but a corpse,[39]
Shakti, who is the primordial goddess.

---

23 This devotional invocation by the author is very loosely based on the *Shivashtakam* by Sri Chaitanya Mahaprabhu (1486–1534).

24 The Ganges River.

25 The kundalini energy rising to the crown chakra.

26 Nandi is the name of the bull who is Shiva's vehicle.

27 Shiva Nataraja.

28 Elements of the primordial chakras located at the genitals, heart, and crown.

29 Ignorance; plus, Shiva is the lord of gurus, and *guru* is Sanskrit for "breaker of darkness."

30 The kleshas.

31 Lord of kundalini energy.

32 Energy flows out of the chakras in his palms.

33 Hat ha, sun, and moon; hence, hatha yoga.

34 Union.

35 Shakti Maa, the mother of all.

36 Eons of time.

37 Sanskrit for "blackness" and "time."

38 Prana.

39 Shabda.

Salutations to Shakti!
You cause the entire universe to
vibrate with your beauty.
You disguise yourself to the unwise[40]
through maya.[41]
You reveal yourself to the vira[42]
with blinding splendor.[43]
You give courage to the fearful
and strength to the weak,
Yet you are loving and consoling[44]
as well as fearless and fearsome,[45]
Shakti, who is the Divine Mother.

Salutations to Shakti!
Your energy gives us shivers of bhoga.[46]
By looking at your yoni,
my lingam springs to strength,
Aching to fulfill its need within
your flowing, sacred springs.[47]
The scent of your yoni is like the
richest oils and perfumes,
Enchanting the universe with
your magickal musk.
Shakti, who is every goddess and
the only goddess.

40 Actually *pashu*, a person caught in his lower, animal nature.

41 The illusion that the universe is not made of energy.

42 Sanskrit for "hero," the type of person who should follow Tantra.

43 The explosion of light that occurs when the kundalini fills the crown chakra.

44 Qualities of her manifestation as Parvati.

45 Qualities of her manifestation as Kali.

46 Sensual enjoyment.

47 Besides the obvious sexual connotation, this also inspires the flow of kundalini.

Salutations to Shakti!
Your divinity earns devotion from all,
even the gods themselves.
Staring at your yoni is worship, the only
worship any need to do.[48]
Honoring your yoni is the goal of
any who seek nirvana.
Worshiping your yoni removes crore[49]
lifetimes of karma.
Shakti, who is the goal of all worship,
and before whom all things bow.

The next part of the ritual is both simple and complex. If Shakti, sitting in the chair, has not spread her legs so her cosmic yoni is visible, she does so now. Shiva meditates upon the beauty and power of her yoni. He should spend ten minutes or more meditating on her yoni, being amazed at it, marveling, seeing it as the source of all things. He may also ask for favors or gifts from Shakti.

This practice may seem easy, but it is a bit more complex than it sounds. During this time it is up to the woman to maintain herself as Shakti. She needs to *be* Shakti, holding herself as the goddess for the entire ritual. Similarly, it is up to the man to maintain himself as Shiva, thinking as Shiva, acting as Shiva, being Shiva. Holding these forms can be challenging, but with practice it will soon become easier and then become natural.

When he is finished, he kneels before Shakti and kisses both her feet. She places her hands on his head and gives him a blessing. What blessing? Allow Shakti to speak through you and say what you feel. Let her give the blessing through you.

48 According to the *Yoni Tantra*.

49 Sanskrit: ten million.

Both participants stand, look into each other's eyes, hug[50] each other, and kiss. Together they say: **I return now to who I am.**

Then they banish the chakra.

....

In some Tantric books, it says that the ideal girl for this type of ritual is sixteen years old. When reading this, many people today were offended by this, especially those in modern Western cultures. However, this was twilight language. It actually means a woman who is sixteen *days* into her menstrual cycle. That is, she is menstruating. This is highly valuable for the creation of the yoni tattva, but it is not necessary for this version of the ritual.

Sometimes people do not have partners but still want to participate in this ritual. One person, male or female, can do this using just visualization. This can be aided by using a murthi of Shakti as a focal point of the ritual.

The Intermediate Yoni Puja for Couples

This is identical to the basic form of this ritual until you get to the part where Shiva meditates on Shakti's yoni. In this version, Shiva worships the cosmic yoni in a more active way. She slides to the front of the chair, with her legs to the sides. He pours the elements, represented by the fluids listed in the chart, over her yoni.

Note that the oil should be edible, such as high-quality olive oil. A large, wide-mouthed container, under the front of the chair, collects the fluids now energized by the contact with the cosmic yoni of Shakti. If she is a young girl of sixteen (i.e., a woman who is menstruating), it is likely that some of her sacred blood will join the mixture. With such a "girl," this is also known as the secret meaning of the *Kumari Puja*.

Shiva should spend ten minutes or more meditating on her yoni, being amazed by it, marveling, seeing it as the source of all things. He may also ask for favors or gifts from Shakti.

The fluids are blended and a few drops of this highly charged magickal fluid are added to water or wine. This is consumed by both Shiva and Shakti.

When finished, Shiva kneels before Shakti and kisses both her feet. She places her hands on his head and blesses him. What blessing? Allow Shakti to speak through you and say what you feel. Let her give the blessing through you.

Both participants stand, look into each other's eyes, hug each other, and kiss. Together they say: **I return now to who I am.**

Then they banish the chakra.

The Advanced Yoni Puja for Couples

Getting a blessing from the God or Goddess is incredible. Giving a blessing to the God or Goddess and achieving his or her gratitude is unbelievable. And when the blessing you give is one of pleasure, words cannot describe the possible results.

In this advanced version, the ritual begins as in the intermediate version. In addition to the chair, there should be a mat or pad for the floor.

---

50 This should be a full "Tantric hug." A Tantric hug is the opposite of the typical Western hug known as a "ladder hug" or an "A-frame hug." This typical Western hug does not allow the chakras to contact each other. Instead, generally only the upper part of the chest and shoulders come into contact, allowing everything below the upper chest to have distance from the other person. From the side, these hugs look like an A-frame house or ladder, a capital A without the horizontal bar. With a Tantric hug, both people move into each other, making body contact from nipples to knees. All of the chakras align and link with the partner's chakras thanks to this intimate, personal space-breaking contact. Take a few moments to silently *conspire* (from the Latin meaning "breathe together") about the power of the ritual.

Fluid	Element	Fluid	Element
Yogurt	Earth	Milk	Air
Water	Water	Oil	Ether or Spirit
Honey	Fire	—	—

Fluids Represented as Elements in the Intermediate Yoni Puja

The ritual continues through the offering of the five elements to the cosmic yoni of Shakti. Afterward, Shiva assists her in standing, moves the chair away, and spreads the pad or blankets on the floor in the center of the chakra.

He faces her and draws her to him. He places his lingam in the Goddess's hand. They kiss, caress, and continue as Goddess and God, Shakti and Shiva, pleasuring each other. The passion should rise until it is almost beyond human comprehension. Eventually they lie down on the mat.

Note: If you have read books on Tantric sex, you have probably heard that there should be little physical motion. The *Yoni Tantra* does not advise this for the ritual.

At this point, Shiva inserts his lingam into Shakti's yoni. When gods unite, fireworks ensue! According to the *Yoni Tantra*, they should have "vigorous intercourse." He should eventually ejaculate within her.

Traditionally, the combined fluids were collected from her yoni on a large leaf from a banana plant. However, we have found it easier to bring back the chair, have her sit on it, and allow gravity to pull the mingled fluids, called *maharasa* (Sanskrit for "great fluid"), into the container placed below.

The fluids are blended and a few drops of this highly charged magickal fluid are added to water or wine. Both Shiva and Shakti consume this.

When finished, Shiva kneels before Shakti and kisses both her feet. She places her hands on his head and blesses him. What blessing? Allow Shakti to speak through you and say what you feel. Let her give the blessing through you.

Both participants stand, look into each other's eyes, hug each other, and kiss. Together they say: **I return now to who I am.**

Then they banish the chakra.

The Basic Yoni Puja for Groups

This follows the same pattern as this ritual for a couple. One woman is chosen to act as Shakti. Everyone else will manifest as Shiva. One person acts as Shiva during the invocation. At the conclusion of the invocation, he leads her to the chair.

Each person, one at a time, will have the honor of worshiping and honoring the cosmic yoni of Shakti. The amount of time each person spends in worship is determined by the number of people participating in the ritual. The puja shouldn't last more than an hour. One by one, each person meditates on the beauty and power of Shakti's yoni. At the end of their meditation, each person kisses her feet. She puts her hands on their heads and blesses them as she sees fit.

When everyone has finished, the person who acted as Shiva during the invocation stands in front of her and helps her to rise. They look into each other's eyes, hug each other, and kiss. Together they say: **I return now to who I am.**

Then banish the chakra.

If there are too many people to worship/honor/meditate upon Shakti's yoni in a timely manner, each person should bring a gift of fresh fruit or candy. They should place it on a plate in front of Shakti, then kneel and kiss her feet. The ritual continues as before. At the end of the ritual, the energized foods are passed out to all participants of the ritual.

The Intermediate Yoni Puja for Groups, Version 1

This follows the same pattern as this ritual for a couple with the modifications for the basic ritual just described. At the conclusion, the elements are mixed and some of the mixture is placed in water or wine. Some chakras prefer to use fruit juice, although it has been claimed that the acidity of some fruit juices can mute the effects of the spiritualized and empowered elements.

The Intermediate Yoni Puja for Groups, Version 2

This follows the same pattern as the Intermediate Yoni Puja for Groups, Version 1. However, after the libation of the yoni with the elements, each participant may give a special blessing to the Shakti's yoni. This may include stroking with feathers, fingers, licking and sucking, chanting, breathing, etc.

In larger groups, there may not be time for this, so each person may give a piece of fruit or candy to the Goddess. After everyone drinks of the wine or water empowered by the sacralized elements, the fruit and candy are passed around to all participants and consumed.

The Advanced Yoni Puja for Groups

This follows the same pattern as the Intermediate Yoni Puja, Version 1, combined with the Advanced Yoni Puja for Couples. The difference in preparation is that pads, mats, or blankets are not limited to the center for Shakti. They also are spread around the circumference of the chakra, one for each couple.

As in the Advanced Yoni Puja for Couples, after all have made the libation of the five elements to the Shakti's yoni, the person who functioned as Shiva comes back to the center and removes the chair. At the same time, the other couples go to the edge of the chakra. Pairs may have been chosen in advance or by the method described in the Rite of the Five Ms (the Panchamakara).

Each Shiva faces his Shakti and draws her to him. He places his lingam in the Goddess's hand. They kiss, caress, and continue as God and Goddess, Shiva and Shakti, pleasuring each other. The passion should rise until it is almost beyond human comprehension. Eventually they lie down on the mat.

Note that although the Shiva and Shakti in the center of the room will need to have at least one woman as Shakti, this is not necessary for the other ritualists. Everyone can manifest the Shiva or Shakti energy, but a born woman (sometimes called a "cis woman") and born man are required to produce the yoni tattva. You may need to adjust the descriptions to meet the needs of the genders of the people involved.

At this point, the Shivas insert their lingams into the Shaktis' yonis. When gods unite, fireworks ensue! According to the *Yoni Tattva*, they should have "vigorous intercourse." Eventually the Shivas will ejaculate within the Shaktis, hopefully after she has had one or more of her own releases.

While the Shakti in the center of the room remains on her back to hold in the *maharasa*, one member of each of the couples, either Shiva or Shakti, collects a small amount of his or her own *maharasa* and anoints the yoni of the Shakti in the center of the room with the magickally charged and spiritualized fluid. When all have finished, the central Shakti again sits on her chair and allows gravity to pull the *maharasa* from within her into the container placed below. In this way, the energy of all the participants is transferred to the mingled fluids of the Shakti and infuses the elements.

The fluids are blended and a few drops of this highly charged magickal fluid are added to water or wine. All participants consume this.

When finished, each Shiva kneels before his Shakti and kisses both her feet. She places her hands on his head and blesses him. What blessing? Allow Shakti to speak through you and say what you feel. Let the Goddess give the blessing through you.

All participants stand, look into each other's eyes, hug each other, and kiss. Together they say: **I return now to who I am.**

Then banish the chakra.

....

Finally, I want to repeat this note: worshiping and honoring Shiva and Shakti does *not* require transmission of disease. People should discuss safer sex practices that will be used *before* the ritual begins. Anyone with any type of communicable disease, even a minor cold, should inform everyone before the beginning of the ritual to give members the opportunity to determine if they wish to work with that person. Transparency and honesty are vital within *Modern Tantra* practices.

The End of the Beginning

I've already used this expression once in relation to the knowledge of the Sri Yantra. My purpose there was to indicate that what I've presented here is just the beginning of understanding the depth of that image. Here, I'm using the expression to show that the concepts in this book are just the beginning of an exciting ancient Pagan path. Although you have now reached the end of this book, you have not reached the end of *Modern Tantra*. I hope you will use the concepts and ideas presented here as a guide. You can take the information and add it to what you're doing. You can change it all you want. Of course, if you change it, you won't be doing *Modern Tantra*; you'll be doing something else, something new that's powerful and meaningful for you. That's exciting, too.

My hope is that you'll take the information here and use it to start your own *Modern Tantra* chakra, a Pagan system that truly has ties going back thousands of years. Then, instead of just changing it, I hope you'll *add* to it. Add things and correct things based on your studies. Add things based on your own experiences.

It is not my goal to have this book become a Tantric Bible, where you must obey what is written or be punished. Rather, I hope you see it as a telescope.

When you look at the night skies through a telescope, you're seeing the light that the stars emitted millions and tens of millions of years ago and more. You're seeing the past. And yet our desire to visit the Moon and Mars and all the galaxies is an indication of our drive for the future.

A telescope allows you to see into the past, live in the present, and strive for a better future, a future filled with hope, love, adventure, science, knowledge, wisdom, health, and spirituality.

Modern Tantra is one spiritual path out of many. If understanding the ideas, using the techniques, and bringing this new and ancient Paganism with roots in the ancient Indus Valley has helped you achieve any of these goals, it will have served its purpose.

Namaste!

(That which is of the gods in me
recognizes and honors that which
is of the gods in you.)

Namaste

APPENDIX ONE: A DEFINITION OF TANTRA

There have been many attempts to define Tantra. One of the problems with doing so is that the exact translation of the term is debatable. Another problem is that because Tantra has existed for thousands of years, the meaning of Tantra has evolved. Today, the term *Tantra* is often used as a catchword for many things that have little or no relation to any traditional Tantric practices.

In their book *Tantra for Erotic Empowerment*, Mark A. Michaels and Patricia Johnson give the following explanation. I think it is good in that, following the very nature of Tantra, it is expansive rather than limiting, explaining the direction of Tantra rather than being dogmatic. The writers have been kind enough to give their permission for this to appear here. I have changed only the order (I have placed their information on what is *not* Tantra first) and the format.

Tantra Defined

By Mark A. Michaels (Swami Umeshanand Saraswati)
and Patricia Johnson (Devi Veenanand)

Tantra is not:

Tantra is not sacred sexuality, although it may include sexual practices among many uses of the body as a tool for spiritual development.

Tantra is not a set of techniques for better sex. Increased pleasure, deeper intimacy, and new lovemaking skills are often the by-products of the practices, and many people are drawn to Tantra out of an interest in developing these abilities. Such goals are valid, but it is unlikely that they will be attained until they are discarded.

Tantra is not psychotherapy, although many practices may have psychological benefits. Some modern teachers use 1960s-era emotional release techniques, which are of questionable efficacy and are potentially dangerous. They have nothing to do with traditional Tantra.

Tantra is not an easy fix for personal or relationship problems. Partnered practice can deepen intimacy, but it can also magnify existing tensions. Similarly, solo practice—particularly meditation—may ease some personal problems, but not always. If the psychological or interpersonal issues are serious, they should be addressed with a trained therapist.

Tantra is not for the faint-hearted, the ungrounded, or the emotionally fragile. We all have these qualities in some respects at some times, but if you feel you are not fearless enough to practice Tantra, there are many other approaches that may serve you better. Whatever path you choose, it is best to make the choice with as much self-awareness as possible.

Tantra is not a healing modality, although practicing can significantly benefit both physical and emotional health.

Tantra is not a religion in the conventional Western sense; however, it has helped shape both Tibetan Buddhism and many branches of Hinduism. Tantric ideas can be found in most of the world's religions.

Tantra is not magic in the popular sense—mere trickery or spellcasting—but many Tantric texts include recipes and instructions for creating amulets, casting spells, and obtaining magickal powers. In addition, the effects of practicing can be quite magickal in an entirely different way.

Tantra is not easy. You can't learn it by reading a book or attending a weekend workshop. It requires sustained experience. (In French, the word *expérience* means experiment, and that definition applies as well.)

Tantra is not a set of physical practices, yogic exercises, or sexual gymnastics. Physical practices are merely tools for conditioning the body and changing the consciousness. In Tantra, everything one does in daily life can function as a tool.

Tantra is not a form of sexual Olympics, even though Tantric sexual practices can transform sexuality into a divine—Olympian—experience.

Tantra is not a massage technique, genital or otherwise. Unfortunately, "Tantric massage" has become a euphemism for erotic massage in many circles. Any form of massage can be given and received Tantrically—with awareness, a sense of sacredness, and as a means to cultivate and direct energy—but calling something Tantric does not make it so.

Tantra is not polyamory, polyfidelity, open marriage, or about having multiple partners. There is no moral judgment here. A person can be Tantric regardless of love-style or relationship style—celibate, single, monogamous, or polyamorous.

Tantra is not for thrill-seekers. It requires patience, self-discipline, and regular practice of non-sexual solo exercises. It may not offer immediate gratification, so it is likely to disappoint anyone looking for a new kind of kick. We do not discourage anyone from seeking new and intense forms of sexual pleasure. People who honestly and consciously engage in sexual adventuring can often possess greater integrity and deeper self-awareness than people who go to great lengths to make sex "sacred" to justify engaging in it. In our view, consensual sex is intrinsically sacred.

Tantra is not an "art," a term that implies it is a skill set or something that you can learn to "do." Since it is a holistic approach to living, it is more all-encompassing than any art form.

Tantra is not sacred prostitution. Indian society, like many other ancient cultures, had a tradition of temple prostitution, but this tradition was at best peripherally related to Tantra. While we respect the contemporary movement to reclaim the spiritual role of the prostitute, it is not accurate to call prostitution, however sacred, Tantra.

Tantra does not have a central doctrine. The written texts are primarily practical manuals, and no one text or group of texts can be considered authoritative.

Tantra is not an easy answer. In fact, practicing is likely to inspire more questions. Tantra is everything we have said it is not, and more.

Truth can only be touched by
embracing the paradoxical.

Tantra is:

Tantra is an ancient tradition that recognizes sexual energy as a source of personal and spiritual empowerment. This sets it apart from most Western traditions and helps explain why most Westerners have reduced it to its sexual elements alone.

Tantra is the magic of transforming your consciousness and thereby transforming your entire being. Your body is the most powerful tool for bringing about this transformation.

Tantra is a spiritual science. Tantric techniques have been tested and have proven effective for many centuries. If you practice diligently, you will experience results.

Tantra can be quite simple. Everyone has had Tantric experiences, but it is not always so easy to notice them.

Tantra can be embraced in whole or in part. A few simple practices can often produce profound and lasting results.

Tantra is goalless, unless exploring and expanding consciousness can be called a goal. Goal orientation is one of the biggest obstacles faced by the aspiring Tantrika. Abandoning specific goals and focusing on what you are doing in the moment, with as much awareness as you can muster, are the keys to effective practice.

Tantra is a way of life. The Tantric approach to exploring your own consciousness is an ever-evolving process of discovery that emerges from daily practice.

Tantra can provide you with the means to deepen your sense of connection to self, to your partner, to all that is.

Tantra is a technology of mind and body that will lead you to know yourself deeply.

Tantra is for people of "heroic" temperament [*viras*] who are already mentally healthy. Ideally, an aspiring Tantrika has done extensive work on the self. Traditionally, this might mean years of Yogic study and practice. For Westerners, psychotherapy may be the best preparation, since it provides tools for the self-exploration that is central to Tantra.[51]

Tantra is a practical way to loosen the bonds of unconscious, habitual behavior and thereby start to live more freely and fully.

Tantra is the discipline of becoming yourself completely. In the end, there is nothing at all to do.

Tantra is pragmatic and non-moralistic. You can utilize whatever tools are at hand for the purpose of expanding consciousness.

51 "In the West, we have a particular type of Yoga ... called psychotherapy; it is one of the most valuable heritages that Western civilization has produced," wrote Dr. Jonn Mumford, noting that psychotherapy is essential for those seriously interested in Yoga. The same applies for Tantra, but the Tantric and psychotherapeutic approaches are radically different, and actually blending them is probably unwise. Dr. Jonn Mumford, *A Chakra & Kundalini Workbook: Psycho-Spiritual Techniques for Health, Rejuvenation, Psychic Powers and Spiritual Realization.* (St. Paul, MN: Llewellyn, 1997), 154.

One way to define Tantra is to say it is ...

The Science of Self-Exploration.

About the Writers

Mark A. Michaels (Swami Umeshanand Saraswati) and **Patricia Johnson** (Devi Veenanand) are a devoted married couple and have been teaching Tantra and Kriya Yoga together since 1999. Their first book, *The Essence of Tantric Sexuality,* won the National Best Books 2007 award in the Health/Sexuality category and was a finalist in the Religion/Eastern Religions category. They have written and appeared in two instructional DVDs: *Tantric Sexual Massage for Lovers* and *Advanced Tantric Sex Techniques* (Alexander Institute, 2007), and have contributed articles to various online and print publications, including *Chronogram* and *Debonair.*

Michaels and Johnson have taught throughout the United States as well as in Canada, Europe, and Australia. They have been featured on television and radio and in numerous publications, including the *Village Voice, Metro, Latina, Jane, RockStar, Breathe, Redbook, The Complete Idiot's Guide to Tantric Sex,* and *The Complete Idiot's Guide to Enhancing Sexual Desire.* Their teaching combines a traditional lineage-based Tantric approach with the best contemporary methods so that students can bring heightened awareness and an expanded capacity for pleasure into all aspects of everyday life.

The authors are senior students of Dr. Jonn Mumford (Swami Anandakapila Saraswati) and have been named lineage holders of the Om Kara Kriya system for the Americas and Europe. Sunyata, coauthor of *The Jewel in the Lotus,* named Michaels his lineage holder in 2001. They have also studied Bhakti Yoga with Bhagavan Das and Tantra with Dr. Rudolph Ballentine.

Michaels is a graduate of New York University School of Law, is a member of the Bar in New York State, and holds master's degrees in American Studies from NYU and Yale. A playwright and translator, he translated and adapted Goldoni's *The Mistress of the Inn* for New York's Roundabout Theatre Company and co-wrote *The Thrill of Victory, The Agony of Debate*, which premiered at New York's Primary Stages. Patricia Johnson is a professional operatic soprano who tours extensively throughout the United States, Europe, and South America and has performed with the New York City Opera, the Houston Grand Opera, and the Komische Oper Berlin. They make their home near New York City.

Together, they are authors of the books *The Essence of Tantric Sexuality*, *Tantra for Erotic Empowerment*, and *Great Sex Made Simple.*

GLOSSARY

A

absorption: A type of magick involving the in-bringing of images and energy to an individual or group with the goal of changing something within the magician or group.

Adinath: First or enlightened lords. One of the nine sects of naths.

agami karma: Karma you create in your current life.

Agarthi-La: Mythical part of the caverns under the Himalayas. A division of Sangara-La.

Agarthinath: Mythical son of the king and queen of Ananda-La who helped lead the people to safety.

aim: The bija mantra of Matangi.

aim klim sauah: The bija mantra of Tripura Sundari.

Ain Sof: The Kabalistic term for the transcendent deity.

Ajña: The sixth (or brow) chakra associated with the third eye between the eyebrows.

akasha: The name of the element of spirit in the Tantric tradition.

akshat: A special type of rice used in rituals.

AMOOKOS: Arcane Magical Order of the Knights of Shambhala. A Tantric order of the Adinath tradition founded by Sri Mahendranath Maharaj (Dadaji) and Sri Lokanath Maharaj (Michael Magee). It has spread the Adinath tradition in a Western fashion and has influenced many Tantric writers and thinkers today.

amrita: A mysterious substance resulting from the movement of kundalini energy to the crown chakra. Traditional Tantrics describe it as an oil that covers the body and gives all the bodily fluids (tears, sweat, phlegm, saliva, lubricating fluids, ejaculations, etc.) a unique sweet smell and flavor. Neo-Tantrics call women's ejaculation fluids amrita.

Anahata: The fourth (or heart) chakra associated with the heart region.

Ananda: Bliss.

Ananda-La: Mythical land where the Laced Triangles Clan settled.

Anandalahari: Wave of bliss; name of a famous hymn to the goddess Parvati.

anandamaya kosha: The sheath of bliss. One of the koshas that collectively form the body, it has been termed the level of God consciousness.

Anandanath: Mythical king of Ananda-La.

Anandavishnu-La: Mythical huge cavern in the center of the caves under the Himalayas.

annamaya kosha: The sheath of food also known as the physical body. One of the five koshas that collectively form the body.

Apana: One of the five pranas, Apana is the vital current that is involved with the excretory systems, including the lungs when used for that purpose.

apas: The name for elemental water in the Tantric tradition.

Ardhanarishvara: The hermaphroditic form of Shiva and Shakti as one deity. Literally, the lord or the god who is half woman.

Aruña Shakti: Tantric goddess of dreams, including dream work, dream interpretation, trance work, and hypnosis.

asanas: Positions held by the body during the practice of hatha yoga.

ashram: Originally a hermitage in India. Now, generally a community of people following a particular spiritual path or leader.

Asita Shakti: Tantric goddess presiding over rites and rituals that restrict, terminate, or end things.

asmita: Egoism. One of the kleshas. Here it means the false sense of who we are and our relationship with the universe.

athame: Western Neopagan ritual dagger.

Atman: Your true self or soul.

avatar: A manifestation of a god. For example, Krishna is a manifestation of Vishnu.

avidya: Lack of knowledge, science, learning, etc. Ignorance.

Ayurveda: Traditional healing methods from ancient India. Includes massage, herbology, acupuncture, hypnotherapy, energy work, and much more.

B

Bagalamukhi: One of the Mahavidyas, she helps people rediscover that they are divine and are encouraged to seek spirituality.

Bhairavi: Warrior goddess aspect of the Mahavidyas. She gives us the strength to destroy problems that confront us inwardly or outwardly.

bhoga: Pleasure.

bhupura: The outer "square" of a Sri Yantra.

Bhuvaneshvari: One of the Mahavidyas. An aspect of Shakti, known as the "Queen of the Universe." The goddess of space into which all things manifest.

bija: Literally, a bija is a "seed." A bija mantra is the simplest mantra available, usually a single sound. For example, the bija mantra for working with the goddess Kali is *krim*. Bija mantras have no known meanings. Rather, their sound triggers certain qualities within us or within the world.

Bindu: The center point of the Sri Yantra. Sperm.

Bodhisattva: A person who has evolved spiritually so that he or she no longer needs to incarnate, but chooses to do so to help guide others.

Brahma: The deity of creation.

Brahma nadi: Extremely fine energy path that flows inside the Sushumna nadi.

Brahman: The transcendent deity of which all other deities are merely a manifestation.

Brahmanism: Practices following the edicts of the Brahmans, the ruling class of ancient India.

breathwork: Term describing the modification of regular breathing to achieve mental, physical, emotional, spiritual, or physiological changes.

C

chakra: (1) A vortex of energy that allows energy to move from one kosha to another. (2) A magick circle. (3) A Tantric chakra is a group of people that practices Tantric rituals.

chakram: A sharp weapon shaped like a wheel or circle.

Chaturasra: One of the three lines that make the outer "square" in a Sri Yantra.

Chhinnamasta: One of the Mahavidyas, she represents the power of sacrifice and courage.

choli: A short shirt or vest worn by women in India.

circadian rhythms: A set of mental, behavioral, physiological, and biochemical processes that repeat in living beings on a daily basis.

coco de mer: The seed of a palm. Native to the Seychelles islands in the Indian Ocean, it is the world's largest seed. It can appear to be a model of a woman's buttocks, hips, and yoni in life size. As a result, it is used by Tantrics to represent the Goddess.

complete breathing: Fully expanding the lungs and using the diaphragm to completely fill them. Used primarily during breathwork,

crore: Indian measure of ten million.

D

Dakshina Marg: Right-hand path. Where rituals described as involving taboos such as intercourse with a person other than your spouse are seen as symbolic and worked with in that way. The opposite of Vama Marg.

damaru: A ritual drum that looks like an hourglass: two conical sides that meet at a single point. It represents conscious and unconscious minds.

danda: A short T-shaped stick that when pressed under the arm can change the body's energy flows.

Dasa: Ten.

detachment: The ability to live in the moment and accept what is taking place rather than being focused on the past or future.

Devanagari: Name of the Sanskrit alphabet.

Dhanwantari: God of health and healing.

dharana: Extreme single focus. A stage of real meditation.

dhatus: Seven fundamental principles that support the body, such as muscles, bones and bone marrow, and fat.

dhum: The bija mantra of Dhumavati.

Dhumavati: The widow goddess aspect of Shakti; one of the Mahavidyas. She can help you eliminate anything blocking your spiritual path and attain health, wealth, strength, and good fortune.

dhyana: The true meditative state, also known as *samadhi*.

digambara: "Clothed with the directions of space." Ritual nudity.

dim mak: Secret Chinese technique of lightly touching a person to disrupt their energy flow, resulting in the person becoming sick or dying days or weeks after the touch.

Diwali: A contraction of Deepavali meaning "row of lights." A festive holiday associated with Lakshmi. Practitioners of *Modern Tantra* celebrate it on October 31.

diya: A small lamp often used in rituals.

dosha: Term used to describe any of the three primary factors that control the five elements.

Durga: The warrior goddess aspect of the goddess Shakti.

Dvapara: The third of the four yugas.

dvesha: Repulsion. One of the five kleshas. The result of responding to any act out of proportion to the nature of the act.

E

ego: A particular piece of jargon indicating not the Western concept but the Tantric concept of a false idea of who you are. Destruction of the ego is not about losing yourself, it's about finding out the truth about your nature.

G

Ganapati: Another popularly used name for Ganesha.

Ganesha: Elephant-headed god known as the "breaker of obstacles." Traditionally called on at the beginning of rituals. Also said to be responsible for writing down the secrets of Tantra as Shiva describes them to Parvati.

Ganesha Chaturthi: Festival of Ganesh. September 1 in the *Modern Tantra* tradition.

Ganga jal: Water from the Ganges River in India, used in rituals.

ghanta: A hand bell used in rituals.

ghee: Purified butter used in lamps, especially for ritual lamps, as a ritual offering, and even in cooking.

gunas: The triad of tendencies from which everything is derived.

guru: Teacher. Literally, one who dispels darkness. In a spiritual sense, a true guru is the manifestation of deity on Earth. Also, a lesser-known chakra.

H

hamsa: Divine white swan on which Brahma rides. The meditative sound of the breath.

Hanuman: Mightiest warrior hero/god, he has the appearance of a monkey.

Harappa: An ancient city in the Indus Valley.

Harina Devi: Tantric goddess of magick for love, sensuality, and sex.

hatha yoga: The form of yoga that is familiar to most Westerners. It outwardly appears as moving the body into various positions known as *asanas* and holding those positions.

havan kund: A type of fire pit used in rituals.

high breathing: Breathing using primarily the upper chest only.

Hinduism: A broad set of faiths originating in India more accurately called *Sanatana Dharma*. It has been described as monotheistic with thousands of gods and goddesses.

hlim: The bija mantra of Bagalamukhi.

Holi: Wild festival held by *Modern Tantra* practitioners on the full moon in March.

hrim: The bija mantra of Bhuvaneshvari.

hsraim hskrim hsrsauh: The bija mantra of Bhairavi.

hum: Bija mantra of Chhinnamasta.

I

Iccha Shakti: Tantric goddess of the will.

Ida nadi: One of the three most important nadis, it is left of the Sushumna (some say it weaves around the Sushumna) and has lunar energy.

Ishta Devata: The deity you choose to cherish and work with the most.

J

japa: Repetition of mantras hundreds or thousands of times.

jivitvasajya: Clinging to life. One of the kleshas.

Jñaña Shakti: Tantric goddess of knowledge and inner wisdom.

jyotish: Tantric or Indian astrology.

K

kalash: A small vase for holding amrita, the elixir of health and immortality. A lota bowl.

Kali: The female counterpart of Shiva in her role as destroyer or transformer. The dark goddess. Also refers to the fourth yuga, the current unenlightened age.

Kali Ma: The female counterpart of Shiva in her role as mother of us all.

kalpa: Day of Brahma. Repeating cycle of 4,320,000,000 years.

***Kama Sutra*:** A dated and overrated text on courtship and behavior made famous by descriptions of sexual positions, including one that can be difficult to attain and maintain.

Kamala: The tenth Mahavidya; goddess of delight and perfect happiness.

kanya danam: The giving away of the bride. Part of a Tantric marriage ritual.

kapala bowl: A bowl traditionally made from the top third of a human skull. It represents the destruction of the ego.

Kapha: One of the three doshas, it controls the elements of water and earth.

Karbura Devi: Tantric goddess of self-control.

karma: The all-pervading law of cause and effect.

Khechari mudra: A Tantric yoga position that involves curling the tongue backward so that the tip touches the soft palate on the top of the mouth.

klesha: Pain or blockage. For the purposes of this book, it is the pain of not being able to spiritually evolve. There are five kleshas: false ego, ignorance, repulsion, attachment, and clinging to life.

koshas: The five bodies, or sheaths, that collectively form a human being.

krim: The bija mantra for the goddess Kali.

Krishna: Avatar of Vishnu. Known for his dark skin, great beauty and licentious appetites. Also a savior deity. Greatly honored and loved in India.

Kriya Shakti: Tantric goddess of physical, spiritual, emotional, mental, and magickal energy.

kriyamana karma: Karma you create and work off immediately.

kumkum: A red paste made from turmeric (Sanskrit: *haldi*) used in ritual.

kund: A fire used in worship.

kundalini: The energy of the body/spirit, waiting at the end of the spine to flow upward toward the head and grant enlightenment. Sometimes considered a fiery energy because it is mistakenly believed to come from the root *kunda*, meaning "fire." However, the source is actually *kundala*, meaning "wound around," describing how the energy is wrapped around the lower tip of the spine.

L

Lakshmana Rekha: The outer edge of a magickal circle that forms a magickal limit that cannot be crossed without permission.

Lakshmi: Female counterpart of Vishnu. Goddess of prosperity and wealth. Also spelled Laxmi.

Laxmi: Alternate spelling of Lakshmi.

lila: Play. Specifically, the play of the goddess Maya. Her play catches our attention so we see only her dance (the physical world) rather than the vibrational reality that appears to us as the physical world.

lingam: The phallus. Shiva's lingam is represented by a special oblong stone polished smooth by the water of the Narada River.

lota: A vessel for holding water frequently used in rituals. It is spherical and has an opening with a lip at the top. Some have handles and spouts.

Lover, You Home?: LoVeR, You HOMe? Mnemonic for memorizing the bija mantras of the chakras.

low breathing: Often called "belly breathing" or "stomach breathing," it uses the diaphragm to fill the lower lungs.

M

madya: Wine. One of the five Ms of the Panchamakara ritual.

magick: The art and science of causing something to occur in conformity with will by means not commonly understood by Western science. Willed change.

maha: Great. Used as an adjective by prefixing it to another word. Thus, *yuga* or *raja* becomes *mahayuga* or *maharaja*.

Maha Navaratri: A festival of nine days occurring five times a year, it is dedicated to Shakti. Celebrated on October 1 among practitioners of *Modern Tantra*.

maha samadhi: Literally, "great enlightenment." Figuratively, the passing into the phase of existence commonly called "death."

Maha Shivaratri: Celebration for Shiva. Followers of *Modern Tantra* celebrate this festival on the new moon in February.

maharas: "Great fluid." The combination of sexual fluids of male and female.

Mahavidyas: Title of the ten great wisdom goddesses (manifestations of Shakti).

mahayuga: Literally "great age." A period of about 4,320,000 years.

maithuna: Ritualized sacred intercourse. One of the five Ms of the Panchamakara ritual.

mala: A string of beads, usually 108 in number, used to count repetitions when chanting. Similar to a Roman Catholic rosary.

Malini Devi: Tantric goddess of wealth in all areas.

mamsa: Meat. One of the five Ms of the Panchamakara ritual.

mandap: An open pavilion used in Tantric wedding rites.

Manipura: The third (or solar plexus) chakra associated, as the name indicates, with the solar plexus area.

manomaya kosha: The sheath of mind. One of the five koshas that collectively form the body.

mantra: Mystical sounds, words, phrases. According to the *Kularnava Tantra*, reciting mantra repeatedly (japa) is useless unless the mantra was given to the student by a teacher (guru). Mantras are the deity in the form of vibration.

Manu: An archetypal figure similar to the Jewish Adam. Like Noah, he was saved from a great flood by Vishnu or Brahma. He is the projenitor of humanity and is given credit for instituting religious practices.

manvantara: Age of Manu. One-fourteenth of a kalpa.

marma: In Ayurveda, areas on the body where energy paths (nadis) and body protrusions (muscle, bone, etc.) intersect and manipulation can cause changes in the body. More secretly, where three lines intersect when the Sri Yantra is projected on the body.

Matangi: One of the Mahavidya goddesses. She helps with teaching and counseling.

matrikas: Sanskrit for "little goddesses." The letters of the Sanskrit alphabet.

matsya: Fish. One of the five Ms of the Panchamakara ritual.

maya: The illusion we call reality.

Maya: Goddess of illusion.

Mehrgarh: Ancient and large city of the Harappan or Indus Valley Culture.

mekhalas: The three circles, or "girdles," inside the outer "square" and outside the metaphoric lotus-petal rings in a Sri Yantra.

Meru Danda: Sanskrit for "axis staff," it is twilight language for the human spine.

middle breathing: Breathing using primarily the lower chest.

monotheism: The belief that there is only one deity.

mouli: Colored thread used in rituals.

mudra: One of several positions, usually of the hands, with a symbolic meaning and certain energetic powers. Also one of the five Ms of the Panchamakara ritual. Sometimes interpreted as parched grain.

Muladhara: The first (or root) chakra associated with the base of the spine.

murthi: Statue in the shape of a deity into which the deity is made manifest and then honored/worshiped.

mythos: An interrelated set of myths and beliefs resulting in the group's values and attitudes.

N

nada brahma: The soundless sound that precedes audible sound.

nadi: Energy path within the body. When the knowledge of nadis was introduced in China, they were adopted as *meridians.*

nakshatras: Division of the year into 27 or 28 parts for astrological purposes. Also, the astrological *lunar mansions.*

Namaste: A greeting. It loosely means "That which is of the gods in me recognizes and honors that which is of the gods in you."

NAMASTE: New Association of MAgical, Sexual and Tantric Explorers. A modern Tantric and sex magick group that teaches people around the world.

Nandi: Name of the bull that is Shiva's vehicle.

Nath: Lord. Name of a Tantric tradition that has nine basic sects.

nava: Nine.

Navanath: Nine lords. General name of the nine Tantric sects with a common heritage. Includes the Adinaths and the Pagal Naths.

navaratna: Jewelry that holds nine gems, one for each of the astrological planets.

Navayoni: A name for the Sri Yantra showing that its central part is composed of nine (nava) triangles (yonis).

Neo-Tantra: A term used by the late Osho (Rajneesh) and Georg Feurstein for a focus on the sexual aspects of traditional Tantra for the purpose of greater pleasure and enhanced spirituality.

Nila Shakti: Tantric goddess who helps you navigate the ups and downs of life without the pain usually associated with such experiences. This is known as "detachment."

O

omkara: Name for the symbol in the Sanskrit alphabet that is pronounced "Om."

P

Pagal Naths: Crazy lords. A sect of the Tantric Navanath tradition. Members are known for doing crazy things in an attempt to awaken others from their normal consciousness that is closer to sleep than reality.

Panchakshara: The name for the famous mantra associated with Shiva, *Om namah Shivaya.*

Panchamakara: The five Ms. Name of a ritual that uses five items, each beginning with the letter "M."

panentheism: The belief that the ultimate deity is both transcendent (beyond our knowledge) and immanent (manifest and available to us).

parabdha karma: That portion of sanchita karma that you are working on in this lifetime.

Parampara: The right to initiate into a particular tradition.

Parvati: Aspect of Shakti in the form of the goddess of fertility, marriage, and love.

Parvatikalidevi: Mythical queens of Ananda-La.

phat: The thunderbolt mantra, used for banishing. It sounds like "top hat" minus the beginning "to-."

Pingala nadi: One of the three most important nadis, it is right of the Sushumna (some say it weaves around the Sushumna) and has solar energy.

Pita Devi: Tantric goddess for improving thinking.

Pitta: One of the three doshas, it regulates the energies of fire and water.

prakruti: Your health constitiution. It is generally described in terms of which doshas are dominant or regressive in your life.

prana: The life-giving energy that flows through the universe and all things. In the West, it is often believed that prana is in the air. This may be due to the fact that a way to trigger the flow of the pranic energy through the body is via breathing exercises known as *pranayama.*

pranamaya kosha: The sheath of energy. One of the five koshas that collectively form the body.

pranas: The five subdivisions, or currents, of pranic energy. They are Prana, Apana, Udana, Samana, and Vyana. In this sense, the prana vital current is involved with the circulatory system and for sending pranic energy to every cell in the body.

pranayama: Breathing exercises that trigger the flow of pranic energy in the body.

pratyahara: The withdrawal of the senses and the normal attention we pay to our environment. A part of true meditation.

prithivi: The name of the earth element in traditional Tantra.

projection: A type of magick involving the projection of images and energy outside of an individual or group with the goal of changing something in the physical world.

proto-Tantrics: Term used in this book to describe the spiritual system of the pre-Hindu Shavites of the Indus Valley whose beliefs and teachings were the forerunners of Tantra and Neo-Tantra, Hinduism, Buddhism, etc.

puja: A traditional Hindu spiritual ritual. Tantric pujas are more in the form of magickal rites and scientific experiments.

Puranas: A group of sacred Hindu texts.

purnima: Full moon.

R

raga: Retention; the false notion that we can retain or be attached to any physical thing.

rajas: The guna, or tendency, toward action.

Rakhi: Short for Raksha Bandhan ("the bond of protection"), a holiday celebrating sibling bonds. Celebrated on August 15 in the *Modern Tantra* tradition.

Rakta Devi: Tantric goddess of vigor and destruction.

rasa: While generally meaning any fluid, it is especially associated with that of plants such as sap. It is also considered to be the sperm or the Sperm of Shiva, which has magickal qualities.

Rasa Tantra: One text gives this name to the practice of drinking one's own urine for physical and spiritual purification.

Rig Veda: One of the three primary Vedas.

ritual: A repeated action or set of actions.

Roy G. Biv: Mnemonic for memorizing the order of the colors of the chakras.

S

sahaja: The path of naturalness, spontaneity, and joyfulness.

Sahasrara: The seventh(or crown) chakra associated with the area at the top of the head.

samadhi: Enlightenment.

Samaveda: One of the three primary Vedas.

Samayachara: The performance of a ritual astrally or in your mind.

sammohan: Ancient Sanskrit word meaning what is today called "hypnosis."

Sanatana Dharma: Sanskrit for "the eternal law," it is the more accurate name for the broad set of religions collectively and commonly called "Hinduism."

sanchita karma: The collected karma from all your past lifetimes.

sandhi: When the Sri Yantra is projected onto the body, a sandhi is where the lines cross.

Sandhya Bhasha: Twilight language. A type of coding that uses everyday words that seem to mean one thing while actually signifying something else. Without understanding the code, you will not understand the true meaning. Literally, "hiding in plain sight."

Sangara-La: Name of a mythical cave society under the Himalayas.

Saraswati: The goddess counterpart of Brahma. Goddess of music, writing, creativity, etc.

Sarvaanandamaya chakra: The tripartite Bindu at the center of the Sri Yantra.

Sarvarogahara chakra: The set of eight red triangles, fourth from the outermost set of triangles, in a Sri Yantra.

Sarvartharakshakara chakra: The set of ten red triangles, third from the outermost set of triangles, in a Sri Yantra.

Sarvarthasadhaka chakra: The set of ten blue triangles, second from the outermost set of triangles, in a Sri Yantra.

Sarvasaubhagyadayaka chakra: The outermost set of fourteen blue triangles in a Sri Yantra.

Sarvashankshobhana chakra: The inner ring of eight metaphoric lotus petals in a Sri Yantra.

Sarvashaparipuraka chakra: The outer ring of sixteen metaphoric lotus petals in a Sri Yantra.

Sarvasiddhipradha chakra: The innermost single triangle in a Sri Yantra.

satapadi: The most important part of the Tantric wedding where the bride and groom take seven steps around a fire pit.

sattva: The guna of balance or harmony.

Satya: The first of the yugas.

Schambhala-La: One of the mythical areas under the Himalayas; a part of Sangara-la.

Schambhaladevi: Mythical daugher of the king and queen of Ananda-La who helped lead the people to safety.

Shakta: A follower of the goddess Shakti, usually in one of her manifestations such as Durga or Kali.

Shakti: (1) The female counterpart of Shiva. (2) The energy that manifests as kundalini energy in the body. (3) Shakes and jerks experienced when the energy flows through the body.

shankh: A conch shell. Can be used to represent the Goddess. With an end cut off, it can be sounded like a trumpet and used in rituals.

Shava: Followers of the god Shiva.

Shavite: Spiritual system that is composed primarily of followers of Shiva; some Shavites are followers of Shiva's consort Shakti.

Shiva: Commonly called the "god of destruction," he is more accurately the "god of transformation." Deity of Shavite Tantrics.

Shivaling: An oblong stone symbolically representing the creative power of Shiva in the form of his lingam.

Shivanayanajala: Mythical doomsday weapon.

siddhis: Magickal powers. If focused upon, they are seen as an enticement away from spirituality.

sindoor: See *kumkum.*

Sri Chakra: Another name for the Sri Yantra.

Sri Paraprasada: Name of the mantra *hamsa.*

Sri Vidya: The study of the Sri Yantra.

Sri Yantra: The most famous yantra in all of India. It is similar to the Kabalistic Tree of Life, but does much more. It consists of nine interlocking triangles surrounded by circles and metaphoric lotus petals.

srim: The bija mantra of Kamala.

Sushumna nadi: Important energy path that traverses the spine.

Svadisthana: The second (or genital) chakra associated with organs of reproduction.

Svecchachara: The path of doing one's own will.

T

tamas: The guna, or tendency, toward inaction.

Tantra: The origin of this word is, at best, conjectural. However, it is generally taken to mean "the expansion of the spirit." There are basically two divisions of Tantra in the West: Neo-Tantra and traditional Tantra. *Modern Tantra* integrates both.

Tantric chakra: A group of people that forms to practice Tantric rituals.

Tantric hug: A full-body hug where participants press against each other fully from breasts to knees.

Tara: Savior goddess. She provides the wisdom that allows us to save ourselves.

tattvas: (Also *tatvas*, *tattwas*, etc.) The five metaphoric elements of air (vayu), earth (prithivi), fire (tejas), water (apas), and spirit (akasha) whose energy pervades everything in existance.

tattvic tides: Time cycles of the day describing which of the tattvas and its energies are most prevalent. Starting with akasha (spirit) at dawn, each cycle lasts for twenty-four minutes. Following akasha is vayu (air), tejas (fire), apas (water), and prithivi (earth). The complete cycle lasts two hours and is repeated a dozen times during a day.

tejas: The Tantric name for the element of fire.

thali: A plate, especially a plate used to hold items in a ritual.

Thelema: Greek for "will," it is the name of the system originated by Aleister Crowley. Many people find that Thelema is very harmonious with Tantra.

traditional Tantra: Modern version of the ancient Tantric tradition that includes religion, divination, healing, and magick, along with the more famous sexual knowledge and techniques.

Treta: Name of the second (or silver) age or yuga.

Tribindu: A term for the point at the center of the Sri Yantra, recognizing its threefold nature.

trikuti chakra: Half of the guru chakra that is linked to the Brahma nadi.

trim: The bija mantra of Tara.

Trimurti: The three-faced deity combining Brahma, Vishnu, and Shiva.

Tripura Sundari: Aspect of the goddess Shakti; one of the Mahavidyas. She allows the energy of Shakti to move through the senses. Overall goddess of the Sri Yantra.

trishul: Shiva's trident.

Trivalya: Collective name for the three circles surrounding the lotus petal rings in a Sri Yantra.

twilight language: Sanskrit: *Sandhya Bhasha*. A seemingly obvious statement that has a secret, inner meaning, if you understand the code.

U

Udana: One of the five pranas, Upana is the vital current that is involved in the way the body creates sounds, including the conscious control of the voice.

uddharani: Ritual spoon.

V

Vama Marg: Left-hand path. A tradition where the Tantric practices of breaking taboos, such as having ritualized intercourse with a person who may or may not be your spouse, are taken literally, not symbolically. The opposite of Dakshina Marg (right-hand path).

Vata: One of the three doshas, it controls air and ether.

Vayu: The Tantric name for the element of air.

Veda: One of the books of sacred Hindu knowledge. There are three primary ones: the Rig Veda, the Yajurveda, and the Samaveda.

veena: A stringed musical instrument that is about four feet long. It is played by Saraswati, Shiva's consort, and also by Matangi.

vhirkuti chakra: Half of the guru chakra that is linked to the Brahma nadi.

vibhuti: Sacred ash.

vidya: Knowlege, science, learning, etc.

vijnanamaya kosha: The sheath of knowledge or intellect. One of the five koshas that collectively form the body.

vira: Hero. A person fit to be a Tantric.

Vishnu: God of maintenance. He who preserves things and keeps living things alive.

Vishuddha: The fifth (or throat) chakra associated with that part of the body.

W

Wicca: A Western form of Paganism.

Y

Yajurveda: One of the three primary Vedas.

yantra: Literally, a "device" or "machine." Yantras are magickal and mystical diagrams. They are the deity in two- or three-dimensional form.

yoga: Literally, "union," but in actual use it means "union with the Divine."

yogini: Tantric subgoddess.

yoni: The female genitals, symbolically represented by a triangle with one point down.

Yoni Tattva: A eucharistic substance with menses and sperm as two of its constituent parts.

yuga: One of four repeating ages of Earth.

Yugadi: New Year. Celebrated on March 21 in the *Modern Tantra* tradition.

BIBLIOGRAPHY

The following pages of bibliography will help you with your study of *Modern Tantra*. This bibliography will continue to grow.

Unless otherwise noted, items with a copyright from Sothis, Sothis-Weirdglow, Weirdglow-Sothis, or AMOOKOS, although uncredited in the actual book or article, were probably either written or translated by or have comments from Michael Magee (Lokanath Maharaj). Also, some photocopied articles were acquired through Mr. Magee. All Tantric practitioners owe him a great debt for all his hard work in bringing forth this wisdom!

One of the difficulties today is finding good books on traditional Tantra. While there are many books that call themselves "Tantric," a good number of them are more creative than based on tradition. That does not make them bad, just not traditional. But if you are looking for traditional information, I could not do better than to recommend the books published by the Bihar School of Yoga. Several of their books are listed here.

Many of the books listed here were published in cities in India, including Delhi, New Delhi, Bombay, Mumbai, Madras, etc. Only city names are given for major cities, with additional information provided for unusual locations of publication.

Magazines, Journals, Articles, and Web Page Resources

I had initially included numerous web pages in this bibliography, but they either became obsolete or changed so frequently that many became totally useless. Therefore, the only URLs I have included are those where I originally found some useful documents.

Anonymous. "Chandamaharoshana Tantra." Photocopy. No location, publisher, or date.

_____. "Fakirs: Religious Mendicants of India." *Scientific American*. 1884.

_____. *Indus Script & More*. http://indusscriptmore.blogspot.com/2011/08/catch-all-group-of-indus-signs.html.

EO. *The Total Tantra Manual.* www.mumyouan.com/i/ae-8.html.

Galadriel, Lady. *The Great Rite, Sex Magick and Wiccan Philosophy.* Cincinnati, OH: Black Moon Publishing, 1988.

Goravani, Das. *Vedic Astrology, Lessons 1–14.* Downloaded from Usenet, 1995.

Greene, Douglas. "How to Be a Yogi." *Mechanix Illustrated.* August 1952.

Jantsang, Tani. *Tibetan Vajreyana-Tantra, Chod Rite & Principles on Pythagorean Pentalpha—Pentamychos.* Photocopy. No location, publisher, or date.

Kaviraj, Gopinath. *Some Aspects of the History and Doctrines of the Nathas.* Photocopy. No location, publisher, or date.

Kellar, Harry. "Personal Observations of High-Caste Magic in India and Africa." *The North American Review.* 1893.

Kenoyer, Johnathan Mark. "Uncovering the Keys to the Lost Indus Cities." *Scientific American Special.* Vol. 15, No, 1. New York: 2005.

MacGregor, Willow. *Sex Magick.* Cincinnati, OH: Black Moon Publishing, 1988.

Magee, Mike. *The 64 Yoginis of Matsyendranath.* 1995. www.shivashakti.com/matsya.htm.

_____. *The Yogavishaya of Minanath.* 1995. www.shivashakti.com/vishaya.htm.

Maharaj, Jai. *A Brief History of Astrology.* www.astrologysource.com/history.html.

_____. *The Gayatri Mantra.* From Usenet. No date.

_____. *Simplified Basic Concepts [of Hindu Astrology].* From Usenet. No date.

Maharaj, Sri Lokanath (Michael Magee), trans. *Kali Hridayam.* London. No publisher ordate.

Mahendranath, Shri Gurudev. *The Magick Path of Tantra: The Orgasm of Ecstasy.* 2002. www.mahendranath.org/magickpath/magickpath.pdf.

McColl, Colin. *The Revelation of Tara.* Sunland, CA. Self-published. No date.

Mumford, Dr. Jonn. "Sex Magic." *Penthouse.* Australia. March 1989.

Romanoff, Kate M. "Rumble in the Cosmic Sheets: A Contextualized Look at Hindu Tantric Sex." Master's thesis at the University of Colorado, 1999.

Sanderson, Alexis. *The Visualization of the Deities of the Trika.* 1990. www.alexissanderson.com/uploads/6/2/7/6/6276908/sanderson_1990_visualization.pdf.

Sargent, Denny. "Energy of the Goddess." *PanGaia.* No. 15.

Shambhala Nath (Donald Michael Kraig). *Select Tantrik Glossary.* 1984. www.shivashakti.com/glossary.htm.

Sprinkle, Annie (Ellen F. Steinberg). "The Total Orgy." *Velvet.* November 1988.

Tantrik Order in America. *Vira Sadhana: International Journal of the Tantrik Order.* American edition.

Various. *Chakra.* Vols. 3 (1971) and 4 (1972). New Delhi, India: Kumar Gallery.

_____. *Critique.* Issue 29 (1988–89). Santa Rosa, CA: Critique Publishing.

_____. *Kalachakra Initiation.* Madison, WI: Deer Park, 1981.

_____. "Maithuna Lessons." *Tantra: The Magazine.* Vol. 1, nos. 1–6. Albuquerque, NM: 1994–1995.

Multiple Issues of Journals and Magazines

Most of the following magazines or journals are no longer available, but they may be found through used book and magazine resources. Several issues of each of these titles were consulted as part of the information provided in this book.

- *Azoth*
- *Cincinnati Journal of Ceremonial Magick*
- *Ecstasy*
- *Gnosis*
- *Gnostica*
- *Green Egg*
- *Kalika*
- *Magical Blend*
- *Mandragore*
- *Mountain Astrologer*
- *New Frontier*
- *Newsletter of the Natha Tantrikas*
- *Occult Observer*
- *Occult Review*
- *Qigong*
- *Sothis*
- *Tantra*
- *Weirdglow*
- *Yoga International*
- *Yoga Journal* (especially issues 37, 48, 19, and 116)

Classes and Initiatory Materials

These are a few of the important trainings I received that generally must be attended in person and require initiation before receiving them. The last two items are available to anyone directly from the publisher.

- Grade papers of AMOOKOS
- Personal letters with Lokanath Maharaj (Michael Magee)
- Personal letters with Sri Mahendranath (Dadaji)
- Grade papers of NAMASTE
- Classes with Sunyata Saraswati
- Class with Jwala
- Workshops with Thomas Ashley-Farrand
- Six-tape set and manuscript of *Philosophy and Methodology of Kriya Yoga* by Goswami Kriyananda, Chicago, IL: Temple of Kriya Yoga, 1996, www.yogakriya.org/php/catalog/philosophyandmethodologyofkriyayoga.php
- IPHM Level 3 Indian Head Massage Practitioner Diploma course with tutoring from Hannah Louise Murphy, JHJ Holistics Ltd. Training Academy, Wrexham, North Wales, UK, no date

Music/Audio

Anand, Margo. *The Art of Sexual Magic.* Boulder, CO: Sounds True, 1996. Six-tape set.

Ashley-Farrand, Thomas. *The Beginner's Guide to Mantras.* Boulder, CO: Sounds True, 2001.

_____. *Great Spiritual Disciplines and Astotaras.* Self-published, 1996.

_____. *Mantra Meditation for Attracting and Healing Relationships.* Boulder, CO: Sounds True, 2003.

_____. *Mantra Meditation for Creating Abundance.* Boulder, CO: Sounds True, 2003.

_____. *Mantra Meditation for Physical Health.* Boulder, CO: Sounds True, 2003.

_____. *Mantra: Sacred Words of Power.* Boulder, CO: Sounds True, 1999.

Electronic musical instruments (Saarang Concerto Artistic Electronic Tambura and Taalmala Digi-60 Electronic Tabla) from Radel Electronics, Bangalore, India.

Gabriel, Peter. *Passion.* Geffen Records, 1989.

Inner Voice. *Gayatri.* Times Music, India, 1999.

Jasraj, Durga. *Gayatri Mantra.* Biswas Records, 1996.

Lewis, Brent. *Pulse... Where the Rhythm Begins.* Ikauma Records, 1995.

Merlin's Magic. *Reiki: The Light Touch.* Inner Worlds Music, 1995.

Multiple Artists. *Jai Shiva!* Sri Rama Publishing, 1987.

Velez, Glen. *Rhythms of the Chakras.* Sounds True, 1998.

Electronic Musical Instruments (Saarang Concerto Artistic Electronic Tambura and Taalmala Digi-60 Electronic Tabla) from Radel Electronics, Bangalore, India.

Videotapes/DVDs

Connor, Cynthia, director. The *Secrets of Sacred Sex.* Healing Arts, 1994.

Douglas, Nik. *Tantra: Indian Rites of Ecstasy.* New York: Mystic Fire Video, 1969.

Edgar, Horace, director. *Kama Sutra of Vatsyana.* Ventura, CA: Telemedia, 1995.

Emerson, Wesley, director. *The Tantric Guide to Sexual Potency and Extended Orgasm.* Chatsworth, CA: Adam & Eve, 1994.

Horner, Mike, director. *Taoist Sexuality.* Hillsborough, NC: Adam & Eve, 2000.

Kalin, Betsy, director. *Hearts Cracked Open.* Los Angeles, CA: Itchy Bee Productions, 2006.

Kallir, Barbara, writer and director. *A Tantric Guide to Greater Sex, Love and Intimacy.* San Francisco, CA: Crystal Clear Communications, 1989.

Perry, Dr. Michael, and Dr. Patti Britton. *Kama Sutra, Tantra & Tao: The World's Most Erotic Sex.* Full Circle Entertainment, 1998.

Rapley, Dr. Suzzane, director. *Intimacy & Sexual Ecstasy.* Santa Barbara, CA: Love Alive Productions, 1989.

Saraswati, Sunyata. *The Jewel in the Lotus.* San Francisco, CA: Kriya Jyoti Tantra Society, 1986. Three-video set.

Stevenson, Jayne, director. *Yoga of the Heart: A Tantric Festival.* Mangrove Creek, NSW, Australia: Big Shakti, 2006.

Stubbs, Kenneth Ray, director. *Kama Sutra of Sexual Positions.* Tucson, AZ: Secret Garden Publishing, 2002.

Tigunait, Pandit Rajmani, PhD. *Sri Chakra: The Highest Tantric Practice.* Honesdale, PA: Himalayan Institute, 1999. Four videos.

Wise, Robert. *Star Trek: The Motion Picture.* Paramount Pictures, 1979.

Young, Lance, director. *Bliss.* Columbia/Tristar Studios, 1997.

INDEX

A

B

C

D

E

F

G

H

L

M

R

S

T

U

V

W

Y

Z

Revised and Expanded • Over 150,000 Copies Sold
MODERN MAGICK
TWELVE LESSONS IN THE HIGH MAGICKAL ARTS
DONALD MICHAEL KRAIG

Modern Magick

Twelve Lessons in the High Magickal Arts

DONALD MICHAEL KRAIG

For over two decades, Donald Michael Kraig's *Modern Magick* has been the world's most popular step-by-step guide to working real magick. Tens of thousands of individuals and groups have used this course as their primary instruction manual. Now, greatly revised and expanded, this set of lessons is more complete and relevant to your life than ever.

Written with respect for the student, *Modern Magick* will safely guide you—even if you know little or nothing—through a progressive series of practical exercises and rituals, complemented by the knowledge, history, insights, and theory you need to become a successful ceremonial magician. Firmly rooted in the Western magickal tradition yet designed to be fully compatible with your contemporary practice, this book will help you attain full mastery of all core topics in magick:

- The inner mysteries of the Kabalah, The most powerful rituals of magick
- How to create and perform your own rituals, True meditation, Magickal ethics
- Astral projection, Tools of magick, Evocation of spirits, Pathworking
- The importance of the tarot, talismans and amulets, Secrets of visualization
- Alchemy, Psychic self-defense, Healing rituals, Tantra and sex magick

Filled with personal stories and helpful illustrations, along with updated and brand-new material, this new edition of *Modern Magick* features a completely new lesson that reveals the concepts, techniques, and rituals of Neuro-Linguistic Programming, Chaos Magick, and Postmodern Magick. Ideal for beginning, intermediate, or advanced students, and perfect as a manual for magickal temples, this is essential reading for every true magician.

978-0-7387-1578-0, 528 pp., 8½ x 11 **$29.95**

Gregory Peters
THE MAGICKAL UNION OF
EAST
AND
WEST
The Spiritual Path to New Aeon Tantra

The Magickal Union of East and West

The Spiritual Path to New Aeon Tantra

Gregory Peters

Can Eastern and Western magickal systems be merged? The magickal order, the Ordo Sunyata Vajra, successfully did so by eliminating the cultural trappings and unnecessary mystery surrounding Hindu and Buddhist Tantric magick and filtering it through the Western Thelemic tradition. This book reveals their secrets, providing exercises for integrating mind and body with the universal energy of the cosmos. It culminates with instructions for their ultimate magickal ritual, the Diamond Sapphire Gem of Radiant Light.

Unlike traditional methods where years of study and practice are required before learning such advanced material, these practices are immediately accessible to students of all levels. Also used is a more universal Thelema that transcends the Crowley-centric view, resulting in a New Aeon of magickal possibility and potential for all spiritual seekers.

978-0-7387-4044-7, 216 pp., 6 x 9 **$19.99**

---

revealing the mysteries of theurgy

REDISCOVER THE

MAGICK

OF THE

GODS

AND

GODDESSES

Jean-Louis de Biasi

Rediscover the Magick of the Gods and Goddesses

Revealing the Mysteries of Theurgy

Jean-Louis de Biasi

The philosophical roots of much of Wicca and Paganism, as well as Western ceremonial magick, come from ancient Egypt. In this thoroughly researched book, the Grand Master of the Aurum Solis shares the history and evolution of the theurgic tradition—including the origins of Hermeticism in Egypt and the Mediterranean world, the birthplace of the theurgic tradition—and how-to instructions for discovering the presence of the divine in the world.

Providing a seven-step system of exercises and rituals to help the reader achieve higher levels of consciousness, Jean-Louis de Biasi also includes tips and techniques for working with sacred texts, information about the five temples of the human being, The Great Work, the three cosmic rituals, and the real planetary days. A valuable resource for those interested in the history and practices of the Western Mystery Tradition.

978-0-7387-3997-7, 360 pp., 6 x 9 **$24.99**

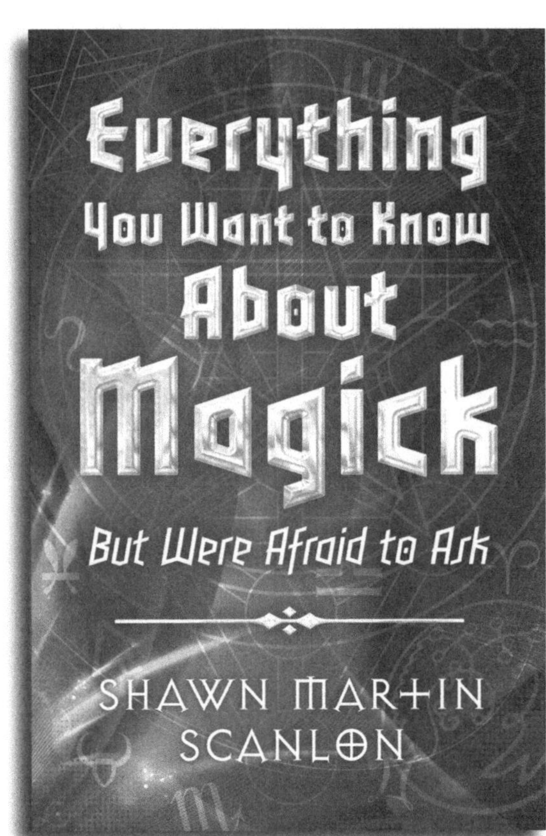
Everything
You Want to Know
About
Magick
But Were Afraid to Ask
SHAWN MARTIN
SCANLON

Everything You Want to Know About Magick

But Were Afraid to Ask

Shawn Scanlon

Real magick scares people as much as it fascinates them. Where does the power come from? Is it real? Is it safe? Can I learn to perform magick myself? This lively and eminently practical guide answers all these questions and every other question readers may have about how to perform magick.

Scanlon presents only the gold of magick and Hermeticism, cutting out the dross entirely. His methods are based on the very best sources in magick and Hermetic literature from Plato and John Dee to Israel Regardie and Aleister Crowley. This manual presents the essential principles of occult magick in a straightforward manner, including clear and detailed steps on how readers can perform their own magick rituals for purposes ranging from attracting wealth, health, and other earthly delights to gaining a deeper sense of purpose and satisfaction in all things.

978-0-7387-3283-1, 360 pp., 6 x 9 **$21.95**

DONALD MICHAEL KRAIG

MODERN SEX MAGICK

SECRETS OF EROTIC SPIRITUALITY

WITH CONTRIBUTIONS BY LINDA FALORIO • NEMA • TARA • LOLA BABALON

Modern Sex Magick

Secrets of Erotic Spirituality

DONALD MICHAEL KRAIG

There has always been a difference between the mystical sexual practices of the East (which focus on the body's energy) and those of the West (which focus on mind and the physical world)—until now.

Modern Sex Magick, by world-famous author Donald Michael Kraig traces the history of Kabalistic sex magick back to the famous Temples in Jerusalem and follows how it was a secret up into modern times. Then he describes the sixteen theorems of magick and sex magick followed by techniques and exercises that will prepare you for sex magick rituals. In this section you will not only learn about male multiple orgasm and female ejaculation, but you will learn how to do them. Then you will learn how to make five types of talismans that you can charge with sex magick.

The book reveals that the true secret of sex magick is how energy raised during sexual arousal is directed. The book gives explicit directions on how you can manifest your desires and goals through the directed use of sexual energy. From this you will learn about monofocal, duofocal and polyfocal sex magick, the different modes of sex magick and more than ten rituals which use sex magick. This book is non-sexist, too, and includes articles by four powerful female sex magicians.

In the most controversial section, Don reveals explicit instructions that others have only hinted at: how to work sex magick with a group. Then, even more revolutionary, are the secrets of using intense sensations and sensory deprivation to enhance your magick. Rituals are included for this work, too.

Already, some have said that this book reveals sex magick for the 21st century. This book is ideal for open-minded adult individuals and groups of any magical level. No matter how much experience you have, this book is a must.

978-1-56718-394-8, 400 pp., 6 x 9 **$19.95**

FREE DVD OFFER INSIDE
TANTRA
FOR EROTIC EMPOWERMENT
the key to enriching your sexual life
Mark A. Michaels & Patricia Johnson

Tantra for Erotic Empowerment

The Key to Enriching Your Sexual Life

MARK A. MICHAELS AND PATRICIA JOHNSON

Surprisingly, most books on Tantra available to Westerners today have very little to do with Tantra and have resulted in massive misunderstandings of the subject. They are usually nothing more than sex guides or relationship manuals. Now, Mark A. Michaels and Patricia Johnson, experts in Tantra and holders of a traditional Indian lineage passed to them by Dr. Jonn Mumford, reveal the true history, philosophy, and practical techniques of this ancient spiritual path in *Tantra for Erotic Empowerment,* the thinking person's guide to Tantra and sexual self-discovery.

This book is literally a course that will train you to become a Tantric in mind, body, and spirit. It's like having a private Tantric guru to instruct you in the underlying concepts and guide you through the practices.

All fourteen chapters follow a specific pattern and are filled with exercises and practices to help you incorporate the Tantric ideas into your life. They begin with a brief quotation from a classic text that sets the mood for the chapter, and then you get a specific meditation to perform. This is followed by the major part of the chapter, which features information and practices that will help you become grounded in Tantric technique and understand more about real Tantra than many of the people who claim to be Tantrics! Although there is a lot of information, Tantra is traditionally experiential, so the many included exercises are designed to help you internalize the information. Finally, you'll get a special message from the authors and several questions you can answer to make sure you understand the material.

Tantra for Erotic Empowerment is not a book about sex. It's a book that reveals ancient secrets, including sexual ones, of personal spiritual development that you can use. Unlike many spiritual traditions that say the body and physical world are unimportant, Tantra holds that sexuality and the physical world can help you on your spiritual path. The body and the world are sacred, and it is almost contrary to nature not to use them in sacred ways, just as they were intended. This book is your personal instruction manual that uses sexual self-discovery to take self-actualization to a new dimension. It is truly a guidebook to personal empowerment, and you can use it to advance your life now. This may well be the most important book on Tantra of the decade.

978-0-7387-1197-3, 288 pp., 7½ x 9⅛ **$21.95**

THE ESSENCE OF
TANTRIC
SEXUALITY
Foreword by Rudolph Ballentine, M.D.
MARK A. MICHAELS & PATRICIA JOHNSON

The Essence of Tantric Sexuality

Mark A. Michaels & Patricia Johnson

Mark A. Michaels and Patricia Johnson have written a modern and comprehensive book that celebrates the sacredness of the body (and desire) within the Hindu Tantric tradition, one which aims to dispel remnants of our Puritan past that define many natural activities of our daily life, including sexual activity and desire, in negative terms.

Based upon the teachings of Dr. Jonn Mumford, their book is much more than an erotic sex manual—though, it is that, too! The authors explain the Tantric philosophy and its principles, demystify it for beginners, and offer authentic exercises and techniques that will help turn your every moment of pleasure into an opportunity to experience the divine.

978-0-7387-0900-0, 240 pp., 7½ x 9⅛ $19.95

Tantric Tips
to
Deepen Intimacy
& Heighten Pleasure
"Patricia Johnson and Mark A. Michaels have written a compassionate and accessible guide to an often mysterious but valuable tradition, and made it relevant for today's readers who want to find more connection, spirituality, and care in their lives and love."
— NAOMI WOLF, author of Vagina and The Beauty Myth
GREAT
SEX
MADE
SIMPLE
Mark A. Michaels & Patricia Johnson
Foreword by Barbara Carrellas, author of Urban Tantra

ECSTASY
THROUGH
TANTRA
Dr. Jonn Mumford

Ecstasy Through Tantra

Dr. Jonn Mumford

Imagine an inner energy which will not only bring you ecstasy beyond your wildest dreams, but also lead you to wisdom, enlightenment and total bliss. You can discover all of this and more in the classic guide *Ecstasy Through Tantra* by Dr. Jonn Mumford.

The practice of Tantra originated thousands of years ago in pre-Hindu India. This India was a truly Pagan society where all people were honored and science was held in high regard. Ancient scholars studied the physical and non-physical bodies. The ancient Tantrics discovered the chakras and the energy known as kundalini, envisioned as a serpent coiled at the base of the spine. When the kundalini is awakened, healing, power, enlightenment, cosmic consciousness, and bliss follow. And as you will learn in this book, one of the best ways to awaken kundalini energy is through the practice of sacred sexuality.

By engaging in specific sexual techniques and positions for ritual intercourse, combined with breathing and visualizations, you'll be flooded with overwhelming physical ecstasy. This ecstasy will trigger expanded states of consciousness. This wisdom, known as Tantric yoga, will show you how to build sexual love and passion to an amazing peak, and then go even higher.

Ecstasy Through Tantra shows you which parts of the body will stir sexual energy into a white heat. Included are color photos of couples engaged in "Asanas of Love," special sexual positions used for kundalini arousal. Discover which sexual positions will "short-circuit" the electric and magnetic currents of the body, leading to an explosive release. Learn how to go beyond the joy of sex to achieve ecstatic union with Divinity.

Ecstasy Through Tantra describes little-known techniques, such as the simple mula bandha exercise that will help women learn to have orgasms more easily while reducing the tendency for premature ejaculation and impotence in men. Discover the secret of the khechari mudra, a way of holding your tongue, which lowers the body's need for oxygen by twenty-five percent with no decrease in energy level. The book also includes beautiful illustrations from ancient sources and modern artists.

Learn what sex magick is and how it differs from Tantra. The "Mass of the Holy Ghost" by Israel Regardie is reproduced here, and with the information in this book the mystical, alchemical, and sexual meanings of this ritual become clear. Contributors include Donald Michael Kraig on how to have a bliss-filled Tantric weekend, and Carl Llewellyn Weschcke on the importance of love and romance.

This makes an ideal book for any loving couple. It is also vital information for anyone who wishes to explore the farthest reaches of sexuality, spirituality, and bliss

978-0-87542-494-1, 208 pp., 6 x 9 **$18.95**

KEITH SHERWOOD

SEX AND TRANSCENDENCE

Enhance Your Relationships Through Meditations, Chakra & Energy Work

BY THE AUTHOR OF *CHAKRA THERAPY*

Sex and Transcendence

Enhance Your Relationships Through Meditations, Chakra & Energy Work

Keith Sherwood

Imagine not only having a sex life that's out of this world, but also a more intimate relationship with your partner—and a life filled with pleasure, love, and joy. Blending tantra, karma, past-lives, and universal consciousness, this book helps you use your body, mind, and energy field to reach new heights of sexual ecstasy and create a profoundly spiritual relationship.

Successful author Keith Sherwood shares practical exercises for releasing karmic baggage, overcoming sexual inhibitions, and using your chakras and energy system to experience complete oneness with your partner. Discover spiritual foreplay techniques for multiple full-body orgasms, and ultimately sustain a relationship built on trust and heightened passion.

978-0-7387-1340-3, 336 pp., 6 x 9 **$18.95**

ROWAN DAVIS
THE Sex FILES
Your Zodiac Guide to
Love & Lust

The Sex Files

Your Zodiac Guide to Love & Lust

Rowan Davis

Astrologer Rowan Davis throws open the bedroom door to the sexual psyche and shines a light on the skeletons inside. *The Sex Files* dissects the hang-ups and bedroom turn-ons of each of the twelve Sun signs, providing an insightful window into the minds of both men and women alike. Davis' profiles are remarkably revealing—sometimes uncomfortably so—and her spot-on honesty is bawdy enough to make you blush. She'll leave you nodding in recognition of your past lovers—and maybe cringing in remembrance of some of your own secrets.

Every naughty fantasy, every psychological game, every debilitating insecurity can be traced back to the horoscope, and Davis' insights prove a handy resource in attracting that perfect carnal companion—and steering clear of emotional train wrecks.

978-0-7387-1354-0, 336 pp., 5 x 6 **$14.95**
